Multilingualism in Public Spaces

Also available from Bloomsbury

Extending Applied Linguistics for Social Impact, edited by Doris S. Warriner and Elizabeth R. Miller

Making Sense of People and Place in Linguistic Landscapes, edited by Amiena Peck, Christopher Stroud and Quentin Williams

Multilingual Memories, edited by Robert Blackwood and John Macalister

Multilingualism, by John Edwards

Reterritorializing Linguistic Landscapes, edited by David Malinowski and Stefania Tufi

Multilingualism in Public Spaces

Empowering and Transforming Communities

Robert Blackwood and Deirdre A. Dunlevy

BLOOMSBURY ACADEMIC
LONDON • NEW YORK • OXFORD • NEW DELHI • SYDNEY

BLOOMSBURY ACADEMIC
Bloomsbury Publishing Plc
50 Bedford Square, London, WC1B 3DP, UK
1385 Broadway, New York, NY 10018, USA
29 Earlsfort Terrace, Dublin 2, Ireland

BLOOMSBURY, BLOOMSBURY ACADEMIC and the Diana logo are trademarks of
Bloomsbury Publishing Plc

First published in Great Britain 2021
Paperback edition published in 2023

Copyright © Robert Blackwood, Deirdre A. Dunlevy and Contributors, 2021

Robert Blackwood and Deirdre A. Dunlevy have asserted their right under the Copyright,
Designs and Patents Act, 1988, to be identified as Editors of this work.

For legal purposes the Acknowledgements on p. xii constitute an extension
of this copyright page.

Cover design by Rebecca Heselton
Cover image: The Shankill Palestine mural in Belfast, by Dee Craig and John
Johnston. Photograph by Deirdre A. Dunlevy.

All rights reserved. No part of this publication may be reproduced or transmitted
in any form or by any means, electronic or mechanical, including photocopying,
recording, or any information storage or retrieval system, without prior permission
in writing from the publishers.

Bloomsbury Publishing Plc does not have any control over, or responsibility for,
any third-party websites referred to or in this book. All internet addresses given in this
book were correct at the time of going to press. The editors and publisher regret
any inconvenience caused if addresses have changed or sites have ceased to exist, but
can accept no responsibility for any such changes.

A catalogue record for this book is available from the British Library.

A catalog record for this book is available from the Library of Congress.

ISBN: HB: 978-1-3501-8659-0
PB: 978-1-3501-8663-7
ePDF: 978-1-3501-8660-6
eBook: 978-1-3501-8661-3

Typeset by Newgen KnowledgeWorks Pvt. Ltd., Chennai, India

To find out more about our authors and books visit www.bloomsbury.com
and sign up for our newsletters.

Contents

List of Illustrations	vii
List of Contributors	ix
Foreword	xi
Janice Carruthers	
Acknowledgements	xii

Introduction: Multilingualism in public spaces: Empowering and transforming communities ... 1
Robert Blackwood and Deirdre A. Dunlevy

1. Multilingual inequality in public spaces: Towards an inclusive model of Linguistic Landscapes ... 13
Durk Gorter

2. Demarcating the space for multilingualism: On the workings of ethnic interests in a 'civic nation' ... 31
Marián Sloboda

3. Empowering multilingualism? Provisions for place names in Northern Ireland and the political and legislative context ... 59
Mícheál B. Ó Mainnín

4. The transformative power of linguistic mobility: Evidence from Italian borderscapes ... 89
Stefania Tufi

5. Invisible presence? Polish in Norwegian public spaces ... 111
Toril Opsahl

6. Place names and the complexity of language recognition in Northern Ireland ... 137
Deirdre A. Dunlevy

7. Postcolonial re-memorization in the public space: A Patrice Lumumba Square in Brussels ... 159
Luk Van Mensel

8. Linguistic Landscape activism as a means of community empowerment: Direct action, Ai'Ta and Breton in France ... 177
Robert Blackwood

9   Multilingualism in the model multicultural city: The influence of
    authors in Leicester's Golden Mile   195
    Michelle A. Harrison
10 Empowering dialect speakers in formal education: The case of the Greek
    Cypriot dialect in preschool education in Cyprus   223
    Andry Sophocleous

Conclusion: Multilingualism in public spaces: Empowering
and transforming communities   241
Robert Blackwood and Deirdre A. Dunlevy

Index   249

Illustrations

Figures

1.1	'Multilingual inequalities in public spaces' (MIPS): A model	19
2.1	A historical German-Czech street-name sign and its present-day Czech equivalent	42
2.2	A damaged historical German-Czech street-name sign	43
2.3	Asymmetrical bilingual design in the Prague metro	44
2.4	Entrance sign, metro network map and informative signs	45
2.5	A commercial advertisement in Vietnamese	47
2.6	The criticized request to use Czech at the Prague Drivers Register Office	48
2.7	A visitor checking the data on his smartphone against monolingual orientation signs and the signs from his perspective	51
4.1	Regions of Italy	90
4.2	Language distribution in Trentino-Alto Adige/South Tyrol	91
4.3	Language distribution in Friuli-Venezia Giulia	92
4.4	Recycling bins for glass and cans	98
4.5	Municipal library in Duino Aurisina	99
4.6	Finance police	100
4.7	Hairdresser's sign	101
4.8	Cafè	102
4.9	Village noticeboard in Sesto	103
4.10	Monolingual regulatory signs displayed in vertical order	104
4.11	Town Hall intercom	105
4.12	Street-name sign (German/Italian)	106
4.13	Sign outside dairy farm 'fresh mozzarella'	107
5.1	Sign at construction site. 'Close the gate after you' in Norwegian and Polish	122
5.2	Billboard campaign, 'Closer to Poland'	123
6.1	Map of the local council areas in Northern Ireland	143
6.2	Town entrance sign in Greyabbey	145

6.3	Street-name sign in English and Ulster-Scots in the Ards Peninsula	146
6.4	Street-name sign in Carrickfergus	147
6.5	Street-name sign in Magherafelt	148
6.6	Road sign for Derry/Londonderry	150
6.7	Mural on the Shankill Road	151
7.1	(Remains of a) Birdseed bust of Leopold II in Brussels (Belgium)	164
7.2	Statue of Leopold II in Ostend (Belgium)	165
7.3	'Patrice Lumumbasquare'/'Square Patrice Lumumba' in Brussels	166
7.4	Location of the 'Square du bastion/Bolwerksquare' and the 'Futur Place Lumumba' in the Matonge neighbourhood	167
8.1	Sign in the Rennes metro system with multiple subordinations of Breton	181
9.1	Multilingual welcome sign outside Belgrave Library	198
9.2	Multilingual welcome sign at St Margaret's bus station	199
9.3	Banners marking the Golden Mile area	200
9.4	Business signs that include Indian Asian scripts or design features	201
9.5	Multilingual signs marking Ramadan celebrations in Highfields	202
9.6	Punjab National Bank sign	203
9.7	Bank of India sign	205
9.8	Cossington Recreation Ground sign, example of fragmentary multilingualism	207
9.9	Business sign, example of fragmentary multilingualism	208
9.10	Business sign, example of fragmentary multilingualism	209
9.11	Leicestershire Police sign, example of duplicating multilingualism	210
9.12	Belgrave Neighbourhood Centre sign, example of duplicating multilingualism	211
9.13	Florist shop sign, example of duplicating multilingualism	212
9.14	Business sign, example of complementary multilingualism	214

Tables

2.1	A News Report on Road-Sign Regulation Changes	37
5.1	Reported Focus-Day Observations	119

Contributors

Robert Blackwood is Professor of French Sociolinguistics at the University of Liverpool, UK, and currently editor of the journal *Linguistic Landscape* with Elana Shohamy. He is the author of a number of articles and book chapters on language policy and regional language revitalization in France, including work on the Linguistic Landscape. He is the co-author with Stefania Tufi of *The Linguistic Landscape of the Mediterranean: French and Italian Coastal Cities* (2015) and co-editor with John Macalister of *Multilingual Memories: Monuments, Museums and the Linguistic Landscape* (2020).

Deirdre A. Dunlevy is a lecturer in Applied Linguistics at the University of Limerick, Ireland. Her research interests focus on Linguistic Landscapes, language and identity, and language policy in minoritized language settings, particularly in Spain and Ireland.

Durk Gorter is Ikerbasque Research Professor at the University of the Basque Country, Spain. He is the head of the Donostia Research group on Education and Multilingualism (DREAM). He does research on multilingual education, European minority languages and Linguistic Landscapes. He has published extensively on those themes and has presented his work at conferences around the world. He also teaches in the European Master in Multilingualism and Education, and he is editor of the journal *Language, Culture and Curriculum*. He received the award of Distinguished Scholar of Multilingualism of the International Association of Multilingualism. For publications, see www.ikerbasque.net/durk.gorter.

Michelle A. Harrison is a teaching fellow in French and Francophone Studies at the University of Leicester, UK. Her research interests focus on French sociolinguistics, regional and minority language-in-education policy, language policy and social media, and the Linguistic Landscape. Her most recent publication is the co-edited volume *French Language Policies and the Revitalisation of Regional Languages in the 21st Century* (2019).

Toril Opsahl is Associate Professor at Center for Multilingualism in Society across the Lifespan (MultiLing), Department of Linguistics and Scandinavian studies, University of Oslo, Norway. Her research interests focus on multilingual language practices in urban contexts; L2-communication in workplace settings; ideologies and language policies; gender, and phenomena associated with the grammar-pragmatics interface.

Together with Stian Hårstad she has published the book *Språk i byen* (Language in the City) (2013).

Mícheál B. Ó Mainnín is Professor of Irish and Celtic Studies at Queen's University Belfast. His research interests focus on Irish and Scottish Gaelic in the medieval and modern periods, and include literature and linguistics. He is the director of the Northern Ireland Place-Name Project at Queen's and has published on various aspects of name studies, including the employment of place names in narrative and as evidence for language contact. His interest in multilingualism is also relevant to his research on the poetry contained in the sixteenth-century Scottish manuscript, the *Book of the Dean of Lismore*.

Marián Sloboda is Assistant Professor in the Department of Central European Studies at Charles University, Prague, Czech Republic. His research interests include the theory and practice of language management or human actions targeting language and communication. He is a member of the Language Management Research Group based at Charles University (http://languagemanagement.ff.cuni.cz). His recent work includes co-editing *The Language Management Approach: A Focus on Research Methodology* (2018) and *Sociolinguistic Transition in Former Eastern Bloc Countries* (2016).

Andry Sophocleous is Assistant Professor of Applied Linguistics at the University of Nicosia, Cyprus. Her research interests focus on dialect use in education, language and identity construction and language and culture. Her publications have appeared in *Sociolinguistic Studies*, *Multilingua*, *Linguistics and Education*, the *Journal of Language, Identity & Education*, *Language, Culture and Curriculum* and in the *International Journal of Multilingualism*.

Stefania Tufi is Reader in Italian Studies and Sociolinguistics at the University of Liverpool, UK. Her main research interests lie within Sociolinguistics, in particular minority and regional languages (including migrant languages), language policy, social dialectology, and the Linguistic Landscape. Most recently she has worked on borderscapes, language and memory, and linguistic constructions of identity in transnational spaces. Her co-edited volume *Reterritorializing Linguistic Landscape: Questioning Boundaries and Opening Spaces* was published in January 2020.

Luk Van Mensel is a postdoctoral researcher at the University of Namur, Belgium, and a visiting lecturer at the KU Leuven, Belgium. He has published on a variety of subjects in Second Language Acquisition (SLA) and sociolinguistics, including the economic aspects of multilingualism, multilingualism in the family, Linguistic Landscapes and language education policy, frequently with a focus on Brussels. He is also co-editor of *Minority Languages in the Linguistic Landscape* (2012) along with Durk Gorter and Heiko F. Marten.

Foreword

Janice Carruthers
Queen's University Belfast

This volume forms part of the MEITS project – Multilingualism: Empowering Individuals, Transforming Societies (www.meits.org). MEITS is led by principal investigator Wendy Ayres-Bennett (University of Cambridge) and funded by the Arts and Humanities Research Council under its Open World Research Initiative.[1] It is a flagship interdisciplinary research project designed to demonstrate the importance of languages in addressing key issues of our time. The project has a large core team of researchers across four universities (the University of Cambridge, Queen's University Belfast and the Universities of Edinburgh and Nottingham), encompassing disciplines as varied as literary-cultural studies, history of ideas, sociolinguistics, education, second-language acquisition, and cognitive neuroscience. MEITS also has a wide range of non-academic partners in a number of sectors, including government departments, charities, schools and grassroots organisations. *Multilingualism in Public Spaces: Empowering and Transforming Communities* has emerged from Strand 3 of MEITS, a sociolinguistic strand based in Queen's University Belfast and led by Janice Carruthers. Strand 3 focuses on questions of identity, diversity and social cohesion in France and (Northern) Ireland; it includes research on contemporary urban varieties of French, on Breton and on Irish, both in Northern Ireland and in the Republic. More specifically, it addresses questions of language policy and practice as they relate to identity and diversity in these different contexts. *Multilingualism in Public Spaces: Empowering and Transforming Communities* has allowed a deepening of the strand's work on language in the public space and a broadening of the range of languages discussed both within and beyond Europe.

The editors are extremely grateful to the AHRC and to MEITS, and in particular to the principal investigator, Wendy Ayres-Bennett, for the funding to support the volume, including financial support for the workshop that laid the groundwork (organized by Robert Blackwood and Deirdre Dunlevy) and for a related public lecture by Unn Røyneland in the University of Liverpool.

Note

1. Award number: AH/N004671/1.

Acknowledgements

The editors would like to thank all those who have contributed to this volume and in particular the Arts and Humanities Research Council (AHRC) for making this volume possible through the *One World Research Initiative* funding. This volume is connected to strand 3 of 'Multilingualism: Empowering Individuals, Transforming Societies' (MEITS) (grant no. AH/N004671/1). We wish to express our particular appreciation to the project PI, Wendy Ayres-Bennet at Cambridge University, and the two co-investigators of strand 3 of MEITS at Queen's University Belfast, Janice Carruthers and Mícheál Ó Mainnín, for their enthusiastic and dedicated support.

The chapters presented in this volume are the result of fruitful discussions that emerged from a workshop held in the beautiful surrounds of Gladstone's Library in Hawarden. We thank all the staff who made our stay there so relaxing, enjoyable and productive.

The timely and considered work of all the authors is much appreciated; their commitment to the project and engagement made the editing process a pleasant experience. We wish to express our gratitude to each of them for engaging with the theme and their creative and thoughtful contributions throughout the entire process.

All the contributors also acted as reviewers for chapters in this volume, and we would like to thank our colleagues who undertook reviews for their constructive considerations of the chapters they engaged with. We are grateful to Will Amos, Nishaant Choksi, Neil Comer, Charles Forsdick, Adam Jaworski, Jeff Kallen, Dimitris Kitis, Guy Puzey, Barbara Soukup, Tamas Szabo and Dominic Watt for their contributions to improving this volume.

Our thanks also go to Cathal Woods at Extra Mural Activity in Belfast and Dee Craig and John Johnston for granting us permission to use their mural for the book cover.

At Bloomsbury, we would like to extend our thanks to Andrew Wardell and Becky Holland for their support and assistance throughout, making it a seamless and straightforward process.

Finally, on a personal level, we would like to thank our families for their patience and support throughout the lifespan of this project; Robert particularly thanks Jude, Luke and Julia. Deirdre would like to thank, as always, her parents, Will and Rafa for their support.

Introduction: Multilingualism in public spaces: Empowering and transforming communities

Robert Blackwood and Deirdre A. Dunlevy

This volume emerges from the Arts and Humanities Research Council (AHRC)-funded Open World Research Initiative (OWRI) project Multilingualism: Empowering Individuals, Transforming Societies (MEITS), an interdisciplinary, multi-institutional research project focused on the opportunities and challenges presented by multilingualism at both an individual and a societal level. This collection arises from a workshop meeting held in 2018 in Gladstone's Library in Hawarden, Wales. The contributors gathered, with the support of the AHRC MEITS grant, to discuss multilingualism in public spaces in their broadest sense, which we explicitly inflect to recognize the complicated and messy nature of both phenomena – points to which we refer below. At the workshop, each contributor brought their own background and research interests to the conversation, leading to the development of a volume that offers a cohesive perspective and diverse cases that contribute to a better understanding of multilingualism and their presence in public spaces as a means for social transformation.

The MEITS project is guided by six overarching strands of research, ranging from cultural studies to cognitive aspects of multilingualism. This particular volume is part of the work of strand 3 of the MEITS project, based at Queen's University Belfast, which is concerned with 'sociolinguistic perspectives on multilingualism: identity, diversity and social cohesion'. Strand 3 of the project seeks to contribute to our understanding of concepts of identity at the intersection with multilingualism, and how they impact social cohesion through the exploration of contrasting scenarios in France and Ireland in particular.

Power and empowerment in the public space

In this volume, we view empowerment explicitly through the prism of multilingualism with a view to exploring the potential for sociolinguistics, and in particular a sociolinguistics of public spaces, to contribute to the ongoing thinking through of this concept. As such, in this introduction, we devote particular space to exploring the concept of empowerment whilst recognizing that both 'multilingualism' and 'the public space' need to be problematized. Other disciplines, including social policy, sociology and social work, have been considering their respective engagement with empowerment for a long time, and, in some cases, have a much more developed disciplinary theorization. In this section, we consider how these areas of scholarship have articulated the issue of empowerment, and how sociolinguistics can both learn from and inflect this discussion.

Etymologically, 'power' is at the heart of empowerment, and – as McLaughlin (2016: 7) notes – a brief exploration of power is a prerequisite for (re)thinking empowerment. Much space has been devoted to (re)defining power, and in this introduction, we are not going to repeat all the debates that have been fought, won or lost, but we will draw on those perspectives that nuance our understanding. Foucault (1984: 28–36) reminds us that power is not something possessed but is rather exercised, and this exercising of power – and explicitly its contestation between different groups within multilingual communities – underpins the following chapters as we trace the unsettling of relationship between individuals, groups and communities in a range of settings across Europe. This contestation reflects the tension that Weber (1978, original 1921) highlights, where power is 'the ability to achieve desired ends despite resistance from others' (Macionis and Plummer 2002: 378). The currents of exercising power and of resistance are themes which span the chapters of this volume, and each of the contributors illustrates how power is not simply held at top of local hierarchies, but can occur at all levels of society. The starting point, therefore, for this volume is the recognition that the exercising of power, and empowerment more broadly, is not a zero-sum gain, despite the urge to frame it in this way by some – usually those who have traditionally enjoyed considerable power (see Gerodimos et al. 2013: 2, who contend that, in authoritarian regimes, the empowerment of the citizenry inevitably comes at a cost to dictatorships).

Just as Foucault views power to be everywhere, and works its way through discourses (Smart 1985), power is to be found at play in everyday encounters (Macionis and Plummer 2002: 378). One of the particular dimensions considered here is the relationship between power and knowledge. Flusser (2003: 95) maintains that 'knowledge has to be transformed into power' and the contributors explore the extents to which awareness of the importance of linguistic diversity and experience of multilingualism can lead to acceptance, resulting in a power transformation. Bourdieu (1991) maintains that language itself is a medium of power, and is to be understood as a product of the relation between a linguistic market and a linguistic habitus. In communicating, we are constantly adapting and changing our language to comply with the intended audience, so that every utterance, no matter how insignificant it may seem, both reinforces and reproduces the social structure. Bourdieu considers language and power particularly in light of issues such as gender and social class, and this can be extended to issues such as identity politics, which emerges throughout the volume, and language rights and protection.

Advances in communication and technology have upset traditional language dichotomies, enabling minority language communities to connect, isolated speakers to make new connections and new speakers to emerge in non-traditional speaker communities (Smith-Christmas et al. 2018). This shift in power dynamics through the removal of barriers that previously existed has empowered speakers to maintain their language in a situation where it previously may have died, or indeed for someone to engage with a language with which they would not otherwise have had the opportunity.

We must also consider, however, the effect that the politics of public spaces and multilingualism bring to the concept of empowerment. In considering empowerment, we take into account the processes and the fact that often it is in conditions of conflict and tension that opportunities for empowerment emerge. It is in the spaces between established structures such as policies, official institutions and legislation that the layers of the everyday occurs; home language cannot be controlled, nor the free thoughts of an individual. As such, a rethinking of the public space as public spaces is helpful, if we consider the contexts explored in this volume, as we see that it is in the friction between the established norm and the plurality of society where agency is located.

A very short history of empowerment

McLaughlin (2016: 2) traces the history of empowerment back to the mid-seventeenth century when, according to the *American Heritage Dictionary of the English Language*, it carried legal significance, signalling the investing of authority. Humphries (1996: 2), entwining empowerment with equal opportunities, pinpoints the 1970s and 1980s in both the UK and the United States as the start of the most recent peak of prominence. Within this timeframe, McLaughlin (2016: 39) identifies Black liberation movements in the 1970s as the beginning of the theorization of empowerment within social policy and sociology, with Solomon (1976: 6) defining the concept as 'a process whereby persons who belong to a stigmatized social category throughout their lives can be assisted to develop and increase their skills in the exercise of interpersonal influence and performance of valued social roles'. Although Solomon's definition does not neatly apply to every single individual, group or community, hers is a particularly useful conceptualization to which we shall return in the concluding chapter. For Gerodimos et al. (2013: 1), empowerment 'implies the acquisition of power' and the processes by which groups and communities have acquired power has been explored across the social sciences, including museum studies, political science, law and anthropology. The reach of empowerment as a concept extended into women's liberation and equality, the disabled people's movement (Price 1996: 40), the Deaf community (McLaughlin 2016: 41–4) and groups identified with the wide spectrum of sexualities (Carabine 1996). With power at its heart, empowerment is modulated by the communication of ideologies by those seeking to empower others, and by those empowered.

Studies on empowerment are wide-ranging and consider topics as diverse as economic, political, social and cultural empowerment. It is in the plurality of voices that conflicts arise, and also where the conditions for real empowerment are formed. Nevertheless, at the centre of all of these studies is the perspective that empowerment involves a level of autonomy and self-determination, and language has a role in each of these empowering processes in some form or another.

Given the longer traditions of exploring empowerment elsewhere in the humanities and social sciences, especially in social work and sociology, we do not seek here to reinvent the wheel when it comes to defining the parameters of empowerment. Rather, we discuss the extent to which sociolinguistics can contribute to this debate. To this end, we exploit the range of findings reached in, for example, social policy. Drawing on Carabine's work on the empowerment of groups representing different sexualities, it is important to recognize that groups understand empowerment in a range of ways and seek it through several processes. Carabine (1996: 17) contends that there are at least three possible approaches: 'People achieve empowerment, first, through self-definition and the development of their own social and political identities; second, through sexual practice in personal relations; third, through seeking rights within social institutions and social contexts.' To refract Carabine's summary through the lens of sociolinguistics, the contributors to this volume consider how individuals self-identify as multilingual, how groups and communities practise multilingualism and how others press their case for the extension of rights as three interconnected methods of empowerment. Across the chapters, the authors draw out the significance of multilingualism in these ongoing processes of exercising power.

Another clear strand of research in this area clarifies how empowerment is something that communities undertake for themselves, rather than have done to them. We do not frame empowerment as some kind of action which is undertaken by 'the powerful' on the 'disempowered', despite the prevailing narratives in some quarters (such as in non-specialist descriptions of social work and in early twenty-first-century political rhetoric in the UK, as highlighted by McLaughlin (2016: 1)). Although there are examples of this patrician approach to empowerment, in this volume we seek to explore how individuals and groups engage multilingually with their situations, rather than, as Ruiz (1991: 264) critiques, empowerment 'portrayed as a gift to the powerless'. Through the development of critical consciousness, what Freire (1970) terms conscientização, one individual voice can be joined with other voices to effect social action on behalf of the community. Central to this idea of critical consciousness is voice and agency (Ruíz 1991: 268), emphasizing the active involvement in the process of the individual and/or community in question, and that empowerment is not something bestowed upon a community by others.

Empowerment and (socio)linguistics

Whilst (socio)linguistic research has not ignored the question of empowerment, there is scope for our field to engage more profoundly and creatively with the exercising of power. Critical sociolinguistics, of course, has a long history of – in the words of Wodak (1989: xiv) – 'uncovering injustice, inequality, taking sides with the powerless and suppressed', and this volume aims to bring this particular perspective to bear on the question of multilingualism and empowerment. Ruíz (1991: 259) draws attention to what he refers to as the 'sociolinguistic and political consequences' of multilingualism (or, more precisely in his terms, bilingualism): 'This goes beyond suggestions that being bilingual can be of some economic or commercial advantage: it entails a general reordering of prevailing societal patterns of stratification.' In other words, multilingualism disrupts existing power dynamics, unsettles traditional hierarchies and has the potential to subvert patterns of domination and subordination. In this volume, the contributors interrogate this disruption in a range of settings, including the classroom (Sophocleous), the city square (Van Mensel), the roadside (Blackwood, Dunlevy) and shops (Harrison).

In their edited volume, Fishman, Pütz and Neff-van Aertselaer (2006: xxi) discuss the 'dynamic processes in which *power* is construed as the ability, whether by overt agency or not, to affect the actions or ideas of others' (emphasis in original), as indicated by the volume's subtitle: 'Explorations of Empowerment through Language'. This framing of power echoes Spolsky's articulation of language management (2004, 2009) whereby individuals, groups or societies with some level of authority seek to change the language practices of *others*. In our volume, we focus our studies of multilingualism so as to shed light on how, adopting the broader definition by Adams (2008: 17), communities 'take control of their circumstances, exercise power, and achieve their own goals' by which 'they are able to help themselves and others to maximize the quality of their lives'. To that end, the chapters approach empowerment from within multilingual communities, many of whom are exercising their relative power as part of wider efforts to address their inequality, however that is articulated across the breadth of European settings.

One aim of this volume is to challenge the shibboleth that multilingualism is in some way negative or detrimental to communal life, as articulated by the widely reported confrontations which can be reduced to the line: 'This is England, speak English.' To this end, the chapters in this volume will explore the notions of powers within a range of communities and countries with a view to, as Esch (1989: 3) notes, establishing 'what the power consists in, what it is for and who precisely has the control'. Edwards (2006: 19) argues that 'language empowerment is commonly seen as a compensatory device', with, he continues, a clear sense of imbalance between those involved, or 'unequal partners' in his exact terms (2006: 20). As such, the chapters here identify those not normally identified with the exercising of power – ranging from the Gujarati florist in Leicester, UK, to the 4-year-olds in Cyprus, and the language activists in Brittany, France – and address Fishman's (2006: 10) challenge to 'specify the outcomes of power, be they material or non-material'. How this unfolds for Polish workers in Norway or Roma in Czechia is considered in the following chapters. By positioning the chapters of the volume around the idea of empowerment, we explore the potential of multilingualism to overcome divisions and build social cohesion. In particular, we discuss how multilingualism can help the individual to become critically conscious and to develop an in-depth understanding of the world, while also benefitting society as whole.

Essential to our approach to understanding empowerment is the work by Lim, Stroud and Wee (2018) on linguistic citizenship as part of their project 'The Multilingual Citizen'. Explicitly taking a Southern theoretical perspective, Stroud (2018a: 8) argues that linguistic citizenship challenges the model of multilingualism identified in postcolonial settings whereby power imbalances are maintained on the basis of monolingual norms, of ideologies which privilege one or two languages to the detriment of others, and of neoliberal governance. As Stroud (2018b: 18) contends, linguistic citizenship should be understood as 'the practices whereby new actors, seeking recognition in the public space in order to determine a new course of events, shift *the location of agency and voice*' (emphasis in original). Although not all in what might be broadly considered as postcolonial settings, linguistic citizenship emerges as a line of enquiry in many of the chapters here, with a range of groups looking for the kind of public acknowledgement to which Stroud refers. In drawing attention to voice, Stroud aligns himself with Ruíz (1991: 260), who nuances our understanding by noting that the inclusion of a given language within – from his perspective – language planning activities can occur at the same time that the group themselves have no voice. In this volume, the contributors grapple with both dimensions in different contexts, teasing out where languages (in the traditional, bounded and named sense) may well be included in public spaces, but where the language group is excluded. This finessing of our understanding of multilingualism-as-empowerment is significant, as summarized by Ruíz (1991: 261): 'To have voice implies not just that people can say things, but that they are heard (that is, that their words have status, influence).' It is this articulating of influence which is contested, for example, in the chapter devoted to direct action (Blackwood), where the activists of Ai'Ta! use the power they exercise in order to be heard as much as to ensure that Breton is seen on the roads of the region.

As noted above, in this introduction, we privilege the hypothesizing of empowerment, recognizing at the same time that multilingualism and the public space are far from uncontested concepts. Rather than grappling with theoretical definitions of public space, we lean to sociologists and geographers who have already problematized the term to thread together much of what we do, and accept the public space as a forum for multilingualism. We can take the public space as a spatial term, considering it to refer to 'where the virtues and capacities of public encounter are learnt and put into practice' (Watson 2006). We have a common, but not necessarily shared, concept of public space. We draw on Gal (2005) to distinguish between public and private spaces. The idea of 'public' space suggests openness and accessibility. However, as emerges across the chapters in this volume, the public space is not equally accessible to all members of society in the same way or at the same time, and so our contributions to the public space can be dependent on a balance of (perceived) social powers.

Fraser's (1990) theoretical considerations of the public sphere lend themselves to our perspective of public spaces consisting of a multiplicity of publics being preferable to a single public sphere. In recognizing the plurality of public spaces, we consider the multiplicity of public arenas with a variety of publics that, as Eley (1992) recognizes, advantages some while disadvantaging others. We see these unequal experiences of public spaces emerge throughout the chapters of this volume, as the tension that emerges from the competition for visibility and agency can in turn become the source of the enactment of social identities and the empowerment of, what Fraser terms, subaltern counterpublics (1990: 67). It is in the space between exclusion and inclusion where the empowerment occurs for a variety of reasons, as members of subordinated social groups construct alternative publics through their actions, as we see in the form of direct action (Blackwood), the staking out of a single street (Harrison) and even in negotiated spaces in kindergartens (Sophocleous), in the following chapters.

We deliberately complicate the concept of public space by pluralizing it in order to recognize not only the variety of inter-related and inter-acting public spaces, but also to acknowledge the productive tensions within public spaces. Rather than accept the concept as inevitably providing a place for consensus and accord, the overlapping and contested nature of public spaces (where, in effect, some are more 'public' than others) contribute to the messiness of multilingualism through the contradictions attested in the chapters in this volume. Whilst it is tempting to view the communities who meet in public spaces as pluralistic and open to multilingualism, we know – as discussed below – that varied practices of language use are not universally appreciated, and are indeed often devalued within some groups and institutions.

From the perspective of language, we see that multilingualism is accepted in private spaces more readily than in public spaces, as the actor's autonomy and control over private domains implies less of a struggle for power and more control of language choice. Equally, some languages are accepted in certain domains more readily (for example, a heritage language in the home versus in a formal public event), and such perceived 'acceptable spaces' for language(s) affect the speakers' attitudes towards the language and their own sense of identity, while also affecting the out-group's perception of the language and its speakers. We understand public spaces broadly, to include domains such as education, online, and the Linguistic Landscape (LL), and explore how language choice in the public space affects the legitimization and normalization of languages in their wider community.

We start this volume from the premise that multilingualism is inherent in our public spaces. As a concept, multilingualism has been the subject of much debate and disparate definitions. Coulmas (2018) documents comprehensively the etymology and evolution of the term 'multilingualism', analysing over twenty definitions of the term. The contested concept is not something we proffer to theorize here; rather, we are working from the understanding of multilingualism as the naturally occurring but competing phenomena of the presence of multiple languages (including variations within what have come to be recognized as bound, named – and often standardized – languages) in societies. In this introduction, we recall the conclusion by Auer and Li Wei (2007: 1) that 'monolingualism may be the exception and multilingualism the norm' since it frames neatly the productive clashes attested in this volume, whereby understandings of modern European settings – such as those discussed in this volume – present monolingual public spaces as idealized. Gorter (2006: 88) notes that 'the idea of monolingualism by country – one state, one language – has become obsolete and has been overtaken by a complicated interplay of many languages' but at the same time, we recognize that there is a spectrum of multilingualism, explored more fully in the following chapters, as ways of organizing meaning-making repertoires. It is this manifestation of the conflicting and contradictory interplay of languages in public spaces that we focus on in this volume.

This volume brings an unequivocally European focus to the issue of empowerment, but it should go without saying that this is not to suggest that multilingualism as a vector for empowerment is limited to Europe. The rationale for this centring on Europe comes as questions of linguistic nationalism, the crisis of hospitality (misleading referred to as a 'migrant crisis'; see Balch 2016) and Brexit intermingle and amplify each other across the continent of Europe. Starting this project not long after the UK's decision by referendum to leave the European Union assumed particular significance for this particular part of the MEITS project, led by an Irish researcher and a British researcher, and based at Queen's University Belfast, in Northern Ireland. At a time when society, especially in Europe, is characterized by transnationalism, superdiversity and hypermobility, a narrative has established itself across the continent that is resistant to multilingualism, and which views the ability to speak, write or read another language not as a strength but as some kind of flaw. According to the increasingly strident rhetoric that cherishes monolingualism, this shortcoming is to be, at best, ignored, and at worst countered, and yet studies consistently point to the benefits of multilingualism in a range of domains, include health, well-being, creativity and economic development. The urgency of the need to articulate clearly the advantages of multilingualism, at this time of fractured relations within the European Union, and during an ongoing crisis of hospitality, is particularly acute in Europe, hence the particular attention of this volume.

Anecdotal evidence abounds of discrimination against speakers of other languages who talk in Urdu, Polish, Lithuanian or any of a host of other languages; this is not a solely European phenomenon, but given the intensification of the resistance to multilingualism, or more accurately, the privileging of monolingualism on the basis of a mythical, single standard language for many of the continent's nation states, the focus on Europe is deliberate and part of the rationale for the wider project.

The contributions to this volume

The authors of the chapters in this volume investigate the range of potential impacts of multilingualism as a lived reality in Europe at a time of social division. By addressing the idea of empowerment in a range of contexts across Europe and from varying perspectives, we can see the commonalities in research concerns across disciplines and the importance of keeping an open dialogue. The chapters foreground challenges of multilingualism for empowerment, pointing to areas where it is contentious, moving to ambivalent contexts under construction and positive examples of empowerment.

As such, following an opening methodological chapter from Gorter, we have grouped the chapters into three main sections. In the first section, Sloboda and Ó Mainnín take two different spatial contexts to explore divided views on empowerment and the tensions and contradictions of the relationship between multilingualism and empowerment. In the second section, Tufi, Opsahl and Dunlevy interrogate the complexity of this relationship with studies that conclude by highlighting the potential for community empowerment in multilingual settings. The final section considers examples where active empowerment through language is taking place. The chapters in the third section each privilege a specific perspective within the wider debates, tackling, respectively, memorialization, direct action, authorship and education.

The volume opens with a methodological chapter by Durk Gorter, proposing a model by which multilingualism in the public space can be evaluated with a bold proposal for a comprehensive model for LL studies. Here, he describes the cyclical sequence in the construction of LLs and how these processes have an effect on the experiences of groups of people and in particular their language practices. Gorter concludes that language policies are affected by reactions of individuals or groups of people to language texts displayed in public spaces, and as a consequence, those reactions can impact future policy development.

In the next chapter, Marián Sloboda focuses on social actors' behaviour that restricts the use of languages other than of the ethnic majority in the Czech Republic. The study shows that various social actors ranging from 'ordinary' citizens to professionals to political representatives, restrict the use immigrant languages, traditional minority languages as well as widely spoken ones, such as Russian, in public. Their behaviour shows how the visibility of different language communities is being (de)legitimized in the country's public space vis-à-vis its national identity. Sloboda concludes that the understanding of how this is done is a precondition for community empowerment.

Mícheál Ó Mainnín's chapter is concerned with minoritized languages in Northern Ireland where language rights are the subject of contention. The absence of a comprehensive language policy has led to an uneven provision of bilingual place-name signage. Ó Mainnín concludes that, while multilingual signage has empowered certain communities in Northern Ireland, this has not had a transformative impact in part because of the scale of political disagreement in a fractured society.

Stefania Tufi undertakes a comparative examination of linguistic and semiotic constructions of border identities in deeply territorialized spaces as they are enacted in two border areas of Italy. In her chapter, she argues that, despite apparent similarities in the two geolinguistic settings, linguistic and cultural motility is deployed differently, and that LL can be key in fostering the transformative potential of local multilingualism for empowerment. She concludes that, as a result, the LL does not just contribute to the construction and display of spatial multilingualism and multiple identities, but it is also instrumental in creating the potential for change and, as such, is a structuring dimension of social life.

Toril Opsahl considers questions of invisibility, migration and empowerment in her chapter which explores and reflects on the presence of Polish in Norway's capital, Oslo. There is little doubt that there are strong and multifaceted linguistic practices involving Polish in Oslo, but these practices seem so far to exist parallel to, and to a lesser degree intertwined with, Norwegian and other languages, in public spaces. Opsahl posits that identities associated with professional life are the most prominent traces of Polish in public spaces, alongside a potential consumer identity connected to market logic, and an important purpose of this chapter is to recognize and reflect on the notion of ambivalence associated with multilingualism in public space. She reasons that a close connection between language and labour may at first glance be seen as a positive sign of empowerment of individuals, but the agency of individuals is challenged – and the potential for transformation limited – when the presence of Polish continues to feed and maintain stereotypical images of available identities, depending not only on a symbolic value but also on market economy.

Dunlevy's study focuses on onomastic approaches to place names and the inclusion or exclusion of different forms of naming on place-name and street-name signs in Northern Ireland. Dunlevy questions the extent to which the display of multilingualism, in the form of inclusion of English, Irish and Ulster Scots, can empower individuals and groups, and how the public space is used to delegitimize specific groups through exclusion in official signage.

In his contribution, Luk Van Mensel engages with the growing body of work on multilingual memorialization as an aspect of empowerment, looking into how the remaining traces of Belgium's colonial past are dealt with (and contested) in the linguistic and semiotic landscape. He focuses on the official renaming of a square in Brussels into the 'Patrice Lumumbasquare/Square Patrice Lumumba'. Van Mensel engages with the debate regarding the recognition in the public space of Congo's first prime minister, contending that this act of renaming may point to the start of a new phase in dealing with the Belgian colonial past. The chapter explores how readjustments of the public space such as these may contribute to the empowerment of the Congolese diaspora in Belgium and – possibly – to a transformation of Belgian society's dealing with its colonial past as a whole.

Robert Blackwood considers direct action, and in particular LL activism, as a tool for empowerment, paying critical attention to the ideologies articulated by the Breton-language collective Ai'Ta! in Brittany, France. In examining the activities of Ai'Ta!, Blackwood contends that minority language activism such as that undertaken in Brittany is used to legitimize the regional language, to obtain justice in what is perceived to be a highly imbalanced relationship, and to force dialogue between citizens and a powerful state.

Michelle Harrison explores in her chapter the presence of the Gujarati language and script in the LL of the English Midlands city of Leicester, adopting an author-centred approach to linguistic empowerment. She investigates the motivations and aims of the individuals and groups who are behind different displays of written information in the city's main centre for its large Indian Asian population, the Golden Mile. Harrison reveals a complex picture of communication in the everyday life of the community, dissecting multilingualism in the public space from an angle that has hitherto not been studied widely, and focusing on a city and a community that have little presence in anglophone sociolinguistic scholarship.

Finally, in her chapter, Andry Sophocleous takes the issue of linguistic empowerment into the domain of education, and in particular she examines language diversity in state preschool education in Cyprus. Sophocleous explores the tension between the potential of Greek Cypriot Dialect to empower children in a learning environment, whilst at the same time Standard Modern Greek is regarded as the official language of learning. She contends that learners (and possibly teachers) are empowered to project a common social and cultural identity but also arrange the foundational stones regarding their confidence, in-class contribution and understanding of the world around them.

References

Adams, R. (2008), *Empowerment, Participation and Social Work*, 4th edn, Basingstoke: Palgrave Macmillan.
Auer, P., and Wei, L. (2007), 'Introduction: Multilingualism as a Problem? Monolingualism as a Problem?', *Handbook of Multilingualism and Multilingual Communication*, 1–12, Berlin: Mouton de Gruyter.
Balch, A. (2016), *Immigration and the State: Fear, Greed and Hospitality*, Basingstoke: Palgrave Macmillan.
Bourdieu, P. (1991), *Language and Symbolic Power*, Cambridge: Polity Press.
Carabine, J. (1996), 'Empowering Sexualities', in B. Humphries (ed.), *Critical Perspectives on Empowerment*, 17–34, Birmingham: Venture Press.
Coulmas, F. (2018), *An Introduction to Multilingualism: Language in a Changing World*, Oxford: Oxford University Press.
Edwards, J. (2006). 'The Power of Language, the Language of Power', in J. A. Fishman, M. Pütz and J. Neff-van Aertselaer (eds), *Along the Routes to Power: Explorations of Empowerment through Language*, 13–34, Berlin: Mouton De Gruyter.
Eley, G. (1992), 'Nations, Publics, and Political Cultures: Placing Habermas in the Nineteenth Century' in C. Calhoun (ed.) *Habermas and the Public Sphere*, 289–338, Cambridge, MA: MIT Press.
Esch, E. (1989), 'English and Empowerment: Potential, Issues, Way Forward' in N. Hussain, A. Ahmed and M. Zafar (eds), *English and Empowerment in the Developing World*, 2–26, Newcastle: Cambridge Scholars.
Fishman, J. A. (2006), Sociolinguistics: More power(s) to You! (On the Explicit Study of Power in Sociolinguistic Research), in J. A. Fishman, M. Pütz and J. Neff-van Aertselaer (eds), *Along the Routes to Power: Explorations of Empowerment through Language*, 3–11, Berlin: Mouton De Gruyter.
Fishman, J. A., Pütz, M. and Neff-van Aertselaer, J. (eds) (2006), *Along the Routes to Power: Explorations of Empowerment through Language*, Berlin: Mouton De Gruyter.
Flusser, V. (2003), *The Freedom of the Migrant: Objections to Nationalism*, Urbana: University of Illinois Press.
Foucault, M. (1984), *Power/Knowledge: Selected interviews and Other Writings 1972–1977*, edited by C. Gordon, New York: Pantheon Books.
Fraser, N. (1990), 'Rethinking the Public Sphere: A Contribution to the Critique of Actually Existing Democracy', *Social Text* (25/26): 56–80.
Freire, P. (1970), *Pedagogy of the Oppressed*, translated by M. B. Ramos, New York: Continuum.
Gal, S. (2005), 'Language Ideologies Compared: Metaphors of Public/Private', *Journal of Linguistic Anthropology*, 15 (1): 23–37.
Gerodimos, R., Scullion, R., Lilleker, D. G., and Jackson, D. (2013), 'Introduction to the Media, Political Participation and Empowerment', in R. Scullion, R. Gerodimos, D. Jackson and D. G. Lilleker (eds), 1–10, London: Routledge.
Gorter, D. (2006), 'Further Possibilities for Linguistic Landscape Research', in D. Gorter (ed.), *Linguistic Landscape: A New Approach to Multilingualism*, 81–9, Clevedon, UK: Multilingual Matters.
Humphries, B. (1996), 'Contradictions in the Culture of Empowerment', in B. Humphries (ed.), *Critical Perspectives on Empowerment*, 1–16, Birmingham: Venture Press.

Lim, L., Stroud, C., and Wee, L. (eds) (2018), *The Multilingual Citizen: Towards a Politics of Language for Agency and Change*, Bristol, UK: Multilingual Matters.

Macionis, J. J., and Plummer, K. (2002), *Sociology: A Global Introduction*, Essex: Pearson Education.

McLaughlin, K. (2016), *Empowerment: A Critique*, London: Routledge.

Price, J. (1996), 'The Marginal Politics of Our Bodies? Women's Health, the Disability Movement, and Power', in B. Humphries (ed.), *Critical Perspectives on Empowerment*, 35–52, Birmingham: Venture Press.

Ruiz, R. (1991), 'The Empowerment of Language Minority Students', in N. H. Hornberger (ed.) *Honouring Richard Ruiz and His Work on Language Planning and Bilingual Education*, 259–69, Bristol, UK: Multilingual Matters.

Smart, B. (1985). *Michel Foucault*. London: Routledge.

Smith-Christmas, C., Ó Murchadha, N. P., Hornsby, M., and Moriarty, M. (eds) (2018), *New Speakers of Minority Languages: Linguistic Ideologies and Practices*, London: Palgrave Macmillan.

Solomon, B. (1976), *Black Empowerment: Social Work in Oppressed Communities*, New York: Columbia University Press.

Spolsky, B. (2004), *Language Policy*, Cambridge: Cambridge University Press.

Spolsky, B. (2009), *Language Management*, Cambridge: Cambridge University Press.

Stroud, C. (2018a), 'Introduction', in L. Lim, C. Stroud and L. Wee (eds), *The Multilingual Citizen: Towards a Politics of Language for Agency and Change*, 1–14, Bristol, UK: Multilingual Matters.

Stroud, C. (2018b), 'Linguistic Citizenship', in L. Lim, C. Stroud and L. Wee (eds), *The Multilingual Citizen: Towards a Politics of Language for Agency and Change*, 17–39, Bristol, UK: Multilingual Matters.

Watson, S. (2006), *City Publics*, Abingdon: Routledge.

Weber, M. ([1921] 1978), *Economy and Society*, Berkeley: University of California Press.

Wodak, R. (1989), 'Introduction', in R. Wodak (ed.), *Language, Power and Ideology; Studies in Political Discourse*, xiii–xx, Amsterdam: John Benjamins.

Multilingual inequality in public spaces: Towards an inclusive model of Linguistic Landscapes

Durk Gorter

1. Introduction

When we walk or drive through a city, we are surrounded by signs, even though we do not pay attention to all of the signs all of the time. Signs can inform us where to go, what is inside a building, what is forbidden to do, and most frequently signs present us with a product or a service to purchase. Advertisements and brand names, along with wayfinding, warning and other information signs, pervade urban public spaces in modern societies. Signs are everywhere, they permeate our daily life, and they can give us a sense of place. Many signs contain messages written in languages we know, can read and understand and this can unite us, but they are also in languages other than our own, which does sometimes lead to divisiveness. Signs can be helpful when written in a language we understand, but signs in a different language can become incomprehensible, mysterious and we may like or dislike them. Signs can thus bind us together as a group, but also can set us apart. Policies may regulate the use of languages on signs but signs usually do not represent languages equally. In other words, signs can and do influence our behaviour and language practices.

Many signs are fixed, others are mobile or transient, and the recent addition of many forms of digital screens leads to profound changes in the presence of dynamic and fluid textual elements in the public space, to which the hand-held screens of smartphones add an additional element. Such changes imply an increase in the complexity of the stream of bits and pieces of textual language that come to city dwellers moving through an urban environment.

Research into the display of languages on signs in public spaces is commonly referred to as the study of Linguistic Landscapes (LL) (Shohamy and Ben-Rafael 2015). Most studies direct their attention to linguistic elements of signs, but it is time for the field to move forward and go beyond existing approaches. What is missing is an overarching model of the entire course of multilingual landscapes that emerges from language policy to language practices. In this contribution a model called Multilingual Inequalities in Public Spaces (MIPS) is proposed, which intends to shed light on linguistic and social inequalities. Its challenge is to uncover language inequality on signs linked to social inequalities in the population and to frame those in a new unified and inclusive perspective. The main idea is to look from a social perspective at LL because population groups differ in their reactions to signage. The aim is to understand better the basic issue of the interrelationships between the processes that lead to the display of multilingual inequalities on signs in public spaces and the perceptions and reactions of people. As a result, this may have enhanced insight and agency and thus may empower individuals or groups to overcome social inequalities. Adopting the model implies a new research agenda for LL studies.

An important assumption, perhaps rather obvious, is that there are differences between people in the ways they are affected by signs in public space. The main conjecture is that the perceptions and reactions of people to signs will be influenced, on the one hand, by language-related factors such as their multilingual repertoires and language biographies and, on the other hand, by intersecting social factors of age, gender, socioeconomic status, ethnicity and residence, among others. The real language practices of an individual in a specific case will further depend on the particulars of the social context, the characteristics and exact placement of the signs and on concrete circumstances such as the purpose or mood of the person concerned.

In the following sections, we will first provide some background information by discussing briefly some trends in the field of LL studies and its relation with multilingualism, as well as two complementary approaches that have recently emerged. Thereafter, we present the new model to enable a more comprehensive study of LL and its implications, together with a research agenda.

2. Trends in Linguistic Landscape studies

Processes of globalization and technological changes lead to visually stimulating and linguistically rich environments in today's urban areas. Over the past ten to fifteen years, numerous LL studies were able to provide an additional view on the relation between language and society, in particular in multilingual contexts. The perspective has become an established specialization of applied linguistics (Gorter 2013) and of sociolinguistics (Van Mensel, Vandenbroucke and Blackwood 2016). The outburst of publications about LL has generated fresh insights about many relevant themes such as multilingualism (Gorter 2006), the role of English (Bolton 2012), language policy (Shohamy 2015) and minority languages (Gorter, Marten and Van Mensel 2012), among many others. This diversity of themes and topics illustrates that the field is heterogeneous and that researchers start out from divergent perspectives. The increased scholarly engagement with the visible display of written languages in public spaces reflects a more general and growing interest in issues surrounding primarily multilingualism, but also multimodality, multiculturalism, and linguistic and cultural diversity.

2.1 The multilingual turn

The study of multilingualism is a field that has recently become one of the 'hottest areas' for linguistic research. A new paradigm is emerging which has been referred to as the 'multilingual turn' (Conteh and Meier 2014; May 2014). This paradigm aims to provide a more sophisticated understanding of how multiple languages influence each other and how language influences people. Today many scholars question the assumption of 'languages' as bounded linguistic systems. The multilingual turn implies a shift from a view of languages as 'givens' to languages as 'resources' and it challenges conventional representations of languages as discrete, countable entities (Makoni and Pennycook 2007; May 2014) also in LL studies.

In relation to these new trends in the study of multilingualism, the concept of translanguaging has gained wide currency. Translanguaging tries to understand flexible and dynamic multilingual practices (Garcia and Li Wei 2014). The term 'translanguaging' has gained currency in applied linguistics in just a few years, and its meaning has evolved. Otheguy, Garcia and Reid (2015) have expanded its meaning to include even monolingual speakers. They defend a psycholinguistically 'unitary view' of a single undifferentiated cognitive competence, although they recognize also that (named) languages are important sociopolitical constructs. Li Wei (2018) went further by proposing translanguaging as a general, practical theory of language, based on the idea that speakers are not using distinct named languages but are 'languaging' and have an 'innate translanguaging instinct' (Garcia and Li Wei 2014: 32). Jaspers (2018) comments on the ideas of Garcia and Li Wei, and he observes two inspirations for translanguaging. First, the concept is based on general sociolinguistic and psycholinguistic insights about dynamic and fluid language practices, and second, it implies a political project of transformation for linguistic diversity at school. After discussing the concept at length, he concludes that the concept of translanguaging can have no less than five different meanings, which *'by any standard ... is a lot for one term'* (Jaspers 2018: 3).

For the study of LL, Gorter and Cenoz (2015) made a tentative proposal to apply the idea of translanguaging to moving between languages while looking from one point of view at linguistic signs. Van Mensel, Vandenbroucke and Blackwood (2016) have already referred to those ideas as 'seminal', although thus far translanguaging has hardly been studied empirically in LL, perhaps because most of the time it refers to the spoken mode. Translingual practices are not the same for everyone and they vary between cities and neighbourhoods depending on, among others, their socio-historic development or degree of social and linguistic diversity. This point is easily understood thinking about the contrast between a central shopping street and a residential area. It is exciting to think about taking a new approach in order to better understand the complexity of translanguaging at the level of individual city residents or visitors and at the same time, obtain knowledge about trends at the level of neighbourhoods with diverse populations. The themes of English as a global language and revitalization of minority languages have been the object of LL studies in various contexts. In some way the two can be seen as at opposite ends of a continuum or a language hierarchy as we will discuss in the next section.

2.2 Top of the hierarchy: English as all around language

In downtown areas of European cities (but also elsewhere), it is somewhat difficult – if not very unlikely – to find a street or square where English has no presence in the LL (Vandenbroucke 2014). English is omnipresent in shop names, brands, slogans and tourist information. It does not matter if English has an official status or if the local population can speak English. A sign in English usually does not index an English-speaking community, but English can just as well be used to symbolize foreign taste and manners (Kasanga 2012; Lawrence 2012; Scollon and Scollon 2003). This ubiquity of English in the LL makes it one of the clearest markers of multilingualism. Reasons to use English on signage may be creative-linguistic or related to the possibility to use English as a lingua franca across many countries. English as a language is mostly associated with modernity, internationalism, fashion and technological advancement – factors that have given English a high status and economic value (Phillipson 2013; Piller 2012; Ricento 2000; Seidlhofer 2003). The special role of English gives rise to specific hierarchical relations among languages. Its use can also lead to new social inequalities, for example, where some groups are able to access what is written on signs and others cannot (Gerritsen et al. 2010). On the one hand, English has spread widely in non-English-speaking countries in the current globalized era, and on the other hand, in English-speaking countries international brand names, shop names and slogans have obtained a presence, especially in Italian or French (Bagna and Machetti 2012). Both processes increase multilingualism in those contexts. Of course, we are not dealing with one unified, standard version of English, but with many different Englishes that come under the umbrella label. English does not immediately replace other languages, but it is used along with them and these multilingual texts display soft boundaries between languages (Cenoz and Gorter 2008). Even in a predominately English-speaking country such as the United States, studies of LL take English into consideration when they look into the role and presence of other languages, such as Chinese in Washington (Leeman and Modan 2009; Lou 2010, 2016), Korean in Oakland (Malinowski 2009), or Spanish in Pittsburgh (Mitchell 2010) or San Antonio (Hult 2014). In the UK, Cook (2013) found that languages are not evenly spread across the different functions of signs and the written languages of signs have a distinctive genre in grammar and typography. In Israel, English is overall gaining importance in combination with either Hebrew or Arabic, to such a degree that according to Ben Rafael et al. (2006: 12) English 'would better be described as a "non-foreign language"'. Hult (2003) observed in Sweden that English is not imposed from above but develops from the ground up into a prominent and thus potentially dominating part of the LL in a complex relationship with the national language, Swedish. A final example are two studies on Mallorca by Bruyèl-Olmedo and Juan-Garau (2009, 2015) who found in a tourist resort that the amount of English displayed was higher than the two official local languages Catalan and Spanish taken together. These examples show that English adds to the multilingual character of LL. At the same time, through its placement at the top of the social hierarchy of languages, it can contribute to inequality among languages on signage.

2.3 Bottom of the hierarchy: Minority languages as subordinate

Research on minority languages has a long tradition of studying topics of language revitalization, language contact and conflict, and the use of LL studies can provide a new lens on those 'old' issues (Gorter et al. 2012, 2019). Signs can reflect hierarchical relations between majority and minority groups in a community, and by looking into how, when and where minority languages are used on signs in combination with or subordinated to majority languages one can gain further insight into structures of inequality (Muth 2012; Tufi 2013; see also Ó Mainnín, this volume, and Dunlevy, this volume).

Ideologies with regard to minority languages can be better and more deeply understood through LL research (Marten 2012; Moriarty 2014). In a case of official bilingualism such as in Wales, the way signs display languages can approve a certain language ideology. How languages are framed demonstrates 'competing ways of visualizing what "being bilingual" actually means' (Coupland 2012: 23).

Visibility is an important issue for minority languages and on a continuum their place may range from being completely ignored, given only token attention, being disputed, obtaining some official support, to a full-fledged revitalization policy. At one end, we find the case of Latgalian in Latvia (Marten 2012) where the role of the regional language is degraded and minimized. The official regulations regarding public signage stipulate the use of the state language Latvian only, although on private signs other languages are tolerated next to Latvian. At the other end of this continuum we can place Basque, a language for which enhancing visibility is the subject of substantial support by regional and local authorities, and this is reflected in the signage (Aiestaran, Cenoz and Gorter 2010). The LL can thus become an arena of contestation of the visibility of a minority language.

Obviously, these considerations are not only of concern to regional minority languages but also of relevance for languages of other minorities, such as languages spoken by immigrants, refugees and other mobile groups. In LL studies, signage related to some of these groups has been studied (Tufi 2010, 2013). A frequently studied phenomenon is the multilingual signage in different Chinatowns in the United States (Leeman and Modan 2009; Leung and Wu 2012; Lou 2010, 2016) or in the UK (Amos 2016; see also Harrison, this volume).

Minority languages at the bottom of a languages hierarchy socially may lack in visibility or may be used as commodities for tourist purposes (e.g. in the case of Sámi, Pietikäinen and Kelly-Holmes 2011). The LL determines differences in appearance and leads to different experiences of cities as a whole and in particular of each of its neighbourhoods (Papen 2012). Signage contributes to a sense of place, because the configuration of the signs in a neighbourhood gives it a certain identity. The ambiance of a neighbourhood can be experienced as united, even if geographic, social or language borders are not clearly demarcated. Every local context has its own constellation of languages in which the languages have hierarchical relationships. The hierarchy of languages is an important variable because some languages are dominating and more powerful (often this is English) and others are subordinated or neglected, which has consequences for the social groups that speak those languages (minorities).

2.4 Two recent approaches in Linguistic Landscape studies

Recently two major, competing, but also complementary approaches seem to have emerged that can give further direction to LL research. On the one hand, there is the 'Ethnographic Linguistic Landscape Approach' (ELLA) and on the other hand, the 'Variationist Linguistic Landscape Study' (VaLLS). The two theoretical and methodological proposals differ strongly in how to carry out studies of the LL.

A detailed outline of the ELLA is provided in Blommaert and Maly (2016) and in a recent extension to include online and offline connections (Blommaert and Maly 2019). Before that, a basis was given by Blommaert (2013), who carried out a qualitative analysis of his own neighbourhood in Antwerp. He argues in favour of LL studies as a form of ethnography in order to 'bring out its full descriptive and explanatory potential' (Blommaert 2013: 16). Using ELLA, researchers are able to diagnose a neighbourhood based on its signage and thus paint a detailed image of its demography, in terms of population distributions and various historical layers. Older and newer groups of inhabitants can be distinguished as well as the organization of practices and relationships between groups. Qualitative elements of the signage are used to show the ambitions and identity aspirations of different groups as part of historical processes of transformation and social change in complex, superdiverse neighbourhoods.

The second and contrasting approach is VaLLS. The principles and standards of VaLLS come from variationist sociolinguistics (Soukup 2016). Its typically quantitative methods are applied to linguistic variation on signs. In her proposal, Soukup emphasizes correlations between social factors and the choice of English on signs, which in her case is explored in the city of Vienna.

These two approaches, ELLA and VaLLS, one qualitative and the other quantitative, can be seen as competing, but also as complementary. Because the two approaches have been only recently developed, it remains to be seen if either (or both) will be widely adopted by other LL researchers (see also Gorter 2019). The current contribution wants to offer a more comprehensive model as an alternative that does not reject but includes both ELLA and VaLLS. The MIPS model developed here aims at an all-inclusive, holistic approach that is distinct from earlier work.

3. Towards a comprehensive model

The objective of the model is to describe, analyse and explain the cyclical sequence involved in the construction of LL and how these processes and outcomes have an effect on the experiences of groups of people and their social behaviour, in particular their language practices. Basically, languages are always unequal because of their social positioning, of the way they are displayed and of both internal and external perceptions of the groups that use them. An encompassing, holistic approach is missing from current research and the model explores a comprehensive manner that attempts to include all or everything. The model has five component parts that are conceived of as the connected dimensions of an interlocking chain (see Figure 1.1).

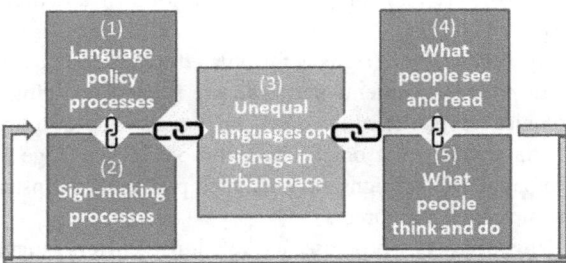

Figure 1.1 'Multilingual inequalities in public spaces' (MIPS): A model of five component parts in an interlocking cycle of Linguistic Landscapes

Components (1) and (2) of the model are the processes that establish the conditions and shape the physical signs and their placement: (1) language policy processes, which regulate or influence how and which languages appear on signs, and (2) sign-making production processes, which are contingent on design, material production and choice of languages, including multimodal aspects. Component (3) is in the centre and consists of the actual signs in urban spaces on which languages are presented in unequal ways. Components (4) and (5) are processes that individual signs, groups of signs or signage as a whole gives rise to: (4) the effect on people who as passers-by perceive, and possibly read in detail the signs. In component (5), after reading and interpreting, people can interact with or react to the linguistic elements on signs, and this can have an impact on what they do and on their language practices.

Putting this all together, it can be stated that language policies, as processes recurring in cycles, are in turn affected by evaluations and reactions of individuals or groups of people to language texts displayed in public space, and as a consequence, those reactions can impact future policy development. In that sense, the interlocking chain works like a feedback loop indicated by the arrow which marks repetition of cycles. A more detailed outline of the components and their interrelationships is provided next.

Component (1): Language policy processes

As stated above, policy determines or at least influences which languages are used on signage, especially on official signs. Johnson (2013: 9) offers the following encompassing definition: 'A *language policy* is a policy mechanism that impacts the structure, function, use, or acquisition of language.' He describes at length that a language policy can be official, top-down or unofficial, bottom-up; it can also be overt or covert, explicit or implicit, de jure or de facto, and its agents can be governments, but also communities, organizations, institutions, families or individuals.

It is not only governments that develop policies for signage, but businesses, private organizations, groups of citizens or individuals also have their own (language) policies, which all contribute to the overall construction of the LL and this may be difficult to control. Policy processes are very complex, not just top-down, and they include covert language policies.

Official language policy about signs is formulated in specific pieces of legislation, or is laid down in policy documents and both are framed by opinions, beliefs and (language) ideologies of public authorities, politicians and influencers of public opinion. Our assumption is that official and non-official language policies do not ensure equality of languages on signs, because such policies are constrained by wider social and economic contextual forces.

The study of language policy processes has to address current language legislation, as well as policy documents, academic and other publications, the media and online debates. Further, the beliefs, opinions and ideologies of key informants with responsibilities related to the governmental language policy have to be considered. Other policy agents have to be taken into account, such as political parties, major companies, advertising agencies and interest groups, but grassroots initiatives and vocal individuals can also play an important role. In investigating policy processes as part of an LL study there are more issues that have to be looked at, such as policy aims in terms of equality of languages, multilingualism in the city, the importance given to English and the role of specific languages for attracting visitors, the use of bilingual or multilingual signs as expression of identity, the use of foreign or migrant languages, contestation and conflict over language use on signs and public debates over language choice (e.g. Moriarty 2014; Rubdy and Ben Said 2015).

Only a handful of LL studies have analysed how language policy influences or determines the languages on signs (Dunlevy 2012), its ideologies or manifestations of contestation (Shohamy 2006, 2015). Authorities usually take responsibility for decisions on language policies and they often attempt to regulate which languages can be used in the public space. Legislation of signage has the intention to control the language (or languages) seen in public. Often there is a gap between the de jure language policy on the use of the official language(s) and the de facto policy of language practices and visibility. LLs can also be an arena where policies are contested, resisted and protested. An example is the regulation about the use of languages other than French, that is, English in the province of Québec (Backhaus 2009). Some investigations demonstrate a complex relationship between language policy and the presence of minority languages on display in public spaces (Szabó-Gilinger, Sloboda, Šimičić and Vigers 2012).These earlier studies are important for the understanding of the relationship between language policy and the LL, but adding research into beliefs or ideologies of policy makers, and what and how they think to influence signage, looks to fill a gap and is part of the model proposed in this chapter.

Language policy processes strongly influence the next component of the model, the sign-making processes as well as the appearance of languages on the physical signs. The chain-links between component (1) and components (2) and (3) indicate that these relationships are not unidirectional, but mutually influence or reinforce each other.

Component (2): Sign-making processes

The largest companies in the sign industry and their clients (frequently chains of shops, restaurants, hotels, etc., but also big-city governments and large organizations) determine what the totality of the assemblage of LLs looks like. These are processes of one step at the time, in fragmented ways, and for the most part in public spaces. Official signage by central or local governments, independent shop owners, private organizations and individuals also contribute to the landscape. Economic considerations can be a constraint for multilingual sign production and placement. Often a sign maker's main concern is to attract the attention of specific target groups, and as such the use of particular linguistic elements can play a role. The sign industry largely has commercial concerns, and an official government policy that regulates the use of languages may be seen more as an obstacle than an opportunity. Sometimes commercial interests prevail over official language regulations. Sign-makers can find creative ways to circumvent policy rules about which languages are mandated to be displayed (as demonstrated by Lamarre (2014) in Montreal). As producers of individual signs (or a series of signs), the LL as a whole of a street, a neighbourhood or a city is at most of secondary importance to the big players in the sign industry. As far as we know, sign-makers usually seem to have little consideration for language equality issues in producing signs. Language only becomes important when they focus on specific target groups and prioritize the visibility of one language, for example, using English. In this regard their work may increase inequalities between languages, even if unknowingly or unintentionally. In contrast, the display of minority languages on signs as part of revitalization efforts by governments and associations or as a display of identity by communities or individuals may be much more concerned with raising issues of language equality.

Sign-making processes first and foremost focus on the question of the design and production of signs and in commercial contexts, in most cases, not on the effect it may have on the unequal representation of languages. Stakeholders from the sign industry, who know about the production process can be an important source of information but have thus far not been included in LL studies, although in advertising studies media professionals have been included (e.g. Martin 2006).

Sign-making processes and production are also laid down in formal documents, such as annual company reports, design guidelines and communication manuals (Hepford 2017). Large multinational companies, such as JCDecaux or Clear Channel Outdoor, produce signage for a multitude of international chains of shops as well as advertisements on street furniture, billboards, transport or shopping malls. Therefore, such companies determine to a substantial degree what people are confronted with in urban LLs around the globe. Next to the big international companies, numerous smaller sign-producing firms are of importance because the sign industry in general is composed of many small- and medium-sized enterprises (SMEs); this includes independent local shop-owners or other entrepreneurs who can have their own responsibility over signage.

A few studies have looked into authorship of signs, for example, of shop owners (Lou 2016; Malinowski 2009). Related to this are some studies that have looked into the relationship between, on the one hand, language policy and texts on signs, and, on the other hand, how the languages on signs and users interact (e.g. Papen 2012, who interviewed shop owners and street artists). What is lacking are studies that collect data from the sign-producing industry.

These first two components of the MIPS model – language policy and sign-making – demonstrate that the physical appearance of the LL as a whole is the outcome of complex processes. The LL is constructed as an assemblage over a longer period of time. Some elements are stable (e.g. inscriptions on monuments), others may have a limited life expectancy (e.g. an advertising campaign on billboards), some signs may appear momentarily (like protest signs in a demonstration) and still others change continuously, such as digital LCD screens with adaptable video messages.

As said, components (1) and (2) are interlocked and together create an assembly of signs, which has thus far been the focus of attention of many LL studies.

Component (3): Unequal languages on signage

The direct influence of policy and sign-production is visible in a dynamic, ever-changing end product, the LL. The reasons why certain languages have a greater and more dominant presence than other languages is related to how people interact with and react to signs (represented in components (4) and (5) of the MIPS model). Our assumption is that the unequal display of languages is made visible more in specific types of signs than in others (e.g. official versus commercial signs). In different urban contexts, there will be differences between public spaces, for example, contrasting a central downtown area with a neighbourhood with a diverse population in terms of origins and home languages of the population. The totality of the LL in public spaces is in most cases largely uncontrolled in terms of signage placed (even when placement of each individual sign needs a permit).

Most LL studies have focused on languages as they appear on signage itself (see Gorter 2013, for an overview) – for example, studies that describe the languages on signs in a shopping street (Dimova 2007; Weyers 2015), a neighbourhood (Maly 2016; Papen 2012), a city (Backhaus 2007) or series of cities (Blackwood and Tufi 2015); or studies that explore the intended meaning of specific signs (Laitinen 2014) or other qualitative aspects (Moriarty 2014); or a study based on linguistic changes in signage that observes social transformations in a neighbourhood related to superdiversity and globalization (Blommaert 2013; Blommaert and Maly 2016). However, most of these studies have limited themselves to an analysis of the signs as physical tokens that contain linguistic elements. In general, researchers have treated the LL as language or meaning on signs to be discovered in the outside world. Signs are treated as pre-given and their linguistic or semiotic properties have to be determined by the researcher in order to figure out their meaning or to look into social implications.

Some locations are more suitable than others (Blackwood 2015) to observe processes of multilingual inequalities, but in principle they are present everywhere, including outside urban contexts. As stated earlier, English has become the ubiquitous language in LL around the globe, but minority languages also play a larger or lesser role in many contexts. This makes it possible to answer questions about the extent to which signage reveals linguistic and social inequalities. A basic idea of the MIPS model is that it can be applied in many different contexts, although it may have to be adjusted to specific local circumstances.

Whereas features of fixed signs are the common focus of LL studies, digital screens have been placed in large numbers in urban environments in recent years. To date, those digital screens have not been the focus of LL research, even though screens are analysed in other fields (Cashmore, Cleland and Dixon 2018; Jewitt and Triggs 2006). In the comprehensive model proposed here, the digital transformation of the LL can be included.

It is obvious that signs can have an influence on people, who may perceive them differently and also react in different ways to elements of the LL around them. Those perceptions and practices have to be part of an integrated study, as well as the links between them.

Component (4): Perception – seeing and reading

There are few studies that have investigated the relation between signage and language users. Ben Said (2011: 68) suggested that LL research 'ought to include voices from the people as an essential part of the interpretation of the linguistic landscape'. Yet, the perspective of actors is only included in few studies. This was the case, for example, to find out preferences for certain languages, in Amos (2016), Garvin (2010) and Trumper-Hecht (2009). The voices of some groups were considered through street interviews with locals and tourists by Onofri et al. (2010, 2013). However, studies that include people's experiences, or try to see through the eyes of users and tap into their interpretations and evaluations, are only beginning to emerge; this is something that is part of the proposed model.

Vingron et al. (2018) used eye tracking to find out more about what people notice when viewing LL (see also Seifi 2015). The method of eye-movement recording is well established in other fields (Roberts and Siyanova-Chanturia 2013), but it is a novelty for LL studies.

A person can look at individual signs or perceive signage as a whole when moving through an urban environment. In general, passers-by will unavoidably look at the languages displayed on signs in public spaces, but not everyone sees or reads in the same way. For example, it makes a difference if a person takes a route every day and passes by numerous signs without paying much attention, compared to first-time visitors who try to find their way. It is important to know what people see and which signs are read by whom and why, what people look at, in which language a person reads a sign and if people notice inequality of languages on signs. It is not clear which languages a person reads on multilingual signs and to which characteristics this is related or if people notice inequality of languages on signs. Our assumption is that people see and read only a small fraction of all signs depending on their familiarity with the specific surroundings (more familiar, less reading) and conditioned by linguistic, social and personal factors. However, this issue of attention is complex. One idea is that if the text of a short bilingual sign is read, the text is usually or almost unavoidably read in both languages. Unequal multilingual competences and different language backgrounds have consequences for the ability to read the languages on the signs and thus the possibility that they influence a person. It is important to find out how many signs people look at and for how long when they move through an urban environment.

The results of a perception study with eye tracking can provide valuable information for the linguistic input received by a person, but it does not tell much about the intake, the actual reading of the written texts in different languages. Thus, a second step is needed in which participants retrospectively answer questions about which signs they read and in which language; component (5) of the model is about that aspect.

Component (5): Reflections, reactions and language practices

Closely linked to what people read in which language(s) is what people think and what they do with the information they process. Their interpretations, meaning-making and evaluations of the signs are crucial for understanding their behavioural reactions and language practices, and how those connect to their linguistic and social background characteristics. For example, commercial signs target specific groups of potential buyers of a certain age, women or men, people who can afford luxury goods and the like. Some signs are aimed at tourists and others target local residents.

Furthermore, a persons' mood or purpose for being in a specific location may have an influence on their interpretation of the LL. It can be argued that how participants in a study evaluate and react to the inequality of languages is correlated with multilingual competence, language background and social factors such as age, class or ethnic group.

The languages we know influence the way we look at the real world, and members of different language groups and people with varying levels of language competence differ in their perceptions, evaluations, reactions and behaviours (see also Stroud and Jegels 2014). In the MIPS model a basic idea is to find out about empirical differences between different social groups, how they deal with language inequalities, and how and why they make use of the languages on signs and how it affects their behaviour in various ways. The model endeavours to point to research that can uncover differences in inequalities between languages and social groups.

4. Potential impact and research agenda

The theoretical model proposed here tries to further LL studies. Thus far, studies have focused mainly on the third component: the characteristics or meanings of the signs itself. The idea is to cast the net wider and to look at the whole cycle from regulation and creation to perception and reaction to LL. Each of the five components can be related to specific issues that can be spelled out as further questions for specific research projects: (1) Do language policies lead to more equality of languages on signage? (2) Do design and production of signs have an effect on unequal representation of languages? (3) To what extent does the signage itself reveal linguistic and social inequalities? (4) In navigating the multiple languages in urban public spaces, how many of all signs do individuals see and how many of the languages on the signs do they read? How much inequality do they perceive? Finally, (5) how do people evaluate and react to the unequal display of languages? And, how does this, in turn as a feedback loop, influence language policy and sign production? The MIPS model has the potential to look into all those questions at the same time as one coherent and consistent whole and make links between the different parts. Many studies focus on component (3) (signs themselves) and some relate the signage to policy, or the authors of signs or to characteristics of a population or to possible interpretations of the meaning of the signs, but the model proposed here wants to go beyond such studies and apply a comprehensive approach that takes into consideration all components and the relationships between them. The model can be transformative for the field in that it addresses some of its shortcomings. The way forward is to treat these questions as parts of one large project in which the researchers make an effort to study all components as an integrated whole, including the feedback loop that points to the ever-changing dynamics of LLs. In this sense the model is part of the research agenda of the field for the coming years.

In terms of social impact, it would inform analyses of LL and underpin an understanding of the types of manipulation of the public space that brings to light inequality and presumably foster the ability to act on this. The outcome of studies based on this model will have social impact because the results are relevant for language policy, city marketing or as a practical application in education. It also speaks to the issue of power of large multinational companies that can manipulate and dominate LL.

The MIPS model helps thinking through multilingualism in the public space. It can help to answer the question to what extent multilingualism in the public space empowers individuals and groups. Or, how multilingualism helps or hinders social groups that want to revitalize, promote or just use their minority language. It can create greater awareness of ways in which the public arena is used to delegitimize specific linguistic groups. Language policy agents can obtain a higher degree of influence of the signage and it can thus empower them. Multilingualism as analysed through the LL in public spaces can make a positive contribution to societal well-being, which in turn has implications for government policy.

The basis of the model is sociolinguistic because it tries to answer questions about linguistic and social issues in society among different groups. Not only is it relevant for LL studies, therefore, but it also opens the road for new research trajectories in sociolinguistics about the fundamental issue of inequality between languages and population groups. Through the model, we come to understand better the traces left behind by unequal languages in the public spaces of multilingual cities.

References

Aiestaran, J., Cenoz, J., and Gorter, D. (2010). 'Multilingual Cityscapes: Perceptions and Preferences of the Inhabitants of Donostia-San Sebastián', in E. Shohamy, E. Ben-Rafael and M. Barni (eds), *Linguistic Landscape in the City*, 219–34, Bristol, UK: Multilingual Matters.

Amos, H. W. (2016), 'Chinatown by Numbers: Defining an Ethnic Space by Empirical Linguistic Landscape', *Linguistic Landscape*, 2 (2): 127–56.

Backhaus, P. (2007), *Linguistic Landscapes: A Comparative Study of Urban Multilingualism in Tokyo*, Clevedon, UK: Multilingual Matters.

Backhaus, P. (2009), 'Rules and Regulations in Linguistic Landscaping: A Comparative Perspective', in E. Shohamy and D. Gorter (eds), *Linguistic Landscape: Expanding the Scenery*, 157–72, London: Routledge.

Bagna, C., and Machetti, S. (2012), 'LL and (Italian) Menus and Brand Names: A Survey around the World', in C. Hélot, M. Barni, R. Janssens and C. Bagna (eds), *Linguistic Landscapes, Multilingualism, and Social Change*, 217–30, Frankfurt: Peter Lang.

Ben Rafael, E., Shohamy, E., Amara, M. H., and Trumper-Hecht, N. (2006), 'Linguistic Landscape as Symbolic Construction of the Public Space: The Case of Israel', in D. Gorter (ed.), *Linguistic Landscape: A New Approach to Multilingualism*, 7–30, Clevedon, UK: Multilingual Matters.

Ben Said, S. (2011), 'Data Triangulation as a Resource in Multilingual Research: Examples from the Linguistic Landscape', in *Proceedings of the Conference on Doing Research in Applied Linguistics*, Bangkok, Thailand: King Mongkut's University of Technology Thonburi and Macquarie University. Available online: http://arts.kmutt.ac.th/dral/PDF%20proceedings%20on%20Web/62-70_Data_Triangulation_as_a_Resource_in_Multilingual_Research.pdf.

Blackwood, R. (2015), 'LL Explorations and Methodological Challenges: Analysing France's Regional Languages', *Linguistic Landscape*, 1 (1): 38–53.

Blackwood, R., and Tufi, S. (2015), *The Linguistic Landscape of the Mediterranean: French and Italian Coastal Cities*, Basingstoke: Palgrave Macmillan.

Blommaert, J. (2013), *Ethnography, Superdiversity, and Linguistic Landscapes: Chronicles of Complexity*, Bristol, UK: Multilingual Matters.

Blommaert, J., and Maly, I. (2016), 'Ethnographic Linguistic Landscape Analysis and Social Change: A Case Study', in K. Arnaut, J. Blommaert, B. Rampton and M. Spotti (eds), *Language and Superdiversity*, 191–211, London: Routledge.

Blommaert, J., and Maly, I. (2019), 'Invisible Lines in the Online-Offline Linguistic Landscape'. *Tilburg Papers in Culture Studies*, no. 223, The Netherlands: Tilburg University.

Bolton, K. (2012), 'World Englishes and Linguistic Landscapes', *World Englishes*, 31 (1): 30–3.

Bruyèl-Olmedo, A., and Juan-Garau, M. (2009), 'English as a Lingua Franca in the Linguistic Landscape of the Multilingual Resort of S'Arenal in Mallorca', *International Journal of Multilingualism*, 6 (4): 386–411.

Bruyèl-Olmedo, A., and Juan-Garau, M. (2015), 'Shaping Tourist LL: Language Display and the Sociolinguistic Background of an International Multilingual Readership', *International Journal of Multilingualism*, 12 (1): 51–67.

Cashmore, E., Cleland, J., and Dixon, K. (2018), *Screen Society*, London: Palgrave Macmillan.

Cenoz, J., and Gorter, D. (2008), 'Linguistic Landscape as an Additional Source of Input in Second Language Acquisition', *IRAL, International Review of Applied Linguistics in Language Teaching*, 46: 257–76.

Conteh, J., and G. Meier. (2014), *The Multilingual Turn in Languages Education: Opportunities and Challenges*, Bristol, UK: Multilingual Matters.

Cook, V. (2013), 'The Language of the Street', *Applied Linguistics Review*, 4 (1): 43–81.

Coupland, N. (2012), 'Bilingualism on Display: The Framing of Welsh and English in Welsh Public Spaces', *Language in Society*, 41: 1–27.

Dimova (2007), 'English Shop Signs in Macedonia', *English Today*, 23: 18–24.

Dunlevy, D. A. (2012), 'Linguistic Policy and Linguistic Choice: A Study of the Galician Linguistic Landscape', in C. Hélot, M. Barni, R. Janssens and C. Bagna (eds), *Linguistic Landscapes, Multilingualism, and Social Change*, 53–68, Frankfurt: Peter Lang.

Garcia, O., and Li Wei (2014), *Translanguaging: Language, Bilingualism and Education*, London: Palgrave Macmillan.

Garvin, R. (2010), 'Responses to the Linguistic Landscape in Memphis, Tennessee: An Urban Space in Transition', in E. Shohamy, E. Ben-Rafael and M. Barni (eds), *Linguistic Landscape in the City*, 252–71, Bristol, UK: Multilingual Matters.

Gerritsen, M., Nickerson, C., van Hooft, A., van Meurs, F., Korzilius, H., Nederstigt, U., and Crijns, R. (2010), 'English in Product Advertisements in Non-English-Speaking Countries in Western Europe: Product Image and Comprehension of the Text', *Journal of Global Marketing*, 23 (4): 349–65.

Gorter, D. (ed.) (2006), *Linguistic Landscape: A New Approach to Multilingualism*, Clevedon, UK: Multilingual Matters. (Originally as a special issue of *International Journal of Multilingualism*, 3 (1)).

Gorter, D. (2013), 'Linguistic Landscapes in a Multilingual World', *ARAL – Annual Review of Applied Linguistics*, 33: 190–212.

Gorter, D. (2019), Methods and Techniques for Linguistic Landscape Research: About Definitions, Core Issues and Technological Innovations, in M. Pütz and N. Mundt (eds), *Expanding the Linguistic Landscape: Multilingualism, Language Policy and the Use of Space as a Semiotic Resource*, 38–57, Bristol, UK: Multilingual Matters.

Gorter, D., and Cenoz, J. (2015), 'Translanguaging and Linguistic Landscapes', *Linguistic Landscape*, 1 (1): 54–74.

Gorter, D., Marten, H. F., and Van Mensel, L. (eds) (2012), *Minority Languages in the Linguistic Landscape*, London: Palgrave Macmillan.

Gorter, D., Marten, H. F., and Van Mensel, L. (2019), Linguistic Landscapes and Minority Languages, in G. Hogan-Brun and B. O'Rourke (eds), *The Handbook on Minority Languages and Communities*, 481–506, London: Palgrave-Macmillan.

Hepford, E. A. (2017), 'Language for Profit: Spanish–English Bilingualism in Lowe's Home Improvement', *International Journal of Bilingual Education and Bilingualism*, 20 (6): 652–66.

Hult, F. M. (2003), 'English on the Streets of Sweden: An Ecolinguistic View of Two Cities and a Language Policy', *Working Papers in Educational Linguistics*, 19: 43–63.

Hult, F. M. (2014), 'Drive-Thru Linguistic Landscaping: Constructing a Linguistically dominant place in a bilingual space', *International Journal of Bilingualismi*, 18 (5): 507–23.

Jaspers, J. (2018), 'The Transformative Limits of Translanguaging', *Language and Communication*, 58: 1–10.

Jewitt, C., and Triggs, T. (2006), 'Screens and the Social Landscape – Editorial', *Visual Communication*, 5 (2): 131–40.

Johnson, D. C. (2013), *Language Policy*, London: Palgrave Macmillan.

Kasanga, L. A. (2012), 'English in the Democratic Republic of the Congo', *World Englishes*, 31 (1): 48–69.

Lamarre, P. (2014), 'Bilingual Winks and Bilingual Wordplay in Montreal's Linguistic Landscape', *International Journal of the Sociology of Language*, 2014 (228): 131–51.

Laitinen, M. (2014), '630 Kilometres by Bicycle: Observations of English in Urban and Rural Finland', *International Journal of the Sociology of Language*, 228: 55–77.

Lawrence, C. B. (2012), 'The Korean English Linguistic Landscape', *World Englishes*, 31 (21): 70–92.

Leeman, J., and Modan, G. (2009), 'Commodified Language in Chinatown: A Contextualized Approach to Linguistic Landscape', *Journal of Sociolinguistics*, 13 (3): 332–62.

Leung, G. Y., and Wu, M. H. (2012), 'Linguistic Landscape and Heritage Language Literacy Education: A Case Study of Linguistic Rescaling in Philadelphia Chinatown', *Written Language & Literacy*, 15 (1): 114–40.

Li, Wei. (2018), 'Translanguaging as a Practical Theory of Language', *Applied Linguistics*, 39 (1): 9–30, https://doi.org/10.1093/applin/amx039.

Lou, J. J. (2010), 'Chinese in the Side: The Marginalization of Chinese in the Linguistic and Social Landscapes of Chinatown in Washington, DC', in E. Shohamy, E. Ben-Rafael and M. Barni (eds), *Linguistic Landscape in the City*, 96–114, Bristol, UK: Multilingual Matters.

Lou, J. J. (2016), *The Linguistic Landscape of Chinatown: A Sociolinguistic Ethnography*, Bristol, UK: Multilingual Matters.

Makoni, S., and Pennycook, A. (eds) (2007), *Disinventing and Reconstituting Languages*, Clevedon, UK: Multilingual Matters.

Malinowski, D. (2009), 'Authorship in the Linguistic Landscape: A Multimodal-Performative View', in E. Shohamy and D. Gorter (eds), *Linguistic Landscape: Expanding the Scenery*, 107–25, London: Routledge.

Maly, I. (2016), 'Detecting Social Changes in Times of Superdiversity: An Ethnographic Linguistic Landscape Analysis of Ostend in Belgium', *Journal of Ethnic and Migration Studies*, 42 (5): 703–23.

Marten, H. F. (2012), 'Latgalian Is Not a Language': Linguistic Landscapes in Eastern Latvia and How They Reflect Centralist Attitudes', in D. Gorter, H. F. Marten and L. Van Mensel (eds), *Minority Languages in the Linguistic Landscape*, 19–35, Basingstoke: Palgrave-Macmillan.

Martin, E. (2006), *Marketing Identities through Language: English and Global Imagery in French Advertising*, London: Palgrave Macmillan.

May, S. (ed.) (2014), *The Multilingual Turn: Implications for SLA, TESOL and Bilingual Education*, London: Routledge.

Mitchell, T. D. (2010), '"A Latino Community Takes Hold": Reproducing Semiotic Landscapes in Media Discourse', in A. Jaworski and C. Thurlow (eds), *Semiotic Landscapes: Language, Image, Space*, 168–86, London: Continuum.

Moriarty, M. (2014), 'Contesting Language Ideologies in the Linguistic Landscape of an Irish Tourist Town', *International Journal of Bilingualism*, 18 (5): 464–77.

Muth, S. (2012), 'The Linguistic Landscapes of Chișinău and Vilnius: Linguistic Landscape and the Representation of Minority Languages in two Post-Soviet Capitals', in D. Gorter, H. F. Marten and L. Van Mensel (eds), *Minority Languages in the Linguistic Landscape*, 204–24, Basingstoke: Palgrave-Macmillan.

Onofri, L., Nunes, P. A. L. D., Cenoz, J., and Gorter, D. (2010),' Economic Preferences for Language Diversity: Myth or Reality? An Attempt to Estimate the Economic Value of the Linguistic Landscape', SUSDIV Paper 15.2010. Milan, Italy: Fondazione Eni Enrico Mattei. Available online: www.susdiv.org/uploadfiles/GC2010-015.pdf.

Onofri, L., Nunes, P. A. L. D., Cenoz, J., and Gorter, D. (2013), 'Linguistic Diversity and Preferences: Econometric Evidence from European Cities', *Journal of Economics and Econometrics*, 56 (1): 39–60. www.eeri.eu/documents/jee/JEE_2013_01_03.pdf.

Otheguy, R., García, O., and Reid, W. (2015), 'Clarifying Translanguaging and Deconstructing Named Languages: A Perspective from Linguistics', *Applied Linguistics Review*, 6 (3): 281–307.

Papen, U. (2012), 'Commercial Discourses, Gentrification and Citizens' Protest: The Linguistic Landscape of Prenzlauer Berg, Berlin', *Journal of Sociolinguistics*, 16 (1): 56–80.

Phillipson, R. (2013), *Linguistic Imperialism Continued*, London: Routledge.

Pietikäinen, S., and Kelly-Holmes, H. (2011), 'The Local Political Economy of Languages in a Sámi Tourism Destination: Authenticity and Mobility in the Labelling of Souvenirs', *Journal of Sociolinguistics*, 15 (3): 323–46.

Piller, I. (2012), 'Multilingualism and Social Exclusion', in M. Martin-Jones, A. Blackledge and A. Creese (eds), *The Routledge Handbook of Multilingualism*, 281–96, London: Routledge.

Ricento, T. (ed.) (2000), *Ideology, Politics and Language Policies (Focus on English)*, Amsterdam: John Benjamins.

Roberts, L., and Siyanova-Chanturia, A. (2013), 'Using Eye-Tracking to Investigate Topics in L2 Acquisition and L2 Processing', *Studies in Second Language Acquisition*, 35 (2): 213–35.

Rubdy, R., and Ben Said, S. (eds) (2015), *Conflict, Exclusion and Dissent in the Linguistic Landscape*, Basingstoke: Palgrave Macmillan.

Scollon, R., and Scollon-Wong, S. (2003), *Discourses in Place*, London: Routledge.

Seidlhofer, B. (2003), *A Concept of International English and Related Issues: From 'Real English' to 'Realistic English'?*, Strasbourg: Council of Europe – Language Policy Division.

Seifi, P. (2015), 'Eye Movements and Linguistic Landscape', Unpublished master's thesis, University of Groningen, The Netherlands.

Shohamy, E. (2006), *Language Policy: Hidden Agendas and New Approaches*, London: Routledge.

Shohamy, E. (2015), 'LL Research as Expanding Language and Language Policy', *Linguistic Landscape: An International Journal*, 1 (1/2): 152–71.

Shohamy, E., and Ben-Rafael, E. (2015), 'Introduction: Linguistic Landscape, a New Journal', *Linguistic Landscape*, 1 (1/2): 1–5.

Soukup, B. (2016), 'English in the Linguistic Landscape of Vienna, Austria (ELLViA): Outline, Rationale, and Methodology of a Large-Scale Empirical Project on Language Choice on Public Signs from the Perspective of Sign-Readers', VIEWS, Vienna English Working Papers, vol. 25, http://anglistik.univie.ac.at/views/.

Stroud, C., and D. Jegels (2014), 'Semiotic Landscapes and Mobile Narrations of Place: Performing the Local', *International Journal of the Sociology of Language*, 228: 179–99.

Szabó-Gilinger, E., Sloboda, M., Šimičić, L., and Vigers, D. (2012), 'Discourse Coalitions for and against Minority Languages on Signs: Linguistic Landscape as a Social Issue', in D. Gorter, H. F. Marten and L. Van Mensel (eds), *Minority Languages in the Linguistic Landscape*, 263–80, Basingstoke: Palgrave-Macmillan.

Tufi, S. (2010), 'Degrees of Visibility of Immigrant Communities in the Linguistic Landscape of Genoa and Cagliari', in A. Ledgeway and A. L. Lepschy (eds), *In and Out of Italy: lingue e cultura della migrazione italiana*, 31–42, Guerra: Perugia.

Tufi, S. (2013), 'Shared Places, Unshared Identities: Vernacular Discourses and Spatialised Constructions of Identity in the Linguistic Landscape of Trieste', *Modern Italy*, 18 (4): 391–408.

Trumper-Hecht, N. (2009), 'Constructing National Identity in Mixed Cities in Israel: Arabic on Signs in the Public Space of Upper Nazareth', in E. Shohamy and D. Gorter (eds), *Linguistic Landscape: Expanding the Scenery*, 238–52, London: Routledge.

Vandenbroucke, M. (2014), 'Language Visibility, Functionality and Meaning across Various Time Space Scales in Brussels' Multilingual Landscapes', *Journal of Multilingual and Multicultural Development*, 36 (2): 163–81.

Van Mensel, L., Vandenbroucke, M., and Blackwood, R. (2016), 'Linguistic Landscapes', in O. García, N. Flores and M. Spotti (eds), *Oxford Handbook of Language and Society*, 423–49, Oxford: Oxford University Press.

Vingron, N., Gullifer, J. W., Hamill, J., Leimgruber, J., and Titone, D. (2018), 'Using Eye Tracking to Investigate What Bilinguals Notice about Linguistic Landscape Images', *Linguistic Landscape*, 3 (3), 226–45.

Weyers, J. R. (2015), 'English Shop Names in the Retail Landscape of Medellín, Colombia', *English Today*, 126 (32, 2): 8–14.

2

Demarcating the space for multilingualism: On the workings of ethnic interests in a 'civic nation'

Marián Sloboda

1. Introduction

Social modernization with nationalism as a prominent ideology has had a monolingualizing transformative effect on Europe; however, postmodernist trends such as increased respect for linguistic minorities and multilingualism have been changing Europe since as early as the 1960s (Neustupný 2006; Wright 2016). Still, we can observe that many of the languages spoken in the territories of European countries are hardly visible in the public space.

This chapter investigates this phenomenon in the context of the Czech Republic (Czechia), East-Central Europe, which displays important prerequisites for openness towards multilingualism in public spaces. First, its Constitution designed the country as a civic nation, in which no ethnic group assumes a privileged position. Second, the country has no legal act that would promote the ethnic majority's language as national or as official explicitly. Third, due to a later onset of social modernization as compared to Western Europe (Hroch 2000), the country has had a rather long history of quotidian multilingualism, and in the nineteenth and twentieth centuries, it also experienced official bilingualism. Finally, the Czech people view themselves as a rather tolerant nation. On the other hand, however, vociferous demonstrations of xenophobic attitudes that surfaced during the Refugee Crisis in Europe (e.g. Berntzen and Weisskircher 2016) had a substantial grassroots component in Czechia (cf. Muhič Dizdarevič 2016, 2017). They have pointed out that, in addition to legislation, official policies or public statements, it is equally important to focus one's attention on ordinary people's behaviour towards the languages of others.

The aim in this study is to focus on such behaviour and to scrutinize the ways in which people react to, and particularly restrict, language choice. Since empowerment involves the development of critical understanding of sociopolitical environments in order for people to gain greater control over their lives (Christens 2011) or, as Perkins (2010: 207) notes, raising awareness about the influence of powerful political and economic structures and interests is important for empowerment, the aim of this study is also to reveal people's orientations to higher-scale interests and social order categories in their behaviour towards language choice.

2. Theoretical perspective

This study can be categorized as pertaining to Linguistic Landscape (LL) studies which show a 'phenomenological orientation' (cf. Zabrodskaja and Milani 2014). In studying behaviour towards languages in public spaces, I assume a praxeological and mobile stance on space (Stroud and Jegels 2014) which focuses on living and engaging with the displays of languages in signage.

The engagement with language displays that is responsive in nature is a type of what Jernudd and Neustupný (1987) describe as 'language management'. In their conceptualization (for recent articulations, see Fairbrother and Kimura 2020; He and Dai 2016; Nekvapil 2016), language management is any metalinguistic or metapragmatic practice triggered by social actors' noting of a phenomenon, such as a language choice in a sign, which deviates from their expectation. From the stage of deviation noting, the process usually proceeds to evaluation and sometimes further to adjustment design and its implementation. Empowerment within this framework is such an adjustment in this process through which power is achieved (Neustupný 2004: 5). Some processes of language management in this praxeological sense take the form of simple acts of individual behaviour, but some become highly organized – involving more social actors, resources, deliberation and ideologies across multiple settings (Nekvapil 2009). *Language* management also clusters with other types of management behaviour, as illustrated by Neustupný (1993) in his analysis of language management for the disadvantaged Romani speakers in Czechoslovakia. Elaborating on his study, Neustupný and Nekvapil (2003) have identified *communicative* management which, in addition to language, concerns non-linguistic components of communication, for example, after Hymes (1974), the management of participation (i.e. inclusion/exclusion which is particularly relevant to empowerment) and the management of setting (relevant to spatiality). The other types are *socioeconomic* management and *sociocultural* management (Nekvapil 2016). These are driven by non-linguistic interests, but as Jernudd and Neustupný (1987) have pointed out, these interests are frequently of major significance in language management and, therefore, the identification of language-to-interest relationships must become an important part of the analysis of language choice management.

Given this book's focus on empowerment in relation to public spaces, the central concern here can further be specified as the question of how social actors' management of language choice contributes to the (dis)empowerment of speaker groups by structuring spaces along the public/private distinction. Bailey (2002) argues that there is 'no essential "private" or intrinsic "public," no obvious psychological or anthropological constant underlying these concepts' (15), but despite the concepts' shifting and sliding character, 'the distinction itself … is pervasive, durable, persistent, and deeply rooted' (ibid.). This applies at least to Western societies, in which, as Gal (2005) notes, the public/private distinction has developed a categorial nature, since people bind multiple characterizations to publicness/privateness. Publicness is usually associated with accessibility, openness, rationality, objectivity, officiality, eminence, national relevance and formality, while the opposing characteristics – that is, inaccessibility, closeness, emotionality, subjectivity, ordinariness, local relevance and informality – are bound to the category of privateness (Gal 2005). As Schegloff (2007) shows in interactional detail, an important feature of categories in contrast to simple 'labels' is that categories can be inferred indirectly in social practice. Therefore, this study does not limit itself to explicit labelling of spaces as 'public' or 'private' but also considers differentiations based on social actors' observable orientations to any characteristic bound to that pair of categories.

The issue is further complicated by the fact that (1) social actors may apply the public/private distinction recursively, that is, reiterate the differentiation within a social phenomenon already differentiated by this distinction, for example, a smaller private space within a larger public space (Gal 2005: 26–7), and (2) the public/private contrast may work as an 'axis of differentiation' (Gal and Irvine 2019: 19) used to differentiate within multiple types of social phenomena – spaces, people, moralities, themes, activities, social practices and/or relations – at once. Social actors may project the distinction onto a different social phenomenon, but its primary anchoring is in one type of social phenomena depending on culture, for example, in space in the United States but in persons in the former socialist states of Central and Eastern Europe (Gal 2005). Such projections are facilitated by the 'erasure' (forgetting, denying, ignoring or eliminating) of some features of the social phenomenon in question when the distinction is projected onto it (Gal 2005: 27; Gal and Irvine 2019: 20). For multilingualism management, this means that social actors may treat languages differentially as a result of a projection of the public/private distinction from a social phenomenon of another type onto them. For example, the occurrence of some languages is taken as legitimate in public *spaces*, while others are to occur in private ones only; public *persons* legitimately use some languages, while only private ones use some others; some languages are legitimate in public *activities*, while others only in private ones; and so on. And all these projections may again be spatialized. This is how a space for a particular language or language class can be demarcated.[1] When projected onto a linguistically defined social group, such language differentiation impacts on the group's recognition, legitimation or participation in public spaces. Thus, language choice management contributes to the reproduction of social divisions and to power inequality between groups.

Some theoretical inspiration for this study stems from ethnomethodology: its understanding of situated 'micro' level social practices as instantiations of the 'macro' social order that reproduce this same social order (Coulter 2001). This entails the understanding of publicness/privateness of a space as a practical accomplishment of differentiation by social actors in their practices. Accordingly, their own, 'emic' views and ordinariness of their practices are of interest here, and the analytical preference is for non-elicited naturally occurring data (ten Have 2004), with reliance on the researcher's in-group knowledge of the collectivity researched (ten Have 2002).

3. Methodology

Following the ethnomethodological inspiration, I utilized my own experience of the places I have lived in and moved through, also including my observations of others' interactions with the LL, as a starting point. I have not employed the walking-based methods used in similarly focused studies (Garvin 2010; Laitinen 2014; Stroud and Jegels 2014; Szabó and Troyer 2017), because according to these, researchers *instruct* themselves or informants to move through certain places and make comments or take notes (see also Opsahl, this volume). Instead, I have decided to work with 'key incidents' – as Emerson (2007) explains:

> Key incidents are not necessarily dramatic matters, significant or noteworthy for those involved. Rather a key incident attracts a particular field researcher's immediate interest, even if what occurred was mundane and ordinary to participants. This 'interest' is not a full-blown, clearly articulated theoretical claim, but a more intuitive, theoretically sensitive conviction that something intriguing has just taken place. (469)

The data generation for this study was thus not motivated by a particular research agenda, but rather a certain overall and varying theoretical sensitivity. Various key incidents were recorded over an extended period of time. Some of them have been selected for this study, not as representative or illustrative of a claim, but in so far as they contribute to theory development. The cases are also not necessarily representative or typical of the situation in Czechia as a whole, but there are taken-for-granted elements in them, as well as a presence/absence of a breach response, which point to some fundamentals of the social order in the polity.

A characteristic feature of key incidents is that they open up new lines of enquiry and analysis (Emerson 2007: 430). I have followed the lines suggested by the language management approach as sketched above: after having noted down and photo-documented an incident, I sought evidence of whether the phenomenon in question was also noted, evaluated and adjusted by other members of society or was part of such management. The data thus comprises not only my notes from observations and photographs but also related official documents, news media reports and internet discussion posts. With two key incidents that do not seem to have provoked public response, an interview and an email enquiry were used.

4. The Czech context

A few notes on the Czech context are pertinent in order to facilitate the understanding of the cases analysed below and to expose similarities to, or differences from, other national contexts.

The historical Czech lands used to be part of the multilingual, yet German-dominated, Austrian Empire. The Czech national movement in the nineteenth century basically aimed at emancipation from German supremacy. Established in 1918 after the empire's disintegration, Czechoslovakia remained a multi-ethnic country due to the presence of three million German speakers and significant Polish, Roma and Rusyn (Ukrainian) minorities. During and following the Second World War, the Czech lands gradually homogenized – as a result of Nazi extermination of Jews and the Roma, the Czechoslovaks' post-war expulsion of Germans and the assimilation of other ethnic groups encapsulated behind the Iron Curtain. Russian was the main foreign language taught in schools during the socialist period. Officially it was the language of an ally, but following the military suppression of the 1968 Prague Spring, it unofficially also became the language of 'the occupiers'. Meanwhile, and as an exception, the population of Slovaks increased due to in-migration from the Slovak part of Czechoslovakia. The bi-national Czech-Slovak federation disintegrated along ethnonational lines in 1993, but the Constitution of Czechia defined the newly established state as a civic one. Although ethnic homogenization continued in the 1990s, Czechia soon became a destination country for international migration (Sloboda 2016). Today, foreign residents make up 5 per cent of its 10.6 million population. In the last census, 89 per cent of residents declared Czech as their mother tongue, 2.5 per cent both Czech and a minority language and 4 per cent a minority language only (the remaining 4.5 per cent refrained from disclosing their mother tongue). Speakers of Slovak, Ukrainian, Russian, Vietnamese and Polish are the most numerous minorities (for details, see Sloboda 2016).

During the past few decades, Czechs have developed the self-image of a tolerant nation, as evidenced in a survey by Public Opinion Research Centre (2008) as well as in public discourse, sometimes despite contradictory evidence (cf. Radio Praha 2000; Raduševič 2011). This public discourse shifted during anti-Roma demonstrations following the Great Recession and especially during the 2014–16 Refugee Crisis in Europe. The nation's positive self-image has been challenged and debated; even those media maintaining the image expressed limitations in its validity (see, e.g. Hovorková 2014; Pisingerová 2018; Polák 2018). Ethnic intolerance has increased not only in discourse but also in practical action, as manifested in the anti-Roma demonstrations and the demonstrations and other acts of hate targeting migrants and Muslims. Since similar trends have been observed in other countries around the world (Park 2019: 405), it is pertinent to examine, using this specific but non-unique Czech case, the ways in which restrictive language management at the 'micro level' of practical action and the involvement of 'macro-level' interests can be identified and analysed.

5. Differentiations along public/private lines

The key incident I would like to start with is an event that I first noted in media and later studied in a research project (Sloboda et al. 2012; Szabó Gilinger et al. 2012). The incident comprised the defacing of Polish names in place-name and street-name signs in the Těšín borderland region, soon after the Polish names were added to the Czech names on signs in 2006. Czech and Polish had been in written use in that region for several centuries. In 1920, the region was divided between the newly independent

Czechoslovakia and Poland after an armed struggle, leaving a significant Polish population on the Czechoslovak side of the border. In 2006, the installation of Polish signs following an amendment to the Minority Act began in the town of Český Těšín, but a great number of signs were damaged or stolen soon after. Akin to reactions to minority language signs in other parts of Europe, this incident features a number of interesting aspects (see Sloboda et al. 2012). Two arguments raised in public debate against the use of Polish are relevant here. Firstly, bilingual street-name signs containing Polish were acceptable in the town centre but not in the town's peripheral residential areas.[2] Secondly, putting up *commercial* bilingual signs was not a problem in contrast to the installation of municipal bilingual signs (Szabó Gilinger et al. 2012: 273). Tourist as well as commercial signs also remained intact. To sum up, Czech-Polish bilingualism was generally acceptable (1) in a particular section of the urban landscape, that is, the town centre, (2) on commercial signs and (3) on visitor-oriented signs.

The three differentiations seem to work as public/private distinctions. Concerning the first one: Europeans usually consider streets as public spaces and the interior of houses as private spaces, but rescaled to the whole town level, the distinction was applied here recursively in the sense that the centre was 'public' and peripheral residential areas 'private'. The second differentiation was also interpreted as public/private: Polish was not acceptable on signs viewed as 'public' in terms of public law, that is, signs installed by the government or government-sponsored subjects (Sloboda et al. 2012: 64–5). Instead, the Polish minority language was acceptable on 'private' signs, that is, those set up by private-law subjects, such as shop owners, and addressing other private-law subjects.[3] In the third differentiation, Polish was acceptable for 'public' communication in terms of outward communication with visitors, while unacceptable for the 'private' marking of the local residential space. Thus, in their management of Czech-Polish bilingualism in public space, locals oriented to the public/private distinction understood in terms of the difference between (1) central versus peripheral urban spaces, (2) public-law versus private-law signs and (3) visitors versus residents.

It has not become clear from this incident whether the attempts at exclusion concerned Polish only or minority languages more generally. Several cases in other parts of the country suggest that the preference for Czech monolingualism in public-law signage is more widespread. Although the official bilingualization policy has not materialized in regions other than the Těšín area, the policy has nevertheless been problematized on a national scale. One key incident here is a TV news report on new traffic sign regulations, broadcast by a popular private television station and presented in the extract in Table 2.1.

Rather than being a survey of just three responses, this news report is better understood as a media product or the TV station's message to its audience. The conclusion of the report suggested that place names in Czechia should be in Czech only. Three preceding discursive moves contributed to this conclusion. First, the narrator's formulation that the town of Český Těšín '*could* be named this [Polish] way' suggested that the Polish name of the town was new. This was underscored by a studio graphic simulation of the bilingualization, while a real sign could have already been photographed in the town, the Polish name of which had existed from time immemorial. The news report thus provided the audience with the possible

Table 2.1 A News Report on Road-Sign Regulation Changes, TV Prima, October 2001 (Transl. from Czech)

Video captures	Sound
ČESKÝ TĚŠÍN / CZESKI CIESZYN	NARRATOR: Since the end of April, signs with city names should look like this: Český Těšín could be named this way.
FILIPOV / PHILIPPSDORF	The sign 'Filipov' would be accompanied by a name in German.
ROSTĚNICE / ROSTERNITZ	'Rostěnice' similarly.

Video captures	Sound
	TRANSPORT MINISTRY SPOKESMAN: The Czech name would come first there, of course, and below there would be a sign, with the same background colour, that is white, and of the same size as the original Czech one.
[four establishing shots zooming in groups of persons recognizable as Roma, shabby houses in the background]	NARRATOR: A directive of the Ministry provides national minorities with the option of applying to the municipal authorities for names to be displayed on signs in their languages. It is sufficient for the minority to make up at least 10 per cent of the population.
	REPORTER: Well, for example, here in Litvínov, the city could rewrite the signs as 'Litvínovos' due to the Roma of Janov [a neighbourhood in Litvínov].
[medium close-up of a person]	CZECH-LOOKING CITIZEN: They understand, don't they? Litvínov as Litvínov.
[medium close-up of a person]	ROMA-LOOKING CITIZEN: Perhaps even as it is now, even without the signs they include us, don't they?
[medium close-up of a person]	CZECH-LOOKING CITIZEN: I think that we are in Czechia, so the names should be Czech, shouldn't they?

interpretation that a new Polish name was being introduced to supplement the 'original' Czech sign. Second, the selection of the town of Litvínov and its 'infamous' Roma community in Janov reveals significant ideological work in the news production. Namely, the number of the Roma in Litvínov did not reach the threshold of 10 per cent, mentioned by the ministry spokesman, so signage in Romani was not an option in Litvínov. Despite this, the producers of the news report decided to focus on this town. The Roma are a significantly marginalized minority in Czechia, and a majority of the Czech population holds rather negative attitudes to the group (Lyons and Kindlerová 2016: 394–405), so by exemplifying the bilingual signage policy with Romani, the producers of the report extended the negative evaluation to the policy as such. On top of this, the reporter overlaid the Czech name 'Litvínov' with a Romani sign, saying that the Romani sign would 'rewrite' (*přepsat*) the Czech one, which was in contradiction even to the ministry spokesman's description several seconds earlier. From this point of view, the news report suggested a reading of the situation as minority languages creating competition for Czech in the public space and promoted the idea that this kind of multilingualism would endanger the majority language (this trope operates more widely in Europe, see Blommaert et al. 2012).

The extent of the desire to prevent the visibility of minority languages in Czech public space can better be determined using the case of Slovak which finds itself on the opposite end of the attitudinal scale to Romani. The Slovaks have long been the most positively viewed minority by Czechs (Public Opinion Research Centre 2019); the Slovak language receives positive evaluations, such as 'beautiful' (*krásná*), 'soft' (*měkká*), 'euphonious' (*libozvučná*), and if spoken by women, 'sexy' (*sexy*), on various occasions (Sloboda, forthcoming). Slovak is also mutually intelligible with Czech to such an extent that speakers of the two languages are routinely able to make themselves understood when each is speaking in their own language without interpreting. The habitual nature of such communicative practice empowers Slovak speakers to take up a variety of social roles and positions in the Czech context (cf. below). Despite all this, there is substantial evidence that Slovak is tacitly avoided or eliminated from Czechia's public space. Slovak is almost absent from the LL of Czechia, but this is most likely due to the intelligibility of Czech to Slovaks and the perceived social and cultural closeness (Dolník et al. 2015: 81–114), which do not motivate Slovak speakers to express themselves in Slovak in Czechia's LL. However, as far as online space is concerned, Czech internet users sometimes contest the mere presence of internet articles (unlike discussion posts) in Slovak in the .cz domain, the argument being that the articles were published on the 'Czech web' (Sloboda and Nábělková 2013). Nábělková (2008) noted that, in the online debate on this issue, Czech users did not take into account that Slovak is a language of a sizeable national minority at home in Czechia but wrote about it only as of a language of Slovaks from Slovakia (139). That is, the Slovak national minority was semiotically erased from the discourse and the resulting image of Czech ethnolinguistic hegemony in the physical space was projected into the online space, in particular the 'public' genre of the article in contrast to 'private' discussion posts.

Restrictions on Slovak have also occurred in spoken communication. Key incidents include a complaint submitted by a Slovak-speaking director of a home for people with disabilities to the Czech ombudsman. The complainant asked the ombudsman for his opinion on the request by her superior who 'would welcome her using Czech, the official language [of the country]' (Varvařovský 2011). The complainant's superior argued the alleged status of Czech as the official (*úřední*) language despite the fact that no official language is specified for most types of communication in the healthcare organization and that Czech law does not use the term. Such contradictions reveal the ideological nature of the request. In a related area of psychiatric care, Satinská (2008) noted similar argumentation with an imaginary legal regulation.[4] Some of the interviewed Slovak psychiatrists reported that their superiors asked them to communicate in Czech at work. Satinská (2008) adds:

> Those of my respondents who encountered this request [to speak Czech] have adapted, except for one. The person who did not was not given the job she applied for but opened a private ambulance where she still speaks Slovak. (own translation)

Satinská (2008) illustrates that not only Czechs but also Slovaks themselves restrict their public use of Slovak. When choosing between the two languages for communication, her informants oriented to the work/private-life distinction (ibid.).

Several incidents testify that the use of Slovak is even normatively inappropriate with public figures such as political representatives. Former mayor of Prague Adriana Krnáčová comes from Slovakia but consistently speaks Czech in public. For another example, current prime minister Andrej Babiš spoke a mixture of Czech and Slovak prior to the 2013 election, when his political movement ran for the Parliament for the first time. He has lived in Czechia for a long time, but it was as late as the election campaign that he shifted to Czech, despite his obvious difficulty in staying in a monolingual mode. Both he and the former mayor of Prague took private Czech lessons around the time of taking up their political functions, which testifies to the desirability to opt for Czech when communicating as a political representative. Similar behaviour can also be observed with other types of public personae, for instance, the Slovak-born spokesman of flag carrier Czech Airlines and some other cases (Sloboda, forthcoming).

What all these cases show is that even a language as intelligible and positively rated as Slovak does not have its place in public, official and professional communication, at least in some areas, such as politics, healthcare and certain media roles and genres. The mutual intelligibility of Slovak and Czech empowers Slovaks to adopt various roles in Czech society, but the pressure to use Czech in public indicates how extensive the orientation to Czech language hegemony is in the public space.

6. Issues with 'foreign'-language dominance

Some cases point out that the acceptance of languages other than Czech also has its limits in communication between clearly private-law subjects. One such case included the reaction of municipal authorities of Karlovy Vary and Mariánské Lázně to Russian. The two spa towns are located in the western region bordering Germany. They have become very popular with Russian speakers, who not only come to visit these towns as tourists, but many of whom have also settled there, bought properties and run businesses from there. The provision of services to Russian-speaking residents and visitors manifests itself in the remarkable presence of Russian in the landscape of the town centres, often without accompanying parallel text in Czech or any other language (Shánělová 2005/2006; Zedník 2009). The local authorities tried to manage the visual dominance of Russian several times in the period from 2009 to 2016. Initially, there were attempts at a municipal regulation (Houdek 2013; Zedník 2009), later the local governments coordinated their efforts with a liberal-conservative party in the Parliament to submit amendments to the Consumer Protection Act and the Advertisement Regulation Act (Kopecký 2014, 2016; Toman 2016). The rationale according to one of the MPs was that 'people are angry that they live in the Czech Republic, but do not feel at home here because of the flood of foreign-language ads. They feel totally overwhelmed and they are angry that we don't do anything about it' (Špačková 2011, own translation). This effort at the obligatory use of Czech in private-law signage suggests that, if a 'foreign' language starts to dominate a landscape overall, the public-law/private-law distinction may become irrelevant and the town's landscape becomes, in a sense, a 'private' space of the ethnic majority.

The following incident suggests that this general conclusion may be limited to certain languages. A news report by Czech Television put forward an analogy between the present domination of Russian and the former, pre-war, domination of German in the landscapes of the two towns (Czech Television 2013). From the native Czech perspective, such a link makes sense: both Russian and German are languages of nations that are perceived as being oppressive in the Czech national narrative, hence the efforts to suppress their local dominance in the Czech public space.

The following four incidents suggest that historical sociocultural symbolism may indeed limit the use of German as well, although the language is otherwise widely used and promoted especially in the Czech-German/Austrian borderlands for its economic significance. First, the above-mentioned policy on national minority languages in signage is de jure applicable to German in some municipalities with a German minority population, but according to a representative of the minority, after the incidents in the Těšín region, the municipal authorities 'have not expressed any interest, among other things owing to concerns around the rise of national chauvinism' (Government Council for National Minorities 2009: 6, own translation). Second, at a German multinational company operating in Czechia, English was preferred for internal communication, inter alia, to manage recollections of the historical German domination over the Czechs that the asymmetric status of German managers versus Czech subordinates could have evoked (Nekvapil and Sherman 2009).[5] Third, Prague had a substantial German-speaking population up until the Second World War and several German-Czech bilingual street-name signs have been preserved until today. Figure 2.1 shows one and a newer standardized monolingual Czech sign above, although the Czech street name (*Křižovnická*) has remained the same, and so it appears twice there. This is superfluous from a purely communicative point of view: the Czech name in the older sign is sufficient for one's localization. But from a sociocultural viewpoint, the contemporary Czech sign says that the bilingual sign underneath no longer has an informative function as a street-name sign, but it is a historical artefact that can be

Figure 2.1 A historical German-Czech street-name sign (below) and its present-day Czech equivalent (above), Prague city centre (50°5'11.5"N 14°24'53"E), August 2018

appreciated by tourists and history lovers (and sociolinguists for that matter). This also means that the German name has been deactivated as a street name; the sign no longer categorizes that street as a Czech-*German* location. Neither does a similar sign shown in Figure 2.2 after the German street name was damaged during the founding of Czechoslovakia in 1918, but it has been preserved 'as an imprint of that historical event' (Heritage Department of the Office of the President of the Czech Republic, email from May 2019).

Finally, Bermel and Knittl (2018) researched language management at a small castle in northern Czechia, close to the former Czech-German ethnic border. Staff working at the castle justified their practice of restricted use of German in orientation signage by citing practical problems and a socioeconomically motivated claim that Czechs constitute the vast majority of their visitors. Nevertheless, incomplete replies in interviews gave one of the researchers 'a feeling that there is another reason [i.e. the historical symbolism] explaining German's absence there' (Bermel 2019). At the same time, staff generally reported their ability and willingness to use German (and Polish) rather than English in *spoken* interactions (Bermel and Knittl 2017). They thus differentiated between the spoken and the written modes of public communication: more languages were acceptable in spoken communication with

Figure 2.2 A damaged historical German-Czech street-name sign, Prague Castle (50°5'27.5"N 14°24'8.5"E), July 2016

individual visitors or groups, while their use was restricted in written communication in signage. This differentiation also seems to orient to the public/private distinction: written signs in public space are more permanent and accessible, whereas spoken utterances disappear from the space immediately and may only remain as private memories of the individual participants.

Figure 2.3 Asymmetrical bilingual design in the Prague metro, Muzeum Station (50°4'46"N 14°25'54"E underground), July 2018

All these cases highlight the difficult acceptance of German and Russian in Czechia's public space even in private-law relations, especially if the language starts dominating a particular space or is unaccompanied by parallel Czech discourse.

If German and Russian form a special category, what about other 'foreign' languages? One key incident here concerns English in the bilingual design of the Prague metro signage. Orientation and informative signs – for example, network maps, the marking of tracks and lift locations – usually have English text in plain letters, while the Czech text is in boldface (Figure 2.3). This asymmetry is more widespread among public service providers, for example, at the Main Railway Station and the National Library. The poor visibility of the English text presents a deviation from the expectation that such signs are also there for foreign visitors. This is evidenced in Figure 2.4 (right): a non-standard and individually produced paper sign displaying 'No tickets / No change' in English was added to two identical standardized and industrially produced bilingual signs conveying approximately the same information ('Tickets are not on sale here'). The communicative failure of the standardized signs' design was apparently managed by emplacing the paper sign next to them. Variations of this duplicating strategy have been observed at three more metro stations in the city centre, where foreign visitors are concentrated. This management behaviour thus documents a recurring conflict

Figure 2.4 Entrance sign (left), metro network map (middle) and informative signs (right), Staroměstská Station (50°5'18.5"N 14°24'59"E underground), July 2019

between the communicative norm of informing foreigners and the sociocultural norm of marking public transport premises as Czech.

As for private-law signage, similarly to Russian, English in Prague has become an object of legislative efforts at the national level. Several bills have attempted to promote Czech as the 'national' and 'official' language of the country. Representatives of the Communist Party, who submitted most of the bills, explicitly referred to the older generation's inability to understand signs in foreign languages, especially English (Czech Television 2017: broadcast time 8.33 pm). However, Parliament has not passed the respective bills. Other management acts against English have not been reported to my knowledge, so the language's acceptance on private-law signage seems to be relatively high. Although English has an image of a world language, I will show in the following section that even the dominance of other languages can be locally unproblematic under certain conditions.

7. Conditions for 'foreign'-language dominance

So far, I have talked about restrictions on the use of languages other than Czech, but it is still possible to observe multilingualism and sometimes even the dominance of 'foreign' languages in public places. Many of these occurrences are not removed, and some do not provoke any public response. What then are the conditions under which multilingualism and 'foreign'-language dominance is tolerated?

In the Prague metro case discussed above, there are two exceptions to the dominance of Czech. English text is more prominent (1) on 'emergency exit' signs, in which an interest in health and safety is evident, and (2) in the signs marking entrances to the paid zone of the metro stations (see the illuminated sign in Figure 2.4). The entrance sign warns that only those with a valid ticket may enter the zone, and the graphic (in English only) suggests that validation involves using the machines placed under the sign (there are no turnstiles on the entrances, tickets are occasionally checked by inspectors). My observation as a frequent passenger is that inspectors seem to select apparent foreigners (i.e. carry out ethnic profiling) for ticket checks, despite their evident limited foreign-language skills. Foreign visitors have also been reported as frequent 'fare dodgers' (Czech Television 2019), although these statistics might be the result of inspectors' possible ethnic profiling. Considering these circumstances, the prominence of English on the paid-zone entrance sign manifests that the socioeconomic interest in having foreign visitors purchase and mark their ticket before they enter the paid zone has overridden the otherwise applied sociocultural interest in marking the public transport space as Czech which, in turn, has overridden the communicative interest in informing foreigners on non-economic matters (such as navigating their way around). In other words, English may be visually prominent even in public-law signage if certain health/safety or socioeconomic interests prevail over sociocultural ones.

Visual domination accepted on socioeconomic grounds has also occurred with 'foreign' languages other than English. For instance, Vietnamese on advertising billboards sometimes dominates locations where higher numbers of Vietnamese speakers live or work. The billboard in Figure 2.5 advertised software for a newly introduced national 'EET' sales register. These billboards appear to have gone unnoticed in the media. Earlier advertisements in Vietnamese by the largest Czech bank (Sloboda 2016: 157–8) attracted some media attention, but the journalists presented an understanding for the economic and demographic grounds for the signs' placement, and their evaluation was neutral (Moniová, Lukášová and Jelínek 2014). Another socioeconomic interest – the freedom to engage in enterprise and/or the free movement of goods – was most likely the reason for the failure of the above-mentioned legislative proposals aimed against the local dominance of Russian in private-law signage (cf. Kopecký 2016, and the documents referred to therein). Finally, in her study on the use of traditional German place names in the formerly German-speaking borderlands, Klemensová (2017) found that it was *business* people, rather than residents, who revitalized these names. That is, socioeconomic management has the capacity to override sociocultural interests in displaying 'Czechness' and to locally produce parallel or even exclusive 'foreign'-language use in the Czech public space.

As hinted at above in connection with the Prague metro case, a similar effect can also be observed when health or safety are at stake: several Czech hospitals have introduced some of their communications in Vietnamese in view of a 'language barrier' (*jazyková bariéra*, a term used on hospital forms) (Sloboda 2016: 165) and, on the national scale, the Ministry of Healthcare issues multilingual cards for communicating

Figure 2.5 A commercial advertisement in Vietnamese, Prague Krč district (50°1'44'''N 14°27'13''E), January 2017

with non-Czech-speaking patients as part of the national policy on integrating foreigners. Thus, some public institutions, as well as private businesses, communicate multilingually if socioeconomic interests or health and safety interests receive priority over the other interests involved.

8. Negative evaluation of the public authorities' non-use of English

Public administration has been an exception to the above-mentioned hierarchy of interests so far, but one incident involving a requirement to use Czech stirred controversy. The requirement was formulated on a sign in English put up in a counter window at the Prague Drivers' Register by staff working there (Figure 2.6). The sign was noticed, photographed and went viral in the online media. A journalist summarized the controversy as follows:

> While some commenters agreed with the employees [of the office] and argued that Czechs also cannot make themselves understood in their mother tongue in Great Britain, others – these comprised a majority – pointed out that English is a world language and employees of administrative bodies should have at least a basic command of the language. (Sattler 2017, own translation)

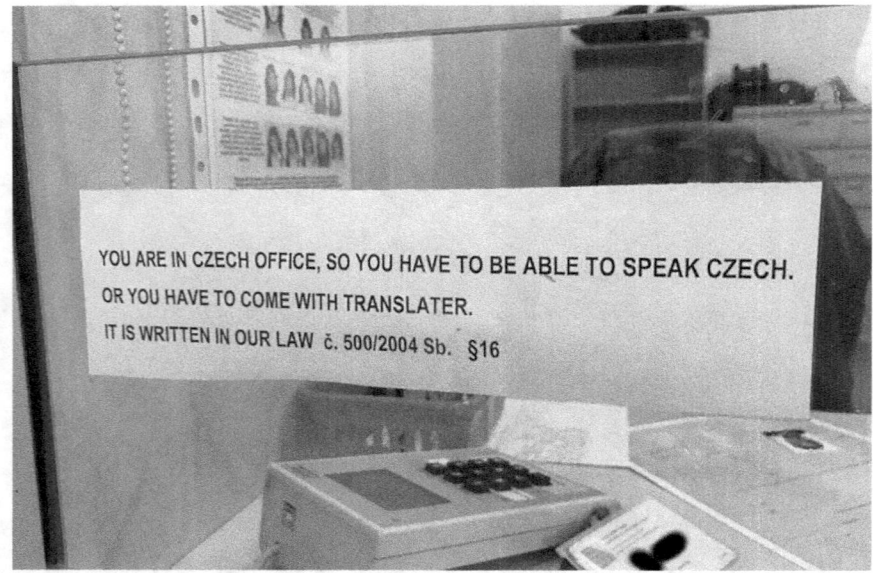

Figure 2.6 The criticized request to use Czech at the Prague Drivers' Register Office (source: Facebook)

Despite the referred-to provision for Czech in the Administrative Code and the widespread practice of marking Czechia's public spaces as Czech, such explicit insistence on using Czech in front of a Czech administrative body because it is a 'Czech office' was received negatively by the public. This may seem strange at first sight, but the negative evaluations also commented on the ungrammatical use of English (see Figure 2.6) and were thus apparently driven by a language ideology according to which 'knowing languages' (*umět jazyky*) is a sign of being intelligent or well educated. The operation of this language ideology in this case was made explicit, for example, in the Prague mayor's comment: 'It [the putting up of that sign] is embarrassing and it tells us a lot about the intelligence of the given person' ('Je to trapné a hodně to vypovídá o inteligenci konkrétního člověka', Sattler 2017). This language ideology seems to echo the acute shortage of foreign-language skills during the country's post-socialist transition, when the Czech economy became suddenly more internationalized (Sherman 2020: 73).

Similar public condemnation of a lack of foreign-language skills among public authority personnel was reported in a Czech Television's news story which exemplified how Czech police officers were unable to communicate in any foreign language with refugees who, in contrast, spoke languages, such as English (Czech Television 2015). Even during a time of heightened anti-refugee sentiments, the message of this news report entitled 'Language barrier between police and refugees' sounded like a criticism of the former.

These two incidents do two things. First of all, they categorize knowledge of English as an attribute of basic education. Secondly, they are key for identifying a split made by social actors within sociocultural management. In other words, not all sociocultural interests bring about a preference for the dominance of Czech. The split can be interpreted in terms of the public/private distinction: when the Czech character of a public space is perceived as endangered, (exclusive) use of Czech is desired (i.e. language management aims at 'privatization' or closure); however, when the image of Czechs' degree of 'educatedness' or openness to the world is at stake, insistence on Czech monolingualism even by public institutions receives negative feedback (i.e. language management aims at openness).

9. Discussion

Having accumulated seemingly unrelated, but substantively similar and theoretically relevant, key incidents, this study has pointed to rather interrelated, systematic and interested acts by an ethnic majority to restrict the public use of others' languages.

Various social actors treated Czech and 'foreign' (often including also traditional minority) languages differentially, by restricting or preventing the latter's occurrence. These differentiating language management activities have taken place despite the country's conceptualization as a 'civic nation' in the Constitution and legal provisions for national minorities, testifying thus to a dissonance between the national identity as conceived officially and as practiced in ordinary social life. Some of the language management activities were carried out consciously as part of explicit public debate, while others in more commonplace or habitual ways, reminiscent of 'banal nationalism' (Billig 1995).

In their overview of language management in Czechia, Neustupný and Nekvapil concluded that it was assimilative towards ethnic minorities (2003: 221). The present analysis has shown the continuation of this trend and has identified some nuances within this behaviour. In some cases, social actors demarcated a space for 'foreign' languages based on the public/private distinction which worked as an ideology of differentiation as described by Gal (2005). The understanding of this distinction as potentially being valid has enabled four analytical steps: (1) to free oneself from the explicit labelling of social phenomena as 'public' or 'private' and to also consider those bound to these categories but named otherwise; (2) to take non-spatial (but spatializable) social phenomena, such as persons and activities, into account; (3) to observe the differentiation at various scales of the same type of social phenomenon; and (4) to observe how various types of social phenomena cluster together. To summarize the cases analysed above, the public/private distinction seems to have been applied to differentiate between the following social phenomena:

1. residential (peripheral) versus central urban areas
2. public-law versus private-law signage
3. public figures versus ordinary individuals
4. written versus spoken communication in public spaces

5. residents versus foreign visitors
6. Czech-speaking residents versus residents not speaking Czech sufficiently well

The social phenomena in the first position on the list – that is, residential urban areas, public-law signage, public figures, written communication, residents and especially Czech-speaking residents – were less open to languages other than Czech. The social phenomena listed in the second position – that is, central urban areas, private-law signage, ordinary individuals, spoken communication and communication with foreign visitors and with residents not speaking Czech well enough – displayed more openness to multilingualism. It is interesting to note that social phenomena that we would consider public in some sense, such as public-law signage, displayed a higher level of closure to 'foreign' languages and so are less public in this sense. This was visible in the conflict over the presence of traditional minority languages – Polish and potentially German and Romani – in place-name and street-name signs. This conflict has also testified that the public/private distinction is no longer anchored in persons in this East-Central European context as in the socialist period (Gal 2005): by opposing the State's bilingualization policy, Czech residents manifested the 'privacy' of their living *space* (town, neighbourhood or street). This seems related to the post-communist transition to democracy, during which citizens have acquired from the State not only some of its property, as shown in Ferenčík's (2015) study of 'private land' signs in Slovakia, but also some responsibility for, and influence on, the public-law spaces they inhabit.

The demarcation outlined above may shift depending on the situated hierarchization of interests involved. The incidents discussed have highlighted that when the sociocultural interest in marking a space as Czech prevails, Czech is preferred. However, there are exceptions to this preference which are also socioculturally motivated, namely cases when outward self-presentation to foreign visitors and the presentation of one's openness or level of 'educatedness' are at stake. The interest in marking Czechness is often overridden by socioeconomic management and health or safety management, which locally generate 'foreign' language use. Recall, for example, the Prague public transport company's signs marking paid zones and emergency exits (for a somewhat different situation in safety signs in other parts of the world, see e.g. Kasanga 2015; Tan and Ben Said 2015).

The relationship of language choice management to empowerment is not always straightforward. Neustupný (2004: 5–6) pointed out that some language management acts may be both empowering and disempowering at the same time and Saruhashi (2018) has shown that not only situational but also long-term perspectives need to be taken into account in assessing the level of empowerment of those involved. In the case of Vietnamese commercial billboards (Figure 2.5), for example, communication in Vietnamese enabled the Vietnamese entrepreneurs to continue their businesses under the new tax registering system. On the other hand, the availability of Vietnamese-speaking cash register providers did not present entrepreneurs with incentives to acquire Czech or other language skills which would pay off in the long run. Instead, they have remained dependant on these providers, who could charge more for their services in the constellation of 'high demand – low offer' in Vietnamese-language services. The relationship of language choice management to empowerment needs to be determined for each case, or type of cases, individually.

Finally, I would like to raise a methodological issue. Even in the highly diversified centre of Prague (cf. Sloboda 2016), public-law signs are usually monolingual in Czech, marking the institutional framework of the city as Czech in the ethnolinguistic sense. Czech monolingualism in direction signage in Prague (Figure 2.7), which fits this category of signs, invites similar interpretation that these *sociocultural* interests have also prevailed here. However, in the Czech towns of Turnov (Bermel and Knittl 2018) and Písek (observed), direction signs are bilingual Czech-English, which indicates that the norm operating there is the *communicative* norm of informing foreign visitors. The Czech monolingualism of direction signs in Prague, which attracts millions of foreign visitors every year (Sloboda 2016: 144), thus presents a deviation from this communicative norm and has indeed been noted and mediatized as such. Kupec (2009) reported that Prague authorities intended to change the language choice, but he identified an obstacle in the status of this signage as 'traffic signs': being subject to national rather than municipal regulation, traffic signs should allegedly be in Czech only and any change to their design would be difficult to achieve (ibid.). In a later news report, the director of the Prague Information Service presented as relevant a different communicative norm that, in contrast, would lead to the exclusive use of Czech: 'the text must be in Czech, because it is in Czech on maps. If the map stated "hrad" and the English sign read "castle", tourists would not understand' (Frouzová 2016, own translation). While maps distributed by the Prague Information Service indeed

Figure 2.7 A visitor checking the data on his smartphone against monolingual orientation signs (a) and the signs from his perspective (b), Prague city centre (50°05'19"N 14°24'58"E), August 2018

feature only Czech place names, the sign *Turistické informace* 'tourist information' in Figure 2.7b points to what is labelled in English as 'Czechtourism IC' or 'Prague City Tourism – Visitor Centre' on Google Maps, and the maps distributed in the former information centre refer to the object named *Karlův most* in Figure 2.7b in English as 'Charles Bridge'. Therefore, the sociocultural interest in marking Prague as a Czech space might indeed be at play here, but the social actors who commented on the signage presented communicative interests as the relevant ones.

This case obviously requires further investigation; here I have only intended to highlight that when analysing language choice in the LL, it is usually not enough to rely solely on photographs and researcher's own member competencies. One solution is that the analytical work would also include an effort at revealing the 'story behind' the LL (Hult 2009). Since interviews (which would provide such a story) cannot be considered as more valid than other types of data but are situated accomplishments by the researcher and the interviewee in interaction (ten Have 2004), I have also suggested looking for the 'stories around' the LL. These consist of the discourse and interactions that people and institutions have already realized in relation to LL objects in their mundane lives for their socially relevant purposes. The collecting of such evidence may focus on observable or reconstructable parts of the language management acts which unfold around the objects suggested for analysis by key incidents.

10. Conclusion

This study has documented that various segments of the Czech population manage language choice in favour of Czech, thereby delegitimizing other language groups' representation or participation, contradicting on different occasions purely communicative needs, the self-image of a tolerant nation and the officially civic conceptualization of the country. In general terms, the study has shown that, whatever the multilingual potential of a country's population and official support for minority languages, the population may restrict language choice extensively. And it may do so not necessarily by means of legal provisions and overt or covert policies but quite effectively in rather banal ways – in line with or even against the law and policies. This depends on various interests which, in a democratic society, need to be disclosed and accounted for.

Acknowledgements

The author wishes to thank Stephanie Rudwick, Jiří Nekvapil, Susan Gal, students of linguistic anthropology courses at Charles University, the reviewers and volume editors for their valuable remarks and suggestions. Any inadequacies which may remain are entirely the author's responsibility. This work was financially supported by the European Regional Development Fund project 'Creativity and Adaptability as Conditions of the Success of Europe in an Interrelated World' (no. CZ.02.1.01/0.0/0.0/16_019/0000734).

Notes

1. In his influential LL study, Blommaert (2013) uses the term 'demarcation' in a different sense of signs (inscriptions) cutting up a larger space into smaller ones with their own regimes of communication. Here, inspired by Gal (2005), demarcation is understood as social actors' differentiation between spaces, or other spatializable social phenomena, according to whether the occurrence of particular languages is legitimate in them or not.
2. An online discussion participant nicknamed 'helenka' formulated the distinction as follows: 'A year ago [i.e. in 2007] when bilingual signs were installed in the town centre, there was no problem, now [when they are installed outside the town centre] the "residents are surprised"' ('Před rokem, když se zaváděly dvojjazyčné nápisy v centru města, tak byl klid, nyní se "obyvatelé diví"') (http://www.ihorizont.cz, 8 September 2008 at 6.30 pm).
3. Some scholars use a similar 'top–down'/'bottom–up' terminology, but there are reasonable doubts about the suitability of these terms (Coupland 2010). In any case, here the public-law/private-law distinction proved to be an 'emic' phenomenon, albeit not labelled as such.
4. The conviction that Czech is declared 'the official language' of Czechia by law is so strong that, in an overview of language legislation, even an MC of a public-service broadcaster claimed that there is an 'Act on the state language of the Czech Republic' (Czech Television 2017: broadcast time 8.16 pm), while in fact no such Act exists.
5. The authors do not formulate it precisely this way, but in his personal communications one of them offered such an interpretation based on his experience of interviews with respondents.

References

Bailey, J. (2002), 'From Public to Private: The Development of the Concept of the "Private"', *Social Research*, 69 (1): 16–31.

Bermel, N. (2019), 'Jazykový management a jazyková ideologie na českých hradech a zámcích [Language management and language ideology at Czech castles]', paper presented in the Circle of Friends of the Czech Language, Charles University, Prague, 10 April.

Bermel, N., and Knittl, L. (2017), 'Managing Multilingual Interactions at Czech Heritage Sites', paper presented at the Fifth International Language Management Symposium, Regensburg, 12–14 September.

Bermel, N., and Knittl, L. (2018), 'The Linguistic Landscape of a Czech Heritage Site: Recording and Presenting the Past and Present of Hrubý Rohozec', in T. Sherman and J. Nekvapil (eds), *English in Business and Commerce: Interactions and Policies*, 194–228, Boston, MA: Walter de Gruyter.

Berntzen, L. E., and Weisskircher, M. (2016), 'Anti-Islamic PEGIDA beyond Germany: Explaining Differences in Mobilisation', *Journal of Intercultural Studies*, 37 (6): 556–73.

Billig, M. (1995), *Banal Nationalism*, Los Angeles: SAGE.

Blommaert, J. (2013), *Ethnography, Superdiversity and Linguistic Landscapes: Chronicles of Complexity*, Bristol, UK: Multilingual Matters.

Blommaert, J., Leppänen, S., Pahta, P., and Räisänen,T. (eds) (2012), *Dangerous Multilingualism: Northern Perspectives on Order, Purity and Normality*, Basingstoke: Palgrave Macmillan.

Christens, B. D. (2011), 'Psychological Empowerment', in K. Dowding (ed.), *Encyclopedia of Power*, 539–40, Thousand Oaks, CA: SAGE.

Coulter, J. (2001), 'Human Practices and the Observability of the "Macro-Social"', in T. R. Schatzki, K. Knorr Cetina and E. von Savigny (eds), *The Practice Turn in Contemporary Theory*, 37–50, London: Routledge.

Coupland, N. (2010), 'Welsh Linguistic Landscapes "from Above" and "from Below"', in A. Jaworski and C. Thurlow (eds), *Semiotic Landscapes: Language, Image, Space*, 77–101, London: Continuum.

Czech Television (2013), 'Boj s cizojazyčnými nápisy [Fight with foreign-language signs]', *Události*, 23 February. Available online: https://www.ceskatelevize.cz/ivysilani/1097181328-udalosti/213411000100223/obsah/246109-zapadoceske-lazne-a-boj-s-cizojazycnymi-napisy (accessed 23 May 2020).

Czech Television (2015), 'Jazyková bariéra mezi policií a uprchlíky [Language barrier between police and refugees]', *Události*, 12 September. Available online: http://www.ceskatelevize.cz (accessed 23 May 2020).

Czech Television (2017), 'Povinné překlady cizích názvů? [Mandatory translation of foreign names?]', *90' ČT24*, 16 January. Available online: https://www.ceskatelevize.cz/ (accessed 23 May 2020).

Czech Television (2019), 'Osm stovek jde utratit líp, varuje Praha černé pasažéry. Turistům pomůžou bezkontaktní terminály [Spend eight hundred crowns better, Prague warns fare evaders. Contactless terminals will help tourists]', *ČT24*, 13 May. Available online: https://ct24.ceskatelevize.cz (accessed 23 May 2020).

Dolník, J., Orgoňová, O., Bohunická, A., Faragulová, A., and Piatková, K. (2015), *Cudzosť, jazyk, spoločnosť* [Foreignness, Language and Society]. Bratislava: Milan Štefanko – Iris.

Emerson, R. M. (2007), 'Working with 'Key Incidents", in C. Seale, G. Gobo, J. F. Gubrium and D. Silverman (eds), *Qualitative Research Practice*, concise paperback edition, 427–42, London: SAGE.

Fairbrother, L., and Kimura, G. C. (2020), 'Introduction: What Is a Language Management Approach to Language Problems and Why Do We Need It?', in G. C. Kimura and L. Fairbrother (eds), *A Language Management Approach to Language Problems: Integrating Macro and Micro Dimensions*, 1–28, Amsterdam: John Benjamins.

Ferenčík, M. (2015), 'Construction of Private Space in an Urban Semioscape: A Case Study in the Sociolinguistics of Globalisation', *Human Affairs*, 25 (4): 365–79.

Frouzová, K. (2016), 'Praze se nelíbí zastaralé cedule, změní design celého orientačního systému [Prague does not like outdated signs, will change the design of the entire orientation system]', *iDnes.cz*, 11 August. Available online: https://zpravy.idnes.cz/ (accessed 23 May 2020).

Gal, S. (2005), 'Language Ideologies Compared: Metaphors of Public/Private', *Journal of Linguistic Anthropology*, 15 (1): 23–37.

Gal, S., and Irvine, J. T. (2019), *Signs of Difference: Language and Ideology in Social Life*, Cambridge: Cambridge University Press.

Garvin, R. (2010), 'Responses to the Linguistic Landscape in Memphis, Tennessee: An Urban Space in Transition', in E. G. Shohamy, E. Ben-Rafael and M. Barni (eds), *Linguistic Landscape in the City*, 254–71, Buffalo, NY: Multilingual Matters.

Government Council for National Minorities (2009), 'Zápis z jednání Rady vlády pro národnostní menšiny [Minutes from the meeting of the Government Council for National Minorities]', 10 December. Available online: www.vlada.cz (accessed 23 May 2020).

He Shanhua, and Dai Manchun [何山华和戴曼纯] (2016), '语言管理理论：源流与发展 [Language Management Theory: origins and developments]', 语言规划学研究/ *Journal of Language Planning*, 2 (1): 32–45.

Houdek, M. (2013), 'Upravte poutače a omezte azbuku, nařídili radní v lázních obchodníkům [Adjust billboards and restrict Cyrillic script, councillors ordered spa business owners]', *iDnes.cz*, 13 February. Available online: http://zpravy.idnes.cz (accessed 23 May 2020).

Hovorková, J. (2014), 'Češi jsou tolerantní, ale xenofobní, říká Lejla Abbasová [Czechs are tolerant, but xenophobic, says Lejla Abbasová]', *Hospital*, 3 (4): 6–10.

Hroch, M. (2000), *In the National Interest: Demands and Goals of European National Movements of the Nineteenth Century: A Comparative Perspective*, Praha: Faculty of Arts, Charles University.

Hult, F. (2009), 'Language Ecology and Linguistic Landscape Analysis', in E. Shohamy and D. Gorter (eds), *Linguistic Landscape: Expanding the Scenery*, 88–103, New York: Routledge.

Hymes, D. (1974), *Foundations in Sociolinguistics: An Ethnographic Approach*, Philadelphia: University of Pennsylvania Press.

Jernudd, B. H., and Neustupný, J. V. (1987), 'Language Planning: For Whom?', in L. Laforge (ed.), *Actes du Colloque international sur l'aménagement linguistique / Proceedings of the International Colloquium on Language Planning*, 69–84, Québec: Les Presses de L'Université Laval.

Kasanga, L. A. (2015), 'Semiotic Landscape, Code Choice and Exclusion', in R. Rubdy and S. Ben Said (eds), *Conflict, Exclusion and Dissent in the Linguistic Landscape*, 123–44, Basingstoke: Palgrave Macmillan.

Klemensová, T. (2017), 'V Gruntě a Špicberk – toponyma německého původu v pohraničí v současnosti (na příkladu vybraných obcí Jesenicka) [V Gruntě and Špicberk – the contemporary situation of toponyms of German origin in the borderlands: a case study of selected municipalities in the Jeseník region]', *Naše řeč*, 100 (5): 300–11.

Kopecký, J. (2014), 'Azbuka nestačí: U cizojazyčné reklamy má být podle poslanců i čeština [Cyrillic is not enough: Czech should be present with foreign-language ads according to MPs]', *iDnes.cz*, 19 June. Available online: https://zpravy.idnes.cz/ (accessed 23 May 2020).

Kopecký, J. (2016), 'Jen ruské nápisy nevadí: Poslanci smetli návrh, který to měl omezit [Russian-only inscriptions don't matter: MPs swept away proposal to reduce them]', *iDnes.cz*, 3 June. Available online: https://www.idnes.cz (accessed 23 May 2020).

Kupec, P. (2009), 'Turistické cedule jsou jen česky, pomoci mohou poslanci [Tourist signs are in Czech only, MPs can help]', *iDnes.cz*, 22 September. Available online: https://zpravy.idnes.cz/ (accessed 23 May 2020).

Laitinen, M. (2014), '630 Kilometres by Bicycle: Observations of English in Urban and Rural Finland', *International Journal of the Sociology of Language*, 228: 55–77.

Lyons, P., and Kindlerová, R. (eds) (2016), *Contemporary Czech Society*, Prague: Institute of Sociology of the Czech Academy of Sciences.

Moniová, E., Lukášová, H., and Jelínek, J. (2014), 'Přiveďte si kamaráda: Česká spořitelna cílí billboardem na Vietnamce [Bring a friend along: Česká Spořitelna's billboards targeting on Vietnamese]', *iDnes.cz*, 4 August. Available online: http://ekonomika. idnes.cz (accessed 23 May 2020).

Muhič Dizdarevič, S. (2016), 'Islamophobia in Czech Republic: National Report 2015', in E. Bayrakli and F. Hafez (eds), *European Islamophobia Report 2015*, 117–30, Ankara: SETA.

Muhič Dizdarevič, S. (2017), 'Islamophobia in Czech Republic: National Report 2016', in E. Bayrakli and F. Hafez (eds), *European Islamophobia Report 2016*, 147–63, Ankara: SETA.

Nábělková, M. (2008), *Slovenčina a čeština v kontakte: pokračovanie príbehu* [*Slovak and Czech in Contact: A Continuation of the Story*], Bratislava: Veda.

Nekvapil, J. (2009), 'The Integrative Potential of Language Management Theory', in J. Nekvapil and T. Sherman (eds), *Language Management in Contact Situations: Perspectives from Three Continents*, 1–11, Frankfurt am Main: Peter Lang.

Nekvapil, J. (2016), 'Language Management Theory as One Approach in Language Policy and Planning', *Current Issues in Language Planning*, 17 (1): 11–22.

Nekvapil, J., and Sherman, T. (2009), Czech, German and English: Finding Their Place in Multinational Companies in the Czech Republic, in J. Carl and P. Stevenson (eds), *Language, Discourse and Identity in Central Europe*, 122–46, Basingstoke: Palgrave Macmillan.

Neustupný, J. V. (1993), Language Management for Romani in Central and Eastern Europe, *New Language Planning Newsletter*, 7(4): 1–6.

Neustupný, J. V. (2004), 'Power of Language across National Boundaries: The Case of Tertiary Education' (Series A: General and Theoretical Papers, no. 630), Essen: LAUD Linguistic Agency. Available online: http://www.linse.uni-due.de/laud-paper.html (accessed 23 May 2020).

Neustupný, J. V. (2006), 'Sociolinguistic Aspects of Social Modernization', in U. Ammon, N. Dittmar, K. J. Mattheier and P. Trudgill (eds), *Sociolinguistics: An International Handbook of the Science of Language and Society*, vol. 3 / *Soziolinguistik: Ein internationales Handbuch zur Wissenschaft von Sprache und Gesellschaft*, 3. Teiband, 2209–24, Berlin: Walter de Gruyter.

Neustupný, J. V., and Nekvapil, J. (2003), 'Language Management in the Czech Republic', *Current Issues in Language Planning*, 4 (3&4): 181–366.

Park, J. S.-Y. (2019), 'Linguistic Anthropology in 2018: Signifying Movement', *American Anthropologist*, 121 (2): 403–16.

Perkins, D. D. (2010), 'Empowerment', in R. A. Couto (ed.), *Political and Civic Leadership: A Reference Handbook*, 207–18, Thousand Oaks, CA: SAGE.

Pisingerová, B. (2018), 'Češi jsou tolerantní národ: Bojí se ale migrantů a teroristického útoku, ukázal průzkum [The Czechs are a tolerant nation, but they are afraid of migrants and terrorist attacks, research shows]', *Frekvence 1*, 2 November. Available online: https://www.frekvence1.cz (accessed 23 May 2020).

Polák, M. (2018), 'Češi jsou tolerantní: Ale jestli je budou zastánci multikulti ještě chvíli prudit, nedopadne to dobře, varuje Markéta Šichtařová [Czechs are tolerant, but if the proponents of multiculturalism keep irritating, things will not go well, warns Markéta Šichtařová]', *Parlamentní listy.cz*, 9 November. Available online: https://www.parlamentnilisty.cz (accessed 23 May 2020).

Public Opinion Research Centre (2008), 'Češi a tolerance [Czechs and tolerance]', press release, Praha: Sociologický ústav AV ČR. Available online: https://cvvm.soc.cas.cz/ (accessed 23 May 2020).

Public Opinion Research Centre (2019), 'Vztah české veřejnosti k národnostním skupinám žijícím v ČR – březen 2019 [The Czech public's views of ethnic groups living in the Czech Republic – March 2019]', press release, Praha: Sociologický ústav AV ČR. Available online: https://cvvm.soc.cas.cz/ (accessed 23 May 2020).

Radio Praha (2000), 'Češi mají sklony k rasismu, ale považují se za tolerantní národ [Czechs are prone to racism, but they consider themselves a tolerant nation]', *Radio Praha*, 28 January. Available online: http://romove.radio.cz/cz/clanek/18337 (accessed 23 May 2020).

Raduševič, M. (2011), 'Češi jsou tolerantní k cizincům, jinověrcům i odlišné sexuální orientaci [Czechs are tolerant of foreigners, other religions and different sexual orientations]', *Literární noviny*, 28 July. Available online: https://literarky.cz (accessed 23 May 2020).

Saruhashi, J. (2018), 'Personal Empowerment through Language Management', in L. Fairbrother, J. Nekvapil and M. Sloboda (eds), *The Language Management Approach: A Focus on Research Methodology*, 231–58, Berlin: Peter Lang.

Satinská, L. (2008), 'Slovenskí psychiatri v českom prostredí: sonda do česko-slovenských jazykových vzťahov [Slovak psychiatrists in the Czech context: a probe into the Czech-Slovak language relations]', *Člověk: časopis pro humanitní a společenské vědy* (13). Available online: http://clovek.ff.cuni.cz (accessed 6 August 2018).

Sattler, R. (2017), 'Jste v Česku, mluvte česky, vzkázaly pracovnice magistrátu cizincům. Můžou i skončit [You are in Czechia, speak Czech, the staff of the City Hall told foreigners. They may even be fired]', *Lidovky.cz*, 17 June. Available online: http://www.lidovky.cz (accessed 23 May 2020).

Schegloff, E. A. (2007), 'A Tutorial on Membership Categorization', *Journal of Pragmatics*, 39 (3): 462–82.

Shánělová, J. (2005/2006), 'Ruština v Karlových Varech [Russian in Karlovy Vary]', *Češtinář*, 16 (1): 3–8.

Sherman, T. (2020), 'Researching Language Management in Central Europe: Cultivation, Social Change and Power', in G. C. Kimura and L. Fairbrother (eds), *A Language Management Approach to Language Problems: Integrating Macro and Micro Dimensions*, 69–88, Amsterdam: John Benjamins.

Sloboda, M. (2016), 'Transition to Super-Diversity in the Czech Republic: Its Emergence and Resistance', in M. Sloboda, P. Laihonen and A. Zabrodskaja (eds), *Sociolinguistic Transition in Former Eastern Bloc Countries: Two Decades after the Regime Change*, 141–83, Frankfurt am Main: Peter Lang.

Sloboda, M. (forthcoming), 'Regulace užívání slovenštiny v Česku: právní a mimoprávní způsoby [The regulation of Slovak language use in Czechia: legal and extra-legal ways]', manuscript.

Sloboda, M., and Nábělková, M. (2013), 'Receptive Multilingualism in 'Monolingual' Media: Managing the Presence of Slovak on Czech Websites', *International Journal of Multilingualism*, 10 (2): 196–213.

Sloboda, M., Šimičić, L., Szabó Gilinger, E., and Vigers, D. (2012), 'The Policies on Public Signage in Minority Languages and Their Reception in Four Traditionally Bilingual European Locations', メディア・コミュニケーション研究 [Media and Communication Studies] (63): 51–88.

Špačková, I. (2011), 'Čechům vadí cizojazyčné reklamy, poslanec je chce počeštit [Czechs bothered by foreign-language ads, an MP wants to Czechify them]', *iDnes.cz*, 18 August. Available online: http://zpravy.idnes.cz/ (accessed 23 May 2020).

Stroud, C., and Jegels, D. (2014), 'Semiotic Landscapes and Mobile Narrations of Place: Performing the Local', *International Journal of the Sociology of Language*, 228: 179–99.

Szabó, P., and Troyer, R. A. (2017), 'Inclusive Ethnographies: Beyond the Binaries of Observer and Observed in Linguistic Landscape Studies', *Linguistic Landscape*, 3 (3): 306–26.

Szabó Gilinger,E., Sloboda, M., Šimičić, L., and Vigers, D. (2012), 'Discourse Coalitions for and against Minority Languages on Signs: Linguistic Landscape as a Social Issue', in D. Gorter, H. F. Marten and L. van Mensel (eds), *Minority Languages in the Linguistic Landscape*, 263–80, Basingstoke: Palgrave Macmillan.

Tan, M. S., and Ben Said, S. (2015), 'Linguistic Landscape and Exclusion: An Examination of Language Representation in Disaster Signage in Japan', in R. Rubdy and S. Ben Said (eds), *Conflict, Exclusion and Dissent in the Linguistic Landscape*, 145–69, Basingstoke: Palgrave Macmillan.

ten Have, P. (2002), 'The Notion of Member Is the Heart of the Matter: On the Role of Membership Knowledge in Ethnomethodological Inquiry', *Forum Qualitative Sozialforschung / Forum: Qualitative Social Research*, 3 (3). Available online: http://dx.doi.org/10.17169/fqs-3.3.834 (accessed 23 May 2020).

ten Have, P. (2004), *Understanding Qualitative Research and Ethnomethodology*, London: SAGE.

Toman, P. (2016), 'Na kolonádě to vypadá jako v cizině. Ruské nápisy ale mohou zůstat [The colonade looks like a foreign country, but Russian signage can remain]', *iDnes.cz*, 6 June. Available online: http://zpravy.idnes.cz/ (accessed 23 May 2020).

Varvařovský, P. (2011), 'Používání slovenského jazyka v zaměstnání [Use of the Slovak language at work]', file no. 164/2010/DIS/JKV. Available online: https://eso.ochrance.cz/Nalezene/Edit/2306 (accessed 23 May 2020).

Wright, S. (2016), *Language Policy and Language Planning: From Nationalism to Globalisation*, 2nd edn, New York: Palgrave Macmillan.

Zabrodskaja, A., and Milani, T. M. (2014), 'Signs in Context: Multilingual and Multimodal Texts in Semiotic Space', *International Journal of the Sociology of Language*, 228: 1–6.

Zedník, V. (2009), 'Азбука? Хватит! Karlovy Vary plánují ochránit češtinu vyhláškou [Cyrillic? Enough! Karlovy Vary plan to protect Czech by a public regulation]', *iDnes.cz*, 20 November. Available online: http://zpravy.idnes.cz/ (accessed 23 May 2020).

3

Empowering multilingualism? Provisions for place names in Northern Ireland and the political and legislative context

Mícheál B. Ó Mainnín

1. Introduction

This chapter is concerned with indigenous and minoritized languages in Northern Ireland (especially Irish) and explores the political and legislative context in terms of support for these languages with reference to specific provisions for place names. In so doing, it paves the way for the following chapter on the Linguistic Landscape in Northern Ireland (which also considers the relationship between policy and practice in detail). The present contribution does not consider the broad swathe of language policy; it focuses on place names as being of interest in a fractured society in which identity is deeply contested and language rights are the subject of contention (Ó Riagáin 2000; de Varennes 2003; Dickson 2003; McMonagle 2010; McMonagle and McDermott 2014).[1] There is some appreciation of the potential of place names of varying origins to contribute to an awareness of a multilingual and shared cultural heritage,[2] and acknowledgement that this, in turn, can empower individuals and communities to countenance greater tolerance of contemporary linguistic diversity. The Northern Ireland Place-Name Project (NIPNP) at Queen's University in Belfast was established with such empowerment in mind in 1987; since then it has deepened the engagement of the public with names as a manifestation of shared languages and shared space through its website (www.placenamesni.org) and on social media (@placenamesni).[3]

Political agreement has been reached recently in Northern Ireland (10 January 2020) to legislate for 'official recognition of the status' of both of the region's indigenous languages, Irish and Ulster-Scots; however, there has been legal provision for some time to allow for the employment of bilingual street signage under certain conditions which will be discussed below. This has empowered some communities, particularly those in which there is strong support for Irish, to request the erection of Irish versions of street and road names alongside the original versions in English;[4] the demand for similar signage in Ulster-Scots has been much more limited. There has been no broad consensus on language visibility in the public space. On the contrary, whereas some support signage as a form of 'resolute action' in promoting a minoritized language,[5] others argue that there is an 'adverse impact' on good relations (and the potential for ghettoization) and advocate for the retention of monolingualism in the majority language, English, as a 'neutral' position.[6] This chapter will begin with a brief account of the background to indigenous and minoritized languages in Ireland. It will then cast some light on ways in which place names have been embroiled in debates on language and identity over recent centuries before considering language politics in Northern Ireland, the broader legislative framework in the UK and internationally, and the provisions for place names in detail.

2. Indigenous and minoritized languages in Ireland

The Irish language, formerly spoken all over Ireland, had receded as a community language to the western seaboard (for the most part) by the time of the partition of Ireland in 1921. Pockets of older speakers remained elsewhere including, for example, parts of Antrim and Tyrone, two of the six counties which have constituted Northern Ireland since 1921.[7] However, as intergenerational transmission had ceased, none of these pockets have survived to the present. The fate of Irish is intimately bound up with the expansion of English, particularly from the seventeenth century. First introduced into Ireland with the Anglo-Norman conquest in the twelfth century, English had expanded and retracted in tandem with the waxing and waning of English power and, by the sixteenth century, survived most strongly in the vicinity of Dublin (in the area known as the Pale). The union of the English and Scottish crowns in 1603 in the person of James I changed the dynamic in some crucial respects; the course was set for English to become the language of monarch and government for the whole of the kingdom. Furthermore, the Plantation of Ulster in 1609 had, as its primary purpose, the reduction of Irish power in the north of Ireland and the breaking of the connection with Gaelic-speaking (i.e. Highland) Scotland. To this end, Protestant settlers, primarily from Lowland Scotland but also from England, were introduced into Ulster; the Lowland Scots introduced a new layer of linguistic complexity into the Irish landscape as they spoke a language akin to English but distinct from it: Scots. As for the Irish, linguistic and confessional identities coalesced with the result that the Irish language became associated with Catholicism, although it was the latter that became the primary marker of national identity in succeeding centuries.[8]

In the contemporary context of Northern Ireland, English is spoken everywhere and both Irish and Scots (now known locally and officially as Ulster-Scots) are minoritized languages. The most recent census figures available are those for 2011; 10.65 per cent of the population claimed 'some ability' in Irish, while 8.08 per cent claimed 'some ability' in Ulster-Scots (Northern Ireland Statistics and Research Agency 2014).[9] In the case of Ulster-Scots, the status of the variety has been contested with some seeing it as a dialect rather than as a language (see Görlach 2000; Falconer 2005; Crowley 2006; Gardner 2015). Speakers are predominantly rural and largely confined to the traditional heartlands of Scottish settlement in Antrim, east Down and east Donegal (the latter in what is now the Irish Republic).[10] The revival of Irish has been strongest in urban areas – particularly West Belfast which has a designated Gaeltacht Quarter, a reflection of the relative strength and visibility of the language in that part of the city – and in the rural district of Carntogher (An Carn) near Maghera in County Derry.[11]

3. 'Barbarous and uncouth'? Language, identity and place names

All three languages have left their mark on the toponymy of Ireland; the majority of the island's place names are of Irish origin but, since the seventeenth century in particular, increasing numbers of names have been coined in English while new names in Scots have been confined to the most northerly of Ireland's four provinces, Ulster. Furthermore, with language shift from Irish to English, Irish place names have been subjected to anglicization, most frequently by means of transliteration whereby a name is borrowed into English, assimilated phonetically, and transcribed in English orthography.[12] The retention of Irish names in this fashion was not warmly endorsed by all concerned with consolidating the conquest of Ireland (and, in order to facilitate this, the mapping of the land) in the seventeenth century; an act dating to 1665 known as the Act of Explanation[13] records the disapproval of the king, Charles II, in the following terms:

> His Majesty taking notice of the barbarous and uncouth names, by which most of the towns and places in this kingdom of Ireland are called, which hath occasioned much damage to diverse of his good subjects, and are very troublesome in the use thereof, and much retards the reformation of that kingdom, for remedy thereof is pleased that it be enacted ... by the authority aforesaid, that the lord lieutenant and council shall and may advise of, settle, and direct in the passing of all letters patents in that kingdom for the future, how new and proper names more suitable to the English tongue may be inserted with an alias for all towns, lands and places in that kingdom, that shall be granted by letters patents; which new names shall thenceforth be [the] only names to be used, any law, statute, custom, or usage to the contrary notwithstanding. (Crowley 2000: 76)

Interestingly, distaste for Irish names was echoed by Jonathan Swift, one of the founding fathers of the Irish literary tradition in English, in his essay 'On Barbarous Denominations in Ireland' which dates to *c.*1740; for Swift it was difficult to imagine any 'gentleman' being able to pronounce place names containing such 'odious sounds ... without dislocating every muscle that is used in speaking' (Davis 1957: 280). To return to Charles II, his desire to replace Irish names with 'new and proper names more suitable to the English tongue' had the support of Sir William Petty (1623–87) who had served as physician-general to the Cromwellian army in Ireland and had been awarded the contract for the great mapping project of the country in 1654 known as the Down Survey. Petty, drawing directly on the words of the king, noted that the 'barbarous and uncouth' names of Ireland were 'unintelligible'; it would be desirable, therefore, if the bulk of them could be 'interpreted, where they are not or cannot be abolished' (Petty [1691] 1861: 73). The wholesale translation and/or replacement of Irish names envisaged by Petty, which would have been a massive undertaking, never materialized; when the first Ordnance Survey of Ireland was conducted between 1824 and 1846 (Andrews [1975] 2002: vii), the Irish names which were engraved on the maps were standardized versions of their pre-existing anglicized forms for the most part.[14] Nonetheless, as articulated by Brian Friel in his acclaimed play, *Translations* (1981), the popular view of the Ordnance Survey was that of a body which was implicated in the destruction and corruption of native names and, therefore, an agent of disempowerment; by adopting anglicized forms (rather than the original Irish forms in Irish orthography), it was rendering Irish place names opaque and devoid of meaning. Friel's depiction of the role of the Ordnance Survey has been challenged but criticism of the Survey's approach had been expressed at the time by Thomas Davis (1814–1845), leader of the Young Ireland movement, who expressed the hope that 'whenever these maps are re-engraved, the Irish words will, we trust, be spelled in an Irish orthography, and not barbarously, as at present' (Davis [1846] 1998: 139). The irony of the use of the term 'barbarous' is striking; for Davis, the anglicized versions of Irish names were barbarous because they were 'English' while for King Charles II they were 'barbarous' because they were Irish. Davis also spoke elsewhere (in an article published in *The Nation* in 1843 entitled 'Our National Language') of Irish names being 'hard to pronounce, and without meaning' for the speaker of English; in this he echoes Petty and Swift although his position is again a contrary one in that the solution is not the destruction of the Irish language (or of its names) but the restoration of Irish throughout society and the re-empowerment of its speakers through the education system:

> To impose another language on such a people is to send their history adrift among the accidents of translation – 'tis to tear their identity from all places – 'tis to substitute arbitrary signs for picturesque and suggestive names ...
> What we seek is, that the people of the upper classes should have their children taught the language which explains our names of persons or places, our older history, and our music, and which is spoken in the majority of our counties.
> (Crowley 2000: 161–3)

The issue of respect for the original forms of Irish place names was specifically raised in the context of the Irish Cultural Revival in the late nineteenth century; in his influential public lecture to the National Literary Society in Dublin in 1892, 'The Necessity for De-Anglicising Ireland', Douglas Hyde (1860–1949), later to become the first president of Ireland, spoke colourfully of the 'shameful corruption' of Irish topographical nomenclature which now would be very difficult to reverse:

> Unfortunately the difficulties attendant upon a realteration of our place-names to their proper forms are very great. ... On the whole, our place names have been treated with about the same respect as if they were the names of a savage tribe which

had never before been reduced to writing, and with about the same intelligence and contempt as vulgar English squatters treat the topographical nomenclature of the Red Indians … I shall not give any more examples of deliberate carelessness, ineptitude and West-Britonising in our Irish topography, for the instances may be numbered by thousands and thousands. I hope and trust that where it may be done without any great inconvenience a native Irish Government will be induced to provide for the restoration of our place-names on something like a rational basis. (Ó Conaire 1986: 166–7)[15]

If Hyde were thinking of the role of the first Ordnance Survey in committing place names to maps, he would have been mistaken in attributing to it a total lack of respect for Irish-language names; its topographical field officer, John O'Donovan (subsequently the first professor of Celtic in Queen's University Belfast), had been authorized to collect the original forms of names (where these were still known) in the course of his fieldwork even though these were not the forms to be engraved on the maps. The possibility of using the Irish forms for any official purpose (including maps) was a different matter and this had been discounted long before the advent of the Survey, as we have seen.[16] In any case, with the foundation of the independent Irish state in 1922 (and attempts since then to revive the fortunes of the Irish language and empower Irish speakers), there has been a concern to reconstruct the original Irish forms of anglicized names for cultural reasons (as Hyde clearly wished) and, in the case of the Irish Republic, the additional requirement of providing Irish forms for use in what is an officially bilingual state.[17] In the latter case, this also necessitates the translation into Irish of place names of English origin (particularly street names in urban areas). In Northern Ireland, the primary focus of research by the NIPNP has been on discovering the linguistic origins of names for the purposes of cultural enrichment and the promotion of pluralism.[18] In more recent years, it has also provided translations of street names in areas where there is demand from local communities (cf. www.ulsterplacename.org).

4. Language legislation and language politics in Northern Ireland

The historical legacy of division in Northern Ireland is such that language has been embroiled in conflicting perceptions of identity as manifested in the contrasting political allegiances of its people (be they Irish or British). Irish, while cherished as the national language by a majority of nationalists, is disowned by the greater number of unionists; Ulster-Scots is supported most strongly by unionists and is treated with indifference (for the most part) by nationalists.[19] Indeed, disagreement on language was a key factor in the suspension of devolved government for three years from the collapse of the Northern Ireland Assembly at Stormont in January 2017 until its restoration in January 2020. Northern Ireland has differed from the other devolved regions of the UK (and from the Republic of Ireland), therefore, in not having had specific legislation to protect either or both of its two minoritized languages.[20] The recent acceptance of the deal sponsored by the British and Irish governments and agreed by the five major political parties in Northern Ireland, *New Decade, New Approach* (Northern Ireland Office 2020), has cleared the way for legislation for indigenous languages for the first time (see Section 5).

The lack of consensus up until the acceptance of this deal in January 2020 had been felt across various domains of governance. For instance, the UK is a signatory (since 1995) to the Council of Europe Framework Convention for the Protection of National Minorities; however, in its update to the Advisory Committee on the implementation of the Framework Convention in 2016, the UK Government did not provide any information on Northern Ireland (*Fourth Report Submitted by United Kingdom Pursuant to Article 25, Paragraph 2 of the Framework Convention for the Protection of National Minorities* (2015)). In commenting on this in February 2017, the Advisory Committee urged the Northern Ireland authorities to 'at least provide information on non-controversial issues' and called upon the central government to 'help build consensus on the reporting process'. It had been given to understand by 'the Northern Ireland authorities' that failure to provide any information was 'the consequence of the lack of agreement on minority and human-rights related issues between the two largest parties of the [Northern Ireland] Executive, particularly on the issue of the Irish language' (*Fourth Opinion of the Advisory Committee on the Framework Convention for the Protection of National Minorities* I, Key Findings, §3). Significantly, the United Kingdom did respond to this by providing some information on Northern Ireland but, in so doing, made no mention of either Irish or Ulster-Scots, even in the section of its response on 'Languages' (Comments of the Government of the United Kingdom on the *Fourth Opinion of the Advisory Committee on the Implementation of the Framework Convention for the Protection of National Minorities by the United Kingdom* 2017).

This is not to suggest that there had been no political or legislative framework within the UK (or provided by the Council of Europe) for the support of Irish and Ulster-Scots.[21] The need to empower speakers of indigenous languages and support linguistic diversity was first articulated by The Good Friday Agreement of 1998 in which all the participants (the British and Irish governments, and all of the political parties in Northern Ireland who signed up to that agreement) 'recognised the importance of respect, understanding and tolerance in relation to linguistic diversity', including Irish, Ulster-Scots and the 'languages of the various ethnic communities' (Northern Ireland Office 1998a: 19, §3).[22] The agreement led to the establishment of six North-South implementation bodies on the island of Ireland including the Language Body comprising Foras na Gaeilge (the Irish Language Agency) and the Ulster-Scots Agency/Boord o Ulstèr-Scotch, both with an All-Ireland remit and funded by the two governments. However, the support enshrined in the agreement was qualified by the stipulation that the new devolved Northern Ireland Assembly would sustain its commitments to the indigenous languages 'in a way which takes account of the desires and sensitivities of the community'; being a divided community, the desires and sensitivities of its people traditionally have differed in relation to languages, as we have seen. The Northern Ireland Act 1998 gave legal effect to the Agreement, and paragraph 28D,[23] which is concerned with 'Strategies relating to Irish language and Ulster-Scots language etc.', specifies that the Executive Committee of the Assembly shall adopt two distinct strategies setting out how it proposes to (i) 'enhance and protect the development of the Irish language' and (ii) 'enhance and develop the Ulster Scots language, heritage and culture' (Northern Ireland Office 1998b: §28D). The Good Friday Agreement was followed in 2003 by the Joint Declaration by the British and Irish Governments. This added little other than to reiterate in paragraph 30 that the British Government will 'continue to discharge all its commitments under the Agreement in respect of the Irish language' and will also 'take steps to encourage support to be made available for an Ulster-Scots academy' (Northern Ireland Office 2003). It also placed particular emphasis on broadcasting in Irish. In the meantime, the British Government, which had signalled its intent to 'actively consider' signing the Council of Europe Charter for Regional or Minority Languages in the Good Friday Agreement, did so on 2 March 2000. The *Charter* was ratified on 27 March 2001 and came into force in the UK on 1 July 2001. While Part II of the *Charter* as ratified applies to both Irish and Ulster-Scots, Part III applies only to Irish and commits to thirty-six provisions in total (DCAL 2005: §14).

The question of support for Irish and Ulster-Scots was raised again in the context of the St Andrews Agreement of 2006. The British Government undertook to introduce an Irish Language Act to enhance and protect the language while reiterating its belief also in the need to enhance and develop not only the Ulster-Scots language but also its 'heritage and culture' (Northern Ireland Office 2006a) – a significant distinction between the two which appears also in the section (28D) added to the Northern Ireland Act of 1998. However, in giving legislative effect to the agreement, the St Andrews Agreement Act (2006) omitted any reference to an Irish Language Act; it committed, instead, the Northern Ireland Executive to adopt strategies for both Irish and Ulster-Scots (Northern Ireland Office 2006b), thereby seeming to empower the devolved political institutions rather than the language communities themselves. Two separate strategies eventually emerged (but were not endorsed by the entire Executive):[24] the *Strategy to Enhance and Protect the Development of the Irish Language* (DCAL 2015b; see also 2016b) and the *Strategy to Enhance and Develop the Ulster-Scots Language, Heritage and Culture* (DCAL 2015a; see also 2016a); these cover the period 2015–35 and include among their aims the desire to facilitate language acquisition and learning, and build sustainable networks and communities. The Northern Ireland government's Department of Culture, Arts and Leisure (DCAL) had formulated these two strategies having previously initiated a public consultation on draft strategies in 2012 (DCAL 2012a, 2012b; see also 2013a, 2013b). The Minister for Culture, Arts and Leisure, Carál Ní Chuilín of Sinn Féin (one of the two parties in government), was also to the fore in initiating a public consultation on an Irish Language Bill in February 2015 (DCAL 2015c); attempts to introduce such a bill in the Northern Ireland Assembly later that year failed to get the necessary cross-community support. There are also Irish-language groups who have advocated for legislation of this kind. Pobal (an umbrella organization for the Irish-speaking community in Northern Ireland) first published a draft of legislative proposals in 2006 and published an updated set of proposals in 2012 (Pobal 2012). More recently, in 2017, Conradh na Gaeilge (which promotes Irish throughout Ireland and abroad) produced a discussion document on an Irish Language Act which differs from that produced by Pobal in some respects; Conradh na Gaeilge provided costings for implementation of the legislation (which were criticized by Pobal as being 'unrealistically low' (Manley 2017)) and suggested timeframes and practical means of delivering some of its proposals (Conradh na Gaeilge 2017). In February 2018, hopes for the restoration of government were raised when the two main political parties, the Democratic Unionist Party (DUP) and Sinn Féin, reached a stage in talks that resulted in the circulation of a potential draft agreement text.[25] The second section of the draft text entitled 'Respecting Language and Culture' proposes three separate bills (Mallie 2018: §2.1) – a general 'Respecting Language and Diversity Bill' and two language-specific bills, an 'Irish (Respecting Language and Diversity) Bill' and an 'Ulster Scots (Respecting Language and Diversity) Bill' – thereby providing official recognition of both Irish and Ulster-Scots (Mallie 2018: §§2.3–4). The *New Decade, New Approach* agreement, formally approved by the Northern Ireland Assembly on 11 January 2020, has endorsed the idea of legislating for 'official recognition of the status' of both Irish and Ulster-Scots (Northern Ireland Office 2020: §27b, §27c) by enacting three bills to amend Section 28d of the Northern Ireland Act 1998. The purpose of these three bills is to (i) 'make provisions to establish [an] Office of Identity and Cultural Expression', (ii) 'make provisions for the Irish Language' and (iii) 'make provisions to establish a Commissioner to enhance and develop the language, arts and literature associated with the Ulster Scots / Ulster British tradition in Northern Ireland' (Northern Ireland Office 2020: Annex E, §5.23). The provisions for Irish will also include the creation of a Commissioner to 'recognise, support, protect and enhance the Irish language' (Northern Ireland Office 2020: §27b) while the aim of the Office of Identity and Cultural Expression is to 'promote cultural pluralism and respect for diversity', 'build social cohesion and reconciliation' and 'celebrate and support all aspects of Northern Ireland's rich cultural and linguistic heritage' (Northern Ireland Office 2020: §27a). Furthermore, provision will be made for facilitating the conduct of business in the Assembly through both languages (Northern Ireland Office 2020: §27g) and for the establishment of a 'central Translation Hub' in the Department of Finance (Northern Ireland Office 2020: §27f). There is also a commitment in the agreement which requires the re-established Executive to produce a draft 'Irish Language Strategy' and a draft 'Ulster Scots Language, Heritage and Culture Strategy' for public consultation within six months (Northern Ireland Office 2020: §5.21.3), but these have yet to materialize.

5. Legislation and provisions for place names: Proposals, public responses and enactments

Legislation has provided for bilingual or dual language street-name signage since the enactment of the Local Government (Miscellaneous Provisions) (Northern Ireland) Order 1995.[26] Article 11 of this act bestows the power on councils to erect street-name signs in a language other than English but the name must always be present in the official English form also. Monolingual street-name signs in Irish or Ulster-Scots would contravene the legislation. On the other hand, the Local Government Act (Northern Ireland) of 2014 (sections 79–80) enables councils to renege on this under their 'general power of competence'.²⁷ There has often been much contention surrounding proposals for bilingual place-name signage at council level, therefore, with the result that such proposals may be blocked. The Good Friday Agreement had committed the British Government, 'where appropriate and where people so desire it', to 'facilitate and encourage' the use of Irish 'in speech and writing in public and private life where there is appropriate demand' (Northern Ireland Office 1998a, 19, §3); the reference to 'public' here can be assumed to include signage in the public sphere, not least because of the reference in the same paragraph of the agreement to the European Charter (as discussed above). Part III, Article 10, of the Charter is concerned with 'administrative authorities and public services' and the undertaking to 'allow and/or encourage ... the use or adoption, if necessary in conjunction with the name in the official language(s), of traditional and correct forms of place-names in regional or minority languages' (European Charter, §§2, 2g). This is qualified to the extent that 'the number of residents who are users of regional or minority languages is such as to justify the measures specified' (European Charter, §2). In reflecting on the obligations of the Charter, a document produced by the DCAL entitled *Guidance on Meeting UK Government Commitments in Respect of Irish and Ulster Scots*,²⁸ the second version of which dates to 2005, notes the legal advice that administrative authorities must have 'the ability to facilitate the use of family and place-names etc. in regional or minority languages (not excluding the use of official languages)' (DCAL 2005: §18). Elsewhere it notes the 'wording and the spirit of Part II [of the Charter] and the findings of recent independent research into public attitudes'; consequently, 'it would be reasonable to expect to see a certain degree of signage' involving the minoritized languages although there is varying practice across government departments and bodies in this respect (DCAL 2005: §33).²⁹ It is recommended, therefore, that because of 'community sensitivities', departments and bodies 'might find it helpful to consider trilingual ... signs in certain locations rather than bilingual signs', that is, a combination of all three languages rather than English and either Irish or Ulster-Scots (DCAL 2005: §34). However, when referring to the use of place names specifically (DCAL 2005: §35), the Guidance does not mention trilingual forms but speaks in terms of departments and associated bodies being encouraged to use 'versions in both languages' in initiating contact with the public and in their documents and publications. At an earlier point in the same paragraph, which is concerned with replying to correspondence or processing applications in which a person has used 'a lawfully adopted Irish or Ulster-Scots language street name',³⁰ the Guidance states that 'both the English and the Irish or Ulster-Scots forms of the street name should be noted on the official record' (DCAL 2005: §35).³¹ This seems to suggest that the reference above to 'versions in both languages' is meant to refer to English and either Irish or Ulster-Scots, but it is not clear how an individual department could make such a judgement (i.e. when to use English and Irish in initiating contact with the public and when to use English and Ulster-Scots). As regards other government departments, it is important to mention the *Bilingual Traffic Signs: Draft Policy and Draft Equality Impact Assessment Consultation* produced by the Department for Regional Development in 2011. It conceived of bilingual signage being limited to welcome signs 'in discrete localised areas to minimise their impact' and to ensure that 'they will get as much local support as possible' (Department for Regional Development, Northern Ireland 2011: 5, §3.4). The possibility of bilingual signage on principal highways, however, was excluded and the proposals were rejected in any case by the minister, Danny Kennedy (Mac an Bhreithiún and Burke 2014: 97–8).

The other European context in terms of legislation relevant to the use of place names and signage in minoritized languages is the *Framework Convention*. Article 11 of the Convention is concerned with the 'use of topographical signage' and the *Advisory Committee's Fourth Opinion on the United Kingdom* (alluded to above) which it published in 2017 has a good deal to say on the situation then current in Northern Ireland:

> In Northern Ireland, the Local Government (Miscellaneous Provisions) Order 1995 permits the erection of bilingual street signs. ... No legal framework exists for bilingual signage for roads and other place-names, and it is a criminal offence to put up an unofficial Irish language sign. The Advisory Committee understands that some councils decided to erect signage other than street names under their 'general power of competence', while other councils (e.g. Mid and East Antrim) have proposed very restrictive policies. ... Interlocutors of the Advisory Committee explained that the language of signage can cause tensions at local level. ... Signage thus appears to have assumed a 'territorial marker' connotation,[32] which continues to lead to an official policy of not posting such signs for fear that they may cause controversy or put at risk public authorities' duty to promote 'good relations'. The Advisory Committee is very concerned by the politicisation of signage ... [and] considers that the use of bilingualism on signage and other public displays should be promoted where possible as a positive tool of integration to convey the message that a given territory is shared in harmony by various population groups. (*Advisory Committee's Fourth Opinion on the United Kingdom*, §111)[33]

It then follows with a recommendation which calls for 'closer dialogue on signage among the government and local authorities in Northern Ireland to identify pragmatic and flexible solutions that accommodate the demands of the population in line with the principles contained in Article 11' (*Advisory Committee's Fourth Opinion on the United Kingdom*, §112).

The source for some of the information obtained by the Advisory Committee was the *Northern Ireland Human Rights Commission's Parallel Report to the Advisory Committee on the Fourth Monitoring Report of the United Kingdom* in March 2016 (Northern Ireland Human Rights Commission 2016). The key sections of this report in the present context are paragraphs §§191–98 ('Traditional Names'). The concerns of COMEX (the Committee of Experts of the European Charter for Regional or Minority Languages) in 2014 are noted in relation to 'delay and obstruction' in dealing with requests for bilingual street names by local councils as is the conclusion that a decision by the Minister for the Department of Regional Development and the Northern Ireland Tourist Board not to introduce bilingual signage 'may be an infringement of the Charter' (Northern Ireland Human Rights Commission 2016: §197).[34] COMEX had also previously raised the issue that measures to promote the Irish language were not always taken forward amid concerns that these would contravene Section 75 of the Northern Ireland Act 1998 which places public authorities under a duty to promote 'good relations' between the main communities in Northern Ireland. The Commission reminds the Advisory Committee of its own position that the implementation of minority rights protected under the Framework Convention does not imply discrimination against the majority population (Northern Ireland Human Rights Commission 2016: §§194–5; see also Northern Ireland Human Rights Commission (2010) and Holder (2018)). Having said all that, it acknowledges that the erection of bilingual signage containing Irish or Ulster-Scots can be viewed by some as 'a territorial marker' (Northern Ireland Human Rights Commission 2016: §196). It suggests in its Executive Summary that the Advisory Committee may wish to put a number of questions to the UK including 'what measures are being taken to overcome the politicisation of language issues in Northern Ireland' and 'how it will fulfil its obligations to promote the use of all minority languages in street names and other topographical indicators in the absence of political consensus' (cf. also §198).

Evidence for the absence of political consensus around bilingual/multilingual place names and signage is to be found in the responses to the public consultation exercises initiated by the Minister for Culture, Arts and Leisure on the draft strategies for Irish and Ulster-Scots (in 2012) and on the Irish Language Bill (in 2015). The response of two of the local political parties to the draft strategy for Irish may be noted here. Traditional Unionist Voice opposed the suggestion that local authorities should facilitate the proper preservation and signposting of Irish place names and the naming of new housing developments to reflect local or national heritage for three reasons: (i) the lack of any desire for this in most parts of Northern Ireland; (ii) the confusion such signposting would cause for drivers and the emergency services; and (iii) the use of Irish place names in bilingual signposting to mark an area as belonging to a particular culture and tradition (DCAL 2013a: 443–4, Response 091). The response from the Alliance Party was very different in tone but also alluded to the demarcation of territory through bilingual signs, be that intentional or otherwise. It failed to see any actions in the draft strategy for Irish that would encourage local authorities to promote a shared identity through place names or the naming of housing developments. This could lead to politicization and further polarization in certain localities. Despite these concerns the party considered the languages themselves to be 'a good means to promote cultural awareness, understanding and diversity' (DCAL 2013a: 406–10, Response 215).

In the case of the Irish Language Bill, the consultation sought responses to five proposals on place names contained in Part 8 of the document. One of these concerned the definition of a place name (DCAL 2015c, 8a) and a second suggested responsibility for place names should be located in the proposed Irish Language Commissioner's Office (DCAL 2015c: 8b). The remaining three questions raised the issue of recognition of Irish forms: the most fundamental question of all being legal and official recognition (DCAL 2015c: 8c) but, also, recognition on bilingual road signage on a par with the English forms (DCAL 2015c: 8e) and on maps and in other publications produced by Land and Property Services, the government agency in which the Ordnance Survey is now located (DCAL 2015c: 8d). Responses on the negative side noted the potential of Irish forms of names to be used as a 'cultural weapon' which would alienate and cause division (DCAL 2015e). Some concerns were voiced by branches of the Grand Orange Lodge of Ireland and include the potential dangers of bilingual signage in terms of road safety (DCAL 2015d: 115); this recalls the response of the Traditional Unionist Voice to the draft Irish strategy above. The issue of finance was also raised, and this was linked to the necessity of equality for Ulster-Scots forms on signage which would add, therefore, to the total cost.[35] Interestingly, Tullygarley Orange Lodge noted that place names are 'shared by all communities' (DCAL 2015d: 164); however, the implication seems to be that, in the case of Irish place names, the communities share the anglicized rather than the original Irish forms. On the positive side, the Northern Ireland Centre for Information on Language Teaching and Research (NICILT) expressed the view that 'a greater awareness and acceptance of placenames as a valuable cultural heritage can foster acceptance of the shared patrimony of Northern Ireland' (DCAL 2015d: 121). NICILT and others also argued (particularly on the basis of practice elsewhere in the UK in the case of Wales and the Western Isles of Scotland) that the original forms of place names be accepted on maps and road signage (DCAL 2015d: 121), and they even argued that monolingual Irish forms be accepted in the case of names of Irish origin. The European Language Equality Network suggested that this would make for a 'consistent place-names policy' and would respect the 'language of the place-name, local history and culture' (DCAL 2015d: 89). St Mary's University, Twickenham, alluded to 'goodwill' in this regard; 'Irish-only signage should be encouraged, except where the local community calls strongly for bilingualism' (DCAL 2015d: 159). The Northern Ireland Human Rights Commission (2015: §57) advised that the Bill should make provision for a broad range of topographical indicators, by which it meant names other than street names which are already provided for in the Local Government Act of 1995 (cf. also DCAL 2013a: 271–2, Response 270). Needless to say, individuals and organizations (such as An Carn, Croí Éanna, Ógras and Ionad Uíbh Eachach) whose concern was the empowerment of Irish speakers supported the proposals strongly (as did some local councils such as Mid-Ulster District Council); in so doing, they stressed the need for official status for Irish, and for public bodies and Royal Mail to accept addresses in the language (DCAL 2015d: 7, 75, 99, 137). The wider point about the responses as a whole is that they reflected community divisions around language (as discussed earlier, in Section 4), and, where local organizations were involved, strong opinions in favour or against legislation were aligned predictably with the cultural and political ethos of those organizations. However, as we have seen, there were significant contributions to the debate from other quarters, some of whom articulated broader UK and European perspectives.

We have noted earlier that the proposal for an Irish Language Bill did not get the necessary support when put to the Assembly in late 2015. However, we have also seen that the draft strategies for both Irish and Ulster-Scots did lead to published strategies the same year. In DCAL's summary of responses to the *Draft Strategy for Irish*, the importance of signage in terms of visibility for Irish was noted in particular. This would facilitate 'normalisation and acceptance of the language' – although care was needed to ensure that signage in Irish would not lead to 'increased community polarisation' (DCAL 2013b: §3.2.52; cf. §§3.2.82–5, 3.2.91 and 3.2.93). The strategies which were subsequently agreed both contained a section on public services in which departments, councils and public bodies were obliged to 'facilitate the proper preservation and signposting of … place-names and the naming of new housing developments' in both Irish and Ulster-Scots (DCAL 2015b: §4.87; 2015a: §4.39 (g)). However, the strategies differ in that the Irish strategy also stresses the 'value and importance' of the Irish language in economic life (including cultural tourism) and the importance of signage in this regard (DCAL 2015b: §4.116, §4.118, §4.130). Visibility and signage have also been highlighted as crucial elements in proposals for an Irish Language Act by Irish-language organizations, and these are articulated in tandem with the call for official recognition for the language. Pobal's proposals speak in terms of legislation conferring 'the same status and validity' on place names in Irish as in English and of the need for public bodies to employ bilingual signage ('using lettering of the same size in the two languages') on the exterior of buildings. They make exception, however, 'for those bodies whose services are primarily directed at or are primarily for the benefit of Irish speakers, which may have a solely or predominantly Irish-language … signage' (Pobal 2012: §§4, §32(i); cf. §32(j), §42); this is reminiscent of the policy applied in the Irish Republic in relation to services in the Gaeltacht. For Conradh na Gaeilge, 'visibility of the language is key for its growth, and to demonstrate that it's part of our shared heritage. To achieve this an act would legislate for bilingual road signage … and official recognition for place-names in Irish' (Conradh na Gaeilge (2017): 11).[36] In distinguishing between road signage and street signs, it states that legislation should be put in place at local council level 'to ensure that bilingual street signage should be available in Irish *where there is a demand for it*' (emphasis added). If 50 per cent of respondents to a plebiscite request street signage in Irish, 'this should be made available and be recognised in law' (Conradh na Gaeilge 2017: 25, §8.6). Significantly, the import of all of this would appear to be that those parts of Northern Ireland which are strongly unionist would never find themselves being forced to accept bilingual Irish-English street signs in their areas but would have to countenance bilingual Irish-English directional road signage throughout the jurisdiction. These matters have continued to be crucial in attempting to achieve political consensus, so much so that in the *New Decade, New Approach* agreement of 2020 (as in the draft agreement of 2018) there could be no mention whatsoever of signage or of bilingual forms of place names.

A more recent contribution to the debate on signage is the report produced by Conradh na Gaeilge, in collaboration with the Committee for the Administration of Justice and Ulster University: *Local Councils, Obligations and the Irish Language: A Framework for Compliance* (2019). This report is concerned with UK commitments to the Irish language and their implementation by local government; in subjecting these commitments to scrutiny, it applies a 'Framework for Compliance' containing five measures derived from the European Charter and other documents which have been discussed above in Section 4 (Conradh na Gaeilge et al. 2019: 3–14). Having set out the policy on street signage provision in the case of each of the eleven local councils in tabular form (Conradh na Gaeilge et al. 2019: 15–17), implementation against the standards set out in the framework is assessed in the light of surveys conducted of local councils at the end of 2016 and updated in 2018 (Conradh na Gaeilge et al. 2019: 21–46). This constitutes an important reflection on provision by actors, therefore. As far as bilingual street signage is concerned, the report finds that policy and implementation vary greatly from council to council; more generally, six councils are not considered to be fulfilling any of their obligations under the report's 'Framework for Compliance',[37] while the other five are perceived to be either 'progressively realising their obligations' or taking positive steps to varying extents in that direction.[38] All 'fall short in some way of the requirements set out in the present framework' (Conradh na Gaeilge et al. 2019: 14) and it may be noted that only two have a policy of promoting awareness of, and respect for, both Irish and Ulster Scots: Derry City and Strabane District Council and Fermanagh and Omagh District Council (Conradh na Gaeilge et al. 2019: 32, 36). The conclusion drawn in relation to place-name signage is that, rather than the diversity of practice which currently pertains, 'a simple, uniform approach would be most suitable so that residents are clear about what they are entitled to in any area'. It also argues, in another significant departure from the position taken by Conradh na Gaeilge in its discussion document on an Irish Language Act in 2017, that thresholds for demand for bilingual signage should be set low as COMEX has regarded 50 per cent as being too high to be compatible with the European Charter and even a much lower figure of 20 per cent as being high in some contexts (Conradh na Gaeilge et al. 2019: 18, 20).

6. Community sensitivities, visibility and the politics of naming

It is interesting that the most significant manifestation of a shared multilingual heritage in Ireland as a whole in the public sphere may be the newly designed Irish passport which was launched in September 2013; for the first time, this contains quotations from literary works in all three languages which are relevant to this chapter: Irish, Ulster-Scots and English. However, this is not to imply that there is a trilingual policy in terms of signage in that part of the Irish Republic in which all three languages are or have been spoken, particularly east Donegal. As regards multilingualism in the Northern Ireland context, the possibility of trilingual signage was alluded to in 2005 in the *Guidance on Meeting UK Government Commitments in Respect of Irish and Ulster Scots*; this report noted varying practices across government departments and bodies in terms of stationery, for example, and recommended, because of 'community sensitivities', the consideration of trilingual rather than bilingual signs 'in certain locations'. However, as we have seen, there was some inconsistency in the document on this and the case was not made for uniform employment of trilingual signage in all domains across the jurisdiction.[39] A comprehensive multilingual policy of this kind was not in mind, therefore, and has not evolved as a policy since.

The question of community sensitivities was alluded to explicitly in the Good Friday Agreement and this has continued to be a key political issue up to the present. Central to this is the idea that there can be no bilingual or multilingual signage without consensus and it is certainly the case that agreement on signage is much to be desired. However, the Northern Ireland Human Rights Commission in its *Parallel Report on the European Charter for Regional and Minority Languages* (September 2009) raised some concern about the appropriateness of a 'long-term search for consensus' as a basis 'on which to conceptualise the protection of human rights, most especially where the rights of linguistic or any other minorities are concerned' as the achievement of consensus is 'not a precondition for giving people access to their rights'. Elsewhere, it noted that, 'in general', the restriction of the use or promotion of Irish 'to accommodate the "sensitivities" of others would be incompatible with freedom of expression' as official acknowledgement of a minority language 'cannot constitute a violation of the rights of those who do not use that language' (Northern Ireland Human Rights Commission 2010). This position, that the promotion of visibility and use of Irish (and by the same token Ulster-Scots) in the public sphere cannot be considered to be an act of discrimination against speakers of English, had also been articulated by COMEX in 2010 in its *UK Third Monitoring Cycle Report* (§123) and in 2011 by the Advisory Committee for CoE's Framework Convention for National Minorities in Their Third Opinion on the UK (§28). Crucially, for the Northern Ireland Human Rights Commission, the sensitivities of non-speakers of a minoritized language and fears of discrimination can be accommodated through the prevention of monolingualism in that language as linguistic pluralism is explicitly codified into the European Charter and promoted implicitly in European Court of Human Rights jurisprudence (Northern Ireland Human Rights Commission 2010).

Another element of the debate on consensus and community sensitivities is the impact on good relations. Section 75 of the Northern Ireland Act 1998 places a duty on councils and other bodies to promote both equality of opportunity and good relations, and COMEX expressed concern in 2010 that potential contravention of section 75 in the form of adverse impact on good relations was being used as justification for not promoting Irish (*European Charter, UK Third Monitoring Cycle Report*, §123). In taking this stance, the monolingual use of the English language in the public space is argued by some to constitute a neutral and reasonable position but the 'neutrality' of English is very problematic, not least when viewed through a historical prism, as we have seen.[40] Furthermore, others have argued that there is no 'universally agreed' neutral position, that section 75 was not intended to operate as a 'political veto', and that it is a 'misapplication' of the Act to find an adverse impact on equality of opportunity 'merely because a policy is politically contentious, or attracts hostility' (Conradh na Gaeilge et al. 2019: 52). The restriction of bilingual signage to certain areas for these reasons was criticized in 2011 by the Advisory Committee as not being 'in line with the spirit of the Framework Convention' the aim of which is 'to value the use of minority languages … with a view to promoting more tolerance and intercultural dialogue in society' (*Advisory Committee on Framework Convention, Third Opinion*, 2011, §126 and §158). It elaborated on this in 2017 in stating that 'bilingualism on signage and other public displays should be promoted where possible as a positive tool of integration to convey the message that a given territory is shared in harmony by various population groups' (*Advisory Committee on Framework Convention, Fourth Opinion*, 2017).

It is the case that the normalization and tolerability of minority languages is facilitated by increased visibility in the public space;[41] indeed, it has been claimed that 'being visible may be as important for minority languages as being heard' (Marten, Van Mensel and Gorter 2012: 1). The argument made very recently by those advocating for

Irish is that the use of bilingual signage provides 'a simple and natural opportunity' to facilitate access to the language in a way which connects with 'shared history and culture' and suggests a 'simple uniform approach' to this across the jurisdiction (Conradh na Gaeilge et al. 2019: 14, 20). However, in the Northern Ireland context, what might be called 'the politics of naming' has proven to be particularly intractable,[42] so much so that the question of visibility for bilingual forms of place names (and for other forms of bilingual signage) has neither been addressed nor resolved in the *New Decade, New Approach* agreement. It is significant that the Agreement speaks of the 'first priority' for the Irish Language Commissioner as being the development of

> best practice standards that facilitate interaction between Irish language users and public bodies, including but not limited to making information or forms available in Irish where required, enabling widely used public websites to have an Irish Language translation available, and ensuring that public bodies reply in Irish where practical to correspondence in Irish. Public bodies will each continue to make their own decisions on other matters to do with the Irish language. (Northern Ireland Office 2020: Annex E, §5.11)

The implication of the last line of this paragraph in particular appears to be that it will still be left to local councils to implement policy on bilingual signage with the result that empowerment of speakers of the minoritized language, be that Irish or Ulster-Scots, will remain uneven across differing council areas. Consequently, the impression of Northern Ireland as 'a patchwork of discrete bounded places with identities that do not overlap' (Mac an Bhreithiún and Burke 2014: 98) will linger into the future.

There is undoubtedly an argument for equality of respect for the two indigenous languages, but the appetite for signage in Ulster-Scots on a par with Irish has yet to be tested, not least in the unionist community where it might be expected to get stronger support, and there would appear to be some who would rather confine its use to the oral medium (see Dunlevy, Chapter 6). Nor have the consequences of the varying proportions of place names in the two minoritized languages been considered; the number of names of Ulster-Scots origin in Northern Ireland is much smaller than the numbers in Irish and English. Consequently, the creation and provision of Ulster-Scots versions for use on signage of the much greater number of names of Irish origin would be a considerable undertaking for those promoting Ulster-Scots at this relatively early stage of its development as it currently lags behind Irish in terms of capacity in this domain.

The provision of directional road signage in all three languages would be infinitely easier as this would involve a limited vocabulary. An obvious parallel for us to consider is Scotland which also has a similar linguistic mix: English, Scots and Gaelic (the latter two genetically linked to Ulster-Scots and Irish, respectively). Signage has traditionally been monolingual here with the exception of the Gaelic-speaking areas where bilingual signs in Gaelic and English may be found (see Puzey 2010: 340–1). More recently, a policy of bilingualism has been introduced into some public domains in the Lowlands where Scots has traditionally been spoken (and Gaelic has not) such as in the transport system and in government (see Hornsby and Vigers 2012; Morgan

2012: 51–2). However, this bilingualism policy does not involve the combination of Scots and English but the provision of a Gaelic version of the name currently employed in English (be that ultimately of Scots or English origin) for use alongside the 'English' name. Clearly, the linguistic convergence of English and Scots in Scotland in recent centuries is a factor here in deciding against attempting to implement a policy involving all three languages. The other parallel is the Republic of Ireland and here the policy is bilingual Irish-English signage across the jurisdiction. It is certainly the case that for some of a unionist persuasion a similar bilingual policy for Northern Ireland is unpalatable in that it would elevate the similarities in the LL between the two parts of Ireland while marking out Ireland as a whole as being different from Britain (although this would be to ignore the bilingualism present in the LL of Wales and Scotland). On the other hand, it would be possible to choose to see the use of Irish on signage in both Northern Ireland and the Republic of Ireland as being 'transnational' in the way that German, for example, is employed on signage in both Germany and Austria.

7. Conclusion

The question reflected in the title of this chapter is the extent to which speakers of indigenous languages have been empowered (or not) in Northern Ireland through political support and legislative provisions for multilingual place-name usage, particularly on signage. This is a matter of some complexity. On the one hand, there is no multilingual approach to signage involving all three languages, English, Irish and Ulster-Scots, nor has there ever been a successful attempt at formulating a uniform and comprehensive policy in order to affect a transformative impact on society as a whole in relation to linguistic diversity. The extent of community division around toleration of indigenous languages, particularly in relation to visibility in the public space, remains high, so much so that this issue could not be addressed in the recent political agreement, *New Decade, New Approach*. On the other hand, there is provision for bilingual place-name signage involving English and either one of the two indigenous languages at local council level. This has enabled speakers of Irish and Ulster-Scots to seek to have bilingual street signage erected in areas where support can be obtained from the majority of residents; nationalist communities, in particular, have seen this as liberating and empowering in terms of equality and respect for Irish national identity. However, the lack of a uniform policy across Northern Ireland as a whole has led to charges of ghettoization and territorial marking; it has been remarked that policy on signage makes it possible for bilingual signs to become part of a 'politicized semiotic system' which includes the marking of territory with flags and the painting of murals and kerbstones (Mac an Bhreithiún and Burke 2014: 97). This is a matter which is considered further in Chapter 6 by Dunlevy.

While the question of visibility and tolerability of indigenous languages in the public space remains divisive, it is appreciated by many that place names have the potential to contribute to understanding of cultural heritage; a notable instance of this in the LL relates to the Shankill area in Belfast and is discussed by Dunlevy in this volume. It is also the case that the emotional attachment to a place name as a marker of local identity may be shared across the community divide irrespective of the linguistic origin of the name (if, indeed, that is known). There can be fierce attachment to a name such as Drumnahuncheon (a name of Irish-language origin, *Droim na hUinseann* 'ridge of the ash-tree'), and pride on the part of the person who received it from their forbears and was in a position to provide the authentic local pronunciation when interviewed in the course of fieldwork by NIPNP. At the same time, there was resistance from the same person to the thought of the name appearing in its original Irish form in bilingual signage in the locality. Nash (1999: 472) concludes from a broader discussion around these issues with Kay Muhr (former senior research fellow in NIPNP) that 'attachments that pivot around the placename can be complicated and contentious, pluralistic and partisan' and this is undoubtedly the case. The question of emotional attachment to particular versions of names, and the perceived legitimacy or not of those versions, has been discussed by Morris (2018) in the context of both Aotearoa New Zealand and Northern Ireland; a related issue is the question of cultural appropriation and 'settler indigenization', which has been examined by Byrnes (2002) in the New Zealand context but which would also be interesting to explore further in the case of Northern Ireland. What might be said here is that NIPNP has played a crucial role in the exploration of rootedness and of place names (which often contain family names and ethnonyms) as a manifestation of a shared multilingual heritage. In so doing, it has created a virtual space (the project website) in which the whole community may retrace its linguistic footprints and recognize in the local landscape the various languages which were historically spoken on the island. The cross-community interest in these matters is evident from engagement with the website (and its related Twitter account); however, for the moment, the successful transfer of that interest from virtual space to public space, and its transformation into greater tolerance and acceptance of multilingual signage in the public sphere, continues to be elusive. That this remains one of the biggest challenges in empowering multilingualism (as far as indigenous languages are concerned) is not surprising given the backdrop of historical contention around language described above; any resolution will necessarily require the involvement of other actors and stakeholders, not least in the field of children's education where at this stage of conflict transformation the seeds might be sown most productively for linguistic encounter.[43]

Notes

1. Skutnabb-Kangas (2018: 13) distinguishes between language rights and linguistic human rights, the latter being the 'more narrow concept'. 'Only language rights that are so fundamental that every individual has them because that individual is a human being, so inalienable that no state is allowed to violate them, and that are necessary for individuals and groups to live a dignified life are linguistic human rights.' See also May (2018: 164) and Skutnabb-Kangas and Phillipson (2017).

2. See Section 5 for evidence to this effect which arose out of responses to draft consultations on an Irish-language strategy for Northern Ireland in 2012 and an Irish Language Bill in 2015.
3. For evidence of this, see the survey of users which is hosted on the website of the Ulster Place-Name Society (https://www.ulsterplacename.org/survey).
4. Some of the English versions of street and road names are of Irish-language origin, however; see Section 3.
5. The reference to 'resolute action' draws on the language of the European Charter for Regional or Minority Languages which refers to the 'need for resolute action to promote regional or minority languages in order to safeguard them' (European Charter 1992, §7(1)c).
6. For discussion of the debate on 'adverse impact' in the context of good relations and equality screening in Northern Ireland, see Conradh na Gaeilge et al. (2019: 47–8).
7. There were also a few speakers remaining in Derry and Armagh; see Ní Bhaoill (2010) and her transcriptions of recordings made in 1931 of speakers from all four counties.
8. For a history of the Irish language, see Doyle (2015); for the eighteenth and nineteenth centuries, in particular, see Wolf (2014). On the background to Scots in Ireland, see Montgomery and Gregg (1997).
9. For some commentary on the figures for Ulster-Scots, see Gardner (2015: 8–9) who notes that it may be more plausible to consider the revival of Ulster-Scots as being 'a literary, or written-language "revival"' (ibid., 8) or as an 'ethnic revival' (ibid., 9).
10. There are very few learners of Ulster-Scots; this is a major point of contrast with Irish where the great majority of speakers in Ireland as a whole are 'new speakers' rather than traditional 'native' speakers.
11. Note also the Turas project in East Belfast and its role in reconnecting members of the Unionist/Loyalist community with the Irish language; see Mac Coinnigh, Ervine and Deeds (2019) and Mitchell and Miller (2019).
12. For discussion of anglicization, and indeed gaelicization and scotticization which may also occur in certain contexts, see Ó Mainnín (2017). The process may be seen at work from the outset of the initial Anglo-Norman conquest in the twelfth century.
13. The full title is An Act for the Explaining of Some Doubts Arising upon an Act Entitled, an Act for the Better Execution of His Majesty's Gracious Settlement of His Majesty's Kingdom of Ireland.
14. On 'the fundamental differences between the object of the survey in establishing a fixed, orthographically standard, and cartographically depicted landscape … and the unfixed, variable, and largely non-cartographic conceptions of place of the local Irish population', see Wolf (2014: 66).
15. Ironically, there are often complaints about the treatment of the Irish versions of names on bilingual signage in the Irish Republic as, on occasion, these have been handled very carelessly by the relevant authorities. See Mac Giolla Easpaig (1992: 84–6).
16. The attitude taken by the Ordnance Survey to issues of language and orthography in mapping names in other parts of the UK, namely in Scotland and Wales, which came later, was different in some respects (see de hÓir 1972–3; Morgan 2012: 50–1; Ó Mainnín 2017).
17. See Mac Giolla Easpaig (2008; 2012) on place-names policy in the Irish Republic and on the role and research of the Placenames Branch of the Department of Culture, Heritage and the Gaeltacht.

18. The importance of place-name projects in Ireland has been described by Nash (1999: 458) in terms of 'their potential to challenge the simple historical narrative and easy politics of the paradigm of colonial naming and post-independence renaming'. She also sees in their approach the combination of 'historical and cultural retrieval with a resistance to fixing Irish culture or simplifying Irish history' (ibid., 475).
19. It was the then leader of the Ulster Unionist Party, David Trimble, who championed the case for Ulster-Scots in the build-up to the Good Friday Agreement of 1998 (Mac Póilín 2018: 47–50). Mac Póilín has also spoken of how both Irish and Ulster-Scots have been 'drawn into a cultural war' and of how Ulster-Scots has been seen by some to 'offer itself as a unionist equivalent to Irish' (ibid., 39, 55–6, 78).
20. Both Wales and Scotland have enacted legislation to that end: the Welsh Language Act 1993, the Welsh Language (Wales) Measure 2011 and the Gaelic Language (Scotland) Act 2005. In the case of the Irish Republic, Irish has had its position as national language and first of two official languages (Irish and English) enshrined in the *Constitution* (1937) and in the Official Languages Act (2003).
21. In terms of the broader framework of linguistic rights, one might also consider the *Universal Declaration of Human Rights* (1948), the first document to treat language as an international human right, the International Covenant on Civil and Political Rights (1966), the International Covenant on Economic, Social and Cultural Rights (1966), the United Nations Declaration on the Rights of Persons Belonging to National or Ethnic, Religious and Linguistic and Minorities (1992) and the Universal Declaration of Linguistic Rights (1996). In the case of the 1992 Declaration, de Varennes (2012: 97) has noted that this document is 'not strictly speaking legally binding on the UK'. More generally, it has been argued that 'no direct and *binding* linguistic human rights or educational rights relating to revitalization exist in international law' (Skutnabb-Kangas 2018: 20).
22. The Democratic Unionist Party, which is now the unionist party with the greatest electoral support, was not a signatory to the Agreement, nor was the Traditional Unionist Voice (as it was not established until 2007).
23. It is important to note that paragraph 28D is a new section in the 1998 Act, which was added in consequence of a provision in the later St Andrews Agreement Act in 2006.
24. When the Irish strategy came before the Executive Committee on 10 March 2016, sufficient cross-community support was lacking. Subsequently, the Irish language organization, Conradh na Gaeilge, lodged an application for judicial review in the High Court which found in favour of the applicant on 3 March 2017.
25. The question of whether or not there was an agreement between the parties was hotly contested but a draft text was leaked and is to be found on the website set up by the journalist Eamonn Mallie (Mallie 2018).
26. The erection of bilingual signs had been officially banned in Northern Ireland in 1947 (O'Reilly 1998). By dual-language street-name signage, it is meant that two separate monolingual name signs are placed one above the other or side by side.
27. Note the anecdotal evidence relating to Craigavon and Ballymoney Councils recorded in Pobal's review of the application of the Charter in the period 2002–5 (Pobal n.d.: §§5.63–4, pp. 69–72). Furthermore, two of Northern Ireland's eleven councils currently have no policy on street signage in place at all because of issues relating to bilingual signage. Mid and East Antrim Borough Council was forced to withdraw its policy after concerns were raised about its legality; Antrim and Newtownabbey Borough Council had a policy to ban bilingual signage until it was forced to withdraw

this policy following judicial review in September 2018 (See Conradh na Gaeilge et al. 2019: 15, 17, 22).
28. At the end of the document, there are two codes of courtesy, one for each language (Annexes C and D). The provisions in both are very similar and echo the guidance given elsewhere in the document.
29. For example, some district councils had adopted bilingual stationery while others employ trilingual stationery and place trilingual signs at the entrance to their buildings (§33).
30. This is a reference to the legal provision in the Local Government (Miscellaneous Provisions) (Northern Ireland) Order 1995. The Guidance notes (§35) that there are no legal restrictions on using Irish or Ulster-Scots versions of other parts of an address, for example, a townland, town or county. This is because there is no legal framework for the use of these categories of place names in the minoritized languages. However, see the comments on topographical signage in the *Fourth Opinion of the Advisory Committee on the Framework Convention for the Protection of National Minorities* (in Section 5).
31. See also the statement which follows and is concerned with scrutiny of documents by third parties; in such circumstances the 'English form of the street address should be shown as well as the Irish or Ulster-Scots version'.
32. Tension around bilingual (Irish-English) signage has frequently resulted in acts of vandalism; 'since 2015 bilingual signs have been attacked on 154 occasions across four councils, costing ratepayers £22,645.50 in repairs and replacement signage' (Hughes 2019).
33. The *Advisory Committee's Third Opinion on the United Kingdom (2011)*, §126 and §158, is also worth quoting:

> the need for keeping good relations has been used as justification for not implementing provisions in favour of persons belonging to minorities, such as the erection of bilingual signs ... [The Committee] finds it problematic that the official policy is to limit the erection of such signs to certain areas where the issue would not raise controversies ... This approach is not in line with the spirit of the Framework Convention ... the aim of which is to value the use of minority languages ... with a view to promoting more tolerance and intercultural dialogue in society.

34. On the controversy surrounding the position of the NITB, see DCAL (2015c), Response 258; DCAL (2015e), Responses, Part 1 (2015).
35. See the responses by Ballindarragh Loyal Orange Lodge (LOL) No. 689; Enniskillen True Blues LOL No. 217; Moneyslane LOL No. 569 (DCAL 2015d: 34, 84, 115).
36. The document adds that it is important that the Irish on signage should be visible and should not be 'in different print or smaller' (Conradh na Gaeilge 2017: §8.3). More generally, signage used by public bodies and by local government should be bilingual; 'signs should be changed as they are naturally updated, but this should be done within a fixed [period of] time' (ibid., §§8.4, 8.5).
37. These councils are Antrim and Newtownabbey; Ards and North Down; Armagh, Banbridge and Craigavon; Causeway Coast and Glens; Lisburn and Castlereagh; Mid and East Antrim (Conradh na Gaeilge et al. 2019: 22, 24, 26, 31, 39, 41).
38. The councils being Derry City and Strabane; Mid Ulster; Newry, Mourne and Down; Belfast City; Fermanagh and Omagh. For the recent proposal by a committee of

Belfast City Council that the threshold for consent to having a street-name sign in Irish be reduced from 66 per cent to 15 per cent of residents, see Madden (2020).
39. The most notable attempt to employ trilingual signage has been by Derry and Strabane District Council; this has not met with universal approval, however. See discussion of this by Deirdre Dunlevy in Chapter 6.
40. On what has been described as 'untrammelled public monolingualism' and the cosmopolitan positioning of English as a 'neutral' language, purely instrumental, 'apolitical' and 'value free', see May (2018: 169, 170).
41. For the 'problem of tolerability' (i.e. convincing majority language speakers of the merits and desirability of minority language rights) and 'tolerance-oriented' language policy, see May (2015: 355; 2018: 173) who also cites Grin (1995) and Kloss (1971; 1977). Muller (2010: 9) discusses normalization in the context of Irish and the important role that legislation has to play in this.
42. For difficulties around the politics of naming in New Zealand, see Byrnes (2002) and Morris (2018). The latter also draws in the controversy surrounding the use of Derry and Londonderry in Northern Ireland.
43. The NIPNP is currently engaged in a collaboration with the Northern Ireland Council for Curriculum, Examinations and Assessment (CCEA) with the intention of creating materials for use in primary schools.

References

Advisory Committee on the Framework Convention for the Protection of National Minorities. *Third Opinion on the United Kingdom*. Adopted on 30 June 2011. Available online: https://rm.coe.int/CoERMPublicCommonSearchServices/DisplayDCTMContent?documentId=090000168008c6c2 (accessed 29 June 2020).

Advisory Committee on the Framework Convention for the Protection of National Minorities. *Fourth Opinion on the United Kingdom*. Adopted on 25 May 2016. Available online: https://rm.coe.int/09000016806fb9ab (accessed 29 June 2020).

Andrews, J. H. ([1975] 2002), *A Paper Landscape. The Ordnance Survey in Nineteenth-Century Ireland*, Dublin: Four Courts.

Byrnes, Giselle (2002), '"A Dead Sheet Covered with Meaningless Words?" Place Names and the Cultural Colonization of Tauranga', *New Zealand Journal of History*, 36 (1): 18–35.

Comments of the Government of the United Kingdom on the Fourth Opinion of the Advisory Committee on the Implementation of the Framework Convention for the Protection of National Minorities by the United Kingdom. Received on 27 February 2017. Available online: https://rm.coe.int/1680703a30 (accessed 29 June 2020).

Conradh na Gaeilge (2017), *Irish Language Act: Discussion Document, Version 1.1* (15 March 2017). Available online: https://cnag.ie/images/Acht_Gaeilge_%C3%B3_Thuaidh/15M%C3%812017_Pl%C3%A9ch%C3%A1ip%C3%A9is_ar_Acht_Gaeilge_%C3%B3_Thuaidh.pdf (accessed 29 June 2020).

Conradh na Gaeilge, the Committee for the Administration of Justice and Ulster University (2019), *Comhairlí Áitiúla, Dualgais agus an Ghaeilge: Creatlach Comhlíonta [Local Councils, Obligations and the Irish Language: A Framework for Compliance]*. Available online: https://www.ulster.ac.uk/__data/assets/pdf_file/0005/

393926/Local-Councils,-Obligations-and-the-Irish-Language.pdf (accessed 29 June 2020).
Constitution of Ireland (1937). Available online: https://www.gov.ie/en/publication/d5bd8c-constitution-of-ireland/ (accessed 29 June 2020).
Council of Europe Charter for Regional or Minority Languages (1992). Available online: https://www.coe.int/en/web/conventions/full-list/-/conventions/rms/0900001680695175 (accessed 29 June 2020).
Council of Europe Framework Convention for the Protection of National Minorities and Explanatory Report (1995). Available online: https://rm.coe.int/CoERMPublicCommonSearchServices/DisplayDCTMContent?documentId=09000016800c10cf (accessed 29 June 2020).
Crowley, Tony (2000), *The Politics of Language in Ireland 1366–1922. A Sourcebook*, London: Routledge.
Crowley, Tony (2006), 'The Political Production of a Language', *Journal of Linguistic Anthropology*, 16 (1): 23–35.
Davis, Herbert (1957), *The Prose Works of Jonathan Swift*, volume 4, Oxford: Shakespeare Head Press.
Davis, Thomas ([1846] 1998), *Literary and Historical Essays 1846*, Washington: Woodstock Books.
de hÓir, Éamonn (1972–3), 'The Anglicisation of Irish Placenames', *Onoma*, 17: 192–204.
de Varennes, Fernand (2003), 'Language Rights and Human Rights: The International Experience', in Dónall Ó Riagáin (ed.), *Language and Law in Northern Ireland*, 5–16, Belfast: Cló Ollscoil na Banríona.
de Varennes, Fernand (2012), 'Summary of the Existing International Legal Obligations of the United Kingdom in Respect of Irish in Northern Ireland', in Pobal, *Acht na Gaeilge do Thuaisceart Éireann* [The Irish Language Act Northern Ireland]. Eisiúint 2. 2nd Issue. Belfast.
Department for Regional Development, Northern Ireland (2011). *Bi-lingual Traffic Signs. Draft Policy and Draft Equality Impact Assessment Consultation 2011*. Available online: https://minutes3.belfastcity.gov.uk/documents/s32939/Appendix%201%20Bi%20Lingual%20Traffic%20Signs%20Consultation.pdf (accessed 29 June 2020).
DCAL (Department of Culture, Arts and Leisure) (2005), *European Charter for Regional or Minority Languages. Guidance on Meeting UK Government Commitments in Respect of Irish and Ulster Scots (Version 2)*. August 2005. Available online: https://www.communities-ni.gov.uk/sites/default/files/publications/dcal/european-charter-for-regional-or-minority-languages%E2%80%93codes-of-courtesy_1.pdf (accessed 29 June 2020).
DCAL (Department of Culture, Arts and Leisure) (2012a), *Strategy for Protecting and Enhancing the Development of the Irish Language. Public Consultation*. July 2012. Available online: https://www.communities-ni.gov.uk/sites/default/files/consultations/dcal/01-consultation-document-draft-irish-language-strategy-july-2012.pdf (accessed 29 June 2020).
DCAL (Department of Culture, Arts and Leisure) (2012b), *Strategy for Ulster-Scots Language, Heritage and Culture. Public Consultation*. July 2012. Available online: https://www.communities-ni.gov.uk/sites/default/files/consultations/dcal/07-consultation-document-draft-ulster-scots-language-heritage-and-culture-strategy-july-2012.pdf (accessed 29 June 2020).
DCAL (Department of Culture, Arts and Leisure) (2013a), *Draft Strategy for Protecting and Enhancing the Development of the Irish Language. Responses to the Public*

Consultation. April 2013. Available online: https://www.communities-ni.gov.uk/sites/default/files/publications/dcal/draft-irish-language-strategy-consultation-responses-april-2013.pdf (accessed 29 June 2020).

DCAL (Department of Culture, Arts and Leisure) (2013b), *Dréachtstraitéis le Forbairt na Gaeilge a Chosaint agus a Fheabhsú. [Draft Strategy for Protecting and Enhancing the Development of the Irish Language]. Achoimre ar Fhreagairtí ar an Chomhairliúchán Phoiblí [Summary of Responses to the Public Consultation]*. April 2013. Available online: https://www.communities-ni.gov.uk/sites/default/files/publications/dcal/04-draft-irish-language-strategy-consultation-report-april-2013-bilingual.pdf (accessed 29 June 2020).

DCAL (Department of Culture, Arts and Leisure) (2015a), *Strategy to Enhance and Develop the Ulster-Scots Language, Heritage and Culture 2015 to 2035*. Available online: https://www.communities-ni.gov.uk/consultations/strategy-enhance-and-develop-ulster-scots-language-heritage-and-culture-2015–2035 (accessed 29 June 2020).

DCAL (Department of Culture, Arts and Leisure) (2015b), *Strategy to Enhance and Protect the Development of the Irish Language 2015 to 2035*. Available online: https://www.communities-ni.gov.uk/consultations/strategy-enhance-and-protect-development-irish-language-2015–2035 (accessed 29 June 2020).

DCAL (Department of Culture, Arts and Leisure) (2015c), *Proposals for an Irish Language Bill (February 2015)*. Available online: https://www.communities-ni.gov.uk/consultations/proposals-irish-language-bill (accessed 29 June 2020).

DCAL (Department of Culture, Arts and Leisure) (2015d), *Proposals for an Irish Language Bill (February 2015). Responses, Part 1 (2015)*. Available online: https://www.communities-ni.gov.uk/sites/default/files/publications/dcal/irish-language-bill-consultation-collated-responses-part-1.pdf (accessed 29 June 2020).

DCAL (Department of Culture, Arts and Leisure) (2015e), *Proposals for an Irish Language Bill (February 2015). Responses, Part 2 (2015)*. Available online: https://www.communities-ni.gov.uk/sites/default/files/publications/dcal/Irish%20Language%20Bill%20consultation%20-%20Collated%20Responses%20-%20Part%202.PDF (accessed 29 June 2020).

DCAL (Department of Culture, Arts and Leisure) (2016a), *Strategy to Enhance and Develop the Ulster-Scots Language, Heritage and Culture 2015–2035. One Year On*. Available online: https://www.communities-ni.gov.uk/sites/default/files/publications/dcal/The%20Ulster-Scots%20Strategy%20-%20one%20year%20on%20-%20March%202016_0.pdf (accessed 29 June 2020).

DCAL (Department of Culture, Arts and Leisure) (2016b), *The Irish Language Strategy. One Year On*. Available online: https://www.communities-ni.gov.uk/sites/default/files/publications/dcal/The%20Irish%20Language%20Strategy%20-%20one%20year%20on%20-%20March%202016_0.pdf (accessed 29 June 2020).

Dickson, Bryce (2003), 'Language Rights and Human Rights: The Northern Ireland Experience', in Dónall Ó Riagáin (ed.), *Language and Law in Northern Ireland*, 17–23, Belfast: Cló Ollscoil na Banríona.

Doyle, Aidan (2015), *A History of the Irish Language. From the Norman Invasion to Independence*, Oxford: Oxford University Press.

European Charter for Regional or Minority Languages (2010), Application of the Charter in the United Kingdom. Third Monitoring Cycle. Report of the Committee of Experts on the Charter. 21 April. Available online: https://rm.coe.int/

CoERMPublicCommonSearchServices/DisplayDCTMContent?documentId=0900001 6806dbb43 (accessed 29 June 2020).

European Charter for Regional or Minority Languages (2014), Application of the Charter in the United Kingdom. Fourth Monitoring Cycle. Report of the Committee of Experts on the Charter. 15 January. Available online: https://rm.coe.int/ CoERMPublicCommonSearchServices/DisplayDCTMContent?documentId=0900001 6806dcc8d (accessed 29 June 2020).

Falconer, Gavin (2005), 'Breaking Nature's Social Union – The Autonymy of Scots in Ulster', in John M. Kirk and Dónall P. Ó Baoill (eds), *Legislation, Literature and Sociolinguistics: Northern Ireland, the Republic of Ireland and Scotland*, 48–59, Belfast: Cló Ollscoil na Banríona.

Fourth Report Submitted by United Kingdom Pursuant to Article 25, Paragraph 2 of the Framework Convention for the Protection of National Minorities. Received on 26 March 2015. Available online: https://rm.coe.int/CoERMPublicCommonSearchServices/Displ ayDCTMContent?documentId=09000016805a8c52 (accessed 29 June 2020).

Gaelic Language (Scotland) Act 2005. Available online: http://www.legislation.gov.uk/ asp/2005/7/contents (accessed 29 June 2020).

Gardner, Peter Robert (2015), 'Unionism, Loyalism, and the Ulster-Scots Ethnolinguistic "Revival"', *Studies in Ethnicity and Nationalism*, 15 (1): 4–25.

Görlach, Manfred (2000), 'Ulster Scots: A Language?', in John M. Kirk and Dónall P. Ó Baoill (eds), *Language and Politics: Northern Ireland, the Republic of Ireland and Scotland*, 13–31, Belfast: Cló Ollscoil na Banríona.

Government of Ireland. Official Languages Act 2003. Available online: http://www. irishstatutebook.ie/eli/2003/act/32/enacted/en/html (accessed 29 June 2020).

Grin, François (1995), 'Combining Immigrant and Autochthonous Language Rights: A Territorial Approach to Multilingualism', in Tove Skutnabb-Kangas and Robert Phillipson (eds), *Linguistic Human Rights: Overcoming Linguistic Discrimination*, 31–48, Berlin: Mouton de Gruyter.

Holder, Daniel (2018), 'Acht na Gaeilge: What Are the Rights of People Who Don't Speak Irish?', *EamonnMallie.Com. Ireland's Home for Independent Thought*, 27 February. Available online: http://eamonnmallie.com/2018/02/acht-na-gaeilge-rights-people-dont-speak-irish-daniel-holder/ (accessed 28 June 2020).

Hornsby, Michael, and Vigers, Dick (2012), 'Minority Semiotic Landscapes: An Ideological Minefield', in Durk Gorter, Heiko F. Marten and Luke Van Mensel (eds), *Minority Languages in the Linguistic Landscape*, 57–73, London: Palgrave MacMillan.

Hughes, Brendan (2019), 'Councils Spend £23,000 Repairing Vandalised Bilingual Signs', *Irish News*, 30 December. Available online: http://www.irishnews.com/paywall/ tsb/irishnews/irishnews/irishnews//news/northernirelandnews/2019/12/30/news/ councils-spend-23-000-repairing-vandalised-bilingual-signs-1801477/content.html (accessed 28 June 2020).

International Covenant on Civil and Political Rights (1966). Available online: https://www. ohchr.org/Documents/ProfessionalInterest/ccpr.pdf (accessed 29 June 2020).

International Covenant on Economic, Social and Cultural Rights (1966). Available online: https://www.ohchr.org/Documents/ProfessionalInterest/cescr.pdf (accessed 29 June 2020).

Kloss, Heinz (1971), 'The Language Rights of Immigrant Groups', *International Migration Review*, 5: 250–68.

Kloss, Heinz (1977), *The American Bilingual Tradition*, Rowley, MA: Newbury House.

Local Government Act (Northern Ireland) 2014. Available online: http://www.legislation.gov.uk/nia/2014/8/contents (accessed 29 June 2020).

Mac an Bhreithiún, Bharain, and Burke, Anne (2014), 'Language, Typography, and Place-Making: Walking the Irish and Ulster-Scots Linguistic Landscape', *The Canadian Journal of Irish Studies* 38 (1/2), special issue, *Text and beyond Text: New Visual, Material and Spatial Perspectives in Irish Studies*: 84–125.

Mac Coinnigh, Marcas, Ervine, Linda, and Deeds, Pól (2019), 'The Irish Language in Belfast. The Role of a Language in Post-Conflict Resolution', in Matthew Evans, Lesley Jeffries, Jim O'Driscoll (eds), *The Routledge Handbook of Language in Conflict*, 556–73, London: Routledge.

Mac Giolla Easpaig, Dónall (1992), 'The Placenames Branch of the Ordnance Survey', in Art Ó Maolfabhail (ed.), *The Placenames of Ireland in the Third Millenium/ Logainmneacha na hÉireann sa Tríú Mílaois*, 76–87, Dublin: Ordnance Survey.

Mac Giolla Easpaig, Dónall (2008), 'Placenames Policy and Its Implementation', in Caoilfhionn Nic Phaídín and Seán Ó Cearnaigh (eds), *A New View of the Irish Language*, 164–77, Dublin: Cois Life.

Mac Giolla Easpaig, Dónall (2012), 'Placenames Research in Ireland', in Mairéad Nic Lochlainn and Brian Ó Raghallaigh (eds), *Placenames Workshop 2012. Management and Dissemination of Toponymic Data Online*, 39–48, Dublin: Fiontar, Dublin City University.

Mac Póilín, Aodán (2018), *Our Tangled Speech. Essays on Language and Culture*, Belfast: Ulster Historical Foundation and Ultach Trust.

Madden, Andrew (2020), 'Belfast City Council Committee Backs New Bilingual Street Signs Policy', *Belfast Telegraph*, 23 October 2020. Available online: https://www.belfasttelegraph.co.uk/news/northern-ireland/belfast-city-council-committee-backs-new-bilingual-street-signs-policy-39659941.html (accessed 22 November 2020).

Mallie, Eamonn (2018), *Full 'Draft Agreement Text'*. EamonnMallie.Com. Northern Ireland's Home for Independent Thought. 20 February 2018. Available online: http://eamonnmallie.com/2018/02/full-draft-agreement-text/ (accessed 29 June 2020).

Manley, John. (2017), 'What Would an Irish Language Act Cost? And What Might the Legislation Contain?', *Irish News*, 2 October. Available online: http://www.irishnews.com/paywall/tsb/irishnews/irishnews/irishnews//news/2017/10/02/news/irish-language-act-content-and-cost-1150668/content.html (accessed 28 June 2020).

Marten, Heiko F., Van Mensel, Luke, and Gorter, Durk (2012), 'Studying Minority Languages in the Linguistic Landscape', in Durk Gorter, Heiko F. Marten and Luke Van Mensel (eds), *Minority Languages in the Linguistic Landscape*, 1–15, London: Palgrave MacMillan.

May, Stephen (2015), 'Language Rights and Language Policy: Addressing the Gap(s) between Principles and Practices', *Current Issues in Language Planning*, 16 (4): 355–9.

May, Stephen (2018), 'Surveying Language Rights: Interdisciplinary Perspectives', *Journal of the Royal Society of New Zealand*, 48 (2–3): 164–76. DOI: 10.1080/03036758.2017.1421565.

McMonagle, Sarah (2010), 'Deliberating the Irish Language in Northern Ireland: From Conflict to Multiculturalism?', *Journal of Multilingual and Multicultural Development*, 31 (3): 253–70.

McMonagle, Sarah, and McDermott, Philip (2014), 'Transitional Politics and Language Rights in a Multi-Ethnic Northern Ireland: Towards a True Linguistic Pluralism?', *Ethnopolitics*, 13 (3): 245–66.

Mitchell, David, and Miller, Megan (2019), 'Reconciliation through Language Learning? A Case Study of the Turas Irish Language Project in East Belfast', *Ethnic and Racial Studies*, 42 (2), 235–53. DOI 10.1080/01419870.2017.1414278.

Montgomery, Michael, and Gregg, Robert J. (1997), 'The Scots Language in Ulster', in Charles Jones (ed.), *The Edinburgh History of the Scots Language*, 569–622, Edinburgh: Edinburgh University Press.

Morgan, Peadar (2012), 'Lifting the Blanket: Dual-Naming for Gaelic Language Planning', in Mairéad Nic Lochlainn and Brian Ó Raghallaigh (eds), *Placenames Workshop 2012. Management and Dissemination of Toponymic Data Online*, 49–55, Dublin: Fiontar, Dublin City University.

Morris, Ewan (2018), ' "H" is for History: Uses of the Past in Place-Name Debates in New Zealand and Northern Ireland', *History Australia*, 51 (1): 113–29.

Muller, Janet (2010), *Language and Conflict in Northern Ireland and Canada: A Silent War*, Basingstoke: Palgrave MacMillan.

Nash, Catherine (1999), 'Irish Placenames: Post-Colonial Locations', *Transactions of the Institute of British Geographers*, 24: 457–80.

Ní Bhaoill, Róise (2010), *Ulster Gaelic Voices. Bailiúchán Wilhelm Doegen 1931*, Belfast: Ultach Trust.

Northern Ireland Human Rights Commission (2009), *European Charter for Regional or Minority Languages. Parallel Report to the Committee of Experts on the Third Periodical Report of the United Kingdom*, September 2009. Available online: https://www.nihrc.org/documents/advice-to-government/2009/parallel-report-on-eu-charter-for-regional-minority-languages-september-2009.pdf (accessed 29 June 2020).

Northern Ireland Human Rights Commission (2010), *Minority Language Rights, the Irish Language and Ulster Scots. Briefing Paper on the implications of the ECRML, European Convention on Human Rights and Other Instruments*, June 2010. Available online: https://www.nihrc.org/uploads/publications/briefing-paper-minority-language-rights-and-ecrml-june-2010.pdf (accessed 29 June 2020).

Northern Ireland Human Rights Commission (2015), *Response on the Proposals for an Irish Language Bill*, May 2015. Available online: http://www.nihrc.org/uploads/publications/Irish_Language_Bill_FINAL_%282%29.pdf (accessed 29 June 2020).

Northern Ireland Human Rights Commission (2016), *Submission to the Advisory Committee on the Framework Convention for the Protection of National Minorities. Parallel Report to the Advisory Committee on the Fourth Monitoring Report of the United Kingdom*, March 2016. Available online: https://www.nihrc.org/uploads/publications/NIHRC_Submission_to_the_Advisory_Committee_on_the_Framework_Convention_for_the_Protection_of_National_Minorities_2016_FINAL.pdf (accessed 29 June 2020).

Northern Ireland Office (1998a), *The Belfast Agreement, Also Known as the Good Friday Agreement*, 10 April 1998. Available online: https://www.gov.uk/government/publications/the-belfast-agreement (accessed 29 June 2020).

Northern Ireland Office (1998b), Northern Ireland Act 1998. Available online: http://www.legislation.gov.uk/ukpga/1998/47/contents (accessed 29 June 2020).

Northern Ireland Office (2003), *Joint Declaration by the British and Irish Governments 2003*. Available online: https://webarchive.nationalarchives.gov.uk/20040705075218/http://www.nio.gov.uk/pdf/joint2003.pdf (accessed 29 June 2020).

Northern Ireland Office (2006a), *The St Andrews Agreement*, October 2006. Available online: https://www.gov.uk/government/publications/the-st-andrews-agreement-october-2006 (accessed 29 June 2020).

Northern Ireland Office (2006b), *Northern Ireland (St Andrews Agreement) Act 2006*. Available online: http://www.legislation.gov.uk/ukpga/2006/53/contents (accessed 29 June 2020).

Northern Ireland Office (2020), *New Decade, New Approach*, January 2020. Available online: https://assets.publishing.service.gov.uk/government/uploads/system/uploads/attachment_data/file/856998/2020-01-08_a_new_decade__a_new_approach.pdf (accessed 29 June 2020).

Northern Ireland Statistics and Research Agency (2014), *Northern Ireland Census 2011. Key Statistics Summary Report*, September 2014, Belfast: A National Statistics Publication. Available online: http://www.nisra.gov.uk/archive/census/2011/results/key-statistics/summary-report.pdf (accessed 29 June 2020).

Ó Conaire, Breandán (1986), *Language, Lore and Lyrics: Essays and Lectures by Douglas Hyde*, Dublin: Irish Academic Press.

Ó Mainnín, Mícheál B. (2017), *Annexing Irish Names to the English Tongue: Language Contact and the Anglicisation of Irish Place-Names*, Maynooth: School of Celtic Studies, Maynooth University.

Ó Riagáin, Dónall (2000), 'Language Rights as Human Rights in Europe and in Northern Ireland', in John M. Kirk and Dónall P. Ó Baoill (eds), *Language and Politics. Northern Ireland, the Republic of Ireland and Scotland*, 65–73, Belfast: Cló Ollscoil na Banríona.

O'Reilly, Camile (1998), 'The Irish Language as Symbol: Visual Representations of Irish in Northern Ireland', in A. D. Buckley (ed.), *Symbols in Northern Ireland*, 43–62, Belfast: Institute of Irish Studies, Queen's University Belfast.

Petty, William ([1691] 1861), *The Political Anatomy of Ireland*, reprinted in James Hewitt Lifford (ed.), *A Collection of Tracts and Treatises Illustrative of the Natural History, Antiquities, and the Political and Social State of Ireland at Various Periods Prior to the Present Century*, volume 2, 1–142, Dublin: A. Thom.

Pobal (2012), *Acht na Gaeilge do TÉ. The Irish Language Act NI. Second Issue 2012* (Belfast).

Pobal (n.d.), *An Chairt Eorpach do Theangacha Réigiúnacha nó Mionlaigh. Feidhmiú na Cairte i leith na Gaeilge. Iúil 2002–2005. Dara Aighneacht ó Pobal chuig Coiste na Saineolaithe ar an Chairt*. Prepared by Marcas Mac Ruairí (Belfast).

Puzey, Guy (2010), 'Place-Names and Language Revitalization in Gaelic Scotland', in Kenneth E. Nilsen (ed.), *Rannsachadh na Gàidhlig 5. Fifth Scottish Gaelic Research Conference*, 339–48, Sydney: Cape Breton University Press.

Skutnabb-Kangas, Tove (2018), 'Language Rights and Revitalization', in Leanne Hinton, Leena Huss, and Gerald Roche (eds), *The Routledge Handbook of Language Revitalization*, 13–21, Milton: Routledge.

Skutnabb-Kangas, Tove, and Phillipson, Robert (eds) (2017), *Language Rights*, 4 volumes, London: Routledge.

The Local Government (Miscellaneous Provisions) (Northern Ireland) Order 1995. Available online: http://www.legislation.gov.uk/nisi/1995/759/contents (accessed 29 June 2020).

United Nations Declaration on the Rights of Persons Belonging to National or Ethnic, Religious and Linguistic and Minorities 1992. Available online: https://www.ohchr.org/EN/ProfessionalInterest/Pages/Minorities.aspx (accessed 29 June 2020).

Universal Declaration of Human Rights 1948. Available online: https://www.ohchr.org/EN/UDHR/Documents/UDHR_Translations/eng.pdf (accessed 29 June 2020).

Universal Declaration of Linguistic Rights 1996. Available online: https://culturalrights. net/descargas/drets_culturals389.pdf (accessed 29 June 2020).
Welsh Language Act 1993. Available online: http://www.legislation.gov.uk/ukpga/1993/38/contents (accessed 29 June 2020).
Welsh Language (Wales) Measure 2011. Available online: http://www.legislation.gov.uk/mwa/2011/1/contents/enacted (accessed 29 June 2020).
Wolf, Nicholas M. (2014), *An Irish-Speaking Island. State, Religion, Community, and the Linguistic Landscape in Ireland, 1770–1870*, Madison: University of Wisconsin Press.

4

The transformative power of linguistic mobility: Evidence from Italian borderscapes[1]

Stefania Tufi

1. Introduction

This chapter is a comparative examination of linguistic and semiotic constructions of border identities in deeply territorialized spaces as they are enacted in two border areas of Italy, namely Trentino-Alto Adige/South Tyrol (ST) and Friuli-Venezia Giulia (VG) in the north-east of the country (nos. 4 and 6, respectively, in Figure 4.1). In these regions language practices are particularly complex and include sets of varieties pertaining to German, Slovenian and Italian repertoires.

The analysis is based on fieldwork carried out in the areas of Trieste/Trst and Sesto/Sexten, which are integrated in socio-historical contexts where the minoritized languages (i.e. Slovenian and German, respectively) have enjoyed both national and regional protection via targeted legislation introduced in the post-war period (Orioles 2003).

The main theoretical framework that the discussion draws upon is the concept of *motility*, or potential for mobility, as proposed in Kaufmann (2002; 2011) and applied to the sociolinguistic production of space. This perspective, which represents a novel approach to Linguistic Landscape (LL) studies, will allow us to investigate to what extent local LL dynamics articulate the construction and consolidation of divergent asymmetrical relations (Fairclough 2015) between language agents and their material and symbolic audiences. The analysis will therefore focus on discursively constructed degrees of motility as they are played out in LL and tease out similarities and differences in spatialization (Lefebvre 1991) practices in the two localities, where multilingual practices are central to the negotiation of different versions of living. It will become apparent that the symbolic and material weight of the local LL is grounded in complex webs of past and present sociolinguistic dynamics as they have sedimented in these highly contested territories. As a result, LL does not just contribute to the construction and display of spatial multilingualism and multiple identities, but is also instrumental in creating the potential for change and therefore it represents a structuring dimension of social life in the observed sites. This is evident both at the macro level, in that institutionalized space impacts on LL mobility or immobility, and at the micro level, in

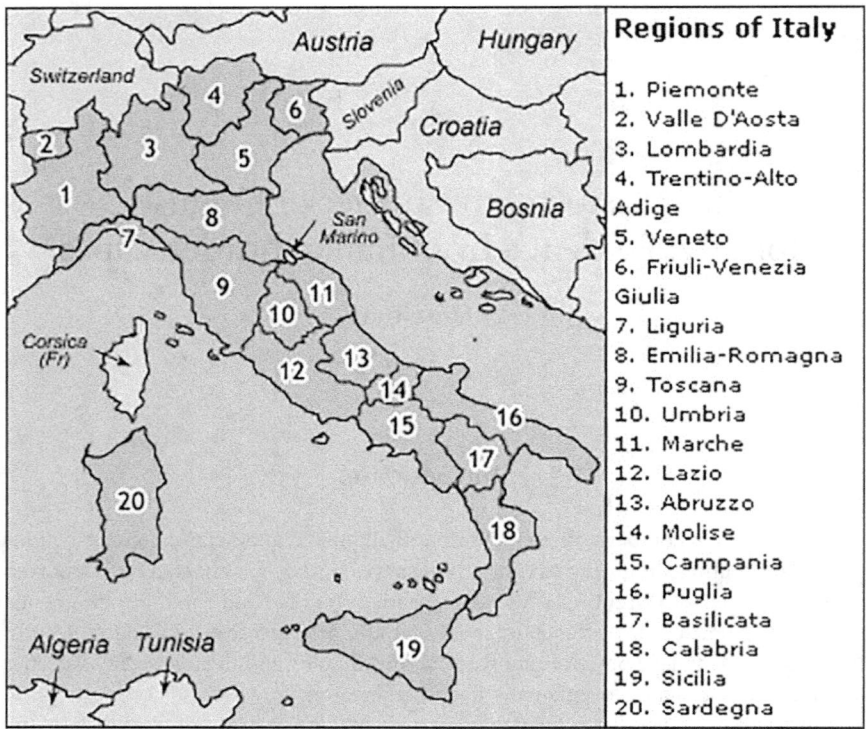

Figure 4.1 Regions of Italy (http://www.big-italy-map.co.uk/)

so far as LL writing acts interact with institutionalized language to manipulate spaces of belonging. The potential for change also translates into different degrees of social empowerment, in that it is directly related to language actors' agency.

In terms of the organization of the chapter, Section 2 provides background information about the two areas from a comparative perspective. This includes an outline of linguistic repertoires, relevant historical information and aspects of language policy. Section 3 examines the theoretical frameworks that have informed the discussion, which is integrated into the presentation of the data (Section 4). Conclusive remarks are provided in Section 5.

2. The context: Similarities and differences between the two areas

The data under consideration for the purposes of this chapter relate specifically to the area outside Trieste/Trst in VG and to the town of Sesto/Sexten in Alto Adige/ST.[2] Both sub-areas lie on the Italian side of the north-eastern border and, similarly to other regions of Italy, legislation includes specific language provision in terms of

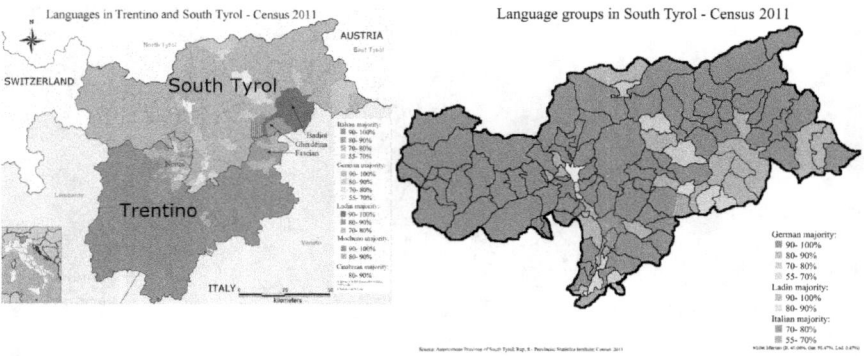

Figure 4.2 Language distribution in Trentino-Alto Adige/South Tyrol (https://it.wikipedia.org)

support for German and Slovenian. This is framed within special statutes which grant a higher degree of autonomy for internal administration than in other regions of Italy, and within both national and regional legislation supporting linguistic specificity and provision (Piergigli 2017).

As regards linguistic practices (Figures 4.2 and 4.3), in VG repertoires include Italo-Romance regional varieties and varieties of Slovenian and Italian, whilst in ST Germanic or Ladin varieties are employed alongside Italian, depending on locality.

Urban Trieste is predominantly Italophone in contrast to the surrounding rural area, where Slovenian is more audible and visible.[3] This situation is replicated in Bolzano (the main city in ST), where Italian dominates language repertoires (ASTAT 2018), whereas in the rest of the region Germanic varieties are prevalent (Figure 4.2). In Sesto, in particular, a near totality of inhabitants self-identify as German speakers (95.37 per cent according to the 2011 census), a situation that is common in the ST region. The sociolinguistics of the two areas therefore presents similarities and differences. The peculiarities of each region are due to the complex linguistic ecologies that characterize the localities, ecologies where the legacy of the past is a major factor.

Over the course of the twentieth century the Italian north-eastern border was highly significant for both the national and the international geopolitical order (Cattaruzza 2007). The events of the First World War caused the dissolution of the Habsburg Empire, and Italian control of the two areas under investigation was sanctioned by the 1919 treaties. Within a consolidated context of nation states which had increasingly articulated ethnic identities via national languages, Italian fascism (1922–43) implemented harsh assimilationist policies which aimed to Italianize heteroglossic groups. These policies caused comparable mass migrations from the two regions, even though the modalities differed. Whilst between fifty thousand and a hundred thousand Italian Slavs moved to (what was then) Yugoslavia to escape the fascist regime (Corni 2011) due to the alliance between Germany and Italy, people in ST were given the opportunity 'to opt out' of Italy and move to Austria (about seventy-five thousand *Optanten* left between 1939 and 1943, of which about fifty

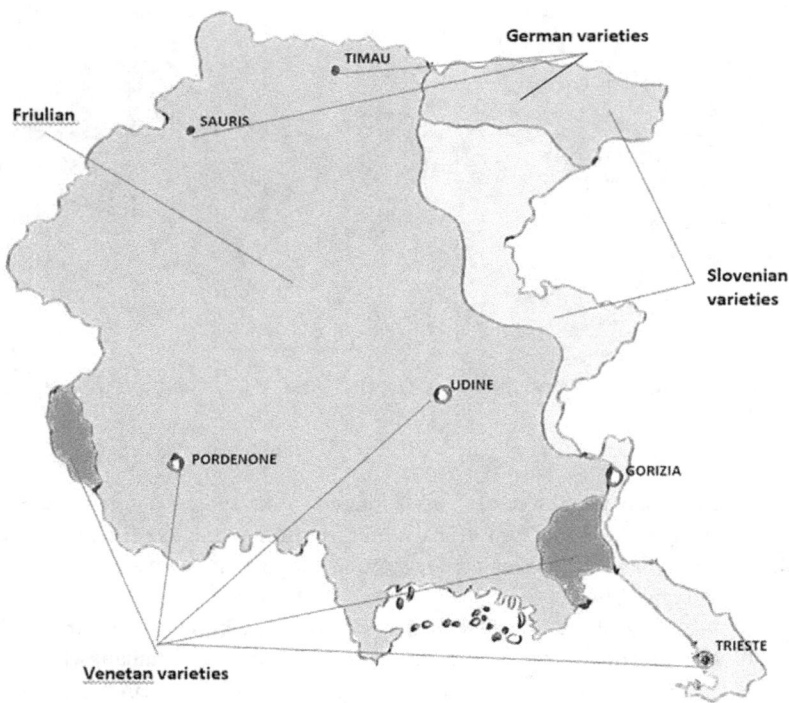

Figure 4.3 Language distribution in Friuli-Venezia Giulia (adapted from Marcato 2001: 26)

thousand returned to Italy after the war) (Grote 2012). Although people returning to Italy from Austria often met with distrust and resentment on the part of both those who had stayed and ethnic Italians, the situation relating to Italian Slavs was further exacerbated by a migration counter-flow of ethnic Italians living in Istria and Fiume (in present-day Croatia) between 1943 and 1956, which included anti-Tito Croatians and Slovenians wanting to leave Yugoslavia (Premik 2004; Pupo 2005). The prolonged period which witnessed the bidirectional transfer of people from the two sides of the border, and the traumatic experiences that characterized it, did not facilitate a process of reconciliation between the two groups. These events have contributed to the consolidation of memorial narratives where language is an essentialized part of the self.

Both outward movement and the return of residents over time would have a lasting effect on collective and individual memory in both areas and contribute to the crystallization of difference in identity-making processes. For example, in VG, Italians are identified with urban dwellers and Slovenians with rural communities, a perception which has become rooted over time and underplays those hybrid identities that have formed as a result of long-term place-sharing on the part of the two groups (Sbisà and Vascotto 2007). In this context, the observed LL in the province of Trieste (by which we refer to an area outside the urban centre which is delimited in administrative terms) is a dynamic agent in the construction of the bounded self, whereas in urban Trieste Slovenian is conspicuous by its absence and is visually silenced (Tufi 2013). Geopolitical and historical aspects have also resulted in a sort of tacit acceptance of the low status of Slovenian, both nationally and internationally:

> The Slovene minority in Italy has been a predominantly closed, exclusive community, both due to historical events that took place in the first half of the 20th century and due to policies of minority protection. As a consequence, no high perceived status of the Slovene minority among Italian speakers has been established. (Brezigar 2009: 213)

On the contrary, in ST, physical and cultural contiguity with other German-speaking territories, a tradition of discourses around ST as a 'German land' since the late nineteenth century (Grote 2012), an awareness that the Dachsprache (i.e. the umbrella language – standard German) is one of the main languages of culture globally, and the privileged socio-economic status that ST enjoys as the wealthiest region of Italy (ISTAT 2018) and one of the richest in Europe, have – amongst other elements – enhanced the type of self-perception and linguistic confidence that LL sanctions, as will become apparent below.

With respect to minority language provision, after the Second World War, and in a much-changed climate where the new international order was keen to consolidate human rights and safeguard individual freedoms, the protection of ethnolinguistic minorities on Italian territory was enshrined in the Italian Constitution (1948). In the decades following the enacting of the Constitution, and together with other minorities, the people of VG and ST have benefitted from both national and regional legislation granting degrees of autonomy in the administration of local matters and supporting ethnolinguistic specificity (Piergigli 2017; Toso 2008). Legislation includes provision for education and envisages both the study of the minority language as a subject and its use as a medium of instruction. The outcomes in the two regions, however, have been different: whilst Slovenian-Italian bilingualism is the norm on the part of ethnic Slovenians but not of ethnic Italians (Sussi 2003) in VG, a segregationist model of bilingualism in ST has been a decisive factor in the slow normalization of bilingual practices (German/Italian) on the part of South Tyroleans (Carli 2003). Recent studies (Wand 2016) about bilingual education in ST show that, similarly to Slovenian in VG, German in ST is deployed as an identity defence mechanism but, unlike Slovenian in VG, it is also a marker of superiority for speakers and an indicator of deficiency in othering processes. Again, these attributions are deep-rooted and date back to times when victimizing discourses were being constructed by the Germanophone group on the occasion, for example, of the First World War and of the following geopolitical settlement. However, as Wand (2016) explains, the current prestige of German is reinforced locally by aspects such as the Italophone parents' choice to send their children to German-medium nurseries as a way to enable German-language acquisition outside the family. In terms of the developments of sociolinguistic aspects, Eichinger (2002) explains that both language attitudes and language practices on the ground have been changing. A growing awareness of the advantages of multilingualism, together with regular contact between German and Italian, have opened up spaces of encounter that feed into forms of regional identity. This is one of the aspects that will account for the peculiar configuration of LL in ST, and it is in direct opposition to local language politics as promoted by local political groups. In the attempt to curb the perceived threat to German identity, these groups advocate, for instance, the testing of language proficiency in the first few weeks of entering German-medium schools, therefore undermining the principle of free choice introduced in 1972 as part of the second autonomy statute (Provincia Autonoma di Bolzano Alto Adige 2009). Although this stance does not necessarily reflect common thinking or actual language practices, it shows that there is no general consensus about how to solve the issue of segregated education.

Finally, even though both VG and ST participated in the swift socio-economic development that characterized post-war Italy, ST has experienced a very successful transition from a rural to a service (mainly tourist) economy and enjoys a very high standard of living (Lechner and Moroder 2012). This cannot be claimed in VG.

All the above aspects contribute to the construction of difference as it is played out in LL, as will emerge from the illustration of the data. Before the discussion of the data, however, some space will be devoted to the sketching of the main theoretical frameworks underpinning the present interpretation of LL.

3. Theoretical background

The differences in the perception (and self-perception) of the two groups can be usefully framed in terms of what Blommaert (2005) calls ascribed (externally attributed) and inhabited (internally endorsed) identity. In the extra-urban context of VG under examination, ascribed and inhabited identity do not coincide. Internal perceptions of the group (and the semiotic practices that actualize them) are characterized by internal prestige norms and the visibility of Slovenian is pervasive (Tufi 2016). On the contrary, ascribed and inhabited identity in ST coincide, in that internal perceptions are reinforced by external perceptions, and LL practices actively contribute to the performance of the different self within the dialectical relationship of unity in diversity of the Germanophone world, a cultural legacy of regional and local autonomy which is rooted in the historical composition of German federalism (Gunlicks 2003).

These aspects complement Berruto's (2016) reflections on sociolinguistic vitality, whereby internal linguistic vitality would characterize forms of inhabited identity, and external linguistic vitality would characterize forms of ascribed identity. It should be borne in mind, however, that in taking these frameworks into consideration, we are not advocating the application of binary interpretive tools. On the contrary, we continue viewing identity in its performative aspects, where different components of identity are deployed differently in daily interactions and where the self is a matter of actualized degrees of embodied existence. We are aware of the limitations of carrying out comparative studies and of the binary categories that they might inadvertently encourage. We therefore wish to remind the reader that the interpretive tools that we propose in this chapter are employed to help us identify critical features relating to linguistic behaviour that, we believe, endows language agents with transformative potential.

In this respect it is interesting to note that the hyphenated names of these regions have contributed to the fossilization of hyphenated identities such as Italo-Slovenians and Italo-Germans in reference to the Slovenophone and Germanophone groups who share the respective regions with Italian groups. Due to the inescapable territorial dimension that is inherent in current geopolitics, this lexical compromise was intended to include the different ethnic identities that share lived space, rather than reflecting the original use of hyphenated terms expressing divided loyalty (as in Higham 1955).[4] In any case, this points to the verbal difficulties of articulating the intersections of history, geopolitics and culture, and the limited descriptive power of naming practices. Hyphenated ethnic terms emphasize, once again, binary conceptions of belonging and banalize identities, which are complex and not simply the sum of two parts. In particular, the Italo-side of the terms foregrounds the nation state (Italy) as the political entity regulating and dictating institutional forms of belonging. The second part of the ethnonyms, on the contrary, engenders the possibility of different, long-standing ethnicities on Italian soil, therefore characterizing a form of *defective* identity if viewed within a traditional understanding of the indissoluble bond between language, culture and the nation state. Such naming practices, therefore, hinder the normalization of hybridization processes and foreground a separation that ignores de facto mixed identities, as illustrated in Section 2. They also militate against social cohesion, in that they encourage a perception of identity which is bounded, immobile and exclusionary and therefore incapable of evolving over time – the very opposite of human experience. Finally, they inhibit processes of both group and individual empowerment, a form of emancipation from crystallized identities that requires a suitable descriptive terminology that the logic of the nation state is not able to engender.

In the attempt to problematize dualistic categories, the main analytical perspective that we wish to take into consideration for the purposes of this chapter is rooted in urban sociology and draws on Kaufmann's (2002, 2011) conceptualization of mobility, both spatial and social. This framework marks a departure from a tradition of studies which have focused on communities or neighbourhoods as concrete and static territories and which provide an areolar view of space, that is, one where groups are geographically delineated and physically bounded. This tradition in turn has influenced concepts of spatial mobility, where the focus has been on movement in space-time rather than on the interaction between actors, structures and context.

The potential for movement with respect to mobile actors is central to Kaufmann's (2002, 2011) theorization of *motility*. Motility, borrowed from biology, is understood as the capacity of entities (e.g. goods, information or people) to be mobile in social and geographic space, and as the way in which entities access and appropriate the capacity for socio-spatial mobility according to their circumstances. Within a 'field of possibilities' (Kaufmann 2011: 57), that is, potential choices that are available in a given context, motility is the way an individual or group exploits opportunities that are available to them to fulfil their aspirations and pursue their objectives.

In particular, Kaufmann (2011: 57) posits that mobility is based on three analytical dimensions. The first dimension, as mentioned above, is the *field of possibilities* – this is based on existing infrastructure in a given locality, the use of space, the job market, the institutions and the laws that govern human activity. The field of possibilities encompasses both given models of achievement and the challenges faced by its members. The second dimension is *aptitude for movement* – within a given physical, economic and social context, these aptitudes provide a degree of motility, that is, an individual's capacity for movement within certain conditions. Motility is the way individuals or groups exploit the field of possibilities with regard to movement in relation to their aspirations and projects. The third dimension is *movement*, which refers to actual moving in physical space, and can include ideas, objects and information in addition to people.

When put together, these three dimensions are likely to produce motility. However, the field of possibilities, engendered by existing infrastructure, is not necessarily conducive to the actual selection of real options on the part of individuals or groups. Conversely, highly developed motility can have the result of anchoring a population to an environment, rather than empowering it to change. Similarly, just because an individual or a group moves a great deal, this does not mean that their field of possibilities is favourable or predisposed to mobility.

By uncoupling movement and mobility, Kaufmann (2011: 57) identifies three main outcomes:

(1) *Moving and being mobile*, where spatial mobility and social mobility go hand in hand. Mobile social actors are empowered to move spatially, too – a prerogative which is afforded by their socio-economic status. In LL terms, this would reflect typical situations in national settings where the status and/or the legislation supporting the majority/standard language warrants its dominant visibility and therefore both its spatial and its social employability.

(2) *Moving without being mobile*, where physical movement does not impact on the actor in terms of role, identity or social position, and where micro-movements ultimately reinforce (social) immobility. An example could be that of actors who travel regularly for work, but whose social status remains immobile. In LL terms, and taking the role of Slovenian in VG into consideration, status elevation via institutional protection in this particular instance can be seen as a micro-movement which does not change real (both ascribed and inhabited) status. The positive impact on linguistic mobility, that is, its employability to enhance its cultural capital and gain centrality in the local linguistic market, is limited.

(3) *Not moving and being mobile*, where (social) change takes place with no spatial component. Virtual movement engendered by connectivity can, for instance, increase the chances of social mobility considerably. In LL terms, this outcome can be exemplified through the role of German in ST in so far as geolinguistic non-movement does not contradict a high degree of sociolinguistic (and LL) mobility. This translates into a maximum usability of all available linguistic resources.

Focusing the analysis on the potential of movement allows us to foreground new aspects of the mobility of LL actors with regard to possibilities and constraints of their manoeuvres. This in turn will enable an appreciation of wider societal consequences of social and spatial mobility, and of the potential of multilingualism in the given settings.

Motility encompasses interdependent elements relating to (a) access to different forms and degrees of mobility, (b) competence to recognize and make use of access and (c) appropriation of a particular choice. If viewed as a form of capital (in a Bourdieusian sense), motility can be mobilized and transformed into other types of capital (i.e. economic, human and social capital). Depending on (local and geopolitical) context, individual actors, groups and institutions differ in access, competence and appropriation, and therefore they have at their disposal different motility options. This framework will inform the analysis of data in Section 4.

Kaufmann's theory has been recently employed in the context of language maintenance and shift in relation to migrant groups. Houtkamp (2018) focuses in particular on language transmission and survival in transnational contexts, such as Turkish groups living in the Netherlands, and analyses the conditions which endow the heritage language with mobility capital, such as the nurturing of transnational ties. The closeness of transnational ties between the two sides of the border is in fact another aspect that VG and ST share in terms of the close cross-border relationships with neighbouring countries where Slovenian and German are the majority (and national) languages. In terms of LL motility, however, this common aspect does not seem to have a high degree of significance, due to the different historical conditions that characterize the long-standing minoritized groups in Italy compared to migrant groups of recent standing, such as the Turkish one living in the Netherlands.

The main purpose of this chapter is to propose and assess the suitability of the theory of motility (Kaufmann 2002, 2011) in LL studies. The presentation of the data will allow us to illustrate the applicability of this notion and its explanatory power in terms of LL motility as observed in borderscapes, and beyond. The discussion will uncover the links between motility and empowerment in the different outcomes engendered by the local realization of the potential for change.

4. The data

Prior to the discussion of the data, a methodological note is necessary to explain the differences in the extent and nature of the LL surveys in the two areas. The data presented for VG in this chapter were collected in 2010 and partly discussed in Tufi (2013, 2016) and in Blackwood and Tufi (2015), albeit within different theoretical frameworks. The data relating to ST, on the contrary, were collected in 2016 and have not been published before. As a result, the two data sets are comparable only to a certain extent, in that the corpus for VG includes a wider area (the entire province of Trieste encompassing five towns and a total population of about thirty thousand) than the corpus for ST, which focuses on one town, Sesto (population two thousand) (ISTAT 2012). This imbalance, however, will add solidity to the analysis as presented below – the LL in VG foregrounded adherence to the standard form of the minoritized

Figure 4.4 Recycling bins for glass and cans – Italian (left) and Slovenian (right)

language consistently even though a wider area was examined, whereas the LL in ST indexed a significantly diverse linguistic repertoire within the limited space of a small centre. In terms of the number of tokens featuring the minority language, the two data sets are broadly comparable (220 in VG and 126 in ST). In addition, an initial comparison as outlined in this research is useful (a) as a preliminary application of motility in minoritized LL settings and (b) to share the concept with a wider audience of scholars in view of further analysis and theorization. For these reasons, we will engage primarily with qualitative aspects of the LL, with the intention of providing a more fine-grained investigation supported by additional data in future research.

As highlighted in Tufi (2013, 2016), data collected in the province of Trieste indicate a pervasive presence of written Slovenian, which is displayed on a wide range of signs pointing to the use of the minority language in all spheres of life. These include both public signs initiated by institutional actors and private ones, such as shop signs and other commercial displays. Signs on recycling bins (Figure 4.4), for example, and on other items pertaining to the local infrastructure, such as public libraries (Figure 4.5) and security (Figure 4.6), are bilingual. Commercial signs range from shop signs (the hairdresser's in Figure 4.7) through to signs indicating establishments such as the café in Figure 4.8, or adverts. We also identified items with longer texts such as party-political communications, and they usually appeared as two monolingual signs, one in Slovenian and one in Italian, displayed parallel to each other or vertically (one above the other).

Figure 4.5 Municipal library in Duino Aurisina (Italian-Slovenian)

Existing sources in fact highlight the high degree of ethno-linguistic awareness of Slovenians in VG and of their dynamism in all social, economic and cultural matters where communication takes place in the minority language (Sussi 2003; Ožbot 2009). Slovenian is therefore the language of business, a significant element in the maintenance of cross-border activities with nearby Slovenia, and of leisure, local politics, religion and media. The language is widely represented in institutional spaces, too (Figures 4.4–4.6). What was noticeable during the surveys was that signs featuring Slovenian and generated by institutional actors (such as municipal, directional, tourist and church signs) were not outnumbered by commercial signs significantly (100 institutional items vs 120 commercial ones, with a proportion of 5:6). This is a peculiar characteristic when compared to other urban or peri-urban contexts in Italy, where commercial signs usually constitute the largest portion of signs (Blackwood and Tufi 2015). The data therefore suggest that the visibility of Slovenian is highest where Slovenian speakers outnumber non-Slovenian speakers and that the strong visual presence of (standard) written Slovenian both indexes and constructs given spaces as spaces of identity and belonging. In addition, the fact that institutional signs appear almost as frequently as commercial signs points to an over-representation of institutionally controlled public space, in an attempt to enhance the visibility and relevance of Slovenian. The result is the production of an imbalance between the (formal) equal status between Slovenian and Italian and the power relations between the two ethnic groups – it can be argued that numerous official signs displaying Slovenian

Figure 4.6 Finance police (Italian-Slovenian)

magnify the institutional manipulation and management of the public space that is not mirrored by the effective social status enjoyed by the minoritized language. The overrepresentation of Slovenian in the management of public space, therefore, reproduces the hegemonic ideology of a majority language situation via discursive processes that are mainly representational – they represent national institutional practices as well as incorporating and re-contextualizing them into local, self-reflexive practices to construct ways of being (Fairclough 2003). As a result, LL discourses contribute to a semiotic construction of social difference (Fairclough 2015). In other words, 'too much' Slovenian inscribed in institutional LL is a meta-semiotic, compensatory device for the perception of low status. This phenomenon underscores a doubly minoritizing effect that might ultimately be detrimental to language maintenance and effectively disempower the minoritized group. In this scenario, the safeguarding of the minority language is an institutional operation that immobilizes language actors in a static linguistic mode (standard Slovenian) that does not release local linguistic energy and dynamism, as will be elaborated below.

Moving to ST, German is dominant in Sesto in the local LL. Similarly to VG, institutional bilingualism has had the effect of producing primarily bilingual inscriptions of the public space where signs generated by bodies endowed with authority and/or organizational power (e.g. local associations) appear regularly. Even though Sesto is only a small centre, the LL survey highlighted that the proportion of institutional versus commercial signs featuring German is not so strikingly in favour of

Figure 4.7 Hairdresser's sign (Italian-Slovenian)

institutional signs – 48 institutional signs were identified as opposed to 78 commercial ones, with an approximate proportion of 5:8. In addition to numerical considerations, however, it is the characteristics of the signs that matter. For instance, and unlike the situation in VG, the minority language was dominant in the LL of Sesto with respect to both the horizontality and the verticality of the signs, that is, the hierarchical order of languages on signs. In addition, signs on the village noticeboard, which is positioned in the very centre of the town and therefore a material as well as a symbolic core structure of local culture, were entirely in German. The local LL therefore contributes to the construction of a monolingual ideology (see also Carli 2003). Local spatialization practices (e.g. the internal organization of languages on signs and the physical positioning of the village noticeboard displaying monolingual German signs), on the one hand, construct German as a community language and a core value and, on the other hand, exploit and consolidate the transactional, commodity value of (written) German as a major world language.

The considerations presented so far stem from an initial analysis of LL in the given settings by taking into account notions such as language ideology, spatialization dynamics and discursive constructions of identity in minoritized contexts with complex historical legacies. However, the role of LL in the observed settings can be such that it exceeds its explanatory potential as exemplified above. Explanatory power can be enhanced by a consideration of the element of movement (and its implications), in that movement is constitutive of borderscapes and of their materialization in given settings. In particular,

Figure 4.8 Cafè (Italian/Slovenian)

and as mentioned earlier, uncoupling movement and mobility will afford novel insights – the capacity of mobility does not necessarily lead to movement (i.e. social change), nor is social change necessarily engendered by mobility. By dissecting the different components of mobility and employing them within an LL framework, we shall be able to identify features that add transformative potential to minoritized settings.

From this perspective, Sesto LL displays a high degree of motility. Different components of motility are mobilized in the public space and LL is significantly involved in the enactment of access, competence and appropriation. LL agents have access to a given linguistic repertoire and choose to prioritize German, as both the semiotics of verticality/horizontality and monolingual German signs testify. In terms of competence, that is, the skills employed by agents to recognize and make use of access, in the LL of Sesto linguistic polycentrism is exhibited through displayed orientation to different norms – Swiss, German, Austrian and South-Tyrolean. The display of different varieties of German is supported by language behaviour that permeates every aspect of local life. As shown in Ciccolone (2009), in ST, speakers consider the entire Germanophone world a linguistic reservoir that they can freely tap into depending on need, and both regional and dialectal uses are employed not just in informal contexts but also in public communication. In addition, a high degree of LL agency is detectable via the numerical superiority of private (commercial) signs relative to institutional signs. As for appropriation (of a particular choice), LL actors exploit a range of available options (i.e. linguistic variety) within the ecology of German.

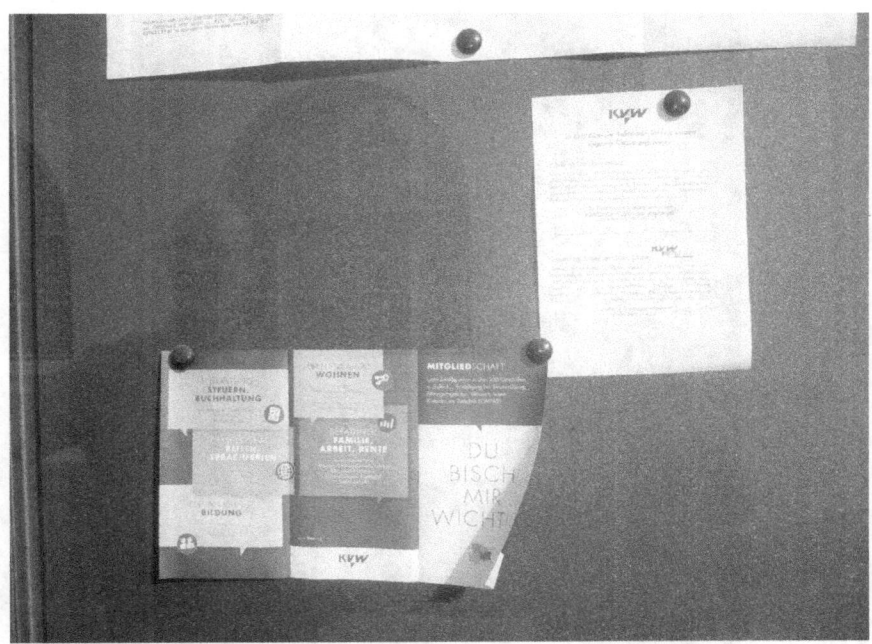

Figure 4.9 Village noticeboard in Sesto (German) – use of BISCH (Austrian German)

Figures 4.9–4.13 provide examples of different varieties of German featuring on different signs.[5] In the phrase DU BISCH MIR WICHTIG (Engl. 'I care about you / You are important to me') in Figure 4.9, 'bisch' (you 'are') is an example of Austrian German (German German – *bist*), whereas 'Unberechtigt' (Eng. 'unauthorized') in Figure 4.10 draws from German German ('Unauthorized vehicles will be removed'). Figure 4.11 is an example of local German with the calque 'Ratsaal', an adaptation from Italian *sala consiliare*, the room where the Town Council meet. 'Dolomitenstrasse' in Figure 4.12 reproduces Swiss German orthography (cf. German German Straße),[6] whilst in Figure 4.13 we have a possible example of grammaticalization – *mozzarella* (feminine in Italian) should be 'Frischer' because cheese is masculine in German.

With respect to VG, we observe a similarity in the ability to access a bilingual linguistic repertoire, but this choice is restricted by language attitudes whereby standard Slovenian is employed consistently in modalities which, in terms of competence, suggest an exhibited monocentrism and compliance with one standard norm. Within our data we can identify occasional instances of local Slovenian such as that represented in Figure 4.6. In Italy, the *Guardia di Finanza* is a special police division responsible for the prosecution of financial crime, and arguably *Finančna Straža* is a Slovenian adaptation of an Italian institution. These types of adaptations, however, are again in relation to local institutions and as such require the application of official bilingualism in the local naming practices – a form of compliance more than of linguistic autonomy.[7]

Figure 4.10 Monolingual regulatory signs displayed in vertical order (German/Italian) – use of German German 'Unberechtigt' (unauthorized)

This is supported by research undertaken by Fusco (2011), who states that the Slovenian community in VG does not agree on the type of linguistic model that should be protected and promoted. Views in fact vary and range from the adoption of standard Slovenian to the use of local varieties as the true expression of linguistic identity and a genuine part of the local heritage. This significant debate, however, does not seem to be part of the LL narrative and is not articulated through LL discourses, thereby contributing to immobility in linguistic terms. As regards appropriation, in VG the materialization of this component of motility points to limited non-institutional LL agency due to the high proportion of institutional signs relative to the incidence of private (commercial) signs.

5. Conclusion

Drawing some preliminary conclusions, similarities between the two settings would support an expectation that motility (as engendered by local multilingualism) is

Figure 4.11 Town Hall intercom (German) – 'Ratsaal' indicating the Council Room (Local German)

similarly deployed in the LL of VG and ST, and that local actors display similar degrees of empowerment in the linguistic management of the public space. These similarities include the peri-urban or rural character of the settings, historical memory and identity formation, the existence of complex linguistic repertoires, legal protection of ethnolinguistic rights and the maintenance of a material and cultural borderscape. LL, however, constructs important differences in the manipulation of the public space in the two geolinguistic settings.

In VG, LL agents adhere to a standard language ideology which crystallizes the minority status, a status which is doubly marginalized in so far as it is underpinned by the perception of Slovenian as a rural language. Spatialization practices and the dominance of Italian in the bilingual LL construct Slovenian as a community language that aims to preserve and defend the local identity, but LL practices foreground standard Slovenian in order to assign legitimacy to the inscribed (and inhabited) borderscape.

Internalized perceptions of peripherality and isolation have been alleviated by the softening of the border with nearby Slovenia since 2004, following the inclusion of the country in the European Union. Whilst this process may have assigned to Slovenian a higher degree of currency and relevance due to intensified, direct contacts with Slovenia, compliance with norms emanating from the nearby country have resulted in the exclusion of local repertoires from LL displays. In addition, it is debatable whether progressive-looking legislation (however slow and ineffective in its implementation) is sufficient in ensuring the maintenance of dynamic language practices which are able to

Figure 4.12 Street-name sign (German/Italian) – Swiss German orthography (German German β)

energize progressively anaemic domains of use (Košuta 2016). The non-availability of contextual information about actual uses of Slovenian (e.g. the public demonstration of numerical superiority that South Tyroleans thrive in) seems to militate against the type of linguistic confidence that would assign a stronger voice to the minoritized group (and add to the field of possibilities), therefore contributing to elevating the status of the language and to maximizing the aptitude for movement for its speakers.

Conversely, in ST, German is dominant in the bilingual LL and its high visibility in peri-urban or rural environments is an element of strength – the LL narrative reinforces a monolingual ideology and validates German as a majority language. In ST, too, spatialization practices construct German as a community language carrying identity functions, but they also exploit and consolidate German as a major world language – German polycentrism is embraced – and both the peculiarities of the local repertoire and those in use elsewhere in the Germanophone world are exhibited in LL.

It follows that it is possible to discern a low level of linguistic (and cultural) motility in the VG LL and a high level of motility in the ST LL. As an asset, motility is engendered by different mobility options available to given individuals and groups (i.e. the local multilingual repertoires), and it enhances the cultural capital of any social reality, but even more so in minoritized settings which, as part of larger national entities, struggle to assert their visibility and voice. The fact that highly developed linguistic motility has in effect firmly anchored South Tyroleans to their environment is an additional

Figure 4.13 Sign outside dairy farm 'fresh mozzarella' (German/Italian)

element of strength and falls under the category of *not moving and being mobile* envisaged by Kaufmann, where (social) change takes place with no spatial component. Linguistic empowerment of local actors is a fact and is supported by language practices that ensure both the internal and the external vitality of German varieties. VG, on the contrary, reflects an outcome similar to *moving without being mobile*, where physical movement (multiple cross-border activities and contacts) does not impact on the local actors in terms of role, identity or social position, or on their ethnolinguistic status. The physical movement reinforces (linguistic) immobility, instead, and in the long term it might continue inhibiting processes of linguistic emancipation through a weakening of both internal and external vitality.

Motility as an analytical category allows a deeper understanding of the multiple factors affecting language practices, especially in areas where the local and geopolitical context is of fundamental importance, and we have identified LL as a significant factor in enhancing social motility. In particular, LL dynamics and linguistic motility are in a symbiotic relationship whereby divergent asymmetrical relations (Fairclough 2015) between language agents and their material and symbolic audiences can be reversed, and where linguistic inequality can be exposed and contested, therefore endowing writing acts with transformative potential. Similarly to linguistic vitality (Berruto 2016), linguistic motility is not decided once and for all. On the contrary, it is susceptible to change and can therefore be manipulated via linguistic citizenship, for example, by initiating change that is not triggered by institutional actors (Tufi 2020). As we have seen for ST, exhibited linguistic polycentrism and local prestige norms empower language agents via the construction of new spaces of ethnolinguistic inhabiting. This can in turn affect externally ascribed identity and upset both vertical and horizontal dimensions of crystallized linguistic positionings due to the inextricable links between social and territorial structures. LL can therefore be instrumental in shifting discourses of subalternity and extremely influential in empowering individuals and groups.

Notes

1. I wish to express my gratitude to all those who contributed to the discussions about signs displaying different varieties of German and Slovenian, and in particular Anke Bohm, Federica Buso, Katia Peruzzo, Francesca Raffi and Giulia Sandrin.
2. For ease of exposition *Trieste* and *Sesto* will henceforth be used, as well as *Venezia Giulia* and *South Tyrol* – the latter being the term employed in English-language texts.
3. Estimates of the Slovenian population in Italy vary between 47,000 and 125,000 (the community refuses to participate in a census). Estimates are therefore controversial in themselves. See Sussi (2003) for an explanation of the nature of the different sources that provide figures.
4. See Cortelazzo (2010) for an explanation of the hyphenated toponym 'Friuli-Venezia Giulia'.
5. Our labelling reflects general agreement among speakers of different varieties of German who were consulted prior to the drafting of this chapter. Unsurprisingly, there was also a degree of disagreement about the variety of German identified on each sign. Local orientation to different norms is, however, confirmed and supports our point about the relaxed attitude towards (written) normativity in ST.
6. The <ss> spelling in, for example, 'Strasse' has also been adopted in recent spelling reforms in Germany, even though not in all phonetic environments.
7. For the Slovenian data, too, we consulted speakers who confirmed the generalized use of standard Slovenian in our corpus, with the exception of signs indexing the presence of police divisions.

References

ASTAT (2018), South Tyrol in Figures. Available online: http://astat.provincia.bz.it/downloads/Siz_2018-eng(1).pdf (accessed 26 November 2018).
Berruto, G . (2016), 'Sulla vitalità delle linguae minores. Indicatori e parametri', in Aline Pons (ed.) *Vitalità, morte e miracoli dell'occitano*, 11–26, Pomaretto: Associazione Amici della Scuola Latina.
Blackwood, R. J., and Tufi, S. (2015), *The Linguistic Landscape of the Mediterranean: French and Italian Coastal Cities*, Basingstoke: Palgrave Macmillan.
Blommaert, J. (2005), *Discourse: A Critical Introduction*, Cambridge: Cambridge University Press.

Brezigar, S. (2009), 'The Slovene Language in Italy: Paths to a Value-Added Position', in Susanna Pertot, Tom M. S. Priestly and Colin H. Williams (eds), *Rights, Promotion and Integration Issues for Minority Languages in Europe*, 207–15, Basingstoke: Palgrave.
Carli, A. (2003), 'Cinquant'anni di tutela linguistica in Alto Adige/Sudtirolo', *Plurilinguismo* 9, 217–26.
Cattaruzza, M. (2007), *L'Italia e il confine orientale*, Bologna: Il Mulino.
Ciccolone, S. (2009), Regionalismi nel tedesco standard in Austria e Alto Adige: valutazioni dei tedescofoni altoatesini. *Quaderni della Sezione di Glottologia e Linguistica. Università degli Studi G. D'Annunzio, Chieti* 19–20, 1–13.
Corni, G. (2011), 'The Exodus of Italians from Istria and Dalmatia, 1945–56', in Jessica Reinisch and Elizabeth White (eds), *The Disentanglement of Populations. Migration, Expulsion and Displacement in Post-War Europe*, 71–90, Basingstoke: Palgrave Macmillan.
Cortelazzo, M. A. (2010), 'L'idea del doppio nome per la regione venne avanzata da Graziadio Isaia Ascoli su "L'Alleanza" nel 1863', *Il Piccolo (gelocal.it)*, 26 November 2010. Availbale online: http://ricerca.gelocal.it/ilpiccolo/archivio/ilpiccolo/2010/11/26/nz_26_apre.html?refresh_ce (accessed 12 November 2018).
Eichinger, L. (2002), 'South Tyrol: German and Italian in a Changing World', in Jeanine Treffers-Daller and Roland Willemyns (eds), *Language Contact at the Romance-Germanic Language Border*, 137–49, Clevedon, UK: Multilingual Matters.
Fairclough, N. (2003), *Analysing Discourse – Textual Research for Social Research*, New York: Routledge.
Fairclough, N. (2015), *Language and Power*, 3rd edn, London: Routledge.
Fusco, F. (2011) 'Il Friuli-Venezia Giulia: mosaico di lingue, lingue di minoranza e dialetti', *Treccani*, 9 November. Available online: http://www.treccani.it/magazine/lingua_italiana/speciali/minoranze/Fusco.html (accessed 10 August 2018).
Grote, G. (2012), *The South Tyrol Question, 1866–2010: From National Rage to Regional State*, Oxford: Peter Lang.
Gunlicks, A. (2003), *The Länder and German Federalism*, Manchester: Manchester University Press.
Higham, J. (1955), *Strangers in the Land: Patterns of American Nativism, 1860–1925*, New Brunswick: Rutdgers University Press.
Houtkamp, C. (2018), 'The Relevance of Motility in Language Shift Research', *Language Problems and Language Planning*, 42 (1): 1–15.
ISTAT (2012), *15° censimento della popolazione e delle abitazioni 2011*. Available online: https://www.istat.it/it/censimenti-permanenti/censimenti-precedenti/popolazione-e-abitazioni/popolazione-2011 (accessed 7 August 2018).
ISTAT (2018), *Anno 2017. Conti economici territoriali*. Available online: https://www.istat.it/it/files/2018/12/Report_Conti-regionali_2017.pdf (accessed 7 August 2018).
Kaufmann, V. (2002), *Re-thinking Mobility*, Burlington: Ashgate.
Kaufmann, V. (2011), *Rethinking the City. Urban Dynamics and Motility*, Lausanne: EPFL Press.
Košuta, M. (2016), 'Del mare tra il dire e il fare. Stato e tutela della lingua slovena in Italia'. Available online: https://www.filologiasarda.eu/files/documenti/pubblicazioni_pdf/bss9/01-kosuta.pdf (accessed 5 November 2018).

Lechner, O., and Moroder, B. (2012), *Ritratto economico dell'Alto Adige*. Available online: https://www.camcom.bz.it/sites/default/files/uploaded_files/Scuola_economia/16873_economia2012_it.pdf (accessed 10 August 2018).

Lefebvre, H. (1991), *The Production of Space*, Oxford: Blackwell.

Marcato, C. (2001), *Friuli Venezia Giulia*, Roma-Bari: Laterza.

Orioles, V. (2003), *Le minoranze linguistiche. Profili sociolinguistici e quadro dei documenti di tutela*, Roma: Il Calamo.

Ožbot, M. (2009), 'Sloveno e italiano in contatto: qualche osservazione sugli scambi linguistici in una zona bilingue', in Carlo Consani (ed.) *Alloglossie e comunità alloglotte nell'Italia contemporanea. Teorie, applicazioni e descrizioni, prospettive. Atti del XLI Congresso internazionale di studi della Società di Linguistica Italiana (SLI), Pescara, 27–29 settembre 2007*, 39–52, Roma: Bulzoni.

Piergigli, V. (2017), 'La Costituzione italiana delle minoranze linguistiche tra principi consolidati, riforme mancate e prossime sfide', *Revista d'estudis autonomics i federals*, 26: 165–206. Available online: https://www.raco.cat/index.php/REAF/article/view/329192/419779 (accessed 26 November 2018).

Premik, K. (2004), *Relazioni italo-slovene 1880–1956*, Trieste: Novi Revija. Available online: http://www.kozina.com/premik/indexita_porocilo.htm (accessed 13 February 2012)

Pupo, R. (2005), *Il lungo esodo. Istria: le persecuzioni, le foibe, l'esilio*, Milano: Rizzoli.

Provincia Autonoma di Bolzano Alto Adige (2009), *Il nuovo statuto di autonomia*. Available online: http://www.provincia.bz.it/news/it/pubblicazioni.asp (accessed 14 December 2018).

Sbisà, M., and Vascotto, P. (2007), How to Conceive of the Other's Point of View. Considerations from a Case Study in Trieste', in Sharon Millar and John Wilson (eds), *The Discourse of Europe: Talk and Text in Everyday Life*, 153–71, Amsterdam: John Benjamins.

Sussi, E. (2003), 'Gli Sloveni in Italia: la situazione attuale e le prospettive', in Vincenzo Orioles (ed.), *La legislazione nazionale sulle minoranze linguistiche. Problemi, applicazioni, prospettive. Atti del Convegno di Studi. Udine, 30 novembre – 1 dicembre 2001. Plurilinguismo* 9, 203–16, Udine: Centro internazionale sul plurilinguismo, Università degli studi di Udine.

Toso, F. (2008), *Le minoranze linguistiche in Italia*, Bologna: Il Mulino.

Tufi, S. (2013), 'Shared Places, Unshared Identities: Vernacular Discourses and Spatialised Constructions of Identity in the Linguistic Landscape of Trieste', *Modern Italy*, 18 (4): 391–408.

Tufi, S. (2016), 'Constructing the Self in Contested Spaces: The Case of Slovenian-Speaking Minorities in the Area of Trieste', in Robert J. Blackwood, Elizabeth Lanza and Hirut Woldemariam (eds), *Negotiating and Contesting Identities in Linguistic Landscapes*, 101–16, London: Bloomsbury.

Tufi, S. (2020), 'Linguistic Landscapes of Urban Italy: Perspectives on Transnational Identities', in Charles Burdett and Loredana Polezzi (eds), *Transnational Italian Studies*, 61–85, Liverpool: LUP.

Wand, A. (2016), ' "Separate but Equal", Segregated or Stymied? Second Language Learning Issues in South Tyrol', *Journal of the Anthropological Society of Oxford*, 8 (3): 330–47. Available online: https://www.anthro.ox.ac.uk/sites/default/files/anthro/documents/media/jaso8_3_2016_330_347.pdf (accessed 15 October 2018).

Invisible presence? Polish in Norwegian public spaces

Toril Opsahl[1]

1. Overview

Poles are by far the largest group of 'immigrants' to Norway represented by more than one hundred thousand individuals. Nevertheless, the presence of Polish has been – at least until recently – somewhat hard to spot in public spaces. Polish presence in Norwegian broadcasting media is limited, and previous studies in educational settings have claimed that Polish pupils are overlooked in schools. So far, there are relatively few sociolinguistic studies of Poles in Norway. This chapter explores and reflects on the presence of Polish in public spaces in an area of the capital Oslo, drawing on parallel field observations from three women. To some extent, the data support an impression of invisibility. However, Polish presence is observed across several dimensions in public space (such as advertising billboards, construction sites and professional settings, e.g. in public hospitals). Parts of the observed Polish presence strengthens stereotypical images of Poles as one-dimensional (blue-collar) workers and professionals. Still, there is little doubt that there exist strong and multifaceted linguistic practices involving Polish in Oslo, but these practices seem to exist parallel to, and to a lesser degree intertwined with, Norwegian and other languages, in public spaces. The dominant language ideologies characteristic of Poland and Norway, respectively, raise questions of how the concept of national identity intersects with multilingualism, as well as to the relationship between cultural and linguistic identity. To the point where one may speak of individual multilingualism, it is in many ways protective of distinctive identities in this specific socio-historical setting. Identities associated with professional life are the most prominent traces of Polish in public spaces, alongside a potential consumer identity connected to market logic. The close connection between language and labour may at first glance be seen as a positive sign of empowerment of individuals. The presence of Polish is ambivalent, however, since the agency of individuals in terms of their daily use of language is challenged when the presence of Polish in public domains continues to feed and maintain stereotypical images of available identities, depending not only on a symbolic value but also on market economy. Methodological insights from the present study support the assumption that research on the relationship between multilingualism in public spaces and the empowerment of individuals needs to include and recognize individuals as interpretative subjects and agents.

2. Poles in Norway

According to Statistics Norway (SSB), immigrants from Poland make up the largest immigrant group in Norway, with 98,700 persons as per 1 January 2019 (SSB 2019). At this time the total number of immigrants was 765,100, accounting for 14.4 per cent of the Norwegian population. The percentage is higher in urban areas, and 33.1 per cent of the capital Oslo's entire population have a migrant background. SSB defines immigrants as 'persons born abroad of two foreign-born parents and four foreign-born grandparents'. Norwegian-born to immigrant parents account for 3.4 per cent of the population. Among these, we find an additional number of 13,300 persons with Polish background. Statistics and the cover term 'immigrant' do not tell us much about the people hidden behind the figures and percentages, but they do tell us that at least 112,000 individuals in Norway lead some sort of transnational lives with ties to Polish networks and communities. As noted by Obojska (2018: 83), the recognition of interconnectivities across and beyond national boundaries in people's experiences is particularly relevant for Poles, due to their long immigration history, constituting one of the twenty largest diasporas in the world (83).

Polish immigration history in Norway started as early as the 1830s (Godzimirski 2011), but the numbers of Poles in Norway were relatively small through the following decades. A small number of Poles ended up in Norway after the turmoil following the Second World War, but what has been called the 'first phase' of modern Polish-Norwegian migrant history did not take place until the 1980s. Approximately two thousand of the political refugees fleeing the martial law of the Jaruzelski regime ended up in Norway. Among them were many prominent intellectuals and artists, today well established within Norwegian society (Friberg and Golden 2014: 12). The second phase, according to Friberg and Golden, was a response to the economic challenges following the end of the communist era and the transition to market economy in the 1990s. A large group of Poles came to Norway for temporary work based on bilateral agreements. The Polish work force was especially connected to agriculture, establishing a stereotypical conception of Poles as being 'strawberry-pickers' supplementing their income with seasonal work abroad. The migration pattern characteristic of the 1990s is largely based on short-term stays and hence circular. Still, Poles made an imprint through the establishment both of more or less permanent professional and social networks, and of cross-cultural marriages and family reunions, as well as through receiving specialist work permits, especially within the healthcare sector (Friberg and Golden 2014: 13).

The third phase in the immigration history starts on 1 May 2004 with European Union (EU) enlargement and the implementation of European Economic Area (EEA) rules, resulting in radical changes of conditions for migration patterns between Poland and Norway. Over the next ten years, the number of Poles in Norway increased from around seven thousand to more than eighty thousand, representing the largest wave of migration to Norway through all times (Friberg and Golden 2014: 15). Since 2006, the growth of Polish labour immigrants to Norway has been accompanied by increased family-related immigration, and in 2007, the Poles became the largest immigrant group in Norway (Godzimirski 2011). There has been a shift from the 2004-typical 'lone man working in the construction sector sending money back to Poland' to trends of entire families moving and reuniting ten years later, also resulting in a more equal gender balance within the Polish immigrant population (Friberg and Golden 2014: 15). Slåke (2018) indicates that we now may be facing a fourth phase in the Polish-Norwegian immigration history since net immigration has decreased in the last few years, possibly as a response to a weaker Norwegian economy. Poland, on the other hand, has had an uninterrupted economic growth for the past 20 years (Slåke 2018: 15). Nevertheless, people from Poland still hold their position as the largest 'immigrant group' in Norway.

Despite this status, Poles in Norway have received relatively little sociolinguistic research attention. Within Norwegian SLA research, a rich tradition has grown for the use of written language corpora, also involving texts from Polish participants, carving way for Polish-Norwegian research cooperation (Golden and Tenfjord 2014; Golden, Jarvis and Tenfjord 2017). Among the existing studies of Polish users of Norwegian, many are thus devoted to their written language use and the acquisition of specific grammatical features such as the Norwegian tense system (Janik 2017) and spatial prepositions (Szymańska 2017). Some studies of spoken use of Norwegian and comparative Polish–Norwegian conversational studies exist as well. Horbowicz's studies (e.g. Horbowicz 2010) suggest that the Polish speakers of Norwegian fail to convey several interactive features by means of adequate structures, which may lead to them being perceived as impolite, aggressive or uninterested. Urbanik (2017, 2020) shows several discrepancies in the grammatical and pragmatic patterns of requests in Norwegian and Polish. The notion of conversational politeness, and thus of socially acceptable requests, differs between the two languages. Research on communication among Poles on Norwegian construction sites, such as the pioneering work performed by Kraft (2017), is of special relevance for this chapter. Kraft sheds light on how the stratification between Norwegian and Polish construction workers relates to language policies, ideologies and practices on construction sites. Of great relevance to this chapter is also Obojska's equally pioneering work on family language policy in Polish families in Oslo, with emphasis on young Poles' language practices and thoughts on language maintenance (Obojska 2017, 2018; Obojska and Purkarthofer 2018). Bygdås's (2016) unpublished MA thesis on language choice and identity among Polish adolescents in Oslo should also be mentioned among the small but growing body of sociolinguistic studies on Polish presence in Norway.

3. Background, motivation and research questions

A notion of under-representation – or even absence – of Poles and Polish in Norwegian public space seems to be a recurring theme in existing studies from different fields. Berezkina's (2018) study of virtual Linguistic Landscapes (LLs) examines language policy on central state websites in Norway and shows how the official practice of promoting multilingualism is in decline, also influencing Polish presence. Berezkina has also performed a traditional LL study of Grønland, one of the most multicultural districts of Oslo, showing that the presence of – especially non-Western – migrant languages is limited and restricted to mostly hand-written, 'bottom-up', unofficial parts of the LL (Berezkina 2012). Among her data, only one example of the use of Polish is mentioned (Polish is one of eleven languages on an official poster from Oslo municipality about available Norwegian language classes). In her study of two major shopping streets in central Oslo, Stjernholm (2013) does not mention any Polish presence at all. Norwegian and English is dominant in her quantitative analysis, alongside some scattered instances of languages such as Italian, French, Spanish, Latin and Swedish (Stjernholm 2013: 81). Stjernholm comments on how 'the low value placed on immigrant languages appears to warrant their exclusion from these linguistic markets' (2013: 83). For Wærdahl (2016), the notion of invisibility turned out to be relevant both as a descriptive and an analytical point in their study of Polish children in Norwegian educational contexts. Information concerning language and cultural background of the Polish children was often missing. This made it difficult to access the children as a researcher, and 'they [i.e. the Polish children] seemed to be overlooked in school as well' (Wærdahl 2016: 95). They find that expectations of school and education are seldom articulated, and there are several examples of poor communication between schools and families, creating the risk of overlooking the social and academic challenges that Polish children face, because cultural differences and differences in pedagogical views are swept under the rug (2016: 102). Slåke (2018) conducted a series of searches in the Norwegian Broadcasting Corporation's (NRK's) internal databases, revealing that the broadcasts covering Poles and Poland have been few compared to the coverage of other nationalities. Slåke assumes further that this under-representation in the NRK's media coverage reflects public discourse in general. Golden and Opsahl (2019) show how the majority of written media's representation of Poles in Norway is one-dimensional, feeding a stereotypical image of a male work migrant often involved in shady business. In 2014, a national research campaign involved school children from all over Norway in the collection of slang and loan words, and while a myriad of languages and cultures were represented, hardly any examples from Polish were reported (Bjorvatn 2015: 45).

Over the last decades, the urban space has been an important focus of interest among Norwegian sociolinguistic researchers. The urban centres were postulated as impact sources for the emergence and spread of linguistic innovations leading to dialect levelling and regional dialects (e.g. Mæhlum 1998; Røyneland 2009). Urban areas have also received research attention as the locus of the emergence of so-called multiethnolectal speech styles (see, for instance, Aarsæther 2010; Opsahl 2009; Svendsen and Røyneland 2008). It is worth noticing that Polish is seldom mentioned among the languages contributing to a multiethnolectal feature pool in these studies. According to Barni and Bagna (2015: 9), the urban contexts represent the most interesting and significant sources for examining and interpreting linguistic dynamics. A city provides the sufficient space for languages to 'manifest their vitality as well as their visibility' (ibid.). Further, Barni and Bagna point to how big cities with a strong multiethnic component may be a place 'where collective and individual identities are able to express themselves, since spaces that are more open to creativity, change, and relations between social and linguistic groups are also more dynamic' (ibid.). The notion of 'invisibility' present in the literature review above makes it uncertain whether the Norwegian capital is a space where collective and/or individual identities are able to express themselves through linguistic resources associated with Polish. Moreover, the question remains as to what extent one may speak of empowerment for users of Polish–Norwegian multilingual repertoires in the Norwegian context.

The notion of invisibility also resonates well with my own impression during unsystematic field observations in Oslo during spring 2018, which triggered a curiosity towards the status of Polish presence in Norwegian public spaces. Hence, the overarching goal of the present contribution is to shed further sociolinguistic light on the largest group of so-called immigrants in Norway, with an emphasis on the interplay between the visibility of Polish in public spaces, and to what extent this specific case of multilingualism relates to the empowerment of individuals. What makes the encounter between Polish and Norwegian even more interesting, seen from a sociolinguistic perspective, are the contradictions regarding linguistic variation and diversity, and the prototypical attitudes thereof, in the two communities.

The research question discussed in this chapter is descriptive, asking in what ways Poles and Polish are visible and/or audible in public places in Oslo. During the search for possible explanations for the (lack of) Polish presence, questions of the relationship between cultural identity and linguistic identity are addressed. Is multilingualism protective of distinctive cultural identities or does it erode them? What does it mean for the agency of individual citizens in terms of their daily use of language? Last, but not least, the chapter discusses the relationship between multilingualism and empowerment of individuals. Empowerment may be seen in close relation to employment. Polish immigrants to Norway are not automatically included in official immigration policies (creating challenges in extracting data on Polish schoolchildren, as mentioned by Wærdahl (2016)). EEA supranational principles regulate Poles' movement and access to Norwegian labour markets, and Polish migrants are not automatically included in integration and language programmes (Iglicka, Gmaj and Wierzejski 2016). According to Iglicka, Gmaj and Wierzejski, 'their adaptation and migration decisions are therefore related heavily to their position at the labour market – their access to jobs and financial security' (2016: 129). Recent initiatives have been made, but until now few in-depth studies of the role of language and communication for an inclusive working life and the welfare for all citizens in Norway exist (Friberg, Dølvik and Eldrine 2013: 46; Opsahl et al. 2019). As pointed to by an anonymous reviewer, there is an important issue at stake here in twenty-first-century Europe, with Poles emerging as totemic for lower-wage manual labour, sometimes scapegoated by nationalist movements. The extent to which they are empowered, marginalized or visible is of great urgency.

4. The notion of invisibility

Shifting structures of power and asymmetrical relations render some types of practices and repertoires more legitimate, and therefore more visible (Kerfoot and Hyltenstam

2017: 8). Securing control over defining what counts as legitimate language thus become an important means for securing access to power (Heller and Duchêne 2012: 5). The *absence* of languages in cities, shops, schools, offices, moving buses, beaches and cyber space – and so on and so forth – is thus important data to be studied, according to Shohamy and Gorter (2009: 2), especially in areas which are politically and socially contested. Silence is not the same as non-communication (Thurlow and Jaworski 2010). A growing body of empirical research recognizes notions of absence and silence as important aspects of discourse studies (Schröter and Taylor 2018). As pointed out by Wærdahl (2016), with reference to Leinonen and Toivanen (2014), the terms 'visible' and 'invisible' have been employed in the study of migrants and minorities for almost 50 years, especially among US scholars, often in connection with certain migrant groups' ability to 'melt' into mainstream society. European scholars have more often turned to concepts like ethnicity, nationality or culture when making distinctions between groups based on their supposed origin (Leinonen and Toivanen 2014: 161). One may easily resist the use of a concept like in/visibility because no human is invisible. However, a focus on in/visibility can help analyse 'how various processes of racialization and practices of 'othering' come about and manifest themselves in Nordic societies' (ibid.). Moreover, the 'immigrant' category traditionally has strong connotations to visible differences in Norway, with skin colour as a prominent factor (Berg 2008: 216; Guðjónsdóttir 2014). Gullestad's influential studies (e.g. Gullestad 2002) show how the term 'migrant' typically invokes images of persons with dark skin, often of a third-world origin, with values that differ from those of the Norwegian majority. This image may have shifted after the 2004 EU enlargement, but still seems to be of relevance. Guðjónsdóttir's (2014) work on Icelandic migrants in Norway in the aftermath of the 2008 economic crisis shows how the migrants themselves construct belonging through racialization:

> Confronting the racial diversity of Oslo, the participants take a hegemonic position and judge who fits and who does not. In their narratives, the participants take part in constructing Norwegian society as 'white' with certain cultural (Christian) values and middle-class norms. Through these narratives, a space is carved out for the inclusion of 'white' Icelanders, while 'non-white' people are marked as non-Norwegian and not belonging to Norwegian society. (Guðjónsdóttir 2014: 180)

There seems to exist a hierarchy of national 'whiteness' as well, and one of the participants in Guðjónsdóttir's study has met hostility when being misrecognized as a Pole [sic], while experiencing friendliness when people discover he is Icelandic (ibid.). The self-constructing practices described by Guðjónsdóttir are also described for Polish migrants in Great Britain, who emphasize their skin colour rather than their ethnicity as a means to bridge the gap between themselves and the host community. 'In contrast to ethnicity, which carries the danger of being associated with Poles from the wrong social class, an emphasis on race assumes membership within the dominant white English group, which also occupies higher social class positions' (Eade, Drinkwater and Garapich 2007: 18). Studies like these highlight the complex nature and entanglement of concepts like 'class' and 'race' (Rosa and Flores 2017) and how the specific socio-historical situations must be taken into account, especially within migrant contexts. Leinonen and Toivanen (2014) emphasize that 'race' alone does not explain why certain groups are more in/visible than others are. In/visibility can also be understood in connection to claiming recognition in society (2014: 164). The concept 'in/visibility' has turned out to be useful in a wider, yet more specific reference in this study, and is henceforth referring to *visibility in public space through language use* (cf. Leinonen 2012), where multilingualism in itself is partly understood as the presence of certain linguistic features associated with different 'languages' in public space.

Participation in working life and good knowledge of Norwegian are mentioned as key principles for inclusion in Norwegian society (Ministry of Culture 2020: 53). One could imagine that the invisibility in public space, as for instance the lack of explicit mentioning of nationality in NRK broadcastings, is an indicator of 'successful integration' (Slåke 2018). Previous research shows, however, that the lack of Norwegian language competence of Polish immigrants hinders integration in the workplace and more generally in society (Friberg 2012; Iglicka, Gmaj and Wierzejski 2016; Kraft 2017). Hence, the question of the relationship between multilingualism, visibility in public space and empowerment of individuals deserves closer inspection, as we now turn to the methodological and empirical parts of the chapter.

5. Methodology and data

Until quite recently, the concepts of place and belonging have been underdeveloped theoretically within sociolinguistic research. A growing body of both empirical and theoretical studies concerning place and space have emerged, based on the conceptualization of place as socially constructed (Cornips and de Rooj 2018: 2). Places are invested with sociocultural meaning through language practices (Quist 2018). Hence, place-making involves 'the assigning – through interaction – of social meaning to (physical) space(s), thereby creating places that are perceived as the basis of belonging' (Cornips and de Rooj 2018: 8). A research tradition that has been concerned with investigating how places are invested with sociocultural meaning through language practices is LL research. Critical LL studies involve the recognition of linguistic facts as strongly connected to general social facts (Ben-Rafael, Shohamy and Barni 2010: xiv). This chapter is influenced by LL research in its 'extended form' (e.g. Shohamy and Gorter 2009). A recognition of LL as social arenas, and the inclusion of *people*, both as interpretative subjects and agents, has emerged over time (Spolsky 2009: 31; Barni and Bagna 2015: 7). This study is qualitative in nature and recognizes the role of the *interpretative subject* as an essential part in the search for deeper understanding of the role of multilingualism in public space. Qualitative analyses are conducted 'to uncover the reasons for the appearance/disappearance of a brand or a sign in a given language, or to explain/describe how groups of speakers react in the face of restrictive regulations concerning the visibility of some languages in a territory' (Barni and Bagna 2015: 12). Speakers use language to construct places and senses of belonging in their daily practices (Quist 2018: 264), a point also mentioned by Stjernholm (2013) in her LL study from Oslo. Knowledge of the language practices perceived as legitimate when places are invested with sociocultural meaning is thus important for empowering individuals within a given sociohistorical context (cf. Kerfoot and Hyltenstam 2017).

The present study recognizes both visual and audible linguistic expressions as relevant semiotic resources in the investment of sociocultural meaning to public spaces. A (public) place is shaped and influenced by both audible and visual expressions, and the place itself influences these practices. An illustrative example of this connection is found in the notes from one of the participants in the study (Table 5.1, co-observer 1, 11.15 am). She reports on how her wearing a name tag on a professional work assignment made strangers approach her in Polish, and how they accordingly were engaged in longer conversations. The visual sign, the name tag connoting 'Polish-ness' (Edelman 2009), generated a space for Polish language practice, adding to the overall impression of a multilingual space, or more precisely, a meaningful multilingual place. Blommaert and Maly (2014) include a sign on the back of a van with a Polish license plate in their ethnographically oriented LL study, arguing that attention to such non-permanent, temporary or even accidental signs 'generates sensitivity to rapid and unpredictable social and cultural change' (2014: 7). The presence of non-permanent linguistic expressions should be included in a description of space and place-making building on the conceptualization of place as socially constructed. Hence, the data collection build on a rather wide conception of 'the patterns of social interaction in which people engage in the particular space' (Blommaert and Maly 2014: 3).

The empirical basis of the study is a combination of three periods of field observations. The first is the author's observations from regular walks through Oslo's inner city over a four-month period during spring 2018, and an additional period during winter/spring 2019. The third more systematic field observation took place on what will be referred to as the 'focus-day', a mid-week working day during spring 2018, with no prior or ongoing public holidays, special events or shattering news bulletins, neither in Poland nor in Norway. This was an attempt to capture 'just another everyday'. To support and adjust my own observations, two women assisted me with their own, separate field observations during the same day. They were simply asked to notice, and make short notes, *every time they saw or heard Polish* from the moment they entered public space in the morning, to the moment they returned to their respective private spaces in the afternoon.

Unlike myself, with only sparse competence in Polish, my co-observers were fluent in both Polish and Norwegian. They were chosen primarily because of their Polish language competence. However, an incautious selection of areas for observation may lead to biased and misleading results (Spolsky 2009: 32). In an attempt to yield a more holistic observation of a defined urban space, the co-observers were chosen because their point of view resembled my own in many respects. We were of the same age, more or less the same educational level, had similar places of residence in two-person households and we all shared a workplace (often) requiring travelling through the similar parts of the inner city. The participants were guaranteed full anonymity throughout the process, and in accordance with relevant research-ethical guidelines (NSD 2018), no further identifiable aspects of their participation or contributions are thus revealed in the following, and third-party information and names are given as 'X'. Table 5.1 offers an overview of our reported observations during the focus day.

Table 5.1 Reported Focus-Day Observations

Main observer (author)	Co-observer 1	Co-observer 2
8.30 am – overhearing Polish conversation between workers at local construction site	7.30 am – Sitting on tram reading a Polish newspaper (*Gazeta Wyborcza*)	06.30 am – Opening Facebook, reading a post about a Norwegian band with Polish name
8.40 am – passing Billboard in Polish (Mycall advertisement)	8.15 am – Greeting a Polish patient at X Hospital	07.45 am – Work colleague jokes and tries to greet me in Polish
9.00 am – Polish (sounding) names on doorbells near tram stop	9.30 am – Interpreting for the patient during surgery procedure	08.30 am – X specialist asks for help in performing a medical procedure on Polish patient
12.00 noon – Overhearing colleagues speaking Polish on their way back/to lunch	11.15 am – Because I am wearing a name tag, I am approached by a stranger in the waiting room during lunch break, 20 minutes small-talk in Polish	11.35 am – Work colleague jokes about my Polish heritage ('there's our Pole') when asking for practical help
1.00 pm – Two Polish language posts in Facebook news-feed during lunch-break surfing (Krakow tourism, FIFA World cup video)	12.00 noon – Texting a Polish friend via Messenger; checking Facebook and Instagram, see 4–6 posts in Polish, click on three of them	4.20 pm – Passing tram number X advertising for the firm Mycall in Polish
	1.00 pm – Interpreting for the same Polish patient	4.50 pm – Overhearing Polish contractors small talking and joking while doing roadworks
	3.00 pm – Overhearing the two women sitting opposite me on the bus on my way home speaking Polish	5.30 pm – Watching a fun Facebook post related to the upcoming FIFA World cup; a great moment from 1974 when Poland beat Argentina 3–2 in their opening match.
	4.00 pm – A Polish song appears in my playlist	
	5.00 pm – Speaking Polish with my mother on the phone	
	8.00 pm – Back on Facebook: See a sports news bulletin in my news feed; click on an article on Polish politics; clicking 'like' on a funny post from a girlfriend in Poland.	

I have chosen to exclude from the present analysis the observations of Polish names on doorbells (Main observer), since these often represent the border between public and private spaces. Even though people's names may serve as contextualization cues and trigger interesting code switches, as was the case in the encounter triggered by the name tag described earlier, as well as generate interesting insights into multilingual language practices (Edelman 2009; Quist 2018), the onomastic dimension will remain a task for future research.

As can be seen from Table 5.1, the co-observers have conscientiously provided detailed accounts of their answers to 'whenever you see or hear Polish during the day'. Hence, the reports also involve observations and participation in language practices that can hardly be associated with the public domain, no matter how liberal one's interpretation of 'public' is. Reports like 'at home talking Polish with my mother on the phone' and 'a Polish song appears in my playlist' (Co-observer 2, assuming she was wearing a headset if listening in public) are excluded from the analysis. At the same time, they are an important reminder of how the relationship between visibility and vitality is not a one-to-one relationship. Both co-observer 1 and 2 are involved in several language practices including Polish during this 'everyday' encounter. The main observer's strikingly shorter list of observations is not in itself striking, since my Polish competence differs significantly from the other observers' competence. There are nevertheless similarities and patterns worth noticing across the observations reported in Table 5.1. These are analysed as falling into four categories, presented further in the next section: the language-skill-based professional site, the construction site, the (billboard) campaign site and the virtual LL site. Based on the nature of the data collection and previous research, I have reason to believe that at least two additional sites are relevant for the presence of Polish in Norwegian public places, that is, the religious site and the educational site. These will be touched briefly upon after a closer look at the main categories that emerge from the data.

6. Analysis

6.1 Categories of Polish presence

The language-skill-based professional site

One category emerging from the observations made during the focus-day is the visible and audible instances of Polish as a form of linguistic capital – in Bourdieu's (1991) sense – in professional settings. My co-observers reported on how their language skills in Polish were recognized and included in problem-solving and professional development in their respective workplaces (e.g. co-observer 2, 8.30 pm, 'X specialist asks for help in performing a medical procedure on Polish patient'). Contrary to the observations and descriptions from blue-collar workplaces (see next section), their

Polish language skill is treated as an additional and positive factor on top of and/or intertwined with their professional skills. The co-observers contribute in translation practices as well as the provision of professional networks, and their Polish background is in several ways recognized as a welcoming addition to the work community. This is especially evident in the report from co-observer 1, whose reports on the focus-day reveal her part-time profession as an interpreter. These observations support Obojska's (2018) findings, where young girls express a strong belief in that their knowledge of Polish will give them better chances on future job markets. In this respect, their individual multilingualism empowers them in their potential for professional success.

There is ambivalence at play here, though, in that certain language skills are recognized in parts of the labour market, while perceived as a drawback in others (Kraft 2017). Moreover, the valorized language practices invoke a kind of multilingualism that relies on an individual's ability to code shift between linguistic features associated with different national languages (i.e. 'Polish' and 'Norwegian') in specialized and professional settings. Both co-observers report on such practices, and I include the language-skill-based professional site as a relevant category for the presence of Polish in Norwegian public spaces.

The construction site

My initial observations leading up to – and following – the focus-day contained several instances of Polish presence on construction and renovating sites. Polish was obtained through eavesdropping into conversations between workers, but also through the observation of visual signs, such as the one presented as Figure 5.1. The sign reads 'Close the gate after you' in Norwegian and Polish, hand-written on a robust piece of wood bolted to the fence. The Norwegian version is on top, but the languages are of similar size and content, right down to the inclusion of a smiley. The observations made during the focus-day strengthen the impression of a strong tie between construction workers and Polish language practices. Two of the participants (Table 5.1, main observer at 8.30 am and co-observer 2 at 4.50 pm) notice the presence of Polish at two different construction sites. I myself was only able to register the language practice as 'Polish', whereas my co-observer reported on 'Polish blue-collar workers throwing jokes at each other during work'.

The Polish immigration group consists of a myriad of professions (Iglicka, Gmaj and Wierzejski 2016), but since the 2004 EU enlargement, Poles are primarily associated with and often stereotyped as blue-collar labour migrants (Baba and Dahl-Jørgensen 2010). The stereotype, and to some extent stigmatization, of the Pole as a more or less uneducated, hard-working man with strong work ethics and limited language competence is also evident in media texts (Golden and Opsahl 2019). In the autumn 2014, the NRK released the television drama series *Kampen for tilværelsen* (The struggle of existence), portraying the Polish linguist Tomasz Novak in search of his father. Novak's intellectual background is erased at almost every encounter with Norwegians, who automatically place him as an unskilled, poor construction worker (who at one point is offered a banana because they presume he is hungry). The series ignited a public debate, also involving the Polish ambassador to Norway, criticizing the use of

Figure 5.1 Sign at construction site. 'Close the gate after you' in Norwegian and Polish

outdated stereotypes (Czmur 2014). Regardless of critical voices, the construction sites still seem to be relevant as a category of Polish presence in Norwegian public spaces (Kraft 2017), and such a connection is present in my data set as well.

According to Friberg (2012: 1919), the vision of Poles as particularly hard-working seems to be a widely held notion, and the superior 'work ethic' of Polish labour migrants is a recurrent theme in Norwegian public debate (ibid.), creating a division between 'Polish jobs' and 'Norwegian jobs'. Consequently, work organizations in the construction industry is often separated along lines of language and nationality (Friberg 2012: 1926; Kraft 2017). Friberg (2012) shows a pattern where Polish construction workers only work alongside other Poles and speak Polish only. Both the main observer and co-observer 2 report on Polish language use isolated from other languages. This pattern, which in fact does not render multilingualism, is ambivalent when it comes to the question of empowerment. Friberg (2012) shows how the capital associated with Polish workers' reputation for being particularly hard-working and compliant is available to all Polish workers, irrespective of their individual abilities: 'Even the feeblest, laziest worker can benefit from this reputation as long as he appears to be Polish' (2012: 1929). Hence, being Polish is a valuable asset in the

Norwegian construction industry, and displaying 'Polishness' through monolingual language practice may be used strategically to signal their competitiveness on the labour market. Where multilingualism involving Norwegian and Polish contributed to empowerment in the previous section, monolingual practices seems to be of essence in this case. The strong, migrant blue-collar-worker stereotype is also indirectly present in the next category: the billboard campaign site.

The billboard campaign site

Two of the participating observers point to an advertisement for a telephone company during the focus-day. Co-observer 2 mentions an advertisement on the tram, written in Polish, and the main observer points to a billboard written in Polish (see Figure 5.2). At first sight, the billboard makes little sense for people expecting the languages that dominated the same advertising spaces earlier during spring, that is, Norwegian and English. Paratexts, logos and pictograms point in the direction of a mobile telephone company, however, so the curious passer-by with no competence in Polish may still understand at least who the sender is. The billboard, reading *Bliżej Polski* (Close(r)

Figure 5.2 Billboard campaign, 'Closer to Poland'

to Poland), is an advertisement for a mobile telephone company specializing in affordable and even free calls from Norway to recipients abroad. The billboard is part of a larger campaign advertising free calls to the EU under the slogan 'Closer to home'. Throughout the campaign, iconic Norwegian urban landmarks – such as for instance the Oslo Opera House or the modern architecture typical of the Oslo harbour area – are combined with parallel landmarks and cityscapes from the respective target countries.

The photograph of the iconic Palace of Culture and Science in Warsaw, originally dedicated to Stalin, may invoke Polish associations among observers without Polish language skills. For Poles, the building brings immediate connotations to Warsaw and Poland. The incorporation into the Norwegian cityscape is done both by the placement of the billboards themselves in the urban landscape, as well as through the aforementioned urban landmarks depicted. What is especially interesting in this billboard is that the iconic Norwegian landmark depicted is not in Oslo. The foreground of the Warsaw palace is in fact *Bryggen* (the Hanseatic dock), a UNESCO cultural heritage site in Norway's second-largest urban centre, Bergen. The *Bryggen* image seems to have been further manipulated through an adjustment of the waterline, floating seamlessly into the blue frame colour associated with the company's logo.

Mycall, the company behind the billboard, has received attention, as well as a 'bridge builder' award (Haugen 2013), for their inclusive company policies towards minorities and multilingualism. Their company web page offers three language choices: Norwegian, English or Polish, with rich opportunities to communicate with customer services in Polish. On their Facebook profile, the majority of their posts seem to be in Polish, although English and Norwegian as well as other languages are present. Their use of languages other than Norwegian or English, and especially Polish, seems to be treated as an unmarked choice in their social media appearance, especially on Facebook. The same may be said about their placing Polish billboards across central Oslo.

According to Spolsky (2009), the mixture of languages in advertisement is a result of growing globalization, and a situation where other languages are more likely to be understood, 'and even if not understood, to carry symbolic associations that can be exploited by the sign-maker' (Spolsky 2009: 36). The campaign and the billboard represent a clear example of the inclusion of Polish language as a relevant semiotic resource for public communication in Oslo. While signalling inclusion, ambivalence is also present: the clear incentives of the opportunity of being 'closer to Poland' and calling 'home' signal exclusion, since 'home' logically must be elsewhere. The tension regarding the status and whereabouts of 'home' is reinforced by the integration of a Polish national monument in the Norwegian cityscape, and at the same time widening the scope from the local place, Oslo, to the national context by involving the Norwegian city of Bergen. At one level, the billboard hence illustrates (stereotypical) notions of global migrant experiences more than local inclusion of multiple language practices.

The choice by a company with clear commercial interests to single out Poles as a target group is interesting. Poles' market value is recognized, so to speak. This speaks to the empowerment of individuals, in securing their ability to engage in customized commercial business. At the same time, the connotations of calling home emphasize the status of Poles as 'visitors', feeding the stereotypical image of the (temporary) work migrant. In this light, it is not clear that the symbolic associations carried by the billboard is exploited in an attempt of including customers with various language backgrounds, as Spolsky (2009) suggests for advertising in a globalized world. Rather, the group size is relevant for targeted advertising. Nevertheless, the data from the focus-day as well as other observations point to advertisement as a clear presence of Polish in Norwegian public spaces. The relationship between the multilingualism represented by the billboard campaign site is ambivalent in terms of the question of empowerment, however, a point to which we will return in the discussion section.

The virtual Linguistic Landscape

An in-depth analysis of the role of social media, and a broader digital diaspora, goes way beyond the limits of this chapter. However, all the observers mention social media as examples of the presence of Polish during the focus-day (also when leaving aside the reports on private communication via Messenger mentioned earlier). They all point to publicly shared Facebook posts, including humorous videos, news bulletins and historical sporting events (due to the then upcoming FIFA World Cup). The importance of including this category as an example of the presence of Polish is evident when taking the question of the empowerment of individuals into account. Obojska (2017) shows how digital practices are important for young Polish girls' identity construction and stance-taking, and further how social media can serve as a site where the members of diasporic communities and the members of the homeland societies come into contact and interact with each other. The reports from the two co-observers fit such a description, where Polish is used in phatic communication with close relatives and friends. Facebook contains shared news and clips that often go viral at a speed and in a manner that makes them present in the minds of large populations at the same time, sharing the same space for (transnational) language practices. Each person accesses a tailored and personal version of a Facebook feed and ads. Hence, it is not straightforward to categorize this as a public shared experience. However, some posts are public and accessible to anyone (even those without an account), and these are included as an example of public space. The Polish presence is manifested also on my own Facebook wall (Table 5.1, Main observer 1.00 pm) and is hence not restricted to members of the diasporic community. Another example of Polish presence in virtual LLs is already touched upon, and that is the language choice-options on websites. Language choice buttons may be considered important for empowerment, both in their recognition and visualization of multilingualism (Berezkina 2017), and in their creating the opportunity for the individual to engage in their language(s) of choice.

I have only access to the reported social media interactions, and no documentation of the interactions themselves (except for my own, which included a short video of a sporting event and a tourism advertising post shared by a Polish friend). One observation worth mentioning is how the linguistic practices I observed on Facebook seem to be free of any signs of code mixing. The use of Polish, English and Norwegian are typically kept strictly apart. This is a point also made by Obojska (2017).

The missing fifth and sixth site

A potential site for Polish presence in Norwegian public places is the religious site. An indication of the relevance of looking into religious sites is the list of Catholic masses held in St. Olav's cathedral in Oslo's city centre. Polish is the second-most frequent choice of language for the saying of masses during the week, after Norwegian and before English and Vietnamese. The website katolsk.no, the official portal for Catholics in Norway, has an information banner in Polish on its front page (contributing to the point made above, of including the virtual LL in the overall picture of the presence of Polish). Polish seems to play a fundamental role in the Catholic congregations in Oslo, but the observers mention no such practices on the focus-day.

As mentioned earlier, the three observers were all members of two-person households. This is an important point, because none of us was likely to notice Polish in schools and/or children's culture and practices, which may represent a site for Polish presence. There exist some reports on the use of parallel language signing in public schools (Bygdås 2016), but as was mentioned in the introduction, a notion of invisibility is mentioned by educational researchers. The Norwegian school has long been regarded as an important factor in reducing social differences through an ideology of 'the unitarity school' (e.g. Telhaug 1994). Norwegian egalitarianism may be one possible explanation for the invisibility of the Polish children's immigrant status, Wærdahl (2016: 104) suggests, pointing to the attempt to focus on similarities and create 'sameness' as 'another way of containing diversity and maintaining the egalitarian Norwegian self-image'. Based on the existing research (e.g. Bygdås 2016; Slany and Struzik 2016; Wærdahl 2016) it is safe to suggest that also the schoolscape contains an element of ambivalence regarding the presence of Polish. Neither the reports from the focus-day observations nor the other observations in the data set can complement this picture, so this remains as an important task for future research.

7. Summary of findings

Polish is not invisible in Norwegian public spaces. The observations have revealed that Polish is present both at construction sites and in other professional contexts. An advertising campaign in Polish was observed twice during the focus-day. In addition, Polish seems to have a strong presence in semi-public language practices on social media sites such as Facebook. Relative to the size of the population, the presence still must be considered limited. A year has passed since the focus-day presented above. When asking my co-observers today whether they are of the impression that things have changed since then, one of them responds as follows (translated from Norwegian): 'There is Polish everywhere: public transport, shops (my local bakery probably only employs Poles!), at work, and so on and so forth. And right now, as we speak, I am watching CNN, listening to President Duda speaking Polish.' The other co-observer agrees and points to even more translation assignments, more Polish-Norwegian romantic couples among her acquaintances, more Polish films in cinemas.

She also points to how Polish tourist destinations become increasingly popular, creating a stronger link between Norway and Poland. Without going so far as to claim that 'there is Polish everywhere', I myself have observed several additional examples of Polish presence in public space. The first restaurant in Oslo serving Polish specialties, *U'mamy*, has been established. The National Theatre's production of a play based on Wisława Szymborska's poems was presented with Polish subtitles and framed with texts in Polish, both on the theatre's website and social media sites (Nationaltheatret 2018). Additional *Mycall*-campaigns have regularly appeared during the year, on billboards, trams and metro stations, and Polish has appeared – alongside other migrant languages – in a billboard campaign for milk cartons from one of the largest dairy producers in Norway. An airport transportation company uses vehicles covered with Polish information, and so on and so forth. Some of these instantiations of Polish in Norwegian public spaces may have been present during the time of the collection of the data presented above and overlooked because of the limitations associated with the design of the field observations. At the same time, my co-observers seem to share my own feeling of an increased presence of Polish.

At least two important points emerge from the cases where Polish appears as especially visible in the data set from the focus-day, and they should be brought into the discussion, since they both relate to the question of empowerment. These points are interrelated and regards the question of multilingualism and the question of stereotypes and available identities. The 'Closer to Poland' billboard campaign and the construction sites, add – to some extent – to a stereotypical image of the (blue-collar) visiting working migrant more than representing an integral part of the local public space. The data create an impression of Polish identities existing parallel to, rather than integrated into, the Norwegian shared public space. Building on the theoretical assumptions presented earlier, one may claim that despite the presence of Polish in public spaces, there are few examples of Polish-Norwegian multilingual public *places*. The billboard, although playing with a level of polyphonic presence of other languages used in the wider campaign, was solely in Polish. The observations of Polish at the construction sites on the focus-day were of Polish with no other languages visible or audible. The observations of the recognition of Polish in professional lives were connected to instances of complete code shifts. Hence, Polish language seems to exist parallel to, and to a lesser degree close to or intertwined with, Norwegian (and other languages) in public spaces. We have also seen traces of ambivalence between the presence of Polish in public space and the maintenance of multilingualism, which should be discussed further. One of the research questions was whether multilingualism is protective of distinctive cultural identities or erodes them. This seems to be a highly relevant question in the Polish-Norwegian context, where the agency of some individual citizens seems to be restricted by strong expectations based on stereotypes directly linked to success at the job market.

8. Discussion

8.1 Mutually reinforcing ideologies

The relationship between multilingualism and empowerment of individuals calls for an investigation of dominant language ideologies. Whereas Norway often has been highlighted as a sociolinguistic 'paradise' (Røyneland 2009), with rich socio-geographic variation and great tolerance towards linguistic diversity, Polish dialects are perceived almost exclusively negatively, and are associated with low education levels and social status (Garbacz 2014). Poland is traditionally seen as a country with a strong standard ideology, where language practices are directly related to ethnic belonging and national identity (Garbacz 2014; Obojska 2018). Different language policies are arguably governing the presence of different languages in the public space (e.g. Blackwood and Tufi 2012). Quist (2018: 241) points to how it is deeply rooted in European ideology to think of speakers and their languages as symbolically linked to cultures and places: 'It is embedded in the ways we speak about language, speakers and places: People in the place named Denmark are called Danes and their language Danish, symbolically indicating an internal coherence between them'. However, the connection between people, places and languages can easily be deconstructed, Quist claims, pointing to the fact that people are engaged in practices involving several national 'languages', and that 'national languages' are widely in use outside of the respective nation states.

The supposed Norwegian openness towards linguistic diversity does not seem to include (all forms of) hybrid linguistic practices, or practices associated with another 'nation language', and resistance against Polish-Norwegian language practices is reinforced by dominant Polish ideologies. The connection between national and linguistic identity seems to be kept very much alive among Poles in Norway. Obojska (2017) portrays how young Polish girls tend to respond negatively to the use of Norwegian in Polish in-group settings, for instance online, where the choice of Norwegian connotes 'people lacking pride and respect for their origins and essentially lacking in "Polishness"' (Obojska 2017: 36). Young girls plan to transfer the Polish language to their future children out of a strong sense of obligation towards the mother tongue, responsive to a one nation-one language ideology, and they call on Polish national discourses to motivate their current and future language choices (Obojska 2018: 88; Obojska and Purkarthofer 2018: 259). According to Leinonen and Toivanen (2014: 163), the way the Nordic nations imagine themselves relies on ideas of cultural, religious and – to a certain extent – linguistic homogeneity. Associations between language and identity are rooted in cultural beliefs and values – that is, ideologies – 'about the sorts of speakers who (can or should) produce particular sorts of language' (Bucholtz and Hall 2010: 2). The ideological views associated with homogeneity are in line with a drift towards the attempt to focus on similarities and create 'sameness' to maintain an egalitarian self-image, as suggested for the 'invisible' status of Polish children in schools (Wærdahl 2016: 104). Monolingual and to some extent purist ideologies are at play in the Norwegian linguistic community (Mæhlum 2011). Conformity to linguistic practices associated with the community is often preferred. Bi-dialectal speakers, for instance, are shown to deliberately flee the risk of being spotted as dialect speakers in the 'wrong' contexts, hence turning to a sort of invisibility strategy (van Ommeren 2016).

A relatively strict separation of language practices associated with 'Polish' and 'Norwegian' (or other languages) is in other words in accordance with ideologies present in both societies. The strong connection between national and linguistic identity may serve as an explanatory factor for the somewhat limited and/or isolated character of the cases of Polish presence in the data, creating an image not so much of multilingualism as of the use of different languages in different settings. There may of course be methodological reasons for the few examples of multilingual presence, but the findings resonate well with previous research. In this light, the presence of Polish in Norwegian public spaces is creating an impression of a Polish space, alongside a Norwegian space, more than that of a multilingual place.

8.2 Reinforcing stereotypes

We have seen how the presence of Polish in public spaces feeds the stereotypical perception of the Polish blue-collar worker. Despite critical voices such as Czmur (2014), a strong stereotype connecting Poles and Polish to the performance of simple, manual labour at construction sites is still alive. This is most probably also connected to a gendered dimension. Most of the young boys in Obojska's studies (2018) had a history of exclusion or bullying at school, where they reported on being called names based on jobs associated with low-skilled 'immigrant' labour. A somewhat subtle example of a reinforcement of this stereotype is found in my data as well, in the reported observations from co-observer 2. At 11.35 am she reports how a 'work colleague jokes about my Polish heritage when asking for practical help'. The impression of Poles as being the ones 'getting things fixed' has also been evident in stereotypical and/or humorous portrayals in the media for two decades (Golden and Opsahl 2019; Slåke 2018).

Some researchers have pointed to patterns where the labour market seems unwilling to accept Poles' entry into other sectors of the labour force (Iglicka, Gmaj and Wierzejski 2016: 129). Moreover, temporary workers are largely selected based on the Polish stereotype, and stereotypes become a self-fulfilling prophecy, where 'workers act in a way that meets employers' expectations' (Iglicka, Gmaj and Wierzejski 2016: 123). Turning to the question of empowerment, and as addressed previously with reference to Friberg (2012), the situation remains ambivalent since Poles (are forced to) exploit the stereotypes in order to succeed in the labour market. As pointed to by Kraft (2017), these strategical moves only succeed to a certain point. There are jobs and tasks only available for the Norwegian-speaking part of the work force. Following Kraft (2017) we may say that it is language skills rather than professional skills that determine opportunities for the workers with Polish background. The process of acquiring specific multilingual linguistic skills may represent an asset for workers, as seemed to be the case for the co-observers providing data to the present study. Multilingualism also creates a restriction on professional opportunities for those who choose not to or are unable to engage in certain kinds of multilingual practices. Hence, some professional arenas, such as construction sites, in as far as they are observable for the public when travelling through the city, is an arena used to delegitimize specific (linguistic) groups. In this light, it is not surprising that some Polish migrants find it important to separate themselves from the Polish group identity, even when such practices may involve discursive hostility towards co-ethnics (Eade, Drinkwater and Garapich 2007: 16). This may be an additional explanatory factor as to the limited cases of Polish presence. Existing heterogeneity – as well as existing language differentiation – undergoes semiotic processes of erasure (Irvine and Gal 2000) causing one-dimensional prototypical identities, which in turn may render communicative challenges for the maintenance of multilingualism. This, in turn, could have a negative effect on other kinds of professions, where individual multilingualism is considered an asset. While the use of Polish adds to the impression of some degree of multilingualism in public space, which empowers individuals through their inclusion into the job market and to their financial security, there is a tension at play towards the maintenance of multilingualism. Not all forms of visibility are necessarily desirable, and certain languages can be reduced by being visible in less empowering ways. The opportunity or space available for negotiating contesting identities and create meaningful places of belonging seems narrow. Obojska (2018) suggests that stereotypes may affect the relationship of young Polish transnationals towards the heritage language and, 'in the long run, also influence the maintenance of Polish in diasporic communities' (Obojska 2018: 82).

8.3 Market forces prevail

Berezkina (2012) and Stjernholm (2013) point to customization and market logic as a reason for the under-representation of languages other than Norwegian and English in the urban LL of inner Oslo. Turning this around, the Polish presence – as demonstrated through the data – can be seen as an expression of language economy and potential profit (Cenoz and Gorter 2009; Duchêne and Heller 2012). The relative size and presence of Poles in Norway make them a suitable target for the construction of a niche market, which must be reached in certain languages and certain communicative styles (Heller and Duchêne 2012: 11). Polish is not necessarily acting as a source of symbolic added value, but literally as marketing authenticity opposite a Polish consumer identity. This was suggested for the billboard campaign site above, as an expression of clear commercial interests. Poles are singled out as a target group with a recognizable market value. The clearest examples of Polish presence in Norwegian public spaces are cases where – to borrow Heller and Duchêne's (2012) dichotomy – 'profit' rather than 'pride' is at stake. The visibility of Polish seems to depend on the language's market value. This value and commodity of the Polish language are to be understood not only symbolically but also economically.

The large group of people with Polish language competence make up a potential group of consumers and a niche market – for instance, for telephone companies and participants in institutional encounters, such as medical procedures in state hospitals, as illustrated in the focus-day data. The close relationship between Polish and renovation and construction sites can also be understood in light of an economic logic, since the strong stereotype maintains an expectation of 'getting the job done', that is, in an economically profitable way. Herein lies again an ambivalence of Polish presence. One may ask whether such stereotypes are typical for Polish migrants per se or whether it applies to groups of labourers from other countries. Friberg (2012: 1929) refers to the fact that many of his Polish respondents were aware that they were competing with other groups of workers in the Norwegian labour market: 'In order to maintain their position, they were dependent on their reputation, as Poles, for having a particularly strong work ethos' (ibid.). Still, it is not impossible that a slow yet evolving recognition of other qualifications is a factor, and that we may be facing a more multifaceted image of Poles in Norway in the near future. Examples of resistance towards the strong stereotype from professionals who have carved out alternative Polish-Norwegian identities exist. I witnessed one case of anecdotal evidence of this a few weeks ago. A colleague with Polish background shared a picture on Facebook, of a sign in Oslo, providing information for customers in Norwegian, English and Polish, side by side, in equally sized and shaped letters. His comment made it clear that this type of language practice in Norwegian public space was not something he embraced, as he read the inclusion of Polish as a signal of a lower expectancy of linguistic competence among Poles. The presence of Polish was interpreted as a case of marginalization more than of empowerment. This case also points to how questions of empowerment can only be answered satisfactorily by including the individual, as interpretative subjects and agents, in the investigation of how public spaces transform into multilingual public places.

9. Concluding remarks

The multilingualism observed in this study, as well as in the previous research reviewed throughout the chapter, is in many ways protective of distinctive identities. Identities associated with the stereotypical professional lives of citizens with Polish backgrounds, and their role as consumers in global as well as local markets, are the most prominent traces of Polish in public spaces. The close connection between language and labour may at first glance be seen as a positive sign of empowerment of individuals. On the other hand, the agency of individuals in terms of their daily use of language is challenged when the presence of Polish in professional domains continue to feed and maintain stereotypical images of 'available' identities, depending not only on a symbolic value, but also on market economy.

The examples of Polish presence presented in this study add to an overall impression of Poles and Polish being a relevant market for economic exchange. The presence of Polish equals potential economic profit. At the same time, the increased amount of cultural expressions and encounters, such as the theatrical and gastronomical sites, and the reports of sporting, literary and musical expressions, point to a stronger sense also of 'pride' in addition to mere 'profit' (cf. Heller and Duchêne 2012). An increased symbolic added value to the presence of Polish may be underway. Space and places are in a way full-fledged 'speakers' in their own right (Gorter, Marten and Van Mensel 2011), and there is a good chance that public spaces in Norway continue to speak Polish in the future. A stronger presence of Polish in public spaces may potentially tear down some hindrances for the negotiation of alternative Polish-Norwegian identities. This, however, involves a risk of a stronger entanglement with Norwegian and a violation of dominant national language ideologies, seen from both a Norwegian and Polish perspective. The separation of language practices associated with 'Norwegian' and 'Polish' may seem necessary for maintaining social cohesion and the maintenance of dominant language ideologies. Seen from an individual's perspective, strong language ideologies of the one-nation-one-language kind may complicate opportunities for social mobility and well-being. Hence, the presence of Polish in Norwegian public spaces – in both visible, often domain-specific forms and more invisible forms – continues to raise important questions of integration and the empowerment of individuals.

Note

1. This work was partly supported by the Research Council of Norway through its Centres of Excellence funding scheme, project number 223265 and 302219. I wish to thank Luk Van Mensel, the reviewers and editors for invaluable input, and I am grateful to my co-observers, and to Anne Golden, Paweł K. Urbanik and my other colleagues at MultiLing, University of Oslo.

References

Aarsæther, F. (2010), 'The Use of Multiethnic Youth Language in Oslo', in P. Quist and B. A. Svendsen (eds), *Multilingual Urban Scandinavia: New Linguistic Practices*, 111–26, Clevedon, UK: Multilingual Matters.

Baba, M. L., and Dahl-Jørgensen, C. (2010), 'Work Migration from Poland to Norway: A New Institutional Approach', *iNtergraph: Journal of Dialogic Anthropology*, 2 (2). Available online: http://intergraph-journal.net/enhanced/vol2issue2/2.html (accessed 29 July 2018).

Barni, M., and Bagna, C. (2015), 'The Critical Turn in LL: New Methodologies and New Items in LL', *Linguistic Landscape*, 1 (1–2): 6–18.

Ben-Rafael, E. (2009), 'A Sociological Approach to the Study of Linguistic Landscapes', in E. Shohamy and D. Gorter (eds), *Linguistic Landscape: Expanding the Scenery*, 40–54, New York: Routledge.

Ben-Rafael, E., Shohamy, E., and Barni, M. (2010), 'Introduction', in E. Shohamy, E. Ben-Rafael and M. Barni (eds), *Linguistic Landscape in the City*, xi–xxviii, Clevedon, UK: Multilingual Matters.

Berezkina, M. (2012), 'Lingvistisk landskap i et av Oslos flerkulturelle områder', in T. Schmidt (ed.), *Målblomar til Margit. Veneskrift til Margit Harsson på 70-årsdagen den 9. juni 2013*, 19–34, Oslo: Novus.

Berezkina, M. (2017), 'Multilingual State Websites in Estonia and Norway. A Study of Language Policy in New Media', PhD diss., Department of Linguistics and Scandinavian Studies, University of Oslo, Oslo.

Berezkina, M. (2018), 'Language Is a Costly and Complicating Factor: A Diachronic Study of Language Policy in the Virtual Public Sector', *Language Policy*, 17 (1): 55–75.

Berg, A.-J. (2008), 'Silence and Articulation – Whiteness, Racialization and Feminist Memory Work', *Nordic Journal of Feminist and Gender Research*, 16 (4): 213–27.

Bjorvatn, D. K. (2015), 'Slang i norsk. Forskningskampanjen 2014', MA diss., University of Oslo, Oslo.

Blackwood, R., and Tufi, S. (2012), 'Policies vs. Non-policies: Analysing Regional Languages and the National Standard in the Linguistic Landscape of French and Italian Mediterranean Cities', in D. Gorter, H. Marten and L. Van Mensel (eds), *Minority Languages in the Linguistic Landscape*, 109–26, Basingstoke: Palgrave Macmillan.

Blommaert, J., and Maly, I. (2014), 'Ethnographic Linguistic Landscape Analysis and Social Change: A Case Study', *Working Papers in Urban Language & Literacies*, WP133, London: King's College.

Bourdieu, P. (1991), *Language and Symbolic Power*. Cambridge: Polity Press.

Bucholtz, M., and Hall, K. (2010), 'Locating Identity in Language', in C. Llamas and D. Watt (eds), *Language and Identities*, 18–28, Edinburgh: Edinburgh University Press.

Bygdås, M. E. (2016), 'Fra Warszawa til Oslo: Språkvalg og identiteter hos polsk-norske ungdommer', MA diss., University of Oslo, Oslo.

Cenoz, J., and Gorter, D. (2009), 'Language Economy and Linguistic Landscape', in E. Shohamy and D. Gorter (eds), *Linguistic Landscape. Expanding the Scenery*, 55–69, New York: Routledge.

Cornips, L., and de Rooj, V. (2018), 'Introduction', in L. Cornips and V. de Rooj (eds), *The Sociolinguistics of Place and Belonging. Perspectives from the Margins*, Studies in Language and Society 45, 1–16, Amsterdam: John Benjamins.

Czmur, S. (2014), 'Basert på foreldede stereotypier om Polen', *Aftenposten*, 9 October. Available online: https://www.aftenposten.no/meninger/debatt/i/1kw3J/Basert-pa-foreldede-stereotypier-om-Polen (accessed 27 July 2018).

Duchêne, A., and Heller, M. (eds) (2012), *Language in Late Capitalism. Pride and Profit*, New York: Routledge.

Eade, P. J, Drinkwater, D. S., and Garapich, M. (2007), *Class and Ethnicity – Polish Migrants in London*. University of Surrey: Centre for Research on Nationalism, Ethnicity and Multiculturalism. Available online: https://www.surrey.ac.uk/cronem/projects/polish/class_and_ethnicity_polish_migrant_workers_in_london.htm (accessed 27 July 2018).

Edelman, L. (2009), 'What's in a Name? Classification of Proper Names by Language', in E. Shohamy and D. Gorter (eds), *Linguistic Landscape: Expanding the Scenery*, 141–54. New York: Routledge.

Friberg, J. H. (2012), 'Culture at Work: Polish Migrants in the Ethnic Division Labour on Norwegian Construction Sites', *Ethnic and Racial Studies*, 35 (11): 1914–33.

Friberg, J. H., and Golden, A. (2014), 'Norges største innvandrergruppe: Historien om migrasjon fra Polen til Norge og om andrespråkskorpuset ASK', *NOA. Norsk som andrespråk*, 30 (2): 11–23.

Friberg, J. H., Dølvik, J. E., and Eldring, L. (2013), *Arbeidsmigrasjon til Norge fra Øst- og Sentral-Europa*. VAM Temanotat. Oslo: Research Council Norway.

Garbacz, P. (2014), 'Dialekter i Norge og Polen: forskjellig status?', *NOA. Norsk som andrespråk*, 30 (2): 24–39.

Godzimirski, J. M. (2011), 'Polsk diaspora og norsk utenrikspolitikk', *Internasjonal Politikk*, 69 (4): 617–43.

Golden, A., and Opsahl, T. (2019), 'Norsk er norsk og polsk er polsk – «and never the twain shall meet»?', Paper presented at the 14th conference on Nordic Languages as a Second Language, Copenhagen, 27–9 May 2019.

Golden, A., and Tenfjord, K. (2014), 'Møte mellom polsk og norsk i Norge', *NOA. Norsk som andrespråk*, 30 (2): 5–9.
Golden, A., Jarvis S., and Tenfjord, K. (eds) (2017), *Crosslinguistic Influence and Distinctive Patterns of Language Learning: Findings and Insights from a Learner Corpus*. Bristol: Multilingual Matters.
Gorter, D., Marten, H. F., and Van Mensel, L. (eds) (2012), *Minority Languages in the Linguistic Landscape*. Basingstoke: Palgrave Macmillan.
Guðjónsdóttir, G. (2014), ' "We Blend in with the Crowd but They Don't" – (In)visibility and Icelandic Migrants in Norway', *Nordic Journal of Migration Research*, 4 (4): 176–83.
Gullestad, M. (2002), 'Invisible Fences: Egalitarianism, Nationalism and Racism', *Journal of the Royal Anthropological Institute*, 8 (2): 45–63.
Haugen, V. (2013), 'Mycall vinner brobyggerpris'. Available online: https://www.tek.no/artikler/mycall-vinner-brobyggerpris/135951 (accessed 29 July 2018).
Heller, M. (2010), 'The Commodification of Language', *Annual Review of Anthropology*, 39: 101–14.
Heller M., and Duchêne, A. (2012), 'Pride and Profit: Changing Discourses of Language, Capital and Nation-State', in A. Duchêne and M. Heller (eds), *Language in Late Capitalism. Pride and Profit*, 1–21, New York: Routledge.
Horbowicz, P. (2010), *How to Be Norwegian in Talk? Polish–Norwegian Interethnic Conversation Analysis*. Oslo: Novus Press.
Iglicka, K., Gmaj, K., and Wierzejski, A. (2016), 'The Poles in Norway: We Wanted Workers but People Arrived', *Myśl Ekonomiczna i Polityczna*, 1 (52): 116–38.
Irvine, J., and Gal, S. (2000), 'Language Ideology and Linguistic Differentiation', in P. V. Kroskrity (ed.), *Regimes of Language: Ideologies, Polities, and Identities*, 35–83, Santa Fe, NM: School of American Research Press.
Janik, M. (2017), 'Positive and Negative Transfer in the L2 Adjective Inflection of English-, German- and Polish-speaking learners of L2 Norwegian', in A. Golden, S. Jarvis and K. Tenfjord (eds), *Crosslinguistic Influence and Distinctive Patterns of Language Learning: Findings and Insights from a Learner Corpus*, 84–109, Bristol, UK: Multilingual Matters.
Kerfoot, C., and Hyltenstam, K. (2017), 'Introduction. Entanglement and Orders of Visibility', in Kerfoot, C. and K. Hyltenstam (eds), *Entangled Discourses. South-North Orders of Visibility*, 1–15, New York: Routledge.
Kraft, K. (2017), 'Constructing Migrant Workers: Multilingualism and Communication in the Transnational Construction Site', PhD diss., Department of Linguistics and Scandinavian Studies, University of Oslo, Oslo.
Landry, R., and Bourhis, R. Y. (1997), 'Linguistic Landscape and Ethnolinguistic Vitality: An Empirical Study', *Journal of Language and Social Psychology*, 16 (1): 24–49.
Leinonen, J. (2012), 'Invisible Immigrants, Visible Expats? Americans in Finnish Discourses on Immigration and Internationalization', *Nordic Journal of Migration Research*, 2 (3): 213–23.
Leinonen, J., and Toivanen, M. (2014), 'Researching In/Visibility in the Nordic Context: Theoretical and Empirical Views', *Nordic Journal of Migration Research*, 4 (4): 161–67.
Ministry of Culture (2020), 'Prop. 108 L (2019 – 2020), Proposisjon til Stortinget (forslag til lovvedtak), Lov om Språk (Språklova) [The Language Law Proposition]', Oslo: Ministry of Culture.

Mæhlum, B. K. (1998), 'Talemålsendring. En presentasjon av prosjektet TEIN, Talemålsendring i Norge', *RISS: magasin for studentar og tilsette ved Institutt for nordistikk og litteraturvitskap*, Trondheim: Universitetet i Trondheim.

Mæhlum, B. K. (2011), 'Det "ureine" språket: forsøk på en kultursemiotisk og vitenskapsteoretisk analyse', *Maal og Minne*, 1: 1–31.

Nationaltheatret [the Norwegian National Theatre] (2018), 'Życie – jedyny sposób'. Available online: https://www.nationaltheatret.no/forestillinger/livet-er-den-enestematen/ycie-jedyny-sposob (accessed 17 June 2019).

NSD Data Protection Official for Research (2018), 'Should I Notify NSD about My Project?'. Available online: http://www.nsd.uib.no/personvernombud/en/notify/index.html (accessed 29 July 2018).

Obojska, M. A. (2017), '"Are You so Ashamed to Come from Poland and to Speak Your Mother Tongue?" – Metalinguistic Talk, Identities and Language Ideologies in Teenagers' Interactions on ASKfm', *Multilingual Margins*, 4 (1): 27–39.

Obojska, M. A. (2018), 'Between Duty and Neglect: Language Ideologies and Stancetaking among Polish Adolescents in Norway', *Lingua*, 298: 82–97.

Obojska, M. A., and Purkarthofer, J. (2018), '"And All of a Sudden, It Became My Rescue": Language and Agency in Transnational Families in Norway', *International Journal of Multilingualism*, 15 (3): 249–61.

Ommeren, R. van (2016), 'Den flerstemmige språkbrukeren: en sosiolingvistisk studie av norske bidialektale', PhD diss., University of Trondheim NTNU, Trondheim.

Opsahl, T. (2009), 'Wolla I Swear This Is Typical for the Conversational Style of Adolescents in Multiethnic Areas in Oslo', *Nordic Journal of Linguistics*, 32 (2): 221–44.

Opsahl, T, Garbacz, P., Golden, A. Svennevig, J. (eds) (2019), 'Second-Language Communication in Workplace Settings – the Case of Polish Migrants in Norway (NorPol)', project proposal presented to the Research council of Norway, University of Oslo, Department of Linguistics and Scandinavian studies. Available online: https://prosjektbanken.forskningsradet.no/#/project/NFR/302219 (accessed 29 May 2020).

Quist, P. (2018), 'Alternative Place Naming in the Diverse Margins of an Ideologically Mono-Lingual Society', in L. Cornips and V. de Rooj (eds), *The Sociolinguistics of Place and Belonging. Perspectives from the margins*, Studies in Language and Society 45, 239–58, Amsterdam: John Benjamins.

Rosa, J., and Flores, N. (2017), 'Unsettling Race and Language: Toward a Raciolinguistic Perspective', *Language in Society*, 46 (5): 621–47.

Røyneland, U. (2009), 'Dialects in Norway: Catching Up with the Rest of Europe?', *International Journal of the Sociology of Language*, 196 (7): 7–31.

Shohamy, E., and Gorter, D. (2009), 'Introduction', in E. Shohamy and D. Gorter (eds), *Linguistic Landscape. Expanding the View*, 1–10, New York: Routledge.

Schröter, M., and Taylor, C. (2018), 'Introduction', in M. Schröter and C. Taylor (eds), *Exploring Silence and Absence in Discourse. Empirical Approaches*, 1–22, Basingstoke: Palgrave Macmillan.

Slåke, A. L. (2018), 'Portraying a Major Minority in Televised Public Service Broadcasting. Portrayal of Polish Immigrants in the Norwegian Broadcasting Corporation', MA diss., Department of Information Science and Media Studies, University of Bergen, Bergen.

Slany, K., and Struzik, J. (eds) (2016), *Doing Family in a Transnational Context. Demographic Choices, Welfare Adaptations, School Integration and Every-day Life of Polish Families Living in Polish-Norwegian Transnationality*. Krakow: Jagiellonian University.

Spolsky, B. (2009), 'Prolegomena to a Sociolinguistic Theory of Public Signage', in E. Shohamy and D. Gorter (eds), *Linguistic Landscape. Expanding the View*, 25–39, New York: Routledge.

SSB Statistics Norway (2019), 'Lower Growth in the Number of Immigrants', 5 March. Available online: https://www.ssb.no/en/befolkning/artikler-og-publikasjoner/lower-growth-in-the-number-of-immigrants (accessed 19 July 2019).

Stjernholm, K. (2013), 'Stedet velger ikke lenger deg, du velger et sted. Tre artikler om språk i Oslo', PhD diss., Department of Linguistics and Scandinavian Studies, University of Oslo, Oslo.

Svendsen, B. A., and Røyneland, U. (2008), 'Multiethnolectal Facts and Functions in Oslo, Norway', *International Journal of Bilingualism*, 12 (1–2): 63–83.

Szymańska, O. (2017), 'On How Polish Learners of Norwegian Render Spatial Prepositions in L2: A Corpus-Based Study of i and på', in A. Golden, S. Jarvis and K. Tenfjord (eds), *Crosslinguistic Influence and Distinctive Patterns of Language Learning: Findings and Insights from a Learner Corpus*, 64–83, Bristol, UK: Multilingual Matters.

Telhaug, A. O. (1994), *Utdanningspolitikken og enhetsskolen. Studier i 1990-årenes Utdanningspolitikk*, Oslo: Didakta.

Thurlow, C., and Jaworski, A. (2010), 'Silence Is Golden: The "Anti-Communicational" Linguascaping of Super-Elite Mobility', in A. Jaworski and C. Thurlow (eds), *Semiotic Landscapes: Language, Image, Space*, 187–218, London: Continuum.

Urbanik, P. (2017), 'Requests in Polish and Norwegian Informal Conversation: A Comparative Study of Grammatical and Pragmatic Patterns', PhD diss., Department of Linguistics and Scandinavian Studies, University of Oslo, Oslo.

Urbanik, P. (2020), 'Getting Others to Share Goods in Polish and Norwegian: Material and Moral Anchors for Request Conventions', *Intercultural Pragmatics*, 17 (2): 177–220.

Wærdahl, R. (2016), 'The Invisible Immigrant Child in the Norwegian Classroom: Losing Sight of Polish Children's Immigrant Status through Unarticulated Differences and Behind Good Intentions', *Central and Eastern European Migration Review*, 5 (1): 93–108.

6

Place names and the complexity of language recognition in Northern Ireland

Deirdre A. Dunlevy

1. Introduction

Northern Ireland is a divided society in which there is ongoing debate around the role of languages that can become a proxy for identity and cultural issues. The Irish language is traditionally associated with the Nationalist community; conversely, for many in the Protestant, Unionist, Loyalist community, Ulster-Scots is a crucial part of their identity. Consequently, support for the two languages has divided political parties and the communities from which they draw their support.

Since the collapse of the Stormont assembly in Northern Ireland from January 2017 to January 2020, division around demands for an Irish Language Act (ILA) was cited as the main stumbling block to the restoration of government. Central to the discourse around the introduction of legislation supporting the Irish language was the issue of its visibility in the Linguistic Landscape (henceforth LL); for communities that do not identify with what they perceive the language to symbolize politically, legitimization of this kind is deeply problematic. Bilingual signage is particularly contentious, and the fear of imposition of such signage across the whole of Northern Ireland as a consequence of an Irish Language Act is seen to be divisive and antagonistic.

This chapter focuses on the complexities of minoritized language recognition in the LL of Northern Ireland and the inclusion or exclusion of different forms of naming (in English, Irish and Ulster-Scots) on place-name and street-name signage. Through an examination of local council language management policies, and the analysis of LL data from council areas that promote an inclusive policy, I question to what extent the display of multilingualism in the form of inclusion of some or all of the languages of Northern Ireland can empower individuals and groups, or in what ways the public space is used to delegitimize specific groups through exclusion in the official signs visible in the LL.

2. Linguistic Landscapes and place-name signage

Studies in onomastics have long considered the key role of place names in the formation of identity at both an individual and societal level. The study of the etymology of place names can uncover geographical, historical, folkloric and local histories of an area, which enriches the understanding of an area and can help to build a sense of identity and belonging in an area (see Ó Mainnín, this volume). As such, signage is seen as the physical manifestation of these histories in an area, the importance of which is echoed in the numerous naming societies and discussions around place names and place-name signage in towns and cities across the globe (see Puzey 2016).

The central role of street names and place names has long been attested in LL studies (Spolsky and Cooper 1991; Landy and Bourhis 1997; Puzey 2009; Järlehed 2017) and as the field has expanded to include newer modes of signage and spheres including the internet, the centrality of place-name and street-name signs to the study of the LL is still pertinent (Gorter and Cenoz 2015). The genre of the toponomastic sign is of prominence in the LL as it is salient in most public spaces, regardless of size, is recognizable as a relatively standardized element of the LL, and, as Blackwood (2015: 42) notes, such signs 'have been emblematic of multilingualism in the public space whilst, simultaneously, achieving prominence in the eyes of the wider public'. It is a marker of official language policy which helps to construct identity perception. Street-name and place-name signs act as functional tools for navigating space, informing the reader of the languages used in an area as well as how the space is organized. They also serve a symbolic function tied to identity and belonging for the community and implement regulatory government policies regarding language use and visibility. Puzey (2009: 823) suggests that 'the function of place-names as markers of identity is a clear indication of the role of place-names in many linguistic landscapes, and not least in those that are contested'. Naming is particularly relevant in the context of Northern Ireland. Due to the contentious status of Irish and Ulster-Scots, the most prevalent manifestation of these languages in the public space is in toponymy and onomastic signage, which is further complicated by the process of anglicization (and re-gaelicization) of Irish place names. Dal Negro (2009: 208) suggests that 'probably nothing is more symbolic for a community than its own name, and in fact place-names, in particular the names of towns and villages, have long been the tangible expression of political power and of subsequent anti-State struggles'. This is evident in the documented acts of transgression on place-name signage which indicate the significance of language display of toponymy to a community. By interacting with the visual display of a place name or street name, the actor is indicating the importance to them of the form in which the name is displayed. In Northern Ireland, the choice of language and linguistic form of the place name is tied to identity. As such, the visual representation of a place name that goes against one's sense of identity (such as the Irish form of a place name in a largely Unionist area) will often lead to acts of transgression and attempts to remove that unit from the LL, rather than having the place name displayed in a language with which that person does not identify. As such, the public space in Northern Ireland embodies an arena where subtle plays of tension become apparent.

Järlehed (2017) outlines the functions of the street-name sign as being threefold. According to Järlehed, the street-name sign serves an urban administration and governance function by enabling the authorities to account for individuals (for census, tax, etc.). The most salient function of the street-name is that of identification and orientation; through the visibility of the sign, the sign reader can orient themselves in the public space and identify their location. The third function, the commemorative and place-making function of the signage, is central to this chapter; through this function, the sign-makers (usually the government authorities in the case of street-name signs) can 'inscribe their version of history into the everyday urban environment' (Järlehed 2017). This can be achieved through the naming of a street or area after particular historical or political figures but also, and central to the linguistic tensions in Northern Ireland, through the choice of language display and order on the place-name or street-name sign. In a community where multilingualism is taken to also represent the binary sectarian divisions, such linguistic choices are indexical of the authorities' attitude towards the minoritized languages in a place.

The role played by a minority language in society can be interpreted by an exploration of the LL; as Marten (2012: 19) suggests, 'LL as a method can contribute to the understanding of the functions that a regional or minority language is assigned to in the ethnolinguistic composition of a region and the underlying language ideology'. It informs the viewer of the existence of a minority language in the area and reveals information about the status of that language in the community, if it is dominant in the LL, or if it is secondary in signage to a more dominant majority language. Gorter (2006: 86) recognizes that 'in bilingual countries or regions signage can also be of great symbolic importance and dispute. In particular the use of place-names in a minority language or in the dominant state language has been a regular issue of linguistic conflict'. The linguistic conflict that Gorter refers to can be further heightened in instances where the minoritized language(s) does not have official status, such as Northern Ireland. As neither Irish nor Ulster-Scots are recognized in legislation as official languages, the visibility of the languages is sporadic in the LL, even within the civic frame. As such, the visitor is presented with a patchwork landscape that marks the traditional community affiliations with a language through the acceptance of a minoritized language in one area and its absence in another. The role of the LL as part of metacultural representation and practice (Coupland and Garrett 2010: 14) is particularly salient in the genre of the place-name sign and street-name sign in the public space in Northern Ireland. This genre of sign explicitly communicates cultural difference, through either inclusive or exclusive policies regarding Irish and/or Ulster Scots. Puzey (2009: 821) notes that 'the choice to include minority place-names on signs can constitute an act of renaming in itself' as the visibility of the minority language in the toponymy is a clear statement of identity. This form of empowerment, however, is a double-edged sword; every inclusionary policy is also potentially exclusionary, as the inclusion of a particular linguistic marker, which is understood to index a particular politico-cultural group may indirectly create an out-group of those who will find it alienating or even threatening (see *Belfast Newsletter* 4 July 2018). Thus, by empowering one speech community, there is the possibility of 'othering' those in the community that do not identify with that language and/or culture, resulting in feelings of disempowerment or delegitimization of one culture in a divided society such as Northern Ireland.

In Northern Ireland, the language choice in the linguistic content of the sign is often socio-politically loaded. In the case of street-name and place-name signs, the absence of a language or languages from a sign is an equally socio-politically loaded decision as the choice of visible linguistic content. In recent history in Northern Ireland, the inclusion of Irish in the public LL was an act of defiance for a community that felt oppressed and restricted from using their language publicly. Through grassroots movements, such as the Shaws Road Gaeltacht, the community empowered themselves by making their language both seen and heard in the public space at a time when it was a very hostile environment for the Irish language (de Brún 2006). The visibility of Irish in the LL thus became an acknowledgement of the presence of the language in that community, and a statement of reclaiming the language and its status for the community, 'to create community feelings of belonging' (Järlehed 2017). During the Northern Ireland Troubles (c.1968–98), the use of Irish in the public space was an in-group marker for Nationalists and contributed to building community solidarity in a time of conflict. The role of Irish in the LL has continued to act as an identity marker for the Nationalist community, and its inclusion in some areas and its exclusion in others, particularly in official signage, is still a site of contestation. Although it is a society emerging from conflict, deep divisions and mistrust still exist between the two main communities. Because of the close ties of the Irish language to the Nationalist community, it is difficult for some for it to become embraced as part of a shared heritage for the wider society.[1]

3. Council signage policies

Article 11 of the Local Government (Miscellaneous Provisions) (Northern Ireland) Order 1995 states clearly that councils have the power to erect street-name signs in any other language; however, the sign must always be present in English also and monolingual street-name signs in Irish or Ulster-Scots would be in contravention to legislation. The management of road signs is the responsibility of the Department of the Environment and are in English only; local borough councils are responsible for all street-name plates. Place-name signs are covered by the Department for Infrastructure under the Traffic Signs Authorisation (8 November 2005), which does not specify language requirements or obligations for such signage, but details fifteen different circumstances in which the content of these signs may be varied. This allows for local policies regarding language visibility to be implemented in the signage.

Of the eleven local councils in Northern Ireland, eight have policies regarding signage that is inclusive of one, or both, of the languages (Irish and/or Ulster-Scots), as outlined in either a language policy or the Street Naming and Numbering Policy for the council area. One council, Antrim and Newtownabbey Borough Council, had an 'English only' policy in relation to street-name signs, which was rescinded in September 2018 due to a judicial review being brought for being in contravention to the Local Government Order 1995, which, as explained above, allows for bilingual signage (*Newtownabbey Times* 30 July 2018). The districts that have Street Naming and Numbering policies only refer to the acceptance of a second language on a street-name sign but do not tend to specify the other languages that are permitted to be used. In four district councils, a bilingual policy that is inclusive of Irish is in place, resulting in varying degrees of visibility of Irish on council signs, ranging from inclusion of Irish in the council logo to signage that is completely bilingual in English and Irish (including dual-language visibility on council-owned properties, where dual-language signs are considered to be two monolingual name signs together). Signage in Ulster-Scots is referenced explicitly in two of the district council policies. Although some districts, such as Mid Ulster, have a promotional policy regarding Ulster-Scots language and culture in place, it does not feature in official signage. The inclusion of Irish or Ulster-Scots in official signage is normally limited to place-name and street-name signage only, apart from instances where the council logo is bilingual, and does not extend to other areas of the civic frame such as regulatory signs (e.g. regarding traffic restrictions). The most inclusive policy is in the Derry and Strabane district council that provides for English, Irish and Ulster-Scots (in that order) on all signage on council-owned properties (Derry City and Strabane District Council 2015a, 2015b). However, there is currently a review of the policy being undertaken, with indications that Ulster-Scots signage will no longer be a requirement (*Derry Now* 13 April 2018; 14 June 2019).

The legislation allows for diversity, resulting in a complex, heterogeneous LL. Although the civic frame is the most regulated, and as such assumed to be the most homogenous, there is room for diversity and variation within the frame due to the policy structure; the regulatory signs and directional signs (road directions, parking restrictions, dog fouling notices, etc.) are all monolingual in English across Northern Ireland. However, the street-name and place-name signs display a level of variety, reflective of the choice of the local councils. This diversity is vulnerable to political changes within the councils and to changes to council boundaries. This vulnerability was evident in 2016 when a Unionist politician called for the replacement of manhole covers on the water supply mains throughout the town of Ballymena because of the inclusion of the Irish word for water, *uisce*, on them (*Belfast Telegraph* 8 March 2016). This area of the civic frame is not covered by the street-naming policy and so such regulatory measures do not extend to other elements of the LL, even those within the civic frame. Although somewhat anecdotal in nature, instances such as that described indicate the tension between linguistic identities and the symbolic value attached to the visual presence of Irish (or Ulster-Scots) in the public space. Furthermore, such arguments index the complicated past and current sociopolitical situation in Northern Ireland, as society is still learning how to deal with the past conflict and build on reconciliation across the communities.

Regarding street-name signage, the visibility of bilingual signage in Irish and English is not a blanket policy in any of the council districts (as protected by the Local Government Order mentioned above), and even within council areas there can be variation in the languages visible in this sign genre, such as Belfast City Council's policy on street-name signs (Belfast City Council 2018). In order for a street to have a bilingual sign a resident must submit a request for signage. Following the acceptance of the request, a plebiscite must be taken in which over two-thirds of the residents of voting age on the street vote in favour of bilingual signage.² This process ensures that the Irish language remains within the confines of largely Nationalist areas (and signs in Ulster-Scots remain in largely Unionist areas), thus adding to the already divided semiotic landscape that is marked by flags, painted kerbstones and political murals (Bryan 2018). The policy disadvantages the minoritized language in that failure by an individual to respond is considered a negative response for that person. However, the policy does allow for bilingual signs and is a compromise that allows for inclusivity in a divided city like Belfast and other areas with a similar policy (Fermanagh and Omagh District Council n.d.; Lisburn and Castlereagh City Council 2018).

4. Methodology

In this article the focus is on the genre of the place-name and street-name sign within the civic frame, as defined by Kallen (2010: 49). The civic frame considers how the authorities regulate behaviour in instructions and orders and how it therefore also regulates language practice and the language visibility of the local landscape through such signs. In a consideration of how authorities engage with the languages of the communities, the civic frame examines the policy-driving practice of language display in communities, by evaluating if and how the authoritative voice(s) behave in the public space, recognizing 'the functional and formal similarities that define a discourse frame devoted to the activities of the state' (Kallen 2010: 46).

Within the civic frame, place-name and street-name signs act as a regulated reference marker for both tourists and locals in an area, thus, the language of that sign is a significant indicator in the LL of the language situation. The presence or absence of languages in place-name signs is indicative of the language relationships in that area, indexing the attitude of the authorities to a language as well as being a clear marker of its presence in the community to the reader. As such, this chapter focuses exclusively on this genre of sign, in order to understand the role it plays for the people using the public space. In considering place-name signs, all types of signs that feature toponomastic content are included, that is to say locational signs such as town boundaries, directional signs and route confirmatory signs, as well as street-name signs.

As the focus of this research is on the genre of toponomastic signs only, towns and areas in each of the council areas were identified that would provide examples of the diversity visible in the genre throughout Northern Ireland. The places analysed include large cities, such as Derry and Belfast, smaller towns and villages, including Greyabbey and Carrickfergus. In each area, street-name and place-name signs were documented along with manifestations of the place or street name in other units outside of that genre.

Towns and villages in each of the council areas were visited over the course four months in 2017 and all place-name signs entering the council area and each town were documented along with examples of the type of street-name signs visible there. The decision of what towns and cities to focus on for the data collection in itself is complex; as the visibility of Irish and Ulster-Scots is a contentious issue, particularly in the current climate where the question of introducing legislation for Irish is the root of some increased tensions in communities, there is no clear indication of areas that do or do not have inclusive signage. Although the council policies exist, as discussed earlier, this does not mean they are fully implemented in each town and city. As such, for this current study it was decided to collect data from at least one town or city in each council area. In order to select the towns and cities, census data was consulted in order to determine where there are reported speakers, with the idea being that if there are reported speakers of either Ulster-Scots or Irish, or both, in the area, there is an increased likelihood of signs in either or both of the varieties being visible. In the 2011 census of Northern Ireland, 10.65 per cent of the population over the age of 3 reported to have some knowledge of Irish, and 8.08 per cent reported to have some knowledge of Ulster-Scots (Northern Ireland Statistics and Research Agency (NISRA) 2014). Speakers of Irish in particular are spread throughout Northern Ireland, with speakers of Ulster Scots being more concentrated in the north and the Ards peninsula. Furthermore, places where issues related to place-name or street-name signs have featured in the media since the collapse of the government in January 2017 were of particular focus, such as Antrim town (*Belfast Telegraph* 7 June 2018), Rathfriland (*Belfast Newsletter* 18 September 2017) and various sites around Belfast.

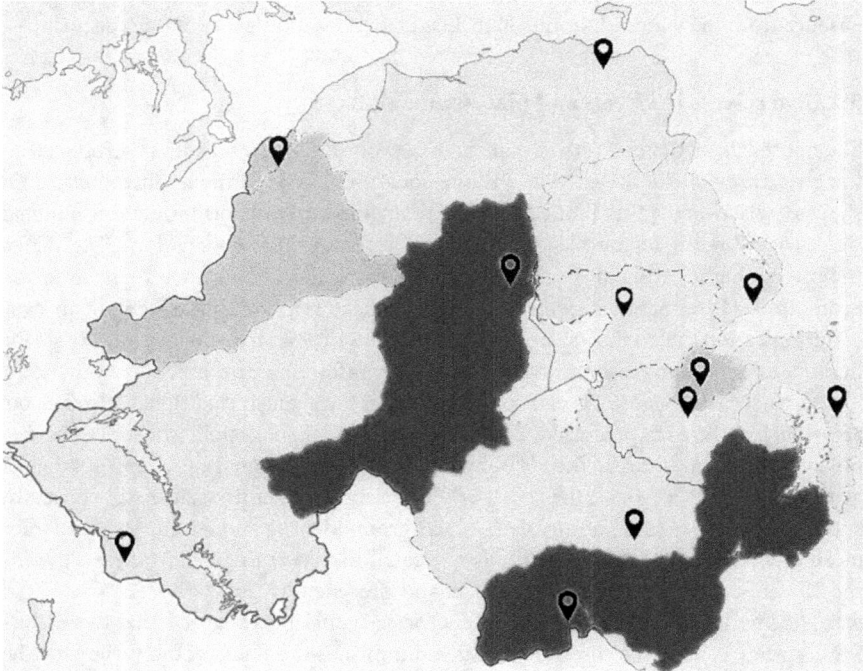

Figure 6.1 Map of the local council areas in Northern Ireland. The location pins mark towns where data was collected

5. Looking at the Linguistic Landscape

Although multilingualism is supported in some of the council areas in Northern Ireland, trilingual street- or place-name signage is not visible in any of the areas. The government policy ensures that all signs must have English (see above), and it is at the discretion of the district or borough council to include another of the autochthonous languages. As such, the LL is varied throughout Northern Ireland, and due to the close link between language and identity for the two main communities, the LL is considered to index community identity when variation in the languages displayed is visible.

In the vast majority of bilingual or dual-language signs, English is placed in the position of dominance on all signs or, in the case of dual-language signs, above the sign in the minoritized language. In instances where it is not placed dominantly, it is more visibly dominant through other visual and typographical forms, such as emboldened when the other language is not. This is in opposition to the widely acknowledged (but not always implemented) policy in minoritized language cases of giving the minoritized language the position of dominance in bilingual signage (Scollon and Wong Scollon 2003: 120). As English is obligatory in all street- and place-name signage, the inclusion of a minoritized language in this genre of signage is optional and at the discretion of the local council, therefore it is further minoritized through the policy. The inclusion of either of the minoritized varieties, on the other hand, can in some ways be more visible despite the dominance of English due to the unexpected inclusion of the language; its absence from the wider LL results in its heightened visibility when it does occur.

5.1 Ulster-Scots in street- and place-name signage

The approach to Ulster-Scots in signage has evolved since it was first introduced to the civic frame of the LL in 1996 (Thompson 1999). When initially introduced into signage, Ulster-Scots was limited to the Ards peninsula and was visible on bilingual signs with English in the place of dominance. The primary focus for Ulster-Scots is now on highlighting the cultural connection to the area, rather than linguistic promotion. Ulster-Scots is clearly valued in signage for its cultural symbolism over communication due to the nature of its visibility; it is presented as a link to the past for heritage and tourism reasons, rather than serving informative or directional functions.

On place-name signs, Ulster-Scots is visible on the signs in traditional Ulster-Scots areas, such as the Ards peninsula, although there is no language policy or street-naming policy in place in the area. The visibility of Ulster-Scots in signage is a clear marker of group identity; as although the status of the variety is contentious, it is still chosen in some communities as representative of their group identity and an important marker of difference. However, the visibility is not equal to that of English on these signs, as the Ulster-Scots text is of a smaller size, and preceded by 'formerly'. The use of the word 'formerly' in Ulster-Scots street- and place-name signs suggests that the Ulster-Scots variety is no longer used and as such diminishes the status of the variety for the sign reader. In the example in Figure 6.2 from Greyabbey, the name of the town is also visible as *Greba*. The village and townland of Greyabbey is named for the monastery

Figure 6.2 Town entrance sign in Greyabbey

that lies to the eastern side of the village. The name may have originated in English (due to the origin of its first monks from Cumberland), but there is also historical evidence for an Irish version of the name, *Mainistir Liath*, and either the Irish or English form, therefore, may be a translation of the other (see The Northern Ireland Place-Name Project). The sign makes no reference to Irish as part of the place's toponymic heritage; however, the Ulster-Scots *Greba* is visible. *Greba* was an informal, Ulster-Scots variety of the name, but in this unit, it is elevated to the appearance of the origin of the name so as to emphasize the connection. Here we have a juxtapositioning of attitudes towards the Ulster-Scots variety; it is elevated to the appearance of an official name for the town, yet it is much smaller in size than the English form of the place name, thus lowering the status of its presence. The inclusion of the word 'formerly' infers that the Ulster-Scots form of the name has historical primacy over the currently used place name, and indeed over the silenced Irish form. However, 'formerly' does also suggest that it is a historical variety no longer in use. All other linguistic content of the sign is visible in English only.

Brown signs in the LL normally index heritage sites or sites of tourist interest in the UK and elsewhere and are characterized by a brown background with white

Figure 6.3 Street-name sign in English and Ulster-Scots in the Ards Peninsula

lettering, in a sans-serif font, and often accompanied by a pictogram to facilitate global understanding. In Northern Ireland, street-name signs in Ulster-Scots often take a form that is similar to that of the established tourist sign, as in Figure 6.3, preceded by the word 'formerly' (as seen also in the place-name sign) or the Ulster-Scots *lang syne* and placed under a street-name sign in English (sometimes accompanied by the Ulster-Scots place-name logo, when financed by the Ulster-Scots Agency[3]). This is indicative of the attitudes towards the language, even by those wishing to promote its visibility; it functions not as a language for communication, but rather as a local marker that can be of interest. Rather than promoting it as a linguistic variety that is used by the local community, the utilization of mitigating terms and forms of including Ulster-Scots further minoritizes the variety through visibility. Even in traditional Ulster-Scots areas, the language is still presented as a cultural or touristic phenomenon rather than the preferred medium of communication in the community. In equating it to a tourist attraction, the language is being minoritized by the nature of its visibility and this is further emphasized by the italicized lettering of the Ulster-Scots form. Its visibility in the LL in the context of the brown tourist sign prevents it from establishing parity with the other languages visible in the LL, or from being considered by the reader as equal to the other languages with which it appears. Such treatment of Ulster-Scots in the public space can be understood to be unintentional linguistic delegitimization of the variety, even by those attempting to increase its visibility.

There has more recently been a move away from the brown Ulster-Scots signs in some areas, such as the one shown in Figure 6.4 from Carrickfergus. Here, the linguistic connection is more tenuous than on other Ulster-Scots signs. Ulster-Scots as a language variety is not used; rather, the connection to Ulster-Scots is indexed by the subpanel,

Figure 6.4 Street-name sign in Carrickfergus

which includes the logo for 'The Scotch Quarter' as part of an initiative of 'Heritage Carrickfergus'. The street is in the historical Scotch quarter of the town, where the original settlement was established in the seventeenth century. Rather than displaying a dual-language sign, the sign is monolingual in English with a border indexing the Ulster-Scots link. Shifting the focus to the cultural-historical link to the area rather than Ulster-Scots as a contemporary language of the community draws on heritage as a marker of identity rather than language and further emphasizes the subordinate status of the language, even in instances where the intention is to promote Ulster-Scots. This approach is endorsed by the Ulster-Scots Agency, who have funded similar signage campaigns elsewhere in Northern Ireland. It is an example of a method of eluding the need to address an official council policy; as the only language visible on the sign is English, it is still compliant with the government order, without going through the process of surveying the people of the area in order to approve the inclusion of other languages.

5.2 Irish in street- and place-name signage

In most council areas that have adopted an inclusive policy in relation to Irish, street-names are permitted in both Irish and English once a plebiscite has been held and receives sufficient support from two-thirds of the residents of the street in question. These signs can take the form of bilingual signs, with English in the dominant position, or in the case of older signs, dual-language signs with a unit in Irish underneath the original English-language sign. In both cases the English and Irish forms use identical lettering and size so as to give equal visibility to both languages, although, as mentioned, English is normally in the dominant position (Scollon and Wong Scollon 2003) of being placed on top. As Irish is not legally recognized as an official language in Northern Ireland, the emplacement of English as the dominant language in official signage is not unexpected. In a divided society like Northern Ireland, where the Irish language is strongly associated with one community, the regulating of English as the dominant language in the LL is an attempt to ensure that no one community is seen to have more status or power than the other.

A concerted effort has been made to develop a strategy for regeneration of the Gaeltacht quarter of Belfast in the Falls Road area in the west of the city, with the Irish language playing a central role (Carden 2012). All street-name signage in the area, including the use of a street or place name in public transport stops, have bilingual or dual-language signage in Irish. This is reinforced in the visual presence of Irish in other frames of the LL within this area, usually in bilingual form, including shop fronts, commercial signage and posters advertising community events. However, there are also instances of Irish monolingual visibility outside of the civic frame. This inclusive visibility of Irish in the civic frame and beyond creates a space for the in-group community of Irish speakers to use their language in the public space. In the past, businesses were reluctant to utilize the language or show an affinity with it so publicly for fear of retaliation. As such, the presence of top-down engagement with the language encourages the use of the language in bottom-up instances in a divided city where the language is a marker of identity. However, as with much of the revitalization movement for Irish in Northern Ireland, it was bottom-up grassroots initiatives that forced the authorities to begin engaging with the language and to take steps to normalize the presence and use of the language in all spheres of public life (Maguire 1991).

In the town of Magherafelt, situated in the Mid Ulster District Council, with an inclusive Irish policy, the street-name signs are an exception in that they display a dominance of Irish both in the distribution of languages and the typographic form of the linguistic content. In Figure 6.5, Irish is on top and is visible in an adaptation of the letterform of the cló Gaelach, the Gaelic/Irish script (O'Neill 1984); however, the letter size is smaller than English and not emboldened. Font choice can be symbolic as well as indexical (Scollon and Wong Scollon 2003: 118) symbolizing an era, style or culture the sign-maker wishes to convey. This semiotic tool is also used to index authenticity and tradition in order to tie the local with international marketability, such as documented by Kallen (2009). Similarly to how different alphabet systems are associated with certain languages, specific typefaces and fonts have also come to be associated with nations and form a marker of identity for that culture. With regard to signs that are constructed using a particular font associated with a culture, Seargeant (2012: 199) states 'their meaning … is a product of code, script, actualisation, and the reader's cultural beliefs about the presence of different languages in the world'. The utilization of the cló Gaelach indexes place and identity (similar to Järlehed 2015 on

Figure 6.5 Street-name sign in Magherafelt

Basque and Galician lettering), further associating the area with the Irish language, and in turn, the Irish identity as a proxy for Nationalist identity. This emphasis on the Irish language and traditional lettering echoes practices in other minoritized languages that endeavour to accentuate the authenticity of the language and its cultural heritage. Järlehed (2017) found that the utilization of Basque lettering in the Basque Country 'in the bilingual street-name sign [is] part of nationalistic claims for visibility, recognition and autonomy'. Similarly, the street-name signs in Magherafelt utilize the cló Gaelach in the lettering that is associated with Irish tradition; as such, the language is exoticized in the sense of a visible difference to English and yet projects authenticity at the same time through the use of the traditional letterform. The distinction presented by the script choice further highlights the language and accentuates its presence in the signage.

Although the visibility of Irish in street-name signs is suggestive of a presence that is more functional than the form of presentation of Ulster-Scots visibility in signage, it does hold a symbolic value also, marking territory and asserting a group identity publicly for a space. The visual reinforcement of Irish in other discourse frames of the LL in some areas emphasizes the sustained effort by the community to normalize and promote the presence of the language as a tool for communication.

5.3 Absence and contestation to onomastic signs in the LL

Järlehed (2017) notes that street-name signs 'offer a rich repertoire of semiotic resources that can be mobilized for creative place-making and identity-work'. This is evident in the linguistic choices made on street-name and place-name signs; however, it is also evident within the linguistic content of a sign. The naming of the city Derry/Londonderry has resulted in many transgressive acts on signage displaying the name. In this instance it is not the choice of language that is an issue, as both forms of the name are in English, but rather the form of the name. Derry, derived from the Irish *Doire* 'oak wood', was officially renamed Londonderry in 1613 by Royal Charter, in recognition of the investment in the city by the livery companies of London; however, both names continue to be used for both the city and county (Morris 2018; Northern Ireland Place-Name Project n.d.). The naming of the city is seen as an identity marker, acting as a shibboleth for Unionist (Londonderry) or Nationalist (Derry) depending on the form the speaker chooses to use. In Figure 6.6, evidence of contestation to the place-name is visible. The route confirmatory sign has been defaced to eliminate 'London' from the place name, with a question mark inserted after the name of the city. This is a common sight across Northern Ireland and indicative of the cultural tensions between the two communities. Although it is usual for each community to use language as a marker of identity, in the case of the city of Derry it is the choice of name within one language variety, the dominant, shared language, that is a proxy for sociopolitical belonging and territory claiming. Unlike the case of An Daingean in Kerry in the Republic of Ireland, discussed in Moriarty (2012), in which the debate around the official place-name hung on which language, Irish or English, to use, the choice of place name for Derry/Londonderry is seen as an identity marker, thus superseding linguistic choice issues and becoming an issue within English also.

Figure 6.6 Road sign for Derry/Londonderry[4]

As the Irish language is traditionally associated with Irish Nationalist identity, the absence of the language in an area can also index the identity of the community, particularly when the language is absent from a unit or genre where it might have been be expected. The mural in Figure 6.7 for example, celebrates the origin of the name of the Shankill area, a traditionally loyalist heartland in Belfast city. Shankill comes from the Irish *Seanchill*, meaning 'old church', which is emphasized by the illustration of a church in the background of the mural. However, the explanation of the origin of the name omits the language from which the name is derived, rather than acknowledging the connection to Irish. Instead, the mural states that the parish of Belfast was formerly called Shankill, with no reference to the original form of the toponym. The inclusion of an ellipsis before the reiteration of Shankill in the mural may index the exclusion of some information, with the use of the word 'formerly' also alluding to a connection with the Ulster-Scots signs discussed earlier. The Shankill is a largely loyalist area, and so the absence of recognition of a connection to Irish is not surprising in a community that does not identify with the language, or its culture and heritage. The colours used

Figure 6.7 Mural on the Shankill Road

in this mural – red, white and blue – are indicative of the community affiliation, as the colours of the British flag are used extensively in loyalist areas, which is reiterated by the presence of the crown in the depiction of the name of the area.

6. Place names, policies and practices

Irish is more common in street-name signs than Ulster-Scots due to both the linguistic demographics of Northern Ireland and the number of council policies that allow for inclusion of another language. As a language which is confined largely to the oral medium (Fenton 2014), the visibility of Ulster-Scots in the LL has been a contentious issue for some within the out-group and also for many who identify with Ulster-Scots heritage. The vision and mission statements of the Ulster-Scots Agency's corporate plan (Ulster-Scots Agency 2014) emphasize the heritage and culture more so than language, responding to the consensus from the Ulster-Scots community as a whole, who are moving towards preference for references to heritage or to cultural-historical connections to certain areas rather than signage in the Ulster-Scots language. As they do not actively seek bilingualism in the LL or other spheres, having an inclusive multilingual policy that includes both Irish and Ulster-Scots does not necessarily serve the speech community of one of those languages. Although place names serve an important role in relation to identity, the use of a language in place names only in the LL can be seen as tokenistic and reinforcing the binary framework that already exists in the public space (Mac an Breithiún and Burke 2014). However, if an inclusive policy is in place and is then removed, it does become an issue because the removal of a language from the public space can be seen to be the delegitimization of a language and the active disempowerment of that community. In a contentious setting, there is a balance to be struck between empowerment through the inclusion of a minoritized language in the public space and the exclusion of the 'other' through the same action, and also supporting the included language in more than just a symbolic nominal manner in its inclusion in the LL reinforcing.

It would be remiss to believe that the councils that have inclusive policies towards Irish and/or Ulster-Scots are harmonious in their approach to multilingualism or without problems. In fact, these policies are often the focus of debate within the councils and result in changing policies, particularly in times of instability within the government, when issues related to language have a heightened political nuance. In April 2018, an Irish-language group based in Antrim town lodged an official complaint to the Equality Commission when plant pots bearing words in Ulster-Scots were placed in the town centre by the local council. The group had previously requested street-name signs in Irish but their request was rejected by the council, citing the English-only road sign policy as the reason. The group considered the exclusion of Irish, and the inclusion of Ulster-Scots, in the public space to be a hypocritical and politicized move. In Belfast, where there is an inclusive language policy and two language officers employed by the city council, protests in September 2019 over the absence of Irish from signage at a new, council-owned leisure centre led to the council being obliged to consider the citywide strategy on bilingual signage. These examples of the multitude of language-related complaints and requests made to the councils illustrate the degree of delegitimization of the language that occurs even at established levels, indicating that delivering on language management strategies and policies is not as straightforward as getting a language supported on paper.

Linguistic rights issues are to the fore in terms of the desires of the Irish-speaking community. The Irish language community are fighting for recognition of their language as they consider language rights to be an extension of civil rights and paramount to a more equal and shared society (Ní Shabhaois 2017). The community actively engage with authorities and policymakers for recognition of their language in all areas of society, with visibility being of vital importance to the campaign (Conradh na Gaeilge 2017). Visibility of a minoritized language can lead to the normalization of its presence in the public space, assist revitalization efforts and lead to cross-community acceptance of Irish in the wider society. In street-name and place-name signage, the visibility of the Irish and Ulster-Scots is heavily regulated, with policies specifying the circumstances under which bilingual or dual-language signage can be implemented in top-down signage, and detailing how the languages should appear in the unit. The policies focus on language placement and size to ensure that the de facto official language, English, is dominant; however, as many policies do not refer specifically to typeface, the utilization of lettering such as the cló Gaelach can further highlight the presence of Irish in a unit.

There is a disparity between the two communities in that the focus on the linguistic aspects is to the fore for the Irish community whereas semiotic factors through the expression of culture are the emphasis for the Ulster-Scots community with regard to signage. This approach is reflective of both the speech communities. The focus for the Ulster-Scots community is on cultural aspects of their heritage, as we see in signage marking the Scotch quarter in towns; the strategy is not to translate names that do not have a historical Ulster-Scots connection, but is moving towards drawing connections and attention to their cultural heritage. In contrast, the Irish community predominantly focuses on bilingualism, with equal status for Irish, as a form of expressing their identity. This balance of priorities reflects the recent debate around the languages in the context of the suspension of the Northern Ireland Assembly; Ulster-Scots was largely absent from all public debates and negotiations around the role of the minoritized languages in the community and was brought into the negotiations by a political party rather than a speech community.

The complexity of identity and belonging and the deep divisions that exist in Northern Ireland are visible in the LL through the policies adopted by councils. Rather than embracing the multilingual heritage and diversity of the community, the councils avoid addressing linguistic issues that have become politicized and so the language(s) used on place-name and street-name signs is dependent on community activism in some instances and vulnerable to instable political decisions in general. Gorter (2006: 86) notes that 'even when the central government officially regulates and accepts bilingual signs, the conflict over which place-names to use and how they are placed on the signs may continue vehemently at regional level'. The introduction of legislation regulating the inclusion of bilingual or multilingual signs in Northern Ireland would undoubtedly result in transgressive acts and tensions initially. However, the embracing and recognition of a multilingual, shared space, can contribute to progress towards reconciliation for a divided society through acceptance of distinctive cultural identities. The current language legislation at council level allows for choice of language in signage (to a limited degree), and as such empowers the local community to utilize signage as a medium of expression of their community identity, as evidenced in areas such as Greyabbey and Magherafelt. This empowerment, however, can also be viewed as disempowering the other, as the inclusion of a contextually highly politicized language in public signage can, at the same time, lead to the exclusion of those in the community who do not identify with the community associated with that language.

7. Conclusion

It is salient that the presence of Irish and Ulster-Scots in the LL in Northern Ireland is a contentious issue and that most progress in supporting their visibility in the LL has been achieved in the genre of street-name and place-name signage. There is wide diversity in policy approaches to the visibility of the minoritized languages at local level; this is open to negotiation with local communities in some council areas. It is also the case that policy at higher levels of governance is not entirely clear or consistent. In the absence of political consensus, grassroots initiatives have been successfully leading the way and have been crucial in initiating and empowering the revitalization and normalization of the minoritized languages in the public space, particularly Irish.

It would appear that for the Ulster-Scots community (and for those who embrace the language as part of their identity) the emphasis is not on visibility in the LL but instead on the acceptance and embracing of elements of broader Ulster-Scots culture. Heritage is valued over communication; the language does not serve a directional function but may serve a symbolic function as an index of historic connections to place. Irish serves a symbolic and an informative function and its presence on signage of this genre on a more equal footing to English echoes the sustained efforts for recognition of the language by the speech community and promotes the normalization of the presence of the language in the public space as a tool for communication.

In the context of ongoing political tensions, it is difficult to envision a wider and more equal embracing of visibility for either of the minoritized languages in the short term. The exclusion of a minoritized language disempowers the group that identifies with the language by not acknowledging that language in the shared public space. However, in a divided community which has two minoritized languages to consider, the inclusion of one minoritized language in signage has been seen to mark out territory and limit the notion of a shared public space. Thus, while empowering some members of the community by the normalization of the visibility of the languages with which they identify, such an 'inclusive' policy can exclude others.

Notes

1. For more on the status of Irish in Northern Ireland, see Chapter 3, this volume.
2. In October 2020, a proposal was carried out by Belfast City Council to reduce the threshold of consent for the erection of bilingual signage on a street from two-thirds of the residents of voting age to 15 per cent. The motion has yet to be ratified by the Council. (*Belfast Telegraph* 23 October 2020).
3. The Ulster-Scots Agency is a cross-border body for Ireland, which was established as a result of the Good Friday Agreement 1998. Its objective is to promote awareness and use of Ulster-Scots culture and language throughout the island of Ireland.
4. The photo of this unit taken by the author was not of sufficient quality. This image is courtesy of Google Maps and was taken in May 2017.

References

Belfast City Council (2018), 'Language Strategy 2018–2023'. Available online: http://www.belfastcity.gov.uk/council/Languagestrategy/Language-strategy.aspx. (accessed 22 July 2018).

Belfast Newsletter (2018), 'Unholy Council Row Over Irish Signs at Cemetery', 4 July. Available online: https://www.newsletter.co.uk/news/unholy-council-row-over-irish-signs-at-cemetery-1-8555076 (accessed 5 July 2018).

Belfast Newsletter (2017), 'What Precedent Is Being Set for Irish Language Act?', 18 September. Available online: https://www.newsletter.co.uk/news/what-precedent-is-being-set-for-irish-language-act-1-8155242 (accessed 2 July 2018).

Belfast Telegraph (2016), 'Irish Words on Ballymena's Manhole Covers Sparks Unionist Demand for Their Removal', 8 March. Available online: https://www.belfasttelegraph.co.uk/news/northern-ireland/irish-words-on-ballymenas-manhole-covers-sparks-unionists-demand-for-their-removal-34519140.html (accessed 18 July 2018).

Belfast Telegraph (2018), 'SF Go Potty over Planters in Ulster Scots but Houl Their Wheesht if You Mention the £25m for Gaelic', 7 June. Available online: https://www.belfasttelegraph.co.uk/opinion/columnists/nelson-mccausland/nelson-mccausland-sf-go-potty-over-planters-in-ulster-scots-but-houl-their-wheesht-if-you-mention-the-25m-for-gaelic-36983928.html (accessed 18 July 2018).

Belfast Telegraph (2020), 'Belfast City Council Committee Backs New Bilingual Street Signs Policy', 23 October. Available online: https://www.belfasttelegraph.co.uk/news/northern-ireland/belfast-city-council-committee-backs-new-bilingual-street-signs-policy-39659941.html (accessed 24 October 2020).

Blackwood, R. (2015), 'LL Explorations and Methodological Challenges: Analysing France's Regional Languages', *Linguistic Landscape: An International Journal*, 1 (1/2): 38–53.

Bryan, D. (2018), 'The Material Value of Flags: Politics and Space in Northern Ireland', *Review of Irish Studies in Europe*, 2 (1): 76–91.

Carden, S. (2012), 'Making Space for Tourists with Minority Languages: The Case of Belfast's Gaeltacht Quarter', *Journal of Tourism and Cultural Change*, 10 (1): 51–64.

Conradh na Gaeilge (2017), *Irish Language Act: Discussion Document, Version 1.0* (10 March 2017) Available online: https://cnag.ie/images/Acht_Gaeilge_ó_Thuaidh/15MÁ2017_Plécháipéis_ar_Acht_Gaeilge_ó_Thuaidh.pdf (accessed 18 July 2019).

Coupland, N., and Garrett, P. (2010), 'Linguistic Landscapes, Discursive Frames and Metacultural Performance: The Case of Welsh Patagonia', *International Journal of the Sociology of Language*, 205: 7–36.

Dal Negro, S. (2009), 'Local Policy Modeling the Linguistic Landscape', in E. Shohamy and D. Gorter (eds), *Linguistic Landscape: Expanding the Scenery*, 206–18, London: Routledge.

De Brún, F. (2006), *Belfast and the Irish Language*, Dublin: Four Courts Press.

Department for Rural Development (2005), 'Traffic Signs Authorisation', 8 November. Available online: https://www.infrastructure-ni.gov.uk/publications/villagetown-name-sign (accessed 16 July 2019).

Derry City and Strabane District Council (2015a), 'Irish Language Policy'. Available online: http://www.derrystrabane.com/gaeilge (accessed 14 July 2018).

Derry City and Strabane District Council (2015b), 'Ulster-Scots Policy'. Available online: http://www.derrystrabane.com/ulsterscots (accessed 14 July 2018).

Derry Now (2018), 'Derry's Council Delay Decision on Possible Removal of Ulster Scots', 13 April. Available online: https://www.derrynow.com/news/derrys-council-delay-decision-possible-removal-ulster-scots/218809 (accessed 15 July 2018).

Derry Now (2019), 'Council Signage Language Policy "Has Never Been Resolved"', 14 June. Available online: https://www.derryjournal.com/news/

council-signage-language-policy-has-never-been-resolved-1-8963625 (accessed 23 July 2019).

Fenton, J. (2014), *The Hamely Tongue: A Personal Record of Ulster-Scots in County Antrim*, 4th edn, Belfast: Ullans Press.

Fermanagh and Omagh District Council (n.d.), Street/Road Naming and Numbering Policy. Available online: https://www.fermanaghomagh.com/app/uploads/2018/01/Street-Road-Naming-and-Numbering-Policy.pdf (accessed 14 July 2018).

Gorter, D. (2006), 'Further Possibilities for Linguistic Landscape Research', in D. Gorter (ed.), *Linguistic Landscape: A New Approach to Multilingualism*, 81–9, Clevedon, UK: Multilingual Matters.

Gorter, D., and Cenoz, J. (2015), 'Translanguaging and Linguistic Landscapes', *Linguistic Landscape: An International Journal*, 1 (1): 54–74.

Järlehed, J. (2015), 'Ideological Framing of Vernacular Type Choices in the Galician and Basque Semiotic Landscape', *Social Semiotics*, 25 (2): 165–99.

Järlehed, J. (2017), 'Genre and Metacultural Displays: The Case of Street-Name Signs', *Linguistic Landscape: An International Journal*, 3 (3): 286–305.

Kallen, J. (2010), 'Changing Landscapes: Language, Space and Policy in the Dublin Linguistic Landscape', in A. Jaworski and C. Thurlow (eds), *Semiotic Landscapes: Language, Image, Space*, 41–58, London: Continuum.

Kallen, J. (2009), 'Tourism and Representation in the Irish Linguistic Landscape', in E. Shohamy and D. Gorter (eds), *Linguistic Landscape: Expanding the Scenery*, 270–83, London: Routledge.

Landry, R., and Bourhis, R. Y. (1997), 'Linguistic Landscape and Ethnolinguistic Vitality: An Empirical Study', *Journal of Language and Social Psychology*, 16 (1): 23–49.

Lisburn and Castlereagh City Council (2018), Street Naming and Postal Numbering Policy.

The Local Government (Miscellaneous Provisions) (Northern Ireland) Order (1995). Available online: http://www.legislation.gov.uk/nisi/1995/759/contents (accessed 14 July 2018).

Mac an Bhreithiún, B., and Burke, A. (2014), 'Language, Typography, and Place-Making: Walking the Irish and Ulster-Scots Linguistic Landscape', *Canadian Journal of Irish Studies*, 38 (1/2): 84–125.

Maguire, G. (1991), *Our Own Language: An Irish Initiative*, Clevedon, UK: Multilingual Matters.

Marten, H. F. (2012), 'Latgalian Is Not a Language': Linguistic Landscapes in Eastern Latvia and How They Reflect Centralist Attitudes', in D. Gorter, H. F. Marten and L. Van Mensel (eds), *Minority Languages in the Linguistic Landscape*, 19–35, Hampshire: Palgrave MacMillan.

Mid Ulster District Council (n.d.), 'Ullans Leid Policy/Ulster-Scots Policy' (2015–2019). Available online: https://www.midulstercouncil.org/languagepolicies (accessed 10 July 2018).

Moriarty, M. (2012), 'Language Ideological Debates in the Linguistic Landscape of an Irish Town', in D. Gorter, H. F. Marten and L.Van Mensel (eds), *Minority Languages in the Linguistic Landscape*, 74–88, Basingstoke: Palgrave Macmillan.

Morris, E. (2018), ' "H" Is for History: Uses of the Past in Place-Name Debates in New Zealand and Northern Ireland', *History Australia*, 15 (1): 113–29.

Ní Shabhaois, U. (2017), Who Are an Dream Dearg? Ag Smaoineamh os Ard. Available online: https://www.smaoineamhosard.com/single-post/2017/01/09/Who-are-An-Dream-Dearg (accessed 27 July 2018).

Newtownabbey Times (2018), 'Irish Language Activists Challenge "English only" Policy', 30 July. Available online: https://www.newtownabbeytoday.co.uk/news/irish-language-activists-challenge-english-only-policy-1-8584239 (accessed 01 August 2018).

Northern Ireland Place-Name Project (n.d.), 'Northern Ireland Place-Name Project: The History Behind Our Place-Names'. Available online: http://www.placenamesni.org (accessed 01 August 2018).

Northern Ireland Statistics and Research Agency (NISRA) (2014), *Northern Ireland Census 2011 Key Statistics Summary Report*, Belfast: National Statistics Publication. Available online: http://www.nisra.gov.uk/archive/census/2011/results/key-statistics/summary-report.pdf (accessed 5 July 2018).

O'Neill, T. (1984), *The Irish Hand. Scribes and Their Manuscripts from the Earliest Times to the Seventeenth Century with an Exemplar of Scripts*, Portlaoise: Dolmen Press.

Puzey, G. (2016), 'Lingusitic Landscapes', in C. Hough (ed.), *The Oxford Handbook of Names and Naming*, 395–411, Oxford: Oxford University Press.

Puzey, G. (2009), 'Opportunity or Threat? The Role of Minority Toponyms in the Linguistic Landscape', in W. Ahrens, S. Embleton and A. Lapierre (eds), *Names in Multilingual, Multi-Cultural and Multi-Ethnic Contact: Proceedings of the 23rd International Congress of Onomastic Sciences*, 821–7, Toronto: York University.

Scollon, R., and Wong Scollon, S. (2003), *Discourses in Place: Language in the Material World*, London: Routledge.

Seargeant, P. (2012), 'Between Script and Language: The Ambiguous Ascription of 'English' in the Linguistic Landscape', in C. Hélot, M. Barni, R. Janssens and C. Bagna (eds), *Linguistic Landscapes, Multilingualism and Social Change*, 187–200, Frankfurt am Main: Peter Lang.

Spolsky, B., and Cooper, R. L. (1991), *The Languages of Jerusalem*, Oxford: Clarendon Press.

Thompson, M. (1999), 'Signs of Encouragement!', *Ullans: The Magazine of Ulster-Scots*, 7. Available online: http://www.ulsterscotsacademy.com/ullans/7/signs-of-encouragement.php (accessed 06 August 2018).

Ulster-Scots Agency (2014), *Ulster-Scots Agency Corporate Plan 2014–2016*. Available online: https://www.ulsterscotsagency.com/fs/doc/publications/ulster-scots-agency-corporate-plan-2014-to-2016-final.pdf (accessed 23 July 2019).

7

Postcolonial re-memorization in the public space: A Patrice Lumumba Square in Brussels

Luk Van Mensel

1. Introduction[1]

One of the purposes of this volume is to critically examine ways in which the Linguistic Landscape (henceforth LL) can be a tool of inclusion for various linguistically and culturally minoritized individuals and communities throughout Europe. This chapter proposes to look into one specific aspect of this topic, namely the contestation and transformation of the remaining glorification of a nation's colonial past in the public space. In former times, statues, monuments and place names referring to a nation's colonial 'endeavours' were often installed to imbue the public with a sense of pride about the accomplishments in the colony and to celebrate the nation's prestige. However, these relics of the past are increasingly becoming a source of unease and shame as the public becomes more aware of the darker sides of colonialism: 'Once celebrated as a symbol of prestige, colonial memories now convey a sense of liability, or even guilt towards the past' (Bragard and Planche 2009: 182). In times of transnational dynamics – or the perception thereof – and the subsequent reactionary folding back on 'one's own people', the way in which a nation deals with the memory of its colonial past is significant. By showing which elements from the colonial legacy a nation wishes to remember in the public space and which elements to forget, a message is conveyed not just about how this nation wants to be remembered, but rather how it wishes to be seen today. Besides the clear impact this may have on citizens with a direct link to the former colony – and their sense of being part (or not) of the former metropole's society – a more wide-ranging effect can be imagined on how the given society deals with different identities and difference more generally and how inclusive or exclusive a national identity it wishes to project. Given this symbolic importance, it should not come as a surprise that calls for a transformation or removal of traces of the colonial memory are often met with (overt and covert) resistance. The reorganization of national memory in the public space may indeed appear to some as undermining the national identity, in the sense that it rewrites some of the nation's founding stories, and therefore poses a potential 'risk to national cohesion' (Smouts 2007: 27, cited in Bragard and Planche 2009).

Focusing on the specific case of Belgium, I will first briefly discuss examples of recent developments in the way the country's colonial past is referred to in the public space, such as through statues or street names.[2] The chapter then turns to the official renaming of a square in Brussels in June 2018 into the Patrice Lumumba Square and discusses in some detail the background and circumstances in which this renaming came about. Patrice Lumumba, who served as the first prime minister of the independent Republic of the Congo between June and September 1960, has become a worldwide symbol of pan-Africanism and anti-colonialism. In January 1961 he was captured and assassinated by his adversaries with the approval and support of Belgium and the United States (see e.g. Goddeeris and Kiangu 2011, for a concise yet informative take on these events). In Belgium, he is particularly associated with the speech he gave on Independence Day (June 30) in 1960, in which he condemned the atrocities committed by the Belgian colonizers, thus presenting a narrative very different from the official one, feeding right into the notions of shame and guilt mentioned above. It is therefore easy to understand why the figure of Lumumba has been contentious in a Belgian context and why, until recently, it was difficult to imagine public recognition of this figure in the urban landscape.

Since this chapter explicitly focuses on memorization and history in public space, it may be useful to add some preliminary remarks on how this topic has been dealt with in linguistic and semiotic landscape research so far before we turn to our own case study.

2. Memory, monuments and place names in the Linguistic Landscape

First of all, one could say that diachronic LL research incorporates history and memory per definition. Textbook examples would include Pavlenko's (2010, 2012) work on Kyiv, Ukraine, in which she illustrates how the distinct language ideologies of consecutive political regimes leave traces in the LL; the work by Spalding (2013) on three centuries of LL in Cork (Ireland); or Vandenbroucke's (2018) diachronic study of the semiotic landscape and LL of the Quartier Dansaert in Brussels, Belgium. These and many other studies view LL as diachronically layered artefacts, as urban palimpsests which can be erased and re-written many times, and take into account 'the role of the past in the construction of the present' (Pavlenko and Mullen 2015: 116).

Secondly, and perhaps more directly relevant to the topic discussed in this chapter, is the work conducted on memorials as part of the expanded LL (Shohamy and Gorter 2009). In the introduction to a special issue of the journal *Linguistic Landscape* (2:3) on memory and memorialization, Ben-Rafael (2016: 207) suggests that 'public memorialization is one of the most salient LL objects' in that memorials are a clear conduit for the symbolic construction of public space. This interest in monuments and memorials (also illustrated in the contributions to the same special issue – see Guilat and Espinosa-Ramírez 2016; Lou 2016; Train 2016; Woldemariam 2016 – as well as in the various chapters of the edited volume entitled *Multilingual Memories*, which focuses on the contribution of LL research to the study of memorialization and multilingualism, Blackwood and Macalister 2020) echoes some of the work conducted under the umbrella of semiotic landscapes, such as the chapters by Abousnnouga and Machin (2010) on war monuments and by Shohamy and Waksman (2010) on the Tel Aviv Ha'apala monument in Jaworski and Thurlow (2010). What these studies have in common is that they emphasize the high visibility and ideological significance of monuments and memorials, considering them architectural embodiments of memories, identities and wider sociocultural discourses. The studies also converge in that they show how, beneath the surface of a very clear and straightforward message, monuments can hide a range of meanings, which Abousnnouga and Machin (2010) call a 'hidden curriculum'. In this sense, Lou (2016) reminds us of Lefebvre ([1973] 1991: 143) noting that 'monumental buildings mask the will to power and the arbitrariness of power beneath signs and surfaces which claim to express collective will and collective thought'. As such, monuments can be regarded as an attempt by top-down forces to establish a symbolic hegemony, 'a way of canonizing ... the memory and ideology of a nation' (Woldemariam 2016: 276). Obviously, the symbolic hegemony can be (and is often) contested in the linguistic and semiotic (virtual) landscape by other actors, who mostly operate bottom-up (Shohamy and Waksman 2012).

This last aspect is aptly illustrated in Guilat and Espinosa-Ramírez's (2016) study on the implementation of the Historical Memory Law (October 2007) in the city of Granada, Spain. Among other things, the law requires local authorities to cleanse the public space from any symbols glorifying or commemorating the former Francoist regime and dictatorship (1939–75). The scholars describe how different interpretations of the law lead to heated debates regarding its implementation, and they provide many illustrations of how the dispute between the different sides is played out in the semiotic and virtual landscape. Perhaps most relevant for the present chapter, they argue (Guilat and Espinosa-Ramírez 2016: 251) that the changes in Spain's public space do not just reflect a transition between political power regimes but between 'regimes of memory' (Foucault 1981). Guilat and Espinosa-Ramírez suggest that the law offers an alternative approach to remembering the traumatic past, which is not just different from the monolithic 'rhetoric of "total victory" under Franco's dictatorship', but equally goes beyond the discourse of 'collective and shared guilt' which typified the transition period after 1975 (Sánchez Léon 2012, cited in Guilat and Espinosa-Ramírez 2016). I will argue below that a similar interpretation may be applicable to Belgium's dealing with its colonial legacy in the public space.

Although they may lack the rhetorical power of monuments and memorials (Armada 1998), place names are also artefacts that can inscribe ideological messages into the LL in subtle yet powerful ways, for they render what (and who) a particular society deems important. For instance, place names can convey a certain version of the (sometimes immediate) past as being a 'natural' part of the local society's frame of reference. As Alderman (2008: 196) asserts, 'place names not only meld history with geography but also conflate place and group identity because of the shared context of using and referring to toponyms'. As such, place names, just like monuments, can be powerful – and possibly empowering – instruments for (top-down) nation-building, when particular (reinvented) nationalist narratives are inscribed into the landscape.

Relatively recent examples in Europe can be found in the LL of post-socialist Eastern European countries, such as former East Berlin (Azaryahu 1997), former Yugoslavia (Robinson, Engelsoft and Pobric 2001), Russia (Gill 2005) or Romania (Light 2004). In LL research, the symbolic importance of place names is well attested in minority language settings, where the mere (co-)presence of minority language toponyms on signs often proves to be a locus of dispute between different powers and language activists (Gorter, Marten and Van Mensel 2012), sometimes boiling down to the presence or absence of a simple diacritical sign (Busch 2013).

Given the symbolic weight of place names, the act of place naming and renaming constitutes an equally interesting research object as the names in and of themselves. After all, the LL is often considered a locus of ideological struggle, not merely a reflection of the outcome of this struggle (Blommaert 2013; Marten, Van Mensel and Gorter 2012; Shohamy 2015; Van Mensel, Vandenbroucke and Blackwood 2016). Moriarty's (2012) take on the debate regarding the renaming of the town of Dingle (Ireland) from a bilingual English-Irish version to a monolingual Irish version, An Daingean, is a nice illustration of this, as she shows how language ideologies are not only reflected but also indexed and performed in the LL.

In sum, the linguistic and semiotic landscape (including place names and memorials) may form an arena of negotiation, contestation, resistance and counter-resistance to prevailing hegemonic narratives between various societal groups and forces. In Belgium (as in other European countries), the sheer abundance of place names and statues referring to the country's colonial past thus reflect a particular vision on the nation's history and its dealing with the past, and calls for renaming (or the removal of statues) can be considered counter-hegemonic proposals, as a 'way of creating new connections between the past and the present' (Alderman 2008: 195). As a corollary, actual renaming can provide a modest yet significant contribution towards the empowerment of diaspora communities, inasmuch as it signals the official recognition of an alternative and perhaps more inclusive view of the past. In the next part, I will briefly discuss the current state of affairs regarding these issues in Belgium.

3. The (post-)colonial memory in Belgium's public space

In Belgium, traces of the Belgian colonial propaganda in the semiotic landscape and LL can be found throughout the country. Stanard (2011: 167) suggests that there are 'dozens, if not hundreds of imperialistic memorials' in Belgium. Most of these were erected in the interbellum period (1925–40) and served among other things to underscore the Belgian nature of the Congo (Goddeeris 2016; Goddeeris and Kiangu 2011; Viaene, Van Reybrouck and Ceuppens 2009). As a result, mainly Belgians are depicted in these memorials instead of foreign travellers or foreign missionaries, for instance, who may have had a more important role in the exploration of the Congo. The Belgians who are depicted often hail from the military, which, as Goddeeris (2016) states, is rather surprising given the lack of a military tradition in Belgium. Similar propaganda issues motivated the naming of streets and squares. Abrassart and Ben Yakoub's (2014) total figure of ninety-eight street names referring to the colonial past for the whole of Belgium seems an underestimation, since in the Brussels Capital Region alone at least thirty-nine streets can be found with a name that refers to this past (Goddeeris 2016). Again, the streets are often named after some military officer who served in the Congo. Most often depicted in monuments and used to name streets is Leopold II, former king of the Belgians (1865–1909), and the de facto owner of the Congo Free State until its annexation as a Belgian colony by the Belgian state in 1908.

Both the place-naming and the memorials thus appear to have been serving the same purpose. Whether these memorials and other propaganda initiatives were successful in their day in terms of what they were supposed to propagate is another issue, but the fact remains that until relatively recently their continued presence met with very little protest. Indeed, Goddeeris states that 'until the end of the twentieth century postcolonial memory [in Belgium] vacillated between nostalgia and disinterest' (2016: 350, my translation). However, a number of publications re-evaluated Belgium's colonial legacy around the turn of the century: Hochschild (1998) accused Leopold II of genocide, Demoulin (2000) called him a 'king with blood on his beard', and the Belgian sociologist De Witte (2001) posited that the Belgian establishment was involved in Lumumba's murder in January 1961. As a result, postcolonial debates surged and, for instance, official excuses were presented to the Congo by the Belgian government in February 2002 (Goddeeris 2016; Goddeeris and Kiangu 2011).

In the aftermath of these events, and in tandem with similar movements contesting memorials, statues and other traces glorifying the colonial past in other (European) countries, the aughts of the present century saw the first instances of protest and criticism of these memorials and street names in Belgium. Statues of Leopold II in particular have been the target of these protests: some of them have been defaced with red paint, sometimes accompanied by tags such as 'assassin' (see Goddeeris 2016, for a detailed list and description). More recently (January 2018), a bust of Leopold II was first stolen from a park in Brussels and then replaced by a duplicate made out of birdseed, resulting in it slowly collapsing into a decomposing heap (see Figure 7.1). In Ostend, a hand was sawn off one of the black statues that stand 'worshipping' underneath the equestrian statue of Leopold II, highlighting the cruelties committed during the exploitation of the Congo Free State (see Figure 7.2).[3] However, in the past, these actions hardly resulted in any modification of the public space: the statues were not removed, no explanatory note was added (one exception aside, namely in Halle, where an information plaque was added) and any requests for a renaming of certain streets and squares were rejected by the local municipalities. Only in Ostend, the cut-off hand was not replaced, meaning its testimony to a less celebratory aspect of Belgium's colonial past remained in place.

It should be noted that the political contestation of these imperialist traces in the public space has often been initiated not only by progressive politicians. Perhaps unexpectedly, it has also been instigated by members of hyper-conservative Flemish nationalist parties, whose motivations are undoubtedly more grounded in their anti-monarchism (which they see on a par with a French-speaking 'old Belgium'). In most cases, the more centralist political parties have been more reticent to change things – or even take up the debate – and they have often used a combination of pragmatic and

Figure 7.1 (Remains of a) Birdseed bust of Leopold II in Brussels (Belgium)

content arguments to resist any changes to street names, statues and other memorials (Goddeeris 2016).

Different from other countries in Europe where similar debates regarding the colonial legacy and postcolonial memory are taking place, the preference in Belgium for a status quo with respect to the display of this colonial legacy could also be partly explained by a fear of stirring up the debate regarding the already complex issue of Belgium's own national identity. In their discussion of the Belgian 'museumification' of colonialism, Bragard and Planche (2009: 187) argue that processes towards a 'sharable' (between colonizers and colonized) narrative of the Belgian colonial past cannot be untied from Belgium's own problematic national identity: 'in addition to being torn between nostalgia and shame, Belgium's colonial memory concurrently needs to integrate into a national memory which is itself torn apart'. According to these scholars,

> the 'colonial dispute' is superposed on another dispute: namely a Belgo-Belgian dispute between the francophones and the Flemings, between the two main communities' conflicting memories, and between separatist and unitarian views on the country's existence. In this context, reappraisals of the colonial past take on a new meaning, as colonialism is often perceived as a mainly francophone bequest, or as Leopold II's alleged abuses are invoked by extremist parties to attack royalty (Vandersmissen 2007) and denied or excused by those willing to preserve what stands as one of the few surviving symbols of the country's unity. (Bragard and Planche 2009: 187)

Figure 7.2 Statue of Leopold II in Ostend (Belgium)

In other words, the (perceived) precariousness of the Belgian national identity in the present impedes a re-memorization of the colonial past, insofar as the latter entails a kind of reorganization of a country's 'national memory'. In Belgium, what this national memory actually consists of is not univocally established and is subject to debate. As a result, if acts such as renaming streets or removing statues are always symbolically salient ways to create new links between the past and present (Alderman 2008), in Belgium, it is not only the embarrassing colonial past which constitutes an obstacle but also the fuzzy present.

In sum, until very recently, we could say that

> the way in which Belgium respects its imperial monuments and fails to erect new ones is symptomatic of its attitude to its colonial past. After heavy turbulence at the turn of the twenty-first century, the country has found a comfortable compromise. It acknowledges mistakes, but continues to paint an overall positive portrait of idealist colonizers. It diminishes left-wing criticism as old-school negativism and

avoids criticism of Belgium's imperial past in view of the country's current political and identity crisis. (Goddeeris 2015: 449)

Now that we have delineated the background and the general outline of Belgium's present handling of its colonial legacy in the public space, let us turn to the case study of the naming of the Patrice Lumumba Square in Brussels.

4. A Patrice Lumumba Square in Brussels

Given what we have discussed above, the renaming of a square as the Patrice Lumumba Square by Brussels city council (Brussels being one of nineteen municipalities that together make up the Brussels Capital Region) may well be considered a surprise by some and a first victory by others. On 23 April 2018, Brussels city council unanimously voted in favour of renaming part[4] of the Bolwerksquare/Square du Bastion as the Patrice Lumumba Square/Square Patrice Lumumba, and the new name was officially inaugurated on 30 June 2018, exactly 58 years after the Congolese declaration of independence. This square is situated on the edge of the city of Brussels' territory, bordering the Ixelles municipality, and near the entrance to the Matonge neighbourhood (see Figures 7.3 and 7.4), which is considered the focal point of the Congolese community living in Belgium, and therefore a highly symbolic location.[5]

At the press conference announcing the city council's decision, the social democrat mayor of Brussels stated the following with respect to the motivations of renaming the square: 'Unfortunately, past actions cannot be undone. But it is possible to bring memories from the past closer together, and so try to reconcile them. The Patrice Lumumba square will be a place of remembrance for the sometimes painful memories of the colonial period' (BRUZZ 23 April 2018, my translation). The political opposition supported the majority's proposal and called the decision 'courageous' (BRUZZ 23 April 2018, my translation).

Figure 7.3 'Patrice Lumumbasquare'/'Square Patrice Lumumba' in Brussels

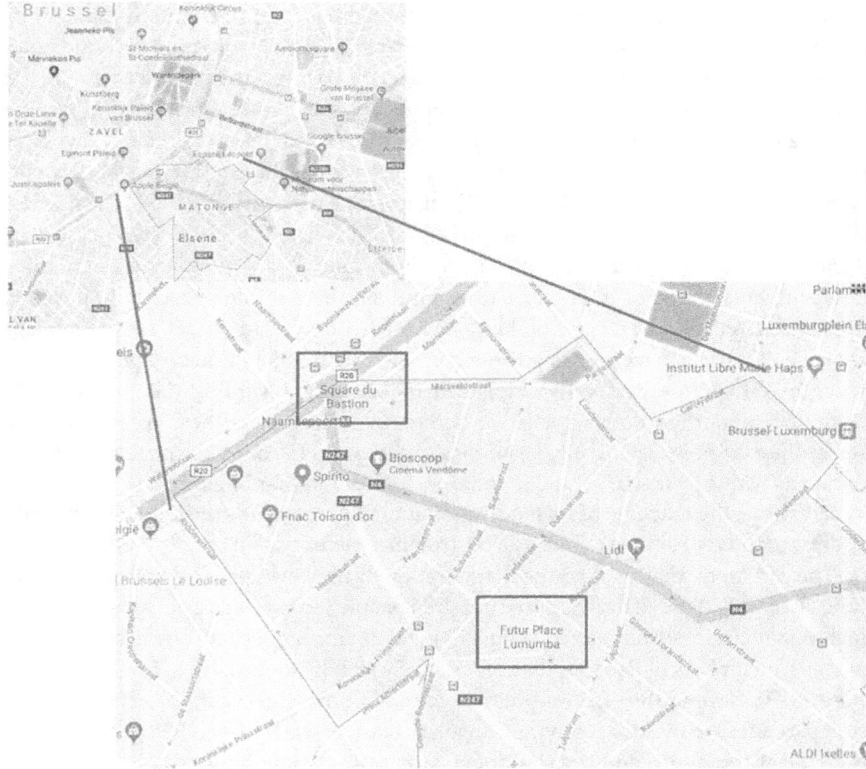

Figure 7.4 Location of the 'Square du bastion/Bolwerksquare' and the 'Futur Place Lumumba' in the Matonge neighbourhood (Google Maps, August 2018)

This apparently unanimous vote and voice across the (ideological and linguistic) political spectrum is surprising and a novelty in comparison to related events in other towns until now, as described above. It should, however, also be mentioned that regardless of the genuineness of the intentions to redress the colonial issue in the public space, local political and electoral motivations may also have contributed to the decision. In the municipal elections taking place a few months after the decision (October 2018), the social democrat mayor of Brussels was going to be challenged by a liberal candidate who belongs to the same party as the mayor of neighbouring Ixelles. Given that the latter had always opposed proposals to name a square after Lumumba (see below) and that in the municipality of Brussels there are more Congolese votes to be won than in neighbouring Ixelles, the mayor of Brussels might have expected some electoral gains.

The odds that the Ixelles part of the same Bolwerksquare/Square du Bastion will also be renamed are indeed low, as the Ixelles municipality has resisted similar proposals on numerous occasions in the past. Since the Matonge neighbourhood is actually located within this municipality (see Figure 7.4), many of the requests to remember Patrice

Lumumba in the public space have been submitted here. Yet the political majority in Ixelles town council has until now always rejected those requests on the grounds that the figure of Lumumba is too contentious. They claim to prefer to honour Africa and the African presence in the municipality in the public space by showcasing less controversial personalities (from other parts of Africa). However, in recent discourse by local policymakers, certain shopkeepers as well as project developers, the neighbourhood is increasingly being referred to as the 'Quartier des continents' (BRUZZ 1 July 2016). According to local activists, the rebranding of 'Matonge' – a clear reference to the African and Congolese identity of the neighbourhood – to a more general 'Quartier des continents' is part of an initiative to rebrand the quartier into an attractive business opportunity for real estate and building developers, hoping to attract a more affluent clientele. The reluctance to recognize a contested figure like Lumumba in the public space may therefore be (partly) explained by concerns regarding the attractiveness of the neighbourhood for a particular audience. Anecdotal as these comments may seem, they do point to the impact of local political and economic considerations on decisions with substantial symbolic value such as the (re)naming (or not) of a square. What's more, the outcome of such decisions arguably transcends the local, as it directly addresses and redresses the country's postcolonial memory.

The ceremony that marked the inauguration of the new name of the square on 30 June 2018 was attended by over three hundred people comprising various stakeholders, including delegates from the city council, many members of the Congolese diaspora, as well as members of Patrice Lumumba's family (RTBF 30 June 2018; *BBC Afrique* 30 June 2018). Beyond the obvious political connotation of the event, the ceremony was set up as a festive event: a 'Fanfare Congolaise' (a big band) played before the start of the official ceremony, and a series of concerts from various artists was organized in the afternoon, including a gospel band and hip-hop, rumba and slam poetry artists 'honoring Patrice Lumumba' (Official program, City of Brussels). Speeches were given by the mayor and by representatives of the various activist associations that have been involved in the fight for public recognition of the figure of Lumumba. In her speech, one of these representatives, Rose Anastasia Mefalessi, stated the following (DH 30 June 2018, my translation):

> This square is here to remind future generations of what schools refuse to teach. It is only a beginning, it is not an end of itself. The fight against colonization continues, it [colonization] is still too present. And reminding people of historical facts is part of this fight.

The notion of the renaming of the square as a beginning and not an endpoint was also reiterated by one of Lumumba's descendants (*De Morgen* 1 July 2018) and by the mayor of the city of Brussels, who talked of the beginning of a 'different history between the Congolese diaspora and the people of Brussels' (*Le Soir* 30 June 2018):

> [Today,] we are writing the name of Patrice Lumumba in the city's collective memory. [...] Now, in the heart of Brussels, we start to write our history. (*De Morgen* 1 July 2018, my translation)

The inauguration received considerable coverage across various news outlets in both the French- and Dutch-speaking press (cf. also the references above), and the portrayal was generally positive, focusing on the novelty of a reference to Lumumba in the public space, while also paying attention to the Congolese diaspora's voice in the matter.

As mentioned, various activist-artist collectives (who joined hands in the overarching *Collectif Mémoire Coloniale*) had been calling for the recognition of Lumumba in the public space for a number of years now. One of their goals was precisely to have Ixelles city council name a small and hitherto unnamed square in the Matonge neighbourhood after Patrice Lumumba. The activists used a variety of online awareness-raising initiatives, such as a Facebook page called *placelumumbaplein*, with more than 1,200 followers, as well as offline initiatives, such as attaching self-fabricated street name plaques to the buildings on the square. Activists also staged a number of events on the same square, including re-enactments of Lumumba's famous speech. Until the actual naming of the present Patrice Lumumba Square, their major accomplishment was the fact that Google Maps added the name 'Futur Place Lumumba' on their online maps (July 2015, see Figure 7.4), which for a long time had been the only reference to Lumumba in Brussels on Google Maps. Also relevant was the placement of a provisional statue of Lumumba, entitled 'Patrice Lumumba, le discours d'indépendance du 30 juin 1960', by artist Rhode Makoumbou, in the central Ravenstein gallery in Brussels (January 2018). According to the campaigners of this event, the statue was made out of sawdust rather than a more durable material to symbolize its transitional state, awaiting placement on a then still hypothetical Lumumba Square. It should be mentioned that the initiative was supported by the French community and cultural venue Bozar (BRUZZ, 21 January 2018), indicating a positive stance from at least part of the political and cultural establishment towards the initiative. According to Mireille Tsheusi Robert from the Bamko collective, which led the campaign for the event, 'Lumumba is a symbol of peace and liberty [...] The statue does not only inform the population about the colonization, but helps us go beyond the traumatic experience. It's a form of collective therapy' (BRUZZ, 21 January 2018, my translation) and constitutes a way 'to finally be able to look the colonial past straight in the eye' (RTBF, 22 January 2018, my translation).

Interestingly, both in the activist's words above ('collective therapy') and the mayor of Brussels' words equally mentioned above ('bring memories closer together and try to reconcile them') reference is made to a *collective* way of dealing with the past. The public recognition of the figure of Patrice Lumumba, and therefore the (implicit) recognition of the atrocities committed by the Belgians in the former colony, is thus regarded by different actors as a step towards the formulation of a narrative of the Belgian colonial past that is *sharable* between the descendants of former victims and former perpetrators, and it is in this sense that it can be considered an act of empowerment. Similar to the Spanish case discussed above (Guilat and Espinosa-Ramírez 2016), I would argue that the naming of the Lumumba Square possibly signals a transition towards a different 'regime of memory' regarding the colonial past: away from the depiction of the former metropole as the saviour of the former colony, away from the clumsy avoidance of the colonial past of the past 20 years, towards a possible path of addressing – and potentially overcoming – the shame and guilt associated with

Belgium's colonial past. The overtly future-oriented perspective expressed and shared by the various stakeholders at hand, namely one where the renaming of the square is explicitly framed as a new beginning, corroborates this new direction. In this sense, a rearrangement of the public space such as the one presented here may well provide a (modest) contribution to empowerment of the Congolese diaspora in Belgium and to a transformation of Belgium's dealing with its colonial heritage.

Before we conclude this chapter, we must address a topic that has been elided in the discussion so far, namely the role of language(s) and language choice in this entire debate. This may be considered surprising, given the linguistico-political situation in Belgium, on the one hand, and the conspicuous multilingual character of the Congo,[6] on the other hand. Yet, at first glance, there does not seem much to say in this regard. The official bilingual Dutch-French legislation in place in the Brussels Capital Region and its municipalities is duly followed, both in the case of the display of the square's official name (with the use of the bilingual 'square' – with its English origins – not to be interpreted as a political choice, but as a simple copying of the square's previous name) and in the mayor's bilingual Dutch-French speech on the day of the inauguration. Many of the bottom-up protests and events mentioned have been conducted in French, given the fact that the linguistic repertoire of the larger part of the Congolese diaspora comprises a working knowledge of French at the very least, besides their knowledge of Congolese languages as well as Dutch if they live in officially Dutch-speaking Flanders. The choice of English for the message depicted in Figure 7.1 can in this sense be considered an exception. Given the activist group's anonymity, we can only conjecture as to their reasons for using English, but aiming for a message that can be (virally) shared with a wider international public (beyond the 'francophonie'), thereby pegging themselves to similar transnational movements (such as Rhodes Must Fall, for instance) seems like a plausible explanation. What may be noteworthy with respect to the role of language in the contemporary postcolonial debate in Belgium in general, and which also applies to the circumstances surrounding the renaming of the Patrice Lumumba Square, is the complete absence of the many (or indeed some of the major) languages spoken in the Congo. If this invisibility can partly be explained by the use of French as a lingua franca among the Congolese diaspora in Belgium, the absence still resonates with other studies attesting to the invisibility of the linguistic legacy of the people being commemorated. For a more in-depth treatment of this issue, see, for instance, Fabrício and Borba (2020).

5. Concluding remarks

A central concern of this contribution, as well as the edited volume as a whole, is the notion of empowerment. We should therefore ask the question who, if anyone, is being empowered by a new Patrice Lumumba Square in the centre of Brussels? Indeed, the current grappling with the country's colonial legacy remains chiefly a Belgian issue, in the sense that it is an issue 'rather remote from the Congolese's present concerns' (Ndaywel 2008, quoted in Bragard and Planche 2009: 182). One may indeed wonder to what extent the people living in the Congo, who have been subject to ongoing periods of conflict and unrest for a couple of decades now, benefit from symbolic struggles about street names and statues in the former metropole. One can only hope that the public recognition of Lumumba as one of the important instigators of Congo's independence may help to turn a page of history and further contribute to a 'healthy' relationship between the two countries, as stated by historian M'Bokolo in JeuneAfrique (26 November 2013, my translation):

> If we want healthy relations between the two countries, the Belgians must recognize those of ours [i.e. the Congolese] who played a role in the independence of the Congo. In my opinion, the independence occupies a very important place in the history of both the Congo and Belgium. For Belgium, this would be the best way to turn the page of colonization and start normal relations with the Congo, as Lumumba advocated in his speech of 30 June 1960.

Turning back to the Congolese diaspora in Belgium, it is clear that this community is affected by the re-memorization of the colonial past in the Belgian public space. Indeed, members of this relatively small community (Schoonvaere 2010), aided by artists and anthropologists (see Goddeeris 2015; Mertens et al. 2013), have become increasingly vocal in challenging the prevalent postcolonial narrative, as attested by their growing activism in recent years. Notwithstanding the possible role of local (small-town) political considerations in the renaming or not of a square, various activist groups' efforts have contributed to a shift in the postcolonial memory among at least part of the public, a potential restart which has led to the recent inauguration of the Patrice Lumumba Square. Indeed, it would appear that the inertia characterizing Belgium's dealing with its postcolonial legacy after the turmoil at the turn of the century (cf. Goddeeris 2015) has been broken to some extent, and a number of events that took place briefly after the inauguration of the square have also renewed discussions on the country's colonial past. So, for instance, the reopening of the Africa Museum at Tervuren (near Brussels) in December 2018 sparked much debate, as did the broadcast of a six-episode television series entitled 'Children of the Colony' on the Dutch-speaking public broadcaster Canvas in the same month, comprising various testimonies by Belgians and Congolese about their colonial and postcolonial experiences. February 2019 saw the presentation of a preliminary UN report on racism towards people of African descent in contemporary Belgium,[7] a report suggesting among other things that Belgium should apologize for the atrocities committed during the country's colonial past, thereby explicitly linking past and present, and applauding the naming of the Patrice Lumumba Square as a first positive initiative.

Since these are all very recent events, their precise impact on postcolonial remembrance is difficult to gauge at the time of writing. And to state that these events, and the grassroots 'guerilla' actions that now and then occur, have sparked a wide-ranging societal debate on the country's colonial past would be an overstatement, as the 'comfortable compromise' – as coined by Goddeeris (2015) – is perhaps too comfortable to abandon. However, one may hope that the discussions that have arisen contribute not only to a gradual recognition and inclusion of a range of narratives about Belgium's harrowing colonial past but also, and perhaps even more importantly, to a continued questioning and recalibration of its postcolonial present.

As such, even if the official naming of the Patrice Lumumba Square in Brussels clearly does not belong to Rice's (2011) favoured category of 'guerilla memorials' (in contrast to the above-mentioned statues made out of sawdust or birdseed, for instance), the recognition of a contested figure like Patrice Lumumba in the capital's public space does contribute to 'transcend(ing) the limited and often chauvinistic national story to remember a more complex and multifaceted (trans)national narrative to help us in the post-colonial present' (Rice 2011: 271). In my opinion, it would therefore be reductive to interpret the inauguration of the Patrice Lumumba Square as a simple means for the Belgian local authorities to display atonement and in this way contribute to achieving the desired political closure on the topic, which would in fact only constitute a marginal sidestep from the comfortable status quo. Equally, I do not believe the naming of the square should be viewed as a cynical ploy to attract voters, thereby dismissing the Patrice Lumumba Square as mere tokenism. Even if these motivations may have played a role, we should not forget that (a) the artist–activist collectives in particular and the Congolese diaspora more generally have, through their continued demands and actions, contributed significantly to the existence of the Patrice Lumumba Square themselves and that (b) this is the very first time the Congolese perspective on the colonial history is being acknowledged in Brussels' public space, and that hence this may be the first step towards offering a counter-narrative to the many Brussels streets quietly celebrating the 'Belgian' colonial history in the former metropole's capital.

Notes

1. Note (30 November 2020): This chapter was written and accepted in its current version before the widespread anti-racist protests in June 2020 following the death of George Floyd in Minneapolis, United States. In Belgium, these protests have also led to renewed and amplified calls for the removal of the Leopold II statues from the public space, as well as the renaming of streets and squares. It remains to be seen at this stage whether these calls will lead to the effective removal of said statues, or the renaming of said streets.
2. Belgium's colonial rule extended over a large part of Central Africa, including present countries the Democratic Republic of the Congo, and, after the First World War, Rwanda and Burundi. The Congo Free State was ruled as a de facto personal possession by King Leopold II between 1885 and 1908, after which the territory was transferred to the Belgian state and became officially the Belgian Congo until it gained independence in 1960.
3. Note that interventionist actions such as these can usefully be described by Alan Rice's (2010, 2011) term 'guerilla memorialization', in that they work to 'rewrite the city and nation's history from the bottom up …, negotiat[ing] new meanings out of the interaction between what is there and what is missing' (Rice 2011: 256).
4. The original Bolwerksquare/Square du Bastion straddled two municipalities, namely Brussels and Ixelles. Note that the use of the word 'square' in both Dutch and French toponyms instead of 'plein/place' is not uncommon in Brussels. The official plaque (see

Figure 7.3) should therefore be read as 'Square Patrice Lumumba' (French)/'Patrice Lumumbasquare' (Dutch). For comparison, in the case of a street the sign would have read 'Rue Patrice Lumumba'/'Patrice Lumumbastraat', with the words 'rue' and 'straat' on the top and bottom of the sign, respectively.
5. If the Matonge neighbourhood is popularly known as the 'African/Congolese' neighbourhood in Brussels, its number of inhabitants from African descent is actually relatively low. However, the presence of food markets, hairdressers and other specialist shops makes it a hotspot for the Congolese living in Brussels and in Belgium more generally. Swyngedouw and Swyngedouw (2009: 68) call the neighbourhood an example of a 'particular urban socio-cultural and socio-economic environment … that function[s] as [a] specific and concrete local anchoring point … for multi-scalar identity formation'.
6. Besides the official language (French) and four national languages (Kikongo, Lingala, Swahili and Tshiluba), it is estimated that over two hundred languages are spoken in the Congo (Bokamba 2008).
7. https://www.unric.org/nl/nieuwsoverzicht/27519-vn-experten-roepen-belgie-op-om-koloniale-verleden-onder-ogen-te-zien.

References

Abousnnouga, G., and Machin, D. (2010), 'War Monuments and the Changing Discourses of Nation and Soldiery', in A. Jaworski and C. Thurlow (eds), *Semiotic Landscapes: Language, Image, Space*, 219–40, London: Continuum.

Abrassart, G., and Ben Yakoub, J. (2014), 'Tijd voor de dekolonisatie van België', Rekto: verso, 62. Available online: https://www.rektoverso.be/artikel/tijd-voor-de-dekolonisatie-van-belgië.

Alderman, D. H. (2008), 'Place, Naming and the Interpretation of Cultural Landscapes', in B. Graham and P. Howard (eds), *The Ashgate Research Companion to Heritage and Identity*, 195–213, Burlington (VT): Ashgate Press.

Armada, B. J. (1998), 'Memorial Agon: An Interpretive Tour of the National Civil Rights Museum', *Southern Communication Journal*, 63 (3): 235–43.

Azaryahu, M. (1997), 'German Reunification and the Politics of Street Names: The Case of East Berlin', *Political Geography*, 16 (6): 479–93.

BBC Afrique (2018), 'Belgique : une place Lumumba inaugurée à Bruxelles', 30 June. Available online: https://www.bbc.com/afrique/region-44667649 (accessed 26 January 2021).

Ben-Rafael, E. (2016), 'Introduction [to a Special Issue]', *Linguistic Landscape*, 2 (3): 207–10. doi: 10.1075/ll.2.3.001int.

Blackwood, R., and Macalister, J. (eds) (2020), *Multilingual Memories. Monuments, Museums and the Linguistic Landscape*, London: Bloomsbury.

Blommaert, J. (2013), *Ethnography, Superdiversity and Linguistic Landscapes: Chronicles of Complexity*, Bristol, UK: Multilingual Matters.

Bokamba, E. G. (2008), 'D.R. Congo: Language and 'Authentic Nationalism', in A. Simpson (ed.), *Language and National Identity in Africa*, 214–34, Oxford: Oxford University Press.

Bragard, V., and Planche, S. (2009), 'Museum Practices and the Belgian Colonial Past: Questioning the Memories of an Ambivalent Metropole', *African and Black Diaspora: An International Journal*, 2 (2): 181–91. doi: 10.1080/17528630902981332.

BRUZZ (2018), 'Officieel: Brussel krijgt Patrice Lumumbasquare', 23 April. Available online: https://www.bruzz.be/samenleving/officieel-brussel-krijgt-patrice-lumumbasquare-2018-04-23 (accessed 26 January 2021).

BRUZZ (2018), 'Tijdelijk Lumumbaplein en standbeeld in Ravensteingalerij', 21 January. Available online: https://www.bruzz.be/politiek/tijdelijk-lumumbaplein-en-standbeeld-ravensteingalerij-2018-01-21 (accessed 26 January 2021).

Busch, B. (2013), 'The Career of a Diacritical Sign: Language in Spatial Representations and Representational Spaces', in S. Pietikäinen and H. Kelly-Holmes (eds), *Multilingualism and the Periphery*, 199–221, Oxford: Oxford University Press.

De Morgen (2018), 'Lumumba heft dan toch zijn eigen pleintje in Brussel', 1 July. Available online: https://www.demorgen.be/nieuws/lumumba-heeft-dan-toch-zijn-eigen-pleintje-in-brussel~baf2a361/ (accessed 26 January 2021).

Demoulin, L. (2000), *Ulysse Lumumba*, Mons: Editions Talus d'approche.

De Witte, L. (2001), *The Assassination of Lumumba*, London: Verso.

DH (2018), 'Bruxelles-Ville: Plus de 300 personnes pour l'inauguration du square Lumumba', 30 June. Available online: https://www.dhnet.be/regions/bruxelles/bruxelles-ville-plus-de-300-personnes-pour-l-inauguration-du-square-lumumba-5b3799555532692547d23f15 (accessed 26 January 2021).

Fabrício, B. F., and Borba, R. (2020), 'Remembering in Order to Forget: Scaled Memories of Slavery in the Linguistic Landscape of Rio de Janeiro', in R. Blackwood and J. Macalister (eds), *Multilingual Memories. Monuments, Museums and the Linguistic Landscape*, 187–212, London: Bloomsbury.

Foucault, M. (1981), *Power/Knowledge: Selected Interviews and Other Writings*, New York: Random House.

Gill, G. (2005), 'Changing Symbols: The Renovation of Moscow Place Names', *Russian Review*, 64 (3): 480–503.

Goddeeris, I. (2015), 'Postcolonial Belgium', *Interventions*, 17 (3): 434–51. doi: 10.1080/1369801X.2014.998253.

Goddeeris, I. (2016), 'Square de Léopoldville of Place Lumumba? De Belgische (post)koloniale herinnering in de publieke ruimte', *Tijdschrift voor geschiedenis*, 129 (3): 349–72. doi: 10.5117/TVGESCH2016.3.GODD.

Goddeeris, I., and Kiangu, S. E. (2011), 'Congomania in Academia. Recent Historical Research on the Belgian Colonial Past', *BMGN-LCHR (Low Countries Historical Review)*, 126 (4): 54–74.

Gorter, D., Marten, H. F., and Van Mensel, L. (eds) (2012), *Minority Languages in the Linguistic Landscape*, Basingstoke: Palgrave Macmillan.

Guilat, Y., and Espinosa-Ramírez, A. B. (2016), 'The Historical Memory Law and Its Role in Redesigning Semiotic Cityscapes in Spain. A Case Study from Granada', *Linguistic Landscape*, 2 (3): 247–74. doi: 10.1075/ll.2.3.03gui.

Hochschild, A. (1998), *King Leopold's Ghost: A Story of Greed, Terror and Heroism in Colonial Africa*, New York: Houghton Mifflin.

Jaworski, A., and Thurlow, C. (eds) (2010), *Semiotic Landscapes: Language, Image, Space*, London: Continuum.

Lefebvre, H. ([1973] 1991), *The Production of Space*, D. Nicholson-Smith (trans.), Oxford: Blackwell.

Le Soir (2018), 'Plus de 300 personnes à l'inauguration du square Patrice Lumumba à Bruxelles', 30 June. Available online: https://www.lesoir.be/165696/article/2018-06-30/plus-de-300-personnes-linauguration-du-square-patrice-lumumba-bruxelles (accessed 26 January 2021).

Light, D. (2004), 'Street Names in Bucharest, 1990–1997: Exploring the Modern Historical Geographies of Post-Socialist Change', *Journal of Historical Geography*, 30 (1): 154–72.

Lou, J. J. (2016), 'Shop Sign as Monument. The Discursive Recontextualization of a Neon Sign', *Linguistic Landscape*, 2 (3): 211–22. doi: 10.1075/ll.2.3.01lou.

Mertens, J., Goedertier, W., Goddeeris, I., and De Brabanter, D. (2013), 'A New Floor for the Silenced? Congolese Hip-Hop in Belgium', *Social Transformations*, 1 (1): 87–113.

Moriarty, M. (2012) 'Language Ideological Debates in the Linguistic Landscape of an Irish Town', in D. Gorter, H. F. Marten and L. Van Mensel (eds), *Minority Languages in the Linguistic Landscape*, 74–88, Basingstoke: Palgrave Macmillan.

Ndaywel, I. (2008), 'Evolution de l'historiographie congolaise: de l'indépendance à nos jours', paper presented to the SOMA-CEGES Symposium Belgium-Congo. History vs. Memory, Brussels, 31 January–1 February.

Pavlenko, A. (2010), 'Linguistic Landscape of Kyiv, Ukraine: A Diachronic Study', in E. Shohamy, E. Ben-Rafael and M. Barni (eds), *Linguistic Landscape in the City*, 133–50, Bristol, UK: Multilingual Matters.

Pavlenko, A. (2012), 'Transgression as the Norm: Russian in the Linguistic Landscape of Kyiv, Ukraine', in D. Gorter, H. F. Marten and L. Van Mensel (eds), *Minority Languages in the Linguistic Landscape*, 36–56, Basingstoke: Palgrave Macmillan.

Pavlenko, A., and Mullen, A. (2015), 'Why Diachronicity Matters in the Study of Linguistic Landscapes', *Linguistic Landscape*, 1 (1/2): 114–32.

Rice, A. (2010), *Creating Memorials, Building Identities: The Politics of Memory in the Black Atlantic*, Liverpool: Liverpool University Press.

Rice, A. (2011), 'Tracing Slavery and Abolition's Routes and Viewing Inside the Invisible: The Monumental Landscape and the African Atlantic', *Atlantic Studies*, 8 (2): 253–74. doi: 10.1080/14788810.2011.563830.

Robinson, G. M., Engelsoft, S., and Pobric, A. (2001), 'Remaking Sarajevo: Bosnian Nationalism after the Dayton Accord', *Political Geography*, 20 (8): 957–80.

RTBF (2018), 'Patrice Lumumba: une statue pour regarder notre passé colonial en face', 22 January. Available online: https://www.rtbf.be/info/societe/detail_patrice-lumumba-une-statue-pour-regarder-notre-passe-colonial-en-face?id=9818789 (accessed 26 January 2021).

RTBF (2018), 'Plus de 300 personnes à l'inauguration de la nouvelle place Lumumba à Bruxelles', 30 June. Available online: https://www.rtbf.be/info/regions/detail_une-nouvelle-place-lumumba-a-bruxelles?id=9960511 (accessed 26 January 2021).

Sánchez León, P. (2012), 'Overcoming the Violent Past in Spain', *European Review*, 20 (4): 492–504. doi: 10.1017/S1062798712000063.

Shohamy, E., and Gorter, D. (eds) (2009), *Linguistic Landscape: Expanding the Scenery*, New York: Routledge.

Shohamy, E., and Waksman, S. (2010), 'Building the Nation, Writing the Past', in A. Jaworski and C. Thurlow (eds), *Semiotic Landscapes: Language, Image, Space*, 241–55, London: Continuum.

Schoonvaere, Q. (2010), *Studie over de Congolese migratie en de impact ervan op de Congolese aanwezigheid in België. Analyse van de voornaamste demografische gegevens*, Brussels: Studiegroep Toegepaste Demografie UCL and Centrum voor Gelijkheid van Kansen en voor Racismebestrijding.

Shohamy, E., and Waksman, S. (2012), 'Talking Back to the Tel Aviv Centennial: LL Responses to Top-Down Agendas', in C. Hélot, M. Barni, R. Janssens and C. Bagna (eds), *Linguistic Landscapes, Multilingualism and Social Change: Multiple Perspectives*, 109–26, Frankfurt am Main: Peter Lang GmbH.

Shohamy, E. (2015), 'LL Research as Expanding Language and Language Policy', *Linguistic Landscape*, 1 (1/2): 152–71.

Smouts, M.-C. (2007), 'Le postcolonial pour quoi faire?', in M.-C. Smouts (ed.), *La situation postcoloniale. Les postcolonial studies dans le débat français*, 25–58, Paris: Presses de la Fondation Nationale des Sciences Politiques.

Spalding, T. (2013), *Layers: The Design, History and Meaning of Public Signage in Cork and Other Irish Cities*, Dublin: Associated Editions.

Stanard, M. G. (2011), *Selling the Congo: A History of European Pro-Empire Propaganda and the Making of Belgian Imperialism*, Lincoln: University of Nebraska Press.

Swyngedouw, E., and Swyngedouw, E. (2009), 'The Congolese Diaspora in Brussels and Hybrid Identity Formation: Multi-Scalarity and Diasporic Citizenship', *Urban Research and Practice*, 2 (1): 68–90. doi: 10.1080/17535060902727074.

Train, R. W. (2016), 'Connecting Visual Presents to Archival Pasts in Multilingual California. Towards Historical Depth in Linguistic Landscape', *Linguistic Landscape*, 2 (3): 223–46. doi 10.1075/ll.2.3.02tra.

Van Mensel, L., Vandenbroucke, M., and Blackwood, R. (2016), 'Linguistic Landscapes', in O. García, N. Flores and M. Spotti (eds), *Oxford Handbook of Language and Society*, 423–49 Oxford: Oxford University Press.

Vandenbroucke, M. (2018), 'Multilingualism, Urban Change and Gentrification in the Landscape of a Brussels Neighbourhood', *Multilingua*, 37 (1): 25–52. doi: 10.1515/multi-2015-0103.

Vandersmissen, J. (2007), 'Cent ans d'instrumentalisation de Léopold II, symbole controversé de la présence belge en Afrique centrale', in S. Jahan and A. Ruscio (eds), *Histoire de la colonisation. Réhabilitations, Falsifications et Instrumentalisations*, 223–40, Paris: Les Indes Savantes.

Viaene, V., Van Reybrouck, D., and Ceuppens, B. (eds) (2009), *Congo in België. Koloniale cultuur in de metropool*, Leuven: Universitaire Pers Leuven.

Woldemariam, H. (2016), 'Linguistic Landscape as Standing Historical Testimony of the Struggle against Colonization in Ethiopia', *Linguistic Landscape*, 2 (3): 275–90. doi: 10.1075/ll.2.3.04wol.

8

Linguistic Landscape activism as a means of community empowerment: Direct action, Ai'Ta and Breton in France

Robert Blackwood

1. Introduction

Activism has served as a tool for empowerment since at least the twentieth century, and a volume, such as this one, which thinks through the issues around empowerment would be incomplete without considering the extent to which action – social, political or direct – contributes to debates on multilingualism. In this chapter, I discuss language activism, specifically in Brittany, in north-west France, and direct action as a means of empowerment for language activists and the wider community. I examine in particular the activities of the collective known as Ai'Ta! (which means 'listen!' in Breton) who seek to disrupt the regularity and uniformity of language in the public space by the emplacement of the regional language in sites managed by Brittany's civic authorities. Analysing the positionings, actions and responses to Ai'Ta!'s undertakings is usefully nuanced by the concepts and critical vocabulary of stance, and in doing so, this chapter responds to the call by Jaffe (2007: 4) to identify salient dimensions of stance research for sociolinguistic scholarship. In invoking stance, I recall the work by Du Bois (2007: 163) who argues that stancetaking implies 'a public act by a social actor, achieved dialogically through overt communicative means, of simultaneously evaluating objects, positioning subjects (self and others), and aligning with other subjects, with respect to any salient dimension of the sociocultural field'. The critical vocabulary of stance, especially the lexicon of alignment, is particularly pertinent in this presentation and analysis of Ai'Ta!.

In particular, in this chapter, I look at the interconnection between stance and Scollon and Scollon's geosemiotics (2003). Scollon and Scollon (2003: 8–23) contend that the intersection of the interaction order, visual semiotics and the semiotics of place, where code preferences, inscription systems and emplacement are privileged, permits the exploration of discourses in place in the material world. To that end, and based on interviews with volunteers from Ai'Ta! and on a critical examination of the group's activities, I explore here the ideologies articulated by language activists in their actions at sites where meaning is intensely activated through performances of social interaction.

The starting point for this discussion are the Linguistic Landscape (henceforth LL) activities undertaken by Ai'Ta! which include – as we discuss more fully below – the removal of monolingual road signs and the emplacing of orange stickers on signage where information is given in French only, calling for a Breton-language version. This use of very visible stickers on monolingual signage can be understood, drawing from scholarship on stance, as the commitment in texts – to adapt Fairclough's 2003 terminology – from the perspective of evaluation, subverting the common-or-garden road sign in what might be considered as a highly non-normative way. Using Du Bois's definition (2007), this activism constitutes disalignment with the language practices of Brittany's regional authorities who commission, pay for and erect the signs which feature only French. The stancetaking by the regional authorities in Brittany is implicit and yet clear: the traditional ideology of the State is conveyed on these road signs by the use French as the only medium of communication. The language activism investigated in this chapter gives voice to individuals who recognize the potential significance of the visibility of Breton in Brittany, but who are normally silenced by all levels of political representation, thereby articulating one way by which direct action is used for empowering a specific community.

In this chapter, I problematize minority language (in)visibility on the basis of the direct actions of Ai'Ta! in the public space and their ideological stances. First, I provide a range of contexts which identify the circumstances in which this linguistic activism is undertaken, including the French State's long-standing language ideologies, an external history of Breton, the local conditions for Ai'Ta!'s activities and recent LL scholarship examining Breton. Second, I identify three distinct but inter-related rationales for this kind of LL activism, drawing out how these positions can be framed as acts of collective empowerment. Finally, I privilege the intersection of stance (Judge 2007) and geosemiotics (Scollon and Scollon 2003) to draw conclusions from the public positioning and activities of Ai'Ta! about direct action as linguistic empowerment.

2. Contexts

2.1 Overview

The fact that this example of language activism comes from France is not insignificant. Competition in the linguistic market of France is not new, and has been comprehensively covered in recent scholarship (Adamson 2007; Judge 2007; Kremnitz 2013; Walter 2012). Over a period that starts well before the Revolution of 1789, the French language, championed by the French court, grammarians, and elites in various guises, neutered its rivals and was established as the national standard language *par excellence*. The myth-making around the supremacy of French in France has been imperfectly counterbalanced by attempts to revitalize France's regional languages, of which there are nine or ten historic languages, plus several varieties closely related to these languages. Inevitably, terminology is contested, hierarchies are created and challenged, and older epithets – dialects, *patois* and the like – persist (see, e.g. Broadridge and Marley 2019; Depau 2019; Joubert 2019 for contemporary coverage from across France). Within the public space, with notable exceptions such as the precincts of schools or within law courts, the regional languages have not been outlawed in a strictly legal sense, although evidence abounds of the stigmatization of speaking Catalan, Corsican or Occitan outwith the family or friendship circle. When it comes to writing, French has been seen as the preferred – and latterly only acceptable – variety for the production of language, but this approach has been increasingly challenged since the end of the twentieth century.

2.2 Breton as a language of France

Breton, as a Celtic language of France, has traditionally been identified with the western side of Brittany, but the number of its speakers has been in decline, stabilizing towards the end of the twentieth century, and it is now used by approximately 5 per cent of the population (Broudic 2013: 441). Breton was one of the languages cited by Barère de Vieuzac in his 1794 report on language variation across the new republic of France. He explicitly linked what he termed as lower Breton with what he referred to as federalism and superstition; federalism, to him, meant the rival Girondin cause whose Breton, Norman and western French supporters had revolted against the centralizing tendencies of the ascendant Jacobins. By superstition, Barère de Vieuzac was referring to the Catholic Church, whose support in Brittany was seen to threaten the Revolution. However, the aggressive campaign to marginalize the regional languages of France has its antecedents in policies originally intended to limit the use of Latin (and thereby limit the power of the Church). This long-standing language policy can be dated back at least as far as the Ordonnance de Villers-Cotterêts of 1539, when King François I decreed that legal documents must be written in French and no other language (Judge 2007: 16–17). From the Revolution through to the twentieth century, the French language was established by successive political regimes as the only appropriate language for all High domains. Since the second half of the nineteenth century, French has bled into Low domains, including the home – regarded as essential for language transmission. By the Liberation in 1945, it is believed that there were no monolingual speakers of any of France's minority languages left (Judge 2007: 27).

With France's regional languages acutely marginalized, it was what Smith (1991: 125) refers to as the third wave of ethnonationalism in the 1960s that heralded the revitalization strategies employed by language activists across France. One dimension to minority language revitalization has been the emplacement of languages such as Breton, Basque, Catalan and Corsican in the public space, not with a view to displacing French, but aiming instead to establish a visible status for these languages for a variety of reasons that we explore below. Meanwhile, the positioning of French as the ultimate language of France has been internalized across the country. There is a broad acceptance of linguistic diversity, and there is even ample evidence of tolerance for multilingualism, but the hegemony of the French language is totemic to the stage where it is possible to see the unquestionable dominance of French as an article of faith for many but, of course, not all citizens of France.[1]

Exploring the tension between a dominant national standard language and dominated minority or regional languages in the public space works particularly well because of the long-established ideologies towards languages other than French. This narrative that France equates to the French language which in turn equates to a single, indivisible people is so dramatically inapplicable to contemporary life with its intensified mobility, its reclaiming of rights and its superdiversity that any research into this contesting of languages in the public space is fruitful.

2.3 The Linguistic Landscape of Brittany

Explorations of the LL across France are always set against the backcloth of the French state's well-known language laws which consistently protect the use of French in many domains of public life, and regulate the deployment of other languages. As discussed elsewhere (Blackwood 2018: 554), the Toubon law of 1994, which focuses on the use of the national standard language in commercial and civic activities, requires the provision of all information used in the public space in French. While Article 21 of the law states that the provisions of this law are not intended to curb the use of languages such as Breton (without actually naming any of France's regional languages), the measures of this legislation effectively challenge the written use of minority languages in a range of areas, including public services. Research thus far into the LL of Brittany has taken a number of perspectives, including the early quantitative studies I undertook (Blackwood 2010, 2011), Hornsby's (2008) exploration of the incongruence of Breton in the LL of the region to young learners of the language and Vigers's (2013) examination of questions of authenticity and memory. Various lines of enquiry have been opened up here, including the potential for road signs, street signs, and toponymic signage to memorialize the Breton language, culture, heritage and traditions (Vigers 2013: 175). It is this 'historicization of memory' (ibid.: 175) that members of Ai'Ta! reject in their calls to transform Breton into a living, written language, rather than qualify it as a regional or heritage language, a point to which we return below. The situation is further complicated by strident voices within French hegemonic discourse (Vigers 2013: 178) who cite internal variation within Breton as rendering the regional language unsuitable for inclusion in the public space, and in particular in official signage. At the very least, it is argued that orthographic choices inevitably made for the use of Breton on public signage have the potential for unintended implications, ranging from creating a hierarchy of varieties of Breton to preventing comprehension completely.

Statistically speaking, the visual arrangement of Brittany – and the city of Rennes, the administrative capital in particular – is overwhelmingly francophone, with the region's written culture, as it appears in the public domain, saturated by French (Blackwood 2010: 303). When Breton does feature in the LL, it is twice as likely to appear alongside French in a given sign as it is to appear on its own (Blackwood 2010: 295), and this raises an interesting issue in the light of the focus of this chapter around the independence of Breton. In particular, given the emphasis on empowerment, the appearance of Breton alongside French in the public space reinforces the hierarchical relationship with the national standard language. In other words, the trend to emplace Breton alongside French, rather than to affix Breton-language signs independent of the French equivalent, reinforces the subordinated position of the minority language in relation to the national standard (see Figure 8.1 for a visual example of this arrangement). Vigers (2013: 178) highlights the paradox of the increased visibility of the Breton language in road signs and of Breton toponyms: 'While gaining visibility in the public space as a reaffirmation of an historical presence and as an aspiration for the future, the very presence of Breton confirms disparity of status.' At first glance, this might well appear inevitable, but as we discuss below, changing the nature of the relationship between advocates of Breton and those of French is a key aim of language activists including Ai'Ta!

From a quantitative perspective, the diachronic approach to LL research, whereby the same streets are surveyed on two different occasions, is particularly informative. Based on my diachronic fieldwork in Rennes, the administrative capital of Brittany, in 2007 and 2014, I concluded (Blackwood 2015: 44–5) that the process of rendering the LL a 'domain of necessity' (Edwards 2007: 244) had stalled, with minimal statistical changes in the presence of Breton in the city's public space. For the handful of Breton signs that had appeared in the LL, a further handful had disappeared. Where Breton had been emplaced on the walls of the city, in two of the three cases, the author-originator of

Figure 8.1 Sign in the Rennes metro system with multiple subordinations (position, font, size) of Breton

the signs was the city council; for the third, a privately owned driving school displayed a trilingual French/Breton/Arabic welcome sign.

Based on the entries in the Zotero LL bibliography,[2] scholarship on language visibility in the public space of Brittany makes up a considerable proportion of the research outputs spatially identified with France, and represents an important contribution to the debates on visibility of minority languages in Europe.

2.4 Linguistic Landscape activism in Brittany

There are a number of organizations and groups which act on behalf of the Breton language in Brittany, as well as those which defend and promote Gallo, the Romance minority language of the region. In this chapter, I focus specifically on the collective known as Ai'Ta! The organisation was formed in 2005 by both Breton-speaking (known as Bretonnant) and non-Breton-speaking individuals, initially from the Trégor district of northern Brittany, with the intention of pursuing direct action to establish a place for the regional language in order to save it (Yekel 2016: 12). Ai'Ta! explicitly positions itself as an independent movement, and is not aligned to any political party, trades union or other association. The group operates on the basis that the invisibility of the regional language is a form of repression.

Members of the action group Ai'Ta! do not style themselves as LL activists, although, in part, this is effectively what they are. Ai'Ta! is a collective of motivated and active individuals who aim to both defend and promote Breton. The defence of Breton takes a number of forms, including the organization of petitions and demonstrations, the writing and distribution of position pieces, the lobbying of civic authorities in the region and – of particular interest to this chapter – direct action, such as the mock 'executions' of the Breton language inside post offices and the removal of monolingual road signs. This kind of direct action falls into the category of 'platform events', proposed by Goffman (1983) and adapted for LL research by Kitis and Milani (2015). As summarized by Kitis and Milani, 'platform events'

> present a performance on an imaginary or highly mediatized performance for a public to watch as spectacle. ... The theatrical character of these performances is heightened by the agents' acute awareness of being filmed, recorded, and watched in one way or another by officials or institutions wishing to delegitimize them and the broader public, which the activists wish to influence. (2015: 274)

The very visible approach to this activism communicates dramatically the ideology that monolingualism disempowers the Bretonnant community in the region, and that direct action plays a significant part in self-determination and representation of a section of society who is metaphorically obscured and concealed by the monolingual road sign.

In the eyes of Ai'Ta!, the climate in Brittany is not particularly propitious for the sustaining of Breton, let alone its revitalization. In 2017, the collective took up the cause of Fañch Bernard, whose parents were forbidden from officially naming him using the tilde on the grounds that <ñ> is not an authorized diacritic for civil status in France. At a local level, the mayor of Quimper, where the Bernard family live, supported the parents' action, but Fañch's parents were summoned to the local High Court for a 'rectification request'. Ai'Ta! has formally complained to the local television channel of the national broadcaster, *France 3 Bretagne*, for the repeated cancellation of Breton-language programmes in favour of national sporting events, or for holiday scheduling. The regional employment offices do not include Breton within the drop-down list for languages spoken for jobseekers completing online applications. The national education department rejected a request by a group of parents and local elected officials to fund a bilingual French-Breton class in a school in Châteaubriant in the Loire-Atlantique *département*. This kind of class (where there is parity in the number of hours of delivery between French and the regional language) takes place across France, and a number of criteria need to be met, including the size of the area, the potential number of pupils and the support of the local authorities. With these requirements satisfied in Châteaubriant, Ai'Ta! have argued that the decision by the education authorities is unfair.

This is the general context which Ai'Ta! identifies as the circumstances in which their defence of Breton has become essential. Based on the information that Ai'Ta! puts into the public domain,[3] the majority of its activities centre on what might be referred to as LL activities, in addition to the lobbying work outlined above. The activists seek to disrupt visually and playfully the monolingual approach adopted by the State in the signage for which it is responsible, negating the existing arrangement of visual resources by the emplacement of highly visible stickers calling for translations into Breton. Broadly speaking, the movement adopts two approaches, both of which see collective action as a participatory event. The first approach is a kind of guerrilla linguistic landscaping, building on what I refer to as 'guerrilla revitalization' (Blackwood 2018: 564) which uses unconventional approaches to exploit low-cost activity for maximum exposure. In the case of Ai'Ta!, this involves the placing of highly visible orange signs on signs which are solely in French. These can be toponyms given only in French, or where either information or instructions are given on signs. These orange signs are very prominent, given their colour and the absence of orange in official signage in France, which – as elsewhere – relies largely on white, green or brown backgrounds.

The second approach is arguably more transgressive, where members of the association meet and remove signs which do not include Breton; this they do without damaging the sign, and they return the materials, down to the screws used, to local town halls. This removal of signs, which is in effect a creation of absence, echoes Kitis and Milani's interpretation (2015: 272) of deterritorialization (Deleuze and Guattari 1983), whereby individuals enact forces 'by removing and contesting the legitimacy of some elements of the built environment [monolingual road signs in this case] and leave destruction and/or void as material traces of their very movements'. These platform events change the materiality of the roadsides of Brittany, thereby reconstituting space (Kitis and Milani 2015: 274), and amplify their message by their approach. This activism is not anonymous: the orange stickers are signed with the action group's name and contact details, and the dismantling and returning of signs is done in full view of the authorities, and – equally significantly – recorded in images and clips for dissemination, thereby magnifying the potential of these platform events. Often, the collective's members pose – unmasked – in front of the sign that they have covered with stickers or dismantled, permitting their identification and undertaking this activism in plain sight, rather than anonymously, under the cover of darkness. The group's actions led in September 2017 to the State pressing criminal charges against the group.

3. Rationales for Linguistic Landscape activism

3.1 Empowerment through activism

In this section – and drawing on analytic tools from LL, sociolinguistics and critical discourse analysis – I consider the positions adopted by Ai'Ta! towards LL activism as articulated by their public-facing material, including their website, press releases and public statements, and by discussions with activists from the movement. Close examination of the information that Ai'Ta! put into the public domain permits the identification of three distinct arguments that underpin the positions adopted by the moment regarding their activism, which I synthesize in the following sections. It is notable that the direct action by members of the collective is justified on the grounds that Ai'Ta! acts on behalf of a specific constituency that includes but is not limited to Bretonnants within the region. The actions of Ai'Ta! are rationalized by members and by the collective's publication on the basis that activities by a handful of individuals working together empowers the wider community by the group's deeds, by their justifications and explanations, and by the responses from the civic authorities.

When investigating the beliefs and activities of Ai'Ta!, we return to an area of interest for earlier LL research, namely road signs. Although not so prominent now in LL research,[4] the road sign – given its visibility, and its force as a mundane yet powerful marker of the State – is a site of ongoing contestation for collectives such as Ai'Ta! In Brittany, this is the case in particular because the State – in the form of the regional authorities – brought road signs into play as part of local-level commitments to supporting multilingualism. A 2015 agreement by Brittany's Regional Authorities to 'transmit the languages of Brittany and develop their use in daily life' was a commitment to establishing bilingual road signs along trunk roads – so the main national arteries – across the region. For three years, no work took place to change the visual arrangement of the signage, hence Ai'Ta!'s direct action in early February 2018 to remove monolingual signs from sections of the N12 across Brittany as the latest part of their campaign of LL activism.

One of the challenges of analysing the approaches, priorities and activities of Ai'Ta! is that the collective organizes itself along the line of direct democracy, eschewing the structures of a more formally constituted organization. As such, there is no president, no leadership committee or even building out of which they operate. Exploring critically Ai'Ta!'s stancetaking and actions depends in part on the individuals with whom one comes into contact. None of the members claim to speak on behalf of the collective, although the aim of defending and promoting Breton is – so Ai'Ta! claims through its website – shared by all supporters as the fundamental doctrine. A consideration of the positions adopted by Ai'Ta! towards the LL of Brittany can be undertaken in this chapter by investigating the collective's public-facing material, including its website, press releases and public statements, and in this chapter, we privilege discussions with activists from the movement. Given the absence of a leadership group within Ai'Ta!, the discussions with activists have to be treated as representative of individual rather than collective positioning. Although there is no evidence of a schism within the movement, or of members diverging from each other over principles or strategies, the findings drawn from the semi-structured interviews should be handled with caution. The individuals I met with are long-standing members of Ai'Ta! and have extensive experience of LL activism, and as such present a distinct perspective, and one that might differ from a new member who has recently joined the collective.

Nevertheless, when we take the views expressed across a number of platforms by Ai'Ta!, what emerges as a coherent standpoint is the rejection of the banal practice of the appropriation of trunk roads as space as performed by the French language alone. This they do on the basis that there exists a basic right of the citizens of Brittany to use 'their language' in the public space. By 'use', we understand Ai'Ta!'s position to mean the consumption of information in Breton, rather than the production of Breton by speakers of the language. At this point, it is helpful to bring geosemiotics, as defined by Scollon and Scollon (2003), back into view, since it dovetails with the discourse used by Ai'Ta! In particular, the arguments put forward by members of the collective correspond to Scollon and Scollon's (2003: 116–41) principles of code preference and inscription. For example, the collective frequently make the case, as in their 2017 open letter to the president of a conglomeration of local communes, that 'there is no reason why the font and size of letters should be different between the two languages. The colours used should also be equally visible'. In other words, signs that are bilingual but which visually privilege French are perceived by Ai'Ta! to be discriminatory and further marginalize Breton. Ai'Ta! identify the local civic authorities as the stance-subject, from which the movement disaligns itself. Equally, the collective disaligns itself from the prevailing narrative regarding the relationship between Breton and French. Ai'Ta! have sought to address this dynamic, given that decisions made in the emplacement of the minority language (from its complete omission, through partially bilingual signage, to smaller or italicized fonts) reinforce the dominance of the national standard. Put differently, the ways in which Breton is included in signage has to, in the eyes of Ai'Ta! and other activists, challenge the entrenched understanding that Breton's existence is dependent on its relationship to French.

Dismantling monolingual road signage as a response to the perceived sidelining of Breton inevitably erases French from the public space in an act of deterritorialization (Deleuze and Guattari 1983), which leaves, in the words of Kitis and Milani (2015: 272), a void as a material trace of movement. This elimination of French is significant, even though the texts (in the broadest sense) are merely a list of toponyms and the distances to each of them. Members of the collective argue that this deletion of French is a consequence of the long-standing hegemonic approach by the State to languages other than national standard. Dismantling signs and returning every last piece to the civic authorities, often in a staged and mediatized way as a platform event, is explained by

Yann[5] from the collective not as an act that disempowers Francophones, but one which emphasizes the marginalization (to the point of omission) of languages such as Breton:

> Effectively, what we're saying is that we don't want this kind of sign so we're giving it back to you. So it's a way to say that we don't like what we're given.

This action disrupts the broadly accepted relationship that subordinates Breton to French by actively removing the French language, and shifting the balance of power in favour of Breton. In other words, rather than expecting Breton to appear alongside (which usually means below) French, Ai'Ta!'s actions contend that without Breton visible, the French language cannot appear in the public space.

At the same time, the activists argue that this approach causes minimal disruption, even when compared with their original preferred strategy of emplacing the orange stickers on road signs. The adhesive backing on the orange stickers was chosen for its strength meaning that, by removing them, the materiality of the road sign was damaged. This is, effectively, vandalism, and so the dismantling of signs is less destructive but no less disruptive. According to Yann, the removal of the monolingual street signs most inconveniences the employees of the local authorities responsible for erecting signs:

> The people who are inconvenienced are the guys who install the signs. [They say] 'Blooming heck, we're going to have to go back out, put the signs back up again' and they convey their frustration to their bosses. And this has a financial hit, and the bosses realise how much time and therefore money is being spent on putting signs back up, they start to wonder whether it wouldn't be cheaper to put Breton on the signs. That doesn't have much of an impact on them, but it makes us happy.

The activist reasons that the economic cost of re-erecting signs can be countered by the manufacture of new signs which feature Breton and which, subsequently, are not dismantled by the activists of Ai'Ta!

Having established the parameters of empowerment through direct action by Ai'Ta!, I now organize the stances adopted by the collective into three arguments which underpin the positions they adopt.

3.2 Activism to legitimize by the very act of emplacement

The first of these lines of argument pursued by Ai'Ta! is the potential for the appearance of Breton in the public space to legitimize the language. The context, as outlined above, has been the consistent denigration of Breton (and the other languages of France) over the course of centuries and its exclusion from High domains across daily life. The pace of exclusion reminds us that language shift in Brittany is a prolonged process rather than an overnight phenomenon, and the transfer of domains from Breton to French was not uniform. In the same way, the reversal of the language shift as a practice by which Bretons as an ethnolinguistic group are legitimized is uneven inasmuch as Ai'Ta! have a route map to revitalization with targets and priorities rather than a single aim. According to Mikael,[6] one of the collective's active and long-standing members, the visibility of Breton on street signs is a method by which the use of Breton can be legitimized, even if the consequences of its emplacement do not lead directly to language acquisition in any measurable way:

> It formalizes the Breton language, it makes it official, it gives it legitimacy for the entire population of Brittany. For us, it's maybe not the top priority, but it is important. For Breton speakers, the ability to speak to other people in Breton is what's important.

Here, he differentiates between Bretonnants, learners of Breton and those who do not speak Breton at all. He argues that, for all residents of the region, regardless of their language abilities, the use of Breton in road signage is important for validating the language. In other words, the emplacement on a publicly owned and subsidized sign plays a major role in the acceptance of Breton by all residents within the region. He immediately distinguishes between the wider population and those who identify as Bretonnant for whom the use of Breton in signage is – possibly – not as important, highlighting instead the significance of opportunities to speak the language. In doing so, he implies that the visibility of Breton is of greater significance to learners and non-speakers than it is to Bretonnants, nuancing the evaluation of the sign arrangement by differentiated stancetakers.

This distinction between categories of citizens is notable insofar that it recognizes that linguistic empowerment means different things to different people, depending on their language abilities. This stance is adopted by a confident speaker of Breton who is active in the promotion of the language; this begs the question as to what a non-speaker or a learner might see as the value of Breton in the LL. This stance also chimes with Hornsby's application of Heller and Labrie's 2003 classification of the orientation of discourses of speaker status, and, in particular, the modernizing theme. Hornsby (2019: 397) argues that this discourse 'in minority language communities relies on political structures, positing the minority as "legitimate", with access to "legitimate rights"'. While Mikael might not believe that he is producing, to use Hornsby's conclusion (2019: 401), 'processes of hierarchisation of speakerhood in the Breton-speaking community', this rationale for activism points to the authority assumed by Ai'Ta! to act on behalf of all residents of Brittany as an act of collective empowerment.

3.3 Activism in the name of justice

A second line of argument is that direct action is the obvious approach to take when seeking to obtain justice – in this case, this is justice for an ethnolinguistic group. Faced with what Mikael refers to as 'a State which refuses to recognise linguistic rights here in France', civil disobedience is perceived by members of Ai'Ta! as a potentially successful method of achieving linguistic and social justice. Much of the discourse employed by Ai'Ta! draws on the rhetoric of civil disobedience and operating at the very edges of legality; the actions of the environmental organization Greenpeace are evoked and highlighted as inspirational. Ai'Ta! frames the positionality of the French State around the myths identified above, whereby 'the French' are one people, within one State, where there are no minority groups, and no linguistic minorities. From the perspective of language activists, this long-held stance by the French State is perceived as somewhere along the spectrum of subjugation and suppression, that, whilst not reaching tyranny, certainly touches on hegemony. However, actions by armed militants at the end of the last century resulted in the death of a woman at a branch of *McDonald's* that heralded a rapid disalignment on the part of the wider population of the region with violence undertaken by Breton nationalists. As a consequence, Ai'Ta!'s emergence as a collective of language activists is explicitly non-violent, and their actions are emphasized as ludic and tongue-in-cheek. As such, the claiming of linguistic rights – as understood by this particular group of language activists – is undertaken by direct action but unambiguously non-violent means.

Direct action as linguistic empowerment has been undertaken by Ai'Ta!, for example, at the refurbished post office in the town of Quimper in the west of Brittany, where the new signage installed after the works on the building omitted Breton. This is a prime example of a platform event undertaken by Ai'Ta! both to challenge the civic authorities responsible for the arrangement of language in the public space and to raise public awareness. Set against the soundtrack of the *biniou kozh*, Breton bagpipes, activists not only protested and distributed leaflets, but enacted the 'death' of the Breton language with individuals representing Breton cut down by the scythe of another activist dressed as the grim reaper. A further example of this kind of platform event are the *Fest Noz*, which are traditional Breton dancing and music festivals, which Ai'Ta! organize inside railway stations where the regional language is absent from the LL. This they do in order to disrupt the routine activities of the station, and thereby draw attention to the group's claims. The collective has also staged football matches inside station concourses. The post offices and railway stations drawn into Ai'Ta!'s activities recall Bock and Stroud's (2019) inclusion of place as a stance-subject; as in the 'zombie landscapes' of Cape Town, these settings are agentive and therefore open to evaluation and subsequent disaligning by the members of the collective. These actions in stations and post offices are justified by members of the collective on the basis that the disruption to daily life draws attention to the causes, attests to the marginalization of the minority groups by the French State and prompts some form of engagement by the civic authorities, with the collective aim of achieving some level of justice.

3.4 Activism as dialogue between the powerful and the voiceless

The engagement with the local councils or the forces of law and order point to the third line of reasoning on the part of the activists, namely that direct action in defence of and for the promotion of Breton is one side of a dialogue with those in power and authority. Linguistic empowerment for Bretonnants and residents of Breton alike embraces values of democracy, while at the same time skating close to the edge of legality in terms of the actions taken. In other words, the third rationale for the activities embraced by Ai'Ta! and others is the democratic validity of their claims for and beliefs towards Breton. The signage targeted by the collective is commissioned, erected, managed and – most significantly – paid for by the various levels of civic authorities in Brittany, and is therefore publicly funded through direct taxation. The civil contract that is based on responsibilities and obligations balanced by rights is used by members of Ai'Ta! to justify the removal of signs on the premise that individuals' taxes have been used to pay for these signs, and therefore individuals, especially those arranged into a collective, have the right to request the kinds of signs that they want.

Together, these three rationales – distinct but clearly inter-related – frame and underpin the central argument that direct action, LL activism in this case, constitute acts of collective empowerment. In the final section of this chapter, I exploit stance and geosemiotics to consider how these two concepts can interact productively to inform debates on multilingualism as empowerment.

4. Conclusions

That the LL is a contested space in Brittany is not in doubt; as in most towns and cities across the world, power relations play out in the public space, with language (or, in this case, named and bounded languages) one dimension in this contest. It is also a given that, in communities, regions and countries where a specific ethnolinguistic group has come to dominate, a minority group emerges as marginalized and is often keen to rectify the imbalance in the distribution of power. In this chapter, I have traced how an organized group of activists have problematized the visual absence of their minority language, and how they have brought the LL into play as part of their efforts to address their diminishment as individuals, as speakers and as a community of practice. In particular, this chapter has offered an exploration of the interconnection between stance and geosemiotics as they collide productively alongside the trunk roads of Brittany.

Direct action as empowerment in the eyes of the collective Ai'Ta! is predicated on more than just adding the regional language to street signs. The claims for recognition, legitimacy and authority are nuanced more subtly than merely demanding that elected representatives in Brittany emplace Breton in road signage. In part, as attested by Vigers (2013) and reinforced by the position papers published by Ai'Ta! and by some of their members, the inclusion of Breton in signs across the region does not address the core of the complaint. While the visibility of Breton is welcomed insofar as it legitimizes the claims made for the language as a valid method of communication within Brittany, by the same token, the way in which it has been emplaced thus far often serves to reinforce prejudices and stereotypes that undermine rather than serve the cause of language activists. In short, the communities who live in Brittany are not empowered by the State's begrudging inclusion of Breton on road signs on trunk roads, and not solely because of the subordinated position and representation of Breton on signage. As a collective, Ai'Ta! recognize the shared benefit of sanctioning the inclusion of Breton in official signage, but at the same time, this action simultaneously disempowers Bretonnants and learners of the language by the ways in which this emplacement has undertaken.

In other words, the linguistic empowerment of supporters of Breton is not achieved by the mere act of the erection of signs that feature Breton, even though this has been a long-standing target for language activists. The precise arrangement of two codes in the same sign, as highlighted by Ai'Ta!, does not revitalize the minority language, precisely because it reinforces the long-standing prejudice that Breton is not suited to writing, is inappropriate for formal usage and requires visual support from French in order to be valid. At the same time, the position of Ai'Ta! can potentially be seen as paradoxical, given the ways in which they affirm the rights of Francophones in Brittany and explicitly state their lack of antipathy towards the French language and its speakers. Linguistic empowerment for Bretonnants and learners of Breton is predicated not on the removal of French in signage, but on the subordination to French in terms of positioning alone.

At this stage, it helps to evoke the critical vocabulary of stance and to bring geosemiotics back to the fore. In these platform events that unfold alongside major trunk roads in Brittany, Ai'Ta! are not the only actors to be stancetaking. The signs are commissioned by the local authorities, and responsibility in its broadest sense for public signage on roads is shared between several agencies, depending on the nature of the road. What is key is that the function of the signs under examination here is informational or regulatory – presenting toponyms and their distances, or giving instructions on the rules of the road. The explicit stance taken by Ai'Ta is referentially grounded by the semiotics of place, in particular emplacement and how these signs are situated. There is clear disalignment here on the part of Ai'Ta!, but it is not with the content of the sign, rather with its visual arrangement. In other words, Ai'Ta! does not dispute the information given or the instructions provided. If we zoom in on the orange stickers calling for Breton to be used, to return to Du Bois's terminology, the stance predicate is the statement which commits the stancetaker – Ai'Ta! in this case – to a clear evaluation of the object, namely the appearance but not the contents of the sign. Ai'Ta! take direct action not against the calculation of the number of kilometres to the cities of Rennes or Vannes, but to how this information is conveyed to the travelling public.

It is exactly at this juncture where Scollon and Scollon's geosemiotics (2003) meet stance. The physical emplacement of the text – the orange sticker which reads 'in Breton' – on another physically emplaced text identifies the stance object. In this case, visual semiotics (in particular colour differentiation and composition) and place semiotics (code preference and inscription) are the most salient dimensions of geosemiotics, identifying the stance object as the way in which the text is presented, not the 'contents' of the text itself. Scollon and Scollon's conceptualization of geosemiotics has the potential to inform work on stance. Given that subjectivity requires orientation to a subject, the emplacement of the sticker indexes both the stance subject (Ai'Ta! in this case) and the stance object (the language of the resources selected on the road signs).

To conclude, the platform events that Ai'Ta! undertake across Brittany are prime examples of activism in the name of empowerment. Inevitably, the positionings adopted by the collective are more nuanced than merely calling for more Breton to be made visible, and direct action as public and mediatized acts of disalignment from France's civic authorities are about more than staking a claim for the value, legitimacy and appropriateness for visible multilingualism across Brittany. These actions are intended to empower speakers and learners of Breton, and yet also at the same time to legitimize multilingualism, and in particular the use of Breton, among non-speakers of the regional language living in Brittany. In short, empowerment counts on the consent of non-Bretonnants in acknowledging that the public space should be presented as multilingual, even if many (most, even) of those who pass through it do not speak, and less so write, the regional language.

Notes

1. By way of example, see Borer's 2014 *De Quel Amour Blessée*, which is both a lament for the corruption of French and a paean to its greatness.
2. The publicly available library (www.zotero.org/groups/216092/linguistic_landscape_bibliography), maintained and updated by Dr Rob Troyer of Western Oregon University, serves as an indispensable resource containing spatially and thematically organized summaries of LL publications.
3. This information can be found primarily through Ai'Ta's website: www.aita.bzh/fr and its publications, such as the 2016 manifesto and history of the movement *Désobéir pour la langue bretonne/Disentiñ evit ar brezhoneg*.
4. There are notable exceptions to this, including Busch's 2013 discussion of the hacek in signs in Carinthia, Amos' 2017 examination of signage in Toulouse, Järlehed's 2017 application of genre to street signs and Tufi's 2019 chapter on street names as rememoration.
5. Members of the collective interviewed for this chapter have been anonymized.
6. Mikael is a pseudonym.

References

Adamson, R. (2007), *The Defence of French: A Language in Crisis?*, Clevedon, UK: Multilingual Matters.

Amos, H. W. (2017), 'Regional Language Vitality in the Linguistic Landscape: Hidden Hierarchies on Street Signs in Toulouse', *International Journal of Multilingualism*, 14 (2): 93–108.

Blackwood, R. J. (2010), 'Marking France's Public Space', in E. Shohamy, E. Ben Rafael and M. Barni (eds) *Linguistic Landscape in the City*, 292–306, Clevedon, UK: Multilingual Matters.

Blackwood, R. J. (2011), 'The Linguistic Landscape of Brittany and Corsica: A Comparative Study of the Presence of France's Regional Languages in the Public Space', *Journal of French Language Studies*, 21 (2): 111–30.

Blackwood, R. J. (2015), 'LL Explorations and Methodological Challenges: Analysing France's Regional Languages', *Linguistic Landscapes*, 1 (1–2): 38–53.

Blackwood, R. J. (2018), 'Revitalization and the Public Space', in W. Ayres-Bennett and J. Carruthers (eds) *Romance Sociolinguistics*, 541–61, Berlin: Mouton de Gruyter.

Bock, Z., and Stroud, C. (2019), 'Zombie Landscapes: Apartheid Traces in the Discourses of Young South Africans', in A. Peck, C. Stroud and Q. Williams (eds) *Making Sense of People and Place in Linguistic Landscapes*, 11–27, London: Bloomsbury.

Borer, A. (2014), *De Quel Amour Blessée: Réflexions sur la langue française*, Paris: Gallimard.

Broadridge, J., and Marley, D. (2019), 'The Evolution of Regional Language Maintenance in Southern Alsace and Northern Catalonia: A Longitudinal Study of Two Regional Languages', in M. Harrison and A. Joubert (eds) *French Language Policies and the Revitalisation of Regional Languages in the 21st Century*, 265–88, Basingstoke: Palgrave Macmillan.

Broudic, Fañch (2013), 'Le breton', in G. Kremnitz (ed.) *Histoire sociale des langues de France*, 439–54, Rennes: Presses Universitaires de Rennes.

Busch, B. (2013), 'The Career of a Diacritical Sign: Language in Spatial Representations and Representational Spaces', in S. Pietikäinen and H. Kelly-Holmes (eds) *Multilingualism in the Periphery*, 199–221, Oxford: Oxford University Press.

Deleuze, G., and Guattari, F. (1983), *Anti-Oedipus: Capitalism and schizophrenia*, London: Continuum.

Depau, G. (2019), 'Diffusion and Transmission of Francoprovençal: A Study of Speakers' Linguistic Conscience', in M. Harrison and A. Joubert (eds) *French Language Policies and the Revitalisation of Regional Languages in the 21st Century*, 129–48, Basingstoke: Palgrave Macmillan.

Du Bois, J. (2007), 'The Stance Triangle', in R. Englebretson (ed.) *Stancetaking in Discourse: Subjectivity, Evaluation, Interaction*, 139–82, Amsterdam: John Benjamins.

Edwards, John (2007), 'Back from the Brink: The Revival of Endangered Languages', in M. Helinger and A. Pauwels (eds) *Handbook of Language and Communication: Diversity and Change*, 241–69, Berlin, Mouton de Gruyter.

Goffman E. (1983), 'The Interaction Order: American Sociological Association, 1982 Presidential Address', *American Sociological Review*, 48: 1–17.

Heller, M., and Labrie, N. (2003), 'Langue, pouvoir et identité : une étude de cas, une approche théorique, une méthodologie', in M. Heller and N. Labrie (eds) *Discours et Identités : la francité canadienne entre modernité et mondialisation*, 9–39, Cortil-Wodon: Editions Modulaires Européennes.

Hornsby, M. (2008), 'The Incongruence of the Breton Linguistic Landscape for Young Speakers of Breton', *Journal of Multilingual and Multicultural Development*, 29 (2): 127–38.

Hornsby, M. (2019), 'Positions and Stances in the Hierarchization of Breton Speakerhood', *Journal of Multilingual and Multicultural Development*, 40 (5): 392–403.

Järlehed, J. (2017), 'Genre and Metacultural Displays: The Case of Street-Name Signs', *Linguistic Landscape*, 3 (3): 286–305.

Jaffe, A. (2007), 'Introduction: The Sociolinguistics of Stance', in A. Jaffe (ed.), *Stance: Sociolinguistic Perspectives*, 3–28, Oxford: Oxford University Press.

Joubert, A. (2019), 'Evolution of Linguistic Identity in a Super-Region: The Case of Catalans and Occitans in *Occitanie*', in M. Harrison and A. Joubert (eds) *French Language Policies and the Revitalisation of Regional Languages in the 21st Century*, 107–28, Basingstoke: Palgrave Macmillan.

Judge, A. (2007), *Linguistic Policies and the Survival of Regional Languages in France and Britain*, Basingstoke: Palgrave Macmillan.

Kitis, E. D., and Milani, T. (2015), 'The Performativity of the Body: Turbulent Spaces in Greece', *Linguistic Landscape*, 1 (3): 268–90.

Kremnitz, G. (ed.) (2013), *Histoire sociale des langues de France*, Rennes: Presses Universitaires de Rennes.

Scollon, R., and Scollon, S. W. (2003), *Discourses in Place: Language in the Material World*, London: Routledge.

Smith, A. D. (1991), *National Identity*, London: Penguin Books.

Tufi, S. (2019), 'Instance of Emplaced Memory: The Case of Alghero/L'Alguer', in R. Blackwood and J. Macalister (eds) *Multilingual Memories: Monuments, Museums and the Linguistic Landscape*, 237–61, London: Bloomsbury.

Vigers, D. (2103), 'Signs of Absence: Language and Memory in the Linguistic Landscape of Brittany', *International Journal for the Sociology of Language*, 223: 171–87.

Walter, H. (2012), *Aventures et mésaventures des langues de France*, Paris: Champion Classique.

Yekel, T. (2016), 'Krouidigezh hag istor vihan Ai'ta!', in Stourmerien Ai'Ta (eds) *Désobéir pour la langue bretonne/Disentiñ evit ar brezhoneg*, 12–14, Fouesnant, France: Yoran Embanner.

Multilingualism in the model multicultural city: The influence of authors in Leicester's Golden Mile

Michelle A. Harrison[1]

1. Introduction

Since the turn of the twenty-first century, Leicester has been recognized by both the UK and international press for constituting a model of a successful multicultural city (Herbert 2008: 2), a narrative that has also been promoted by its City Council (Singh 2003: 42). Multiculturalism, and its associated multilingualism, does not appear to have divided communities in this East Midlands city in the same way as in other parts of England, which is illustrated by the relative absence of violent tensions between ethnic groups, in contrast with Bradford, Burnley and Oldham, which experienced racially motivated riots in 2001 (Herbert 2008: 2), and also Birmingham, where riots occurred in 2005. England has traditionally taken a hands-off approach to language management in terms of legislation (Ager 1995: 47), which allows actors in the private sector to exert their own language policies. Thus, business owners in the country's commercial centres have a significant influence on shaping local Linguistic Landscapes (LL) through their signs. Malinowski (2009: 108) observes that LL researchers tend to overlook the agency of individuals as authors of multilingual signs and instead focus on the position of linguistic codes or distinctions between the public and private sectors. Featuring as a case study the Golden Mile, the main centre for Leicester's Indian Asian population, this chapter considers how multilingualism is managed by public and private actors while considering the motivations and aims of the individuals who are behind the displays of written information. It analyses the role of different authors of signs in shaping the LL of this area, the language policy choices that they make and the effects of these on readers. *Signs*, *authors* and *readers* are employed as blanket terms in this chapter; as underlined by Sebba (2012: 100), these concepts are multidimensional, and each would merit a more in-depth investigation than is possible here. Multilingual signs can appear in various forms and be analysed in many ways. Authors and readers of multilingual signs have distinct linguistic repertoires, language attitudes and motivations, and thus each individual's interaction with any written text is unique.

Owing to the diversity of written multilingual texts, Sebba (2012: 100) observes the difficulty in producing a one-size-fits-all analytical framework. Reh (2004) devises a model to describe and analyse multilingual written texts that correlates how languages are presented in displays of multilingual writing with the linguistic knowledge of readers. In this chapter, Reh's model will be employed from a different perspective, to present an author-oriented rather than a reader-oriented typology. Drawing on the results of a preliminary study undertaken in 2018, which included an LL survey of the Golden Mile area and interviews with business owners and individuals working in local shops and public services, this chapter will investigate the intentions of authors when they include, and when they consciously exclude, languages of the local community in their written communications.

The chapter begins with an overview of the development of Leicester's South Asian community and the emergence of Gujarati as the city's second language. The transformation of Leicester into a city that is characterized by cultural diversity will be examined, before the Golden Mile area is introduced. This will provide essential contextualization before the focus of the chapter moves on to the case study that forms its main part. The survey area and research methods will be summarized before an analysis of the written signs recorded in the survey is presented. This will be followed by an examination of the motivations for the inclusion or non-inclusion of languages in the LL as explained by the authors themselves. In the final part, conclusions will be drawn on the contemporary policies of authors as managers of the LL, and what these might mean for the local community.

2. The development of Leicester's South Asian community

Home to residents from over fifty countries (Leicester City Council 2012), Leicester has emerged as one of Britain's main Indian Asian centres since the 1950s, following the 1947 Independence of India Act and the 1948 British Nationality Act, which allowed Commonwealth citizens to move to the UK and resulted in the arrival of people of Indian, Pakistani, and Afro-Caribbean origins (Martin and Singh 2002: 8). In the late 1960s and early 1970s, a larger wave of immigration occurred when Indian Asians arrived in Leicester from East Africa, following political shifts and forced expulsions (Martin and Singh 2002: 10–11). The arrival of an estimated 20,000 Ugandan Asians is considered to have had the greatest impact on the transformation of Leicester into a strongly multi-ethnic city (Herbert 2016: 338; Vetrovec 1994: 260). Members of this group, who were mainly of Gujarati origin, generally had higher levels of education and were more likely to be proficient in English compared to those who arrived from India and Pakistan (Vetrovec 1994: 261). Many quickly achieved economic and social success in their new home city (Herbert 2012: 297) and contributed to Leicester's prosperity, as well as the development of the city's Golden Mile.

Despite its contemporary recognition as a successful multicultural city, immigrants were not always welcomed warmly in Leicester, particularly in the 1960s and 1970s (Herbert 2016: 338; Hussain, Haq and Law 2003: 42; Martin and Singh 2002: 11). However, this anti-immigration stance began to decline by the end of the 1970s, and this was followed by a move towards a civic multicultural policy from the end of the decade (Singh 2003: 44), the success of which has led to Leicester being hailed as a model of best practice for multiculturalism (see Hassen and Giovanardi (2018) and Singh (2003) for discussions of the 'Leicester Model'). Since the last decade of the twentieth century, the City Council has openly and purposefully celebrated Leicester's ethnic diversity, leading to the creation of the 'One Leicester' city brand in 2008 (Hassen and Giovanardi 2018: 49).

With its multicultural population, modern-day Leicester is also a site of multilingualism. Today, Gujarati is the city's second most widely spoken language after English, with 36,318 (11.5 per cent of the city's population) naming Gujarati as their main language in the 2011 census (Office for National Statistics 2011b). After English (72.4 per cent) and Gujarati (11.5 per cent), other main languages declared include Punjabi (2.4 per cent), Polish (2 per cent), Somali (1.1 per cent), Urdu (1.1 per cent), Chinese (all varieties) (1 per cent), Arabic (0.8 per cent), Bengali (0.6 per cent) and Portuguese (0.6 per cent) (Office for National Statistics 2011b). According to the census, Leicester has the highest proportion (7.5 per cent) of residents outside of London who claim to not be able to speak English well, or not at all (Office for National Statistics 2011c). In its Corporate Equality and Diversity Strategy for 2018–2022, Leicester City Council acknowledges this and states '[this means] that it is important that we are flexible in our approach to delivering services and are able to respond to the fluctuating diversity of the population' (Leicester City Council 2018: 17). The Council's symbolic support of the city's multicultural and multilingual identity was evidenced during the data collection for this project, with the display of multilingual signs at the entrance to public services supported by the Council, including a welcome sign featuring forty-six languages displayed outside Belgrave Library (Figure 9.1). A parallel can be drawn between the function of this sign and the Council signs displayed at its customer service centre and the main bus and coach station (Figure 9.2); only 'welcome' is translated into different languages, while the information on the function of the buildings is available exclusively in English. These signs include both languages spoken by local communities and other national languages; Jaworski (2015: 227) contends that in multilingual welcome signs the former 'create a sense of authenticity and distinction', while the latter '[orient] to or [accommodate] the visiting tourists'. Jaworski (2015: 229) suggests that such mass-oriented signs 'seem to work predominantly as tokens of synthetic personalization'; as only the word 'welcome' is presented in different languages, this represents a symbolic level of support of multilingualism rather than a commitment to meaningful inclusivity.

A 2017 Leicester City Council community languages report explains that 'in line with central government policy, the council encourages the use of English as the city's main language' (Leicester City Council 2017: 2). Hence, the dominant standard

Figure 9.1 Multilingual welcome sign outside Belgrave Library

language is prioritized, and in most spaces 'hegemonic monolingualism' prevails, as is common practice in contemporary societies (Sebba 2012: 100).

The 2011 census revealed that Leicester has the highest proportion of people identifying as part of the Indian ethnic group in England and Wales, representing 28.3 per cent of the local population (Office for National Statistics 2011a). Today, the Indian Asian population is present throughout Leicester, yet a high proportion of migrants originally settled, and many remain, in the inner-city areas around Belgrave Road and nearby Spinney Hills (Martin and Singh 2002: 8). The suburb of Belgrave, located to

Figure 9.2 Multilingual welcome sign at St Margaret's bus station

the north-east of the city centre, is home to a significant number of Gujarati Hindus (Hussain, Haq and Law 2003: 64).

The Golden Mile is formed of a stretch of Belgrave Road and Melton Road that runs through the heart of Belgrave. It has developed into a thriving commercial area that attracts visitors from all over the UK (Martin and Singh 2002: 14); in addition to a comparatively high number of jewellers (the reason for its popular name), one can find an array of shops selling traditional Indian foods and clothing, and several Indian banks. Each year, the area hosts the largest Diwali festival celebrations outside of India, which attracts visitors of different ethnic backgrounds from across the city and beyond (Herbert 2016: 330). The emerging national and international renown of the Golden Mile has led to the suggestion that it has 'the potential to develop into an "Asia Town", akin to London's Chinatown' (Herbert 2016: 330). If such an evolution were to take place in the future, this could lead to a further commodification of Indian Asian culture and a reshaping of the LL of the area. However, Leicester's Golden Mile is unlikely to undergo a transformation on the scale of that of Chinatowns in major popular tourist cities, such as that which has occurred in Washington, DC (Leeman and Modan 2009).

3. Research methods and survey

3.1 Preliminary analysis of the survey area: The languages of the Golden Mile

This project focuses on the wider Golden Mile area, which includes the Golden Mile itself and several adjacent streets that include businesses and public services such as Belgrave Neighbourhood Centre, Cossington Recreation Ground and Belgrave Library.

When entering the Golden Mile, it soon becomes apparent to the visitor that this space is distinct from surrounding areas, with an increase in non-English-language signs and scripts, and other semiotic resources that indicate an Indian Asian local identity. One can also hear the difference, with Indian Asian languages being spoken widely on the streets and in businesses and services. Signs including a diverse range of languages (namely Arabic, Bengali, Gujarati, Hindi, Mandarin, Polish, Portuguese, Punjabi, Somali, Tamil and Urdu) are displayed, but the most present language in the public space after English, which is predominant, is Gujarati. The area is also demarcated by the presence of lamp post banners produced by the city's tourist information service, Visit Leicester, which on one side read 'Golden Mile' and on the other feature brightly coloured Indian-inspired designs (Figure 9.3).

It is noteworthy that while the Golden Mile banners feature Indian-inspired designs, the only language included on them is English. As in the case of the Leicester City Council signs discussed in the previous section, this can be viewed as a token gesture of support rather than a symbol of meaningful inclusivity. Moreover, as it is

Figure 9.3 Banners marking the Golden Mile area

Figure 9.4 Business signs that include Indian Asian scripts or design features

a commercial area, it can be considered as an effort to commodify the culture of the local community.

In addition to signs in other languages, one also finds several signs on which the authors have used the Latin alphabet, but in a script that simulates different Indian Asian scripts. For example, the sign of the takeaway restaurant Punjabi Tarka (Figure 9.4) is written in a style that replicates the Gurmukhi script of the Punjabi language. Other proprietors have chosen to include a design feature that one would associate with South Asia, such as the inclusion of a representation of an elephant in the sign of the restaurant Sri Ganapathi, or the bright golden lettering on the sign of the saree shop Anokhi (Figure 9.4). Here, the authors can be said to impose what Seargeant (2012: 192) describes as 'the visual equivalent of a foreign accent', which is symbolic of the Indian Asian cultural identity of the Golden Mile; this also exemplifies a commodification of that cultural identity.

Figure 9.5 Multilingual signs marking Ramadan celebrations in Highfields

Unlike examples from Chinatowns, such as in Washington, DC, where city design regulations have an impact on the look of signs produced (Leeman and Modan 2009: 34), Golden Mile proprietors are not bound by such rules, which gives the authors of private signs a greater level of agency.

Visible signs of Leicester's multilingual reality are not confined to the Golden Mile area, unlike Amos's observation of Liverpool's Chinatown, where there is a 'stark contrast' between this ethnically defined space and the rest of the city (2016: 128). Although English is the dominant language throughout Leicester, multilingual signs are visible in most areas. Notably, one finds multilingual signs on Narborough Road, to the south-west of the city centre, one of the UK's 'super-diverse' high streets, where 79 per cent of proprietors speak more than one language (Hall, King and Finlay 2015: 7). Multilingualism is also visible in the inner-city suburb of Highfields, where, during the Muslim festivals of Ramadan and Eid, celebratory signs are displayed with messages in Arabic (Latin script), Bengali, Gujarati, Somali and Urdu (Figure 9.5). However, the

Figure 9.6 Punjab National Bank sign

Golden Mile does stand out in the city for its concentration of signs in Indian Asian languages, particularly Gujarati.

3.2 Research methods

This project primarily adopts an ethnographic and qualitative approach to research, although there are also some quantitative elements in the analysis of the LL. To analyse the motivations and consequences of the inclusion of Gujarati in the public space in the Golden Mile area, Reh's (2004) reader-oriented typology model will be employed with a different focus, to analyse multilingual written texts from the position of the author – to understand the motivations and aims of sign writers. Ager (2001: 2–4) underlines the non-neutral nature of language policy; 'senders' are normally conscious of the influence of their language choices on their 'receivers' in any communication. Reh (2004) proposes the use of three parameters to analyse written signs: their spatial mobility (whether the object is stationary or mobile), visibility of multilingualism (if texts in different languages are displayed in the same space) and how multilingual information is arranged (in what she terms as being in a 'duplicating', 'fragmentary', 'overlapping' or 'complementary' manner). The first two parameters will be touched upon here, but it is the arrangement of information on multilingual signs and its effects that form the central part of the analysis.

In addition to a survey of the LL of the area, twenty-five short, semi-structured interviews (lasting between five and fifteen minutes) were undertaken with business owners and individuals working in shops and public services. The interviewees included individuals of different ethnic backgrounds, the interviews were mainly conducted on the spot, and all interviews were conducted in English. The interviews were completed in businesses, services and the like during the working day, thus concision and flexibility were required on my behalf, as the interviewer, to elicit the information required while the interviewees continued their work. For businesses or services that displayed a sign/signs in Gujarati, three main questions formed the basis of the interview: Who established the sign? Who is the intended reader/what is the purpose? How was it decided what part(s) of the message would be presented in Gujarati? In the cases where no signs were presented in Gujarati, the interviewees were asked why the business or service did not display any written information in the language and if they felt that this had an influence on language practices.

4. Analysis

4.1 The visual presence of Gujarati in the Golden Mile area

In total, 335 business properties and public services were surveyed as part of the project, thirty-seven of which (representing 11 per cent of sites) displayed at least one sign including the Gujarati language, or transliterations of English words using Gujarati script. Signs written in a variety of languages (namely Arabic, Bengali, Gujarati, Hindi, Mandarin, Polish, Portuguese, Punjabi, Somali, Tamil and Urdu), could be seen along the Golden Mile, although English was very clearly dominant in the LL, including its sole use in street signs (which, along with other signs managed by local authorities and national government, can be described as top-down (Gorter 2006: 3)). In total, thirty-nine multilingual signs including Gujarati were displayed, comprising handwritten, self-printed or professionally produced signs commissioned and displayed by individual business owners (bottom-up signs), and professionally produced signs displayed on or in local public service buildings, commissioned by Leicester City Council and Leicestershire Police (top-down signs). In thirty-four out of thirty-seven locations (91.9 per cent) multilingual signs were put up by individual business owners, with public sector signs appearing only on the Leicester City Council-supported Belgrave Neighbourhood Centre, Belgrave Library and at the entrance to the local Cossington Recreation Ground.

No clear correlation could be made between the type of business and the likelihood to display multilingual information, but signs featuring Gujarati are more likely to be found in businesses owned or managed by Indian Asians. The Belgrave Road branch of Punjab National Bank features signs in Gujarati, Hindi and Punjabi alongside English; at the time of writing, this is the only branch in the UK to feature Gujarati on its main sign (Figure 9.6), which indicates the bank's awareness of its local customer base, among whom there are a high number of first-language Gujarati speakers. A staff member stated that the main purpose of the signs is to indicate to customers the languages that they can use for transactions in the bank, which correlates with an informational function of language (Landry and Bourhis 1997: 25). The Belgrave Road branch of Bank of India also displays a welcome sign in English, Gujarati, Hindi and Punjabi (Figure 9.7).

It is important to note that Punjab National Bank and Bank of India have their headquarters in India, thus conducting business in Indian languages is not exceptional and these institutions cannot be compared straightforwardly with Leicester's local

Figure 9.7 Bank of India sign

authorities and businesses. In contrast to Punjab National Bank and Bank of India, non-Asian international banks and non-Asian national businesses such as betting shops, food outlets and supermarkets that are present on the Golden Mile do not adapt their standard, English only, corporate signage. Apart from the signs produced by the City Council and the police, all of the multilingual signs including Gujarati were authored by members of the Gujarati-speaking community. This indicates that the provision of written information in Gujarati is predominantly driven by the community, rather than there being a wider campaign for linguistic inclusion. Hence, actors from within the community, such as business owners, play an important role in helping to empower speakers by providing information in community languages, facilitating their participation in everyday life. Access to information is not the only key to unlocking an individual's empowerment to play an active part in society, but a lack of access can act as an important barrier to an individual feeling empowered.

4.2 Type of multilingualism displayed

Following Reh's (2004) framework to analyse multilingualism in the public space, the signs recorded in this survey that included written Gujarati were predominantly stationary, with a newsagent's shop displaying Gujarati-language magazines in its window constituting the only example of mobile inscribed objects. The prevalence of stationary signs is consistent with Reh's (2004: 3) observation that this type of written display is aimed at a spatially mobile readership (i.e. passing trade) and often includes information that is relevant to the particular location, such as a sign detailing the services available in an individual shop. Some of the signs recorded during the survey were of a temporary relevance, for example, posters advertising upcoming entertainment events or day trips and holidays in a travel agent's shop. These kinds of signs, described by Blommaert (2013: 54) as event-related signs, might only be displayed for a short time, until the event occurs, which underlines the transient nature of the LL of any inhabited public space.

All displays of multilingualism recorded in the survey were visible within the same space, with no instances of 'covert multilingualism' found, distinguished by Reh (2004: 5) as occurring when monolingual signs relay the same message at different locations. Moreover, the distribution of multilingual signs was spread throughout the survey area, which suggests that the Golden Mile as a whole is viewed as a multilingual space, as opposed to there being particular locations that are associated with the use of one language.

4.3 Fragmentary multilingual signs

In 51.3 per cent of the multilingual signs including Gujarati recorded in the survey, the authors follow a model of fragmentary multilingualism. Fragmentary[2] multilingual signs refer to examples wherein parts of the text are presented in multiple languages, but the entirety of the message is only available in one language (Reh 2004: 10). Fragmentary signs are usually employed in a multilingual society where the individual reader could be monolingual or multilingual (Reh 2004: 16), but not all monolingual readers will have access to the entirety of the message. In almost all cases of fragmentary multilingualism recorded, the entirety of the information was presented in English and part of the message in Gujarati.

At the entrance to Cossington Recreation Ground, Leicester City Council displays an information sign that follows a model of fragmentary multilingualism (Figure 9.8). This example includes a welcome message in Bengali, Gujarati, Hindi,

Figure 9.8 Cossington Recreation Ground sign, example of fragmentary multilingualism

Figures 9.9 Business sign, example of fragmentary multilingualism

Punjabi, Somali and Urdu, and additional information is provided in Gujarati and Hindi, translating the message in English that food should not be dumped. Several pieces of information are written in English only. The arrangement of information on this sign is in line with the Council's policy of treating English as the main language, and Gujarati and Hindi are given an elevated secondary status here. Other languages spoken by the local community are recognized, but they are given less priority in this case. To offer supplementary information for the parts where the message is written only in English, universally recognizable symbols accompany the text. However, the information at the bottom of the sign is accessible to an English reader only; although a telephone symbol is presented next to the contact numbers, 'for further information' and 'for emergency out of hours' would only be understood by an English reader. The multilingual language policy applied here, with the message that is translated into most languages being the welcome notice, is in line with the earlier observation that the City Council wishes to project an image of embracing multilingualism, but the fragmented information provided in different languages suggests a lack of commitment to empower all readers and aim to achieve meaningful inclusivity.

In one business, the business name and the services offered are communicated in both languages, but details of opening times and contact details are presented in English only (Figure 9.9). In another example, the message that the products are freshly made is communicated in both languages, as is the information on the items being sold, but the pricing details are presented only in English (Figure 9.10). Hence, the English-language reader can understand the entire message, but the prices and the words 'each items below' are not available in Gujarati.

Multilingualism in the Model Multicultural City 209

Figures 9.10 Business sign, example of fragmentary multilingualism

Several business owners who were interviewed explained that they presuppose that their customers can read numerical-based information using Arabic numerals, even if they are not proficient in reading texts in English. When creating signs that follow a model of fragmentary multilingualism, authors make a judgement on the information that is necessary to empower readers as consumers, based on their perceptions of their readers' needs.

4.4 Duplicating multilingual signs

In 30.8 per cent of the multilingual signs including Gujarati recorded in this survey, the authors duplicated complete messages in different languages (Reh 2004: 8). Each of the signs produced by Leicestershire Police, which were displayed on noticeboards in the entrance to Belgrave Library and Belgrave Neighbourhood Centre, follow a model of duplicating multilingualism, with identical information repeated in English and Gujarati within the same sign or on separate signs that are positioned adjacently (Figure 9.11). Duplicating multilingual writing is generally employed when multilingualism is present at the societal level but not at the individual level, which means that it is necessary to repeat the message in different languages to ensure that the message is communicated to the highest number of people possible within a community. It is important to acknowledge that Leicester City Council and Leicestershire Police, as public service providers, have a different duty of care to the local community compared to private business owners. Moreover, the anticipated reader is different, with public service notices generally being aimed at a broader audience. The Belgrave North police unit confirmed that their multilingual posters are produced in-house by Leicestershire Police at the request of local police units; normally these are written and proofread by multilingual police staff. In addition to this technical aspect, the duplication of a message in different languages can also have an affective aspect, as it signals an equal valorization of different linguistic and cultural communities (Reh 2004: 9).

The local police confirmed that in addition to the posters serving a technical function – conveying information about personal safety and crime prevention to

Figure 9.11 Leicestershire Police sign, example of duplicating multilingualism

readers – the inclusion of community languages (in this case Gujarati, but other locally spoken languages are also sometimes used) serves an affective function, which relates to the 'symbolic value condition' set out by Spolsky and Cooper (1991) in their sign rules. The police stated that communicating with the local population in their first languages also allows for a rapport to develop between officers and the community and helps to build a relationship of trust. In addition, it serves to put people at ease with communicating with the police in a common language, which has an important impact on the public reporting or providing information on crime. The police also communicate in community languages orally, for similar purposes. For example, they provide information talks in the local area in community languages and, in January 2018, a video message in Gujarati was delivered by a Police Community Support Officer to appeal for help with a local murder investigation (Jarvis 2018). The duplication of messages in community languages by the police helps to empower local residents, enabling them to play a fuller role in their community and to access information to help to keep them safe.

At the entrance to Belgrave Neighbourhood Centre, Leicester City Council displays multilingual welcome signs in several languages spoken in the local community (Figure 9.12). In contrast with the welcome signs discussed earlier (Figures 9.1 and 9.2), only languages of the local community are featured, indicating that their aim is not to accommodate visitors from outside the area. In an interview, the manager of

Figure 9.12 Belgrave Neighbourhood Centre sign, example of duplicating multilingualism

the centre stated that it is not required for staff at the Belgrave Neighbourhood Centre to be multilingual, but most can speak another language in addition to English. However, there is no guarantee that users of the centre will be able to communicate with its staff in the languages displayed on the signs at any given time. He explained that the signs serve a dual function: to inform monolingual readers of the purpose of the building, and to make everyone feel welcome in this shared space. He suggested that in the past both functions may have been equally important, but today the purpose is more linked to an affective rather than a technical purpose: the main aim is to make community members feel welcome; the Council do not feel that they need to put up more signs in written Gujarati because an increasing number of people understand English.

A parallel can be drawn between this example and the fragmentary multilingual signs displayed by Leicester City Council in other locations, which were discussed in the opening section of this chapter. The duplication of the welcome message does not signal that services are available in all the mentioned languages, but instead aims to signal that the Council recognizes the city's cultural diversity.

In one case, the owner of a florist's shop that was located within a small unit of shops displayed a handwritten sign on which the same message was communicated in English and Gujarati (Figure 9.13). This sign replaced a similar written sign that the same business owner displayed when data was being collected earlier in the project; this example underlines the transient nature of the LL. Although the positioning of the message in English first and the tendency to devote more space to English could be read as being representative of a prioritization of this language, the business owner and author of the sign stated that she was not conscious that she had presented the languages in a specific order. Moreover, she added that the disparity in the amount of

Figure 9.13 Florist shop sign, example of duplicating multilingualism

space devoted to each language was a result of it being written quickly, using pen and paper. On the front of the retail unit (which also included a convenience shop, a travel agent and a mobile phone repair shop), the florist displayed two professionally printed signs displaying contact details and products offered in English. This would suggest that, in spite of her declared language attitudes, the florist does prioritize English, the language of the permanent markers of her business. Hence the empowerment of community language speakers as consumers is a secondary concern, with the primary focus of the business owner being the communication of information in English, the lingua franca of the area.

The model of duplicating information is also exemplified in the Punjab National Bank and Bank of India signs (Figures 9.6 and 9.7, respectively). As explained in the discussion above, this type of multilingual arrangement of information renders the message accessible for monolingual and multilingual English/Gujarati speakers. It is noteworthy that the Bank of India sign (Figure 9.7) positions Hindi, the most widely spoken language in India, before English; this arrangement underscores the non-neutral nature of language policy.

4.5 Complementary multilingual signs

Lastly, 17.9 per cent of the multilingual signs including Gujarati followed the model of presenting multilingual information in a complementary manner, whereby different parts of the message are presented in different languages, and, unlike fragmentary signs, the entirety of the message is not rendered in any language (Reh 2004: 14). No examples of signs following the model of overlapping multilingualism (Reh 2004: 12) were recorded in the survey. One complementary multilingual sign displayed on a convenience shop (within the retail unit described in the previous section) advertised 'Sweet pan' (a traditional South Asian speciality) in English, and a list of traditional South Asian drinks in Gujarati (Figure 9.14). Images to the side of the inscriptions indicate the meaning, but the whole message could only be understood by a reader of both languages.

In another example of this approach to presenting multilingual information, on one poster, displayed in several shops along the Golden Mile, the explanation of the content of an entertainment event advertised was presented in Gujarati, while all other details were presented in English. The target reader of texts where different parts of the message are presented in different languages is imagined to be multilingually competent (Reh 2004: 14). This type of multilingual sign disempowers monolingual readers, as they will only be able to access part of the message. Reh (2004: 23) suggests that this is a more attractive way of presenting information for individuals who are multilingual, rather than duplicating all parts of the message. For sign producers, it could also be advantageous as rendering the message only once requires less space, which means that more information can be included, or production costs may be lower.

Figure 9.14 Business sign, example of complementary multilingualism

4.6 The order and position of languages on multilingual signs

In almost all signs recorded as part of this survey, where different languages were presented within one sign, the author had chosen to present the message in English first. Where the different languages were presented vertically, the sections of text in English were more frequently presented at the top of signs, or at the top and bottom, hence 'sandwiching' the other language(s), and more often to the left when presented horizontally, meaning that the reader would be drawn to that text first, which suggests a preference for the language in written communication (Scollon and Scollon 2003: 120). No clearly distinguishable differences in the size of writing in each language were noted, apart from in the signs produced by Leicester City Council, wherein the words in English are sometimes presented larger. This correlates with the Council's position on managing multilingualism, whereby English is always considered to be the main language.

5. The motivations of authors

The main aim of this project is to understand the reasons why the authors of signs choose to present information in different ways. As posited earlier in this chapter, the authors of signs, particularly those in the private sector, have a high level of agency in the context of this case study – they are empowered to shape the LL of the community without being restricted by legislation. Public sector actors have more responsibility to serve their communities, but legally they have the freedom to decide their own language policies. In all cases the business owners or service providers were responsible for the displays of written information; there were no examples of signs being 'inherited' from previous owners, which can be an important factor to consider when examining authorship in the LL (e.g. in Malinowski's study of authors of Korean signs in California, almost none of the proprietors interviewed had designed the signs themselves (2009: 113)).

Twenty-five interviews were undertaken; eighteen people (72 per cent of respondents) were interviewed in businesses and services that did display signs including written Gujarati (full or partial messages) and seven people (28 per cent) from those that did not include any written information in the language. Ten interviewees out of eighteen (55.6 per cent) from businesses or services that presented full or partial information in Gujarati stated that the signs were targeted specifically at older members of the community who originally came from India. In addition, six interviewees (33.3 per cent) from that category declared that the signs were also aimed at newly arrived people from the Indian state of Gujarat. This highlights the multifaceted nature of the local community, which has been shaped by different waves of immigration, and the complexity of the author's task in developing signage.

5.1 Authors choosing to present complete messages in Gujarati

An interview with an officer from the Belgrave North police unit revealed a technical motivation to duplicate entire messages in English and Gujarati (see Figure 9.11) to ensure that key information is conveyed to as many members of the community as possible. The officer stated that the local police are acutely aware that a significant proportion of residents cannot read English, and as some crimes specifically target the Indian Asian community, the police see full translations as being essential to their work. In addition, an affective motivation was stressed; local police officers communicate in community languages both orally and in writing to make residents feel at ease and to build a relationship with them. Presenting a complete message in Gujarati acts to empower both community members and the local police force, by creating an effective channel of communication that is mutually beneficial.

The technical function of duplicating multilingualism was also cited by the author of the signs in the florist's shop discussed above (Figure 9.13). The business owner stated that she recognized that in the local community some people could not read any English and some only a little; her sole motivation for presenting the message equally in both languages was to ensure that as many customers as possible understand that more products are kept inside of the shop during hot weather. Here, the author's motivation can be categorized as being economic; the decision to duplicate the message in different languages is targeted at attracting more customers.

The informational function of duplicating multilingualism was explained as a further reason for including handwritten Gujarati on signs. One interviewee from a bank and one from a solicitor's office stated that the purpose of having the company name or a welcome sign presented in different languages is to signal to potential customers the range of languages in which the services are available. They stated that it was not necessary to include translations on every sign, but that the duplication of languages on a name or welcome sign served the aim to communicate to customers that those languages can be used in that location. Again, the language policy of the author is driven by an economic motivation to increase the number of customers.

5.2 Motivations for the partial inclusion of written Gujarati

As examined earlier in the chapter, in 51.3 per cent of the multilingual signs recorded, a fragmentary multilingual approach was taken, normally with only part of the messages communicated in Gujarati, and 17.9 per cent exemplified complementary multilingualism. When asked why all the message is not communicated in both languages, one business owner stated that only what he considered to be the essential part of the information was translated for reasons of space, and that the information presented in English only (namely contact details and opening hours) could be understood by most readers. Thus, a practical or economic motivation is sometimes behind the decision to not present the full message in all languages. This is especially pertinent when signs are produced professionally and the amount of text included has an impact on the production costs.

Economic constraints are presented as one of the main reasons for Leicester City Council's policy to limit the number of texts or amount of text that it translates:

> The appropriate steps to be taken, whether translation or interpretation, will be decided on a case by case basis. ... Translation is considerably more costly than interpreting and therefore for every case you should consider if it is necessary and practical to do so, for example it is often the older population who do not speak English as a first language. ... Council services therefore need to assess the situation and the target audience before any printed material is translated. (Leicester City Council 2013: 2)

This underlines again the multilayered nature of language policy and the decisions that can precede the production of signs; here the commissioner of a sign must assess the necessity of the availability of written information in a different language in conjunction with the practical (namely financial) implications of having the sign produced. The question of the necessity of translation is particularly complex and reduces the potential of multilingual texts to serve anything other than a technical function. In a 2017 report (Leicester City Council 2017: 3), the Council stressed that its decision to offer interpretation or translation is rooted in their duty to providing equal access to residents: 'Council staff will not translate material into other languages or provide interpretation as a matter of course. However, our Public Sector Equality Duty requires us to ensure that there are no barriers to residents accessing the services when they need.' The report explains that individual Council staff members are responsible for assessing this need, with the support of the Community Language Service and following the Council's Interpretation and Translation Policy (Leicester City Council 2017: 4).

One business owner who authored signs displaying fragmentary multilingualism claimed that it was not necessary to duplicate all information in Gujarati because at least one member of the family would be able to read English and they could act as an interpreter. The multilingual signs on this shop front were created and printed by the business owner, hence the question of financial cost is less pertinent. Here, the author of the sign indicated no motivation to empower the reader as an individual, instead viewing empowerment as being achieved through the community. Another interviewee, the author of an event sign displaying complementary multilingualism, stated that he presents the description of the shows that he is promoting in the main language of the target audience (in this case, Gujarati speakers) and any other information in English. In the case of a monolingual Gujarati speaker, he suggested that a family member would be able to explain details presented only in English. In these cases, the authors have decided to include only the information that they deem essential for the Gujarati reader's comprehension. The suggestion that members of one's family could act as interpreters can be linked to the traditional characterization of the Indian family, the members of whom primarily look to each other for support, as Sooryamoorthy (2012: 2) explains: 'The Indian family as a strong, cohesive, integral and fundamental unit is a solid foundation of the Indian social structure. … For the individual the family is the first place where one could look for everything that is needed for her/his growth and development.' The expectation of reliance for help from family members impacts the empowerment of individuals who cannot read the dominant language, as this can result in the non-inclusion of multilingual texts in addition to fragmentary multilingualism.

5.3 Motivations for the non-inclusion of written Gujarati

The authors of monolingual signs are equally important to consider in an overview of the shaping of the multilingual LL. The prevalence of spoken Gujarati amongst business owners in the Golden Mile area compared to the relatively low proportion of businesses that include written Gujarati in their signage suggests that the absence of the language is the result of choice. However, other factors could be influential, such as a lower rate of literacy compared to oracy, both among older members of the community, who arrived having not completed formal education, and Gujarati speakers of subsequent generations who have learned it in an informal setting.[3] Moreover, as there are several ethnic groups living in the area, another factor could be a reluctance to indicate a preference for one community, hence English acts as a neutral code.

Amongst the seven interviewees who were asked why their shops or businesses do not display written information in Gujarati, all stated that customers know that they can practise the language in most businesses in the area, and that the lack of signage in the language does not act as a barrier for its use. Hence, the perception that the community does not need to see written Gujarati to know that it is accepted and valorized is proposed as one reason for the authors of signs to present messages in English only, as it has a privileged status as the lingua franca. No concern was expressed about newly arrived Gujarati speakers, which suggests that it is expected that even those new to the area are aware of its reputation or will have existing connections within the community. Of the six pharmacies recorded in the survey, only one displayed written information in Gujarati on its shopfront at the time the data was recorded. Interviewees from two of the pharmacies that do not display any written information in Gujarati stated that it is felt that it would not be necessary to do so, as their customer base is aware that they speak Gujarati and other community languages, and that new customers would presume that they could because of the reputation of the area and the visible signs of the ethnic backgrounds of the shop assistants. This viewpoint challenges the importance of the informational function of multilingual signs suggested above. In one branch of a non-Asian international bank, an assistant stated that although there are no written signs in languages other than English, he estimates that 85 per cent of transactions in the bank take place in another language, including Gujarati, but also in other Indian Asian languages and Eastern European languages. Owing to the multicultural nature of the city, although there is no specific policy to employ multilingual staff, several employees can speak other languages.

A wish to be seen as being modern was proposed as another reason for business owners to exclude any signs in written Gujarati. Three interviewees stated that they did not feel that it is relevant to display written information in Gujarati today, as an increasingly significant number of customers can read English. One business owner stated that although a small number of businesses display signs in Gujarati to make their older customers feel more at ease, he prefers to use English only on his shopfront as he sees this as an indication of 'moving with the times'. Nonetheless, all three interviewees acknowledged the prevalence of multilingual oral communication on the Golden Mile and expressed a willingness to speak Gujarati with customers.

Furthermore, the interviews revealed that a lack of competence or confidence in writing Gujarati can be a reason for a sign writer choosing not to produce multilingual signs. One travel agent who stated that he speaks Gujarati with almost all his customers specified that he provides documentation in English only, his dominant written language, as any errors could lead to him being liable. He suggested that even when customers are not proficient in reading English, they are able to comprehend what he deems to be the most essential written details for his business, namely dates, departure times and prices. An error on his behalf could lead to customers asking for a refund or damage the reputation of his business, which again links to an underlying financial motivation behind language policy.

Lastly, in two shops the interviewees stated that they did not view written signs in any language as being important as the goods displayed communicated to the customer what was on offer. Here, the items displayed in the shop windows are perceived to be the most important semiotic resources to engage with customers.

6. Conclusions

Akin to the way in which Leicester presents a melting pot of different cultures, the data that have emerged from this study suggest that there exists a fusion of different language policies on the ground in the Golden Mile area. One commonality in policy that transpires from the data analysis is the preference for English, which reflects the status of the language in society – English, the sole de facto official language, is omnipresent in public life. The main public body that shapes the LL of the area, Leicester City Council, adopts an unequivocal English-first approach to language management, although its signage does reflect a recognition of de facto multilingualism. In the private sector, individual business owners throughout the Golden Mile exercise individual language policies, but they also tend to privilege English in the production of monolingual and multilingual signs.

The results of the interview data collected suggest a range of reasons for both the inclusion and the conscious non-inclusion of written information in Gujarati. Motivations for authors to include the language on signs can be broadly categorized as follows: being technical, pre-supposing a monolingual reader who otherwise would not be able to understand the message; being informational, to indicate to monolingual or multilingual readers the languages that they can expect to be able to speak within a location; or being affective, trying to make monolingual or multilingual readers feel welcome, comfortable and part of the local community. In all cases, the inclusion of multilingual signs can be linked to a wish for the author to engage with the local community, which could be for economic purposes (in the case of business owners trying to extend their customer base), or for the efficiency of a service (such as increased communication between the police and members of the community). As discussed earlier in this chapter, if the Golden Mile does evolve into a more widely popular tourist attraction in the future, this could impact the development of the LL of the area. However, the authors interviewed for this study did not indicate that the inclusion of Gujarati seeks to commodify Indian Asian culture for visitors from outside of the local community at the present time. Reasons for authors to exclude or to partially include Gujarati can be categorized as being linked to the following: judgements of necessity, presupposing a multilingual reader or a monolingual Gujarati reader who has access to an interpreter within the family; economic constraints, which is particularly relevant when a third party is involved in producing the content or the material; a wish to be seen as modern, hence favouring English over the traditional language; linguistic insecurity on behalf of the author; or the preference of other semiotic resources over written language. Although the interview data did not reveal any examples of this, the question of visual attractiveness and a reluctance to present readers with what is deemed to be too much text could also be a reason for sign writers to limit or exclude different languages (Reh 2004: 23).

A parallel could be drawn between the proportion of Gujarati speakers in Leicester and that of businesses/public services displaying signs in Gujarati on the Golden Mile according to this survey; both represent approximately 11 per cent. However, the relative minority presence of Gujarati in the LL does not reflect the predominance of spoken Gujarati that one hears on the ground; on every corner of the Golden Mile Gujarati is spoken and accepted as a valid means of everyday communication. Although English is visually dominant in the LL, Gujarati is not confined to a minority position in oral communication. Moreover, the cultural identity of the Indian Asian community is imprinted on the Golden Mile not only through the written word but also through visual symbols of the traditional culture, including large shopfronts displaying brightly coloured saris, golden jewellery, savoury foods and sweets.

Where written information is made available in Gujarati, this can be seen to act to help to empower individuals, primarily those who are older or who have arrived recently from India, meaning that they do not need to rely on other people to relay information. The results of this case study suggest that there is a consensus that Gujarati speakers are empowered in oral communication regardless of the presence of written information; even where the LL is not marked by Gujarati, the language is spoken. However, the traditional reliance on family amongst the Indian Asian community might mean that individual agency is not prioritized in the same way that it might be within other ethnic groups.

The suggestion that written information is provided in Gujarati on a basis that is age-graded, to cater to the needs of the first generation of Indian Asians, may indicate that the need for inscribed objects in the language will not persist in the future. However, the language might take on a symbolic, affective function for subsequent generations, representing a link to their cultural heritage. Given the continued popularity of the Golden Mile area for the settlement of newly arrived Gujarati speakers, as well as the robust popularity of the area amongst Gujarati-speaking visitors, it seems likely that the language will continue to feature in the local LL.

Notes

1. I would like to express my gratitude to Jaiwanda Patel and Kamini Patel for their invaluable help with the translation of signs from Gujarati to English for this project. Special thanks to Jay, for sharing her local knowledge and for giving her time so generously.
2. The choice of the term 'fragmentary' is problematic, since the message is not incomplete for all readers; the term is maintained in this chapter, but it is recognized that it does not describe effectively the experience of all readers.
3. Gujarati education (up to A level) is offered at several supplementary schools in Leicester, but it is not widely taught in mainstream education.

References

Ager, D. (1995), *Language Policy in Britain and France: The Processes of Policy*, London: Cassell.

Ager, D. (2001), *Motivation in Language Planning and Language Policy*, Clevedon, UK: Multilingual Matters.

Amos, H. W. (2016), 'Chinatown by Numbers: Defining an Ethnic Space by Empirical Linguistic Landscape', *Linguistic Landscape*, 2 (2): 127–56.

Blommaert, J. (2013), *Ethnography, Superdiversity and Linguistic Landscapes: Chronicles of Complexity*, Bristol, UK: Multilingual Matters.

Gorter, D. (2006), 'Introduction: The Study of the Linguistic Landscape as a New Approach to Multilingualism', *International Journal of Multilingualism*, 3 (1): 1–6.

Hall, S., King, J., and Finlay, R. (2015), 'City Street Data Profile on Ethnicity, Economy and Migration: Narborough Road, Leicester'. Available online: https://lsecities. net/wp-content/uploads/2015/12/SuperDiverseStreets_Leicester.pdf (accessed 15 June 2019).

Hassen, I., and Giovarnardi, M. (2018), 'The Difference of "Being Diverse": City Branding and Multiculturalism in the "Leicester Model"', *Cities*, 80: 45–52. Available online: https://doi.org/10.1016/j.cities.2017.06.019 (accessed 31 July 2018).

Herbert, J. (2008), *Negotiating Boundaries in the City: Migration, Ethnicity, and Gender in Britain*, Aldershot: Ashgate.

Herbert, J. (2012), 'The British Ugandan Asian Diaspora: Multiple and Contested Belongings', *Global Networks*, 12 (3): 296–313.

Herbert, J. (2016), 'Immigration and the Emergence of Multicultural Leicester', in R. Rodger and R. Madgin (eds), *Leicester: A Modern History*, 330–46, Lancaster: Carnegie.

Hussain, A., Haq, T., and Law, B. (2003), *Integrated Cities: Exploring the Cultural Development of Leicester*, Leicester: University of Leicester, Centre for the History of Religious and Political Pluralism.

Jarvis, J. (2018), 'Leicestershire Police Release Belgrave Road Murder Investigation Appeal in Gujarati', *Leicester Mercury*, 27 January. Available online: https://www. leicestermercury.co.uk/news/leicester-news/leicestershire-police-release-belgrave-road-1127272 (accessed 15 June 2019).

Jaworski, A. (2015), 'Welcome: Synthetic Personalization and Commodification of Sociability in the Linguistic Landscape of Global Tourism', in B. Spolsky, I. Inbar-Lourie and M. Tannenbaum (eds), *Challenges for Language Education & Policy*, 214–31, London: Routledge.

Landry, R., and Bourhis, R. Y. (1997), 'Linguistic Landscape and Ethnolinguistic Vitality: An Empirical Study', *Journal of Language and Social Psychology*, 16 (1): 23–49.

Leeman, J., and Modan, G. (2009), 'Commodified Language in Chinatown: A Contextualized Approach to Linguistic Landscape', *Journal of Sociolinguistics*, 13 (3): 332–62.

Leicester City Council (2012), '*Diversity and Migration*'. Available online: https://www. leicester.gov.uk/media/177367/2011-census-findings-diversity-and-migration.pdf (accessed 27 July 2018).

Leicester City Council (2013), *Leicester City Council's Interpretation & Translation Policy*. Available online: http://www.cabinet.leicester.gov.uk/documents/s53109/FINAL%20 IT%20Policy%20-%20Jan%202013%20v3.pdf (accessed 7 August 2018).

Leicester City Council (2017), *Community Languages: Report to the Director of Delivery, Communications and Political Governance*. Available online: http://www.cabinet. leicester.gov.uk/documents/s88433/Community%20Languages.pdf (accessed 15 June 2019).

Leicester City Council (2018), 'Leicester City Council Corporate Equality and Diversity Strategy 2018–2022'. Available online: https://www.leicester.gov.uk/media/184953/ corporate-equality-strategy-2018-2022.pdf (accessed 7 August 2018).

Malinowski, D. (2009), 'Authorship in the Linguistic Landscape: A Multimodal-Performative View', in E. Shohamy and D. Gorter (eds), *Linguistic Landscape: Expanding the Scenery*, 107–25, New York: Routledge.

Martin, J., and Singh, G. (2002), *Asian Leicester*, Stroud: Sutton Publishing.

Office for National Statistics (2011a), 'Ethnicity and National Identity in England and Wales: 2011'. Available online: https://www.ons.gov.uk/peoplepopulationandcommunity/culturalidentity/ethnicity/articles/ethnicityandnationalidentityinenglandandwales/2012-12-11 (accessed 27 July 2018).

Office for National Statistics (2011b), 'Census Table QS204EW Main Language (Detailed)'. Available online: https://www.nomisweb.co.uk/census/2011/QS204EW/view/1946157130?rows=cell&cols=rural_urban (accessed 15 June 2019).

Office for National Statistics (2011c), 'Language in England and Wales: 2011'. Available online: https://www.ons.gov.uk/peoplepopulationandcommunity/culturalidentity/language/articles/languageinenglandandwales/2013-03-04 (accessed 27 July 2018).

Reh, M. (2004), 'Multilingual Writing: A Reader-Oriented Typology – with Examples from Lira Municipality (Uganda)', *International Journal of the Sociology of Language*, 170: 1–41.

Scollon, R., and Scollon, S. W. (2003), *Discourses in Place: Language in the Material World*, London: Routledge.

Seargeant, P. (2012), 'Between Script and Language: The Ambiguous Ascription of 'English' in the Linguistic Landscape', in C. Hélot, M. Barni, R. Janssens and C. Bagna (eds) *Linguistic Landscapes, Multilingualism and Social Change*, 187–200, Frankfurt am Main: Peter Lang.

Sebba, M. (2012), 'Multilingualism in Written Discourse: An Approach to the Analysis of Multilingual Texts', *International Journal of Bilingualism*, 17 (1): 97–118.

Singh, G. (2003), 'Multiculturalism in Contemporary Britain: Reflections on the "Leicester Model"', *International Journal of Multicultural Societies*, 5: 40–54.

Sooryamoorthy, R. (2012), 'The Indian Family: Needs for a Revisit', *Journal of Comparative Family Studies*, 43 (1): 1–9.

Spolsky, B., and Cooper, R. L. (1991), *The Languages of Jerusalem*, Oxford: Clarendon.

Vetrovec, S. (1994), 'Multicultural, Multi-Asian, Multi-Muslim Leicester: Dimensions of Social Complexity, Ethnic Organization and Local Government Interface', *Innovation: The European Journal of Social Science Research*, 7 (3): 259–74.

10

Empowering dialect speakers in formal education: The case of the Greek Cypriot dialect in preschool education in Cyprus

Andry Sophocleous

1. Introduction

One of the main goals of formal education is for learners to develop knowledge, skills and competencies so that they can thrive academically, personally and socially as law-abiding members of a specific society, culture and nation. The cultivation of a set of beliefs and values, whether these are culturally, ethnically, religiously or politically bound is very much related to the mastery of language. As the social philosopher Michael Walzer argues, education is 'a program for social survival [that is] always relative to the society for which it is designed' (1983: 197). Inglehart (1990) even suggests that education is the most important factor that shapes our lives as one's educational level can limit or expand career type, earnings, social prestige and how much one 'influences the communication networks one is exposed to throughout life' (228).

Societies are, in the majority, multilingual and multicultural; multilingual, bilingual – or, in the case of Cyprus, bidialectal – education has always supported the inclusion of children's language and culture in the school curriculum for better school achievement (Ruiz 1991; Yiakoumetti 2006, 2007). Consequently, the school is regarded as a public space where we can investigate how languages are treated; what values they are attributed by educational administrators, curriculum designers and teachers; and what values they carry in actual usage, as theory regarding language use is often not in agreement with actual language practice (see Ioannidou 2009; Sophocleous 2011). The central purpose of this study, therefore, is to investigate sociolinguistic issues relevant to the use of different varieties in the public space of school to understand the extent to which preschoolers are empowered so as to project a certain identity and to seek social cohesion. In other words, empowerment is understood as the tolerance and encouragement of complex, compound identities through which groups within a given society can be connected and demonstrate solidarity. This is achieved by focusing on language use particularly in formal preschool education in Cyprus, in the part of the daily lesson where narration and structured play take place. Justifications for observing these activities are provided below.

Preschool education was selected out of all other levels of formal education (primary, secondary, tertiary) for various reasons. As outlined more fully below, the linguistic repertoire of Greek Cypriots (GCs) consists of two language varieties[1] that they use in their daily interactions: Standard Modern Greek (SMG) and the Greek Cypriot Dialect (GCD). Children born to GC parents live their first 2–3 years at home hearing and acquiring GCD from their familial environment. Systematic learning of SMG begins when they begin state schooling. The reasons why state schooling is in SMG and not GCD are briefly mentioned in Section 1.1. As such, preschool education as a site for exploring multilingualism and empowerment is particularly pertinent, given that this is the site where children begin to develop their early literacy skills, develop a personal identity and are schooled to use their two varieties in different settings. Preschools are where they begin to learn that SMG is associated with schooling, and GCD with less formal and friendly environments (for more about language use in other levels of Cypriot education see Ioannidou and Sophocleous 2010; Papapavlou and Sophocleous 2009; Sophocleous 2009; Tsiplakou 2007).

1.1 Preschool education in Cyprus

I prefer to describe the linguistic ecology of the Republic of Cyprus as bidialectal (Papapavlou and Pavlou 2005), rather than diglossic. SMG serves as the official language of Cyprus (and Greece), and it is used in writing and in formal settings such as in the media, education, church and law. Currently the GCD is not standardized, even though attempts have been made to codify it and, hence, it mainly serves oral interaction in less formal settings among family and friends. It is also the first variety attained in the home environment by children, being the 'default' language spoken, as opposed to SMG that is formally learnt at school. It should also be noted that GCD is also used in writing and broadcasting for specific purposes, normally concerned with folk literature and societal issues (Sophocleous 2011). Apart from being the official language of the Republic of Cyprus and hence the 'prestigious' variety, SMG serves as a strong ethnic bond between Greeks and Greek Cypriots who share similar cultural values, beliefs and religion. The modern history of Cyprus, in particular the 1974 invasion by Turkey, has divided the island into two, the north and the south. The north is under Turkish occupation (36.2 per cent of Cypriot territory) and is where now all Turkish Cypriots live, in a territory that they recognize as the Turkish Republic of Northern Cyprus (TRNC). GCs live in the southern part of the island that is known as the Republic of Cyprus. Prior to the creation of the Republic of Cyprus in 1960 (following the British colonial rule of 1878–1960 and the Ottoman Empire of 1571–1878) Cypriot education was heavily influenced and supported by mainland Greece, and up to the present day the books on Greek-language learning (Γλώσσα) [Language] and history are delivered to all Cypriot schools from Greece. According to the Ministry of Education and Culture (MoEC), language practice in the classroom should be in SMG as is 'the common linguistic code of all Greeks' [original in Greek] (MoEC 28 August 2002). All students attending formal education are expected to 'shift from the linguistic idiom to the pan-Hellenic demotic' (MoEC 1994) once they begin to attend formal state education. There is an official recognition, in other words, that the school is a site of multilingual activities but that there is an expectation that teachers will lead the change in language practices. We explore below the question of the (dis) empowerment of preschool children.

Regarding differences between the two varieties, there are lexical, phonological, syntactic and morphological differences between SMG and GCD, and the lexical inventory of GCD is heavily influenced by the languages of the invaders who occupied Cyprus over the years. There is heavy mixing between SMG and GCD in most domains, even formal ones, and for this specific reason this type of sociolinguistic canvas does not fit into the clearly distinct values attached to a High and a Low variety as described in a classical Fergusonian diglossic model. It is not possible to identify separate High and Low varieties which carry completely different functional loads.

This is one of the reasons why the GC setting is not regarded as diglossic but as bidialectal. Another reason is because GCD comprises a dialectal continuum where different subvarieties are present. These differ in terms of phonology, lexis and morphology and can either co-exist in one region or differ as a result of geographical differences between speakers. Their number has not been agreed upon as there is no clear distinction between some of them (see Tsiplakou 2006) and overlap between them is very common.

This GCD continuum consists of basilectal (most distinct from SMG in terms of phonology and lexis), mesolectal (bearing both SMG and GCD features) and acrolectal features (similar to SMG). Studies indicate that the more basilectal features one employs in his/her speech the more s/he is associated with peasantry and low education (Papapavlou and Sophocleous 2009, 2011; Tsiplakou 2009). These societal attitudes are a result of Cyprus's historical past, its occupation and of the fact that the GCD is a variety that comprises Greek and the languages of the conquerors that have ruled the island. Since Cyprus was under the Ottomans (1571–1878) and the British (1878–1960), GCs wanted to keep their identity, religion and culture alive, and that was achieved by going to night schools and classes (when under Ottoman rule) that were run and taught by priests where children continued to learn Greek in a setting where its use island-wide and across domains was restricted. One can understand how the preservation, protection and even strengthening of Greek as a language was vital for the survival of GC ethnic identity. To this day, the state school curriculum mirrors that of Greece as noted above to enhance and project their Hellenic identity.

GCD constitutes the acquired language of home, and systematic learning of SMG begins in formal kindergarten (3–5 years old) and preschool (4.8–5.8 years) education. The language of formal education is SMG, and teachers are advised to encourage its use in all levels of formal education (MoEC 2002). As already discussed, SMG serves as a strong linguistic and cultural symbol of belonging, and its speakers share the same ethnicity, cultural, and religious identity that is supported by politics and the Greek Christian Orthodox Church in Cyprus. In the context of formal education, even though the use of GCD is less encouraged within classroom walls, the MoEC (2002) acknowledges that it is the language young learners bring to school with them and states that the Greek Cypriot Dialect is respected and can be used by students in certain cases for communication, such as in role plays representing scenes from everyday life, when reciting poems etc.. [original in Greek] (MoEC 28 August 2002)

Often the language policy in education in Cyprus is described as rather covert and at times unclear (Country Report 2004: 31; Papapavlou and Pavlou 2005) due to its vagueness regarding the use of the 'mother tongue', a term that might be used to refer to GCD and at other times to SMG (see Country Report 2004). This has an impact on GCs' sense of belonging, growing up with a different variety at home and using another variety during class time and this is why often when they become adults some regard themselves as 'Cypriots' and others as 'Greeks'. Teachers from primary education are reported to comment on this ambiguity regarding language policy and argue that clearer instructions should be provided by the MoEC as regards the place of GCD in formal education (see Papapavlou and Pavlou 2005).

1.2 The importance and goals of preschool education

Children begin to develop their early literacy skills through interaction; access to children's books; stories and songs they hear at school; and even pointing out, learning and naming objects in a supportive environment (Bohrer 2005; Daimant-Cohen 2007). These activities are regarded as important not only to help children expand their vocabularies, encourage brain development, but also to help develop their experience and understanding of the world around them.

For this particular reason, Early-Years education is increasingly regarded as a significant part of children's learning experiences, often linked to later educational success and metalinguistic awareness (Drigas et al. 2017). Additionally, research indicates that good preschool programmes provide children with improved school readiness, reduced grade retention, reduced need for special education services, as well as improved educational test scores (see Zigler, Gilliam and Jones 2006: 262). Furthermore, research suggests that children's engagement in narrative and after-reading activities, that is, classroom activities that follow storybook reading or teacher narratives such as drawing, role playing, retelling a story, sequencing story events or connecting a story to their personal life as follow-up activities during class time, enhance their imagination, creativity and critical thinking skills which are no less important than their social and emotional development in being active members of a society (Daimant-Cohen 2007; MoEC 2016; Van Kleeck, Stahl and Bauer 2003).

Children's literacy knowledge varies as they enter preschool education. However, fundamental emergent literacy skills such as phonological awareness, vocabulary and concept development are of vital importance (see Casey and Sheran 2004) so children can be able to actively participate in a language-rich environment that promotes a common national language, identity and culture (see Hornberger 2002; Kymlicka and Patten 2003 on multilingual language policies). Talking to children, sharing social experiences together and telling stories will help them to understand their social world and their relationship to others, to enrich their vocabulary and to develop literacy in the school language. The narration of stories in school – both by teacher and learners – is a fundamental practice that strengthens the relationship between interactants, encourages frequent verbal interaction, brings 'home' experiences in the classroom – as in the case of children sharing information about things they do at home like the games they play and trips they have been to with their families – and develops children's creative thinking and language complexity. This is the rationale for examining language use, identity projection and empowerment in this specific part of the preschool curriculum. Hence, to examine how GCD as the less prestigious variety is employed in the classroom, observation was deemed necessary in the parts of the lesson where children bring 'home' and related issues into the classroom environment. This way, the connection between observing the school variety, SMG, during the teacher's narrations, and the activities that followed in both SMG and GCD, gives us a clearer understanding of how children use the two varieties and most importantly how they voice their personal and social identities. In doing so, we see the extent to which the children's practices create a multilingual classroom and how the teachers, with their task of transitioning pupils to using SMG in the formal academic setting, empower these pre-schoolers.

1.3 Structured play and its importance in preschool education in Cyprus

Currently, preschool education in Cyprus serves approximately 75 per cent of children aged 3.0–5.8 and it is free for all children of 4.8 to 5.8 years old (Pashiardis 2007: 212). The daily programme of preschool education begins at 7.45 am and ends at 1.05 pm. Particular focus is placed on play as this constitutes the most important medium through which a child's holistic development takes place. It is through play that the socio-dramatic, symbolic, imaginary, creative and investigative aspect of a child's development unfold (MoEC 2016). Learning about and experiencing social and daily activities can take place through structured play. It connects learning with daily interests and young learners' contributions to class.

Structured play takes place in accordance with structured activities with all children that the teacher plans in advance. These structured activities can be activities of narration (as in story-book reading) by the teacher or children which might involve a whole set of follow-up learning activities such as language development, kinesthetic play, further narration, sociocultural involvement, linguistic exercises and creative writing, just to name a few.

According to MoEC (2016), structured play can contribute to the development and reinforcement of imagination and curiosity, aspiration to experiment, perseverance and inventiveness. Through inquiry and interaction, children can learn through structured play that is 'complemented with linguistic goals and an opportunity to relax and have fun whilst learning' (MoEC 2016: 12, original in Greek). Consequently, structured play encompasses the largest part of the daily programme of children in preschool education and acts as the steering wheel that guides the organization of all other activities taking place. This short section highlights the importance of structured play, which informs the selection of the excerpts that follow and children's language choices in these structured activities.

2. Method

The data collected comes from an ethnographic study whose aim was to examine how children are empowered by their use of the 'home' variety (GCD) and its subsequent reinforcement in structured activities. Furthermore, this study identifies the implications this usage has on the social and personal identities young learners express in the classroom. All the data were collected from a preschool state school in the city of Nicosia, the capital of Cyprus, during the academic year of 2018. All interactions were voice-recorded after obtaining the relevant permit from the MoEC, the school, children's parents and children themselves who orally agreed to be observed and recorded during their lesson. Additionally, handwritten notes were taken during the observations that would later on complement the information from the transcribed data.

2.1 Data collection techniques and data analysis

Data collection began in January 2018 and was completed in May 2018, after visiting the specific preschool classroom once per week for approximately sixty minutes each time. A rich set of data was collected, totalling to twenty hours of class observations, note taking and voice-recordings. The additional notes taken proved to be quite useful later on when transcriptions were undertaken as it was possible to note paralinguistic features too such as voice quality, gestures, facial expressions and expressive body language (see Auer 2007).

The analysis of talk-in-interaction in these naturally occurring conversations between children and their teacher was based on conversation analysis focusing on the analysis of interaction between children and their teacher, as well as any patterns arising as a result of the ways in which speakers produce and recipients comprehend language addressed to them as actions to fulfill specific interactional goals.

The class was composed of twenty-five mixed-aged children of 4–5.5 years old. All children were born to GC parents and raised in Cyprus (twelve boys and thirteen girls).

The teacher was a 47-year-old GC, born and raised in Cyprus. She has been working as a kindergarten/preschool school teacher for twenty-eight years (since 1990). The teacher completed her degree in pre-primary education after completing a three-year program at the Pedagogical Academy of Cyprus in 1990.

3. Results

The excerpts that follow have been selected to address the main focus of this study, namely to examine how GCD is used in the formal environment of school to empower learners.

3.1 Transcription conventions

Transcribed data that is not underlined or in bold is the same in SMG and the GCD

<u>Underline</u>: Greek Cypriot Dialect
Bold: Standard Modern Greek
- :: consonant or vowel lengthening
- ; is the question mark in Greek
- ↑ or ↓ Sharp rises or falls in pitch
- (.) Noticeable stop
- . Falling intonation followed by noticeable stop
- ? Rising intonation followed by noticeable stop
- ! Enthusiasm expressed in utterance
- (0.2) Elapsed time in silence in tenths of a second
- = No gap between speakers' utterances

In the following three examples we examine extract interactions from the classroom environment in preschool education which unfolded in activities designed to reinforce teacher narrations. This we do in order to explore the ways in which children are empowered to use their dialect, GCD, in the formal environment where SMG serves as the language of instruction. The two varieties are seen to co-exist harmoniously and children spontaneously interact with their fellow students and teacher in the language that they bring from home, that is, GCD. In other words, these vignettes illustrate the potential for teachers to empower preschoolers by permitting the use of GCD in order to transition to SMG.

Excerpt 1: The Robin and the Poppy

This first excerpt unfolded the week prior to the closing of the school before the Easter holidays. The teacher was about to begin reading to the children a traditional folk story which relates to Jesus Christ and His crucifixion. The same story was narrated to them the previous week. This explains below the response that some children give, as they remembered what the story was about. During the previous week the story was only read to them. This day, the teacher set additional learning objectives for this lesson. As clarified by the teacher prior to the activity, the learning outcomes of the story entitled 'The Robin and the Poppy' (ο Κοκκινολαίμης και η Παπαρούνα) were twofold: (1) to sensitize young learners to Christian teachings about the suffering of Jesus Christ to save the world and to honour Him during the Easter holidays; and (2) to teach learners to make up compound words in SMG as a continuation of what she started a few weeks back. Hence, the previous week's class on the specific story is a continuation of what is about to follow. The teacher begins this activity by first holding up a small poster with different pictures of a Robin with its red breast and starts to ask questions about it:

01   Teacher: **παιδιά τι βλέπετε εδώ;**

Children what do you see here?

02 Yiannis: Μέλισσα =

'bee' =

03 Nikos: = πκια μέλισσα ρε εσούνι;

= which bee, you?

04 Teacher: είναι μέλισσα;

Is it a bee?

05 Children: όχι! ↑

No! ↑

06 Teacher: **γιατί όχι**; =

Why not? =

07 Maria: = κυρία εν πουλί! ↑

= Miss it's a bird! ↑

08 Teacher: μπορώ να είμαι χελιδόνι; (0.4) **Περιγράψτε με να σας πω πως με λένε!**

Can I be a swallow? (0.4) Describe me so I tell you what my name is!

09 Agapi: **έχει κόκκινη βούλα** =

He has a red spot =

10 Marios: = κοκκινοβούλλης; (compound: kokkino-voulis)

= Redspot? (compound: red-spot)

12 Georgia: **κόκκινο στο λαιμό**! Κοκκινολαίμης! (compound: kokkino-lemis)

Red on the neck! Red-neck! (compound, robin)

13 Teacher: **πως έγινε έτσι**;

How did he become like this? (with red on his neck?)

14 Demetra: έτρεξεν το αίμαν του Χριστού πάνω του↓ =

The blood of Christ run down on him↓ =

15 Giorgos: = επειδή εθύμωσες!

= Because you got angry!

16 Andreas: μπορεί να εβαφτηκέν με το πινέλον! ↓

Maybe he painted himself with a brush! ↓

As is clear, five of the ten pupil responses are in GCD (underlined), three responded using SMG and two used a neutral medium. The teacher's attempt to encourage the children to speak in the formal variety, SMG, is quite obvious. After beginning with a question (01), she asks specific questions in utterances 04, 06, 08 and 13 to encourage them to use SMG to respond to her questions. Worthy of note here is the teacher's attempt to ask all questions in SMG, a pattern that brings children back to the language of school.

Yet, we also see children's utterances in GCD. Interesting to note is the fact that many of these utterances (specifically 03, 07 and 15) took place without any pause between utterances where the next speaker grabbed the floor without any hesitation. This spontaneity of the children, where their focus seems to be on providing a response rather than what variety to employ in their response, explains their use of GCD. Moreover, instances like utterances 14 and 16, which might be regarded as turns where students express own opinion, are also in GCD, the language that comes more naturally to them and the one in which they feel empowered to express themselves in this formal learning environment. The issues of spontaneity, addressing specific questions of the teacher and expressing own opinion will be discussed in more detail below.

Excerpt 2: The Red Poppy

On the same day, children go out for a short break and upon their return into the classroom, the teacher wants to see if they remembered from the previous week how the story they started before the break continued. Employing the same technique as in Excerpt 1 above, she begins this interaction by showing them a photo of a poppy this time.

01 Teacher: **αυτό, τι είναι;**

What is this?

02 Elena: **έχει μαύρη γύρη**

It has black pollen

03 Dionisia: **και κόκκινα πέταλα**

And red petals

04 Vasilis: **κυρία είναι παπαρούνα. Ένα αγριολούλουδο!**

Miss, it's a poppy. A wildflower!

05 Teacher: πολύ σωστά Βασίλη. Τι έχουν κοινό αυτά τα δυο λοιπόν; Πέστε μου. ↑
Very right Vasilis. What do these two have in common then? Tell me. ↑ =
(the robin and the poppy)

06 Marilia: = έσταξε <u>το γαίμα</u> του Χριστού **και** <u>εγίνικε</u> **κόκκινο**

= <u>the blood</u> of Christ spilt **and** <u>it became</u> **red**

07 Teacher: **ωραία παιδιά.** Ποιος θυμάται να μας πει την ιστορία;

Nice children. Who can remember this story to tell us about it?

08 Georgia: **ο Χριστός έπαιρνε τον σταυρό και** έσταξε το <u>γαίμα</u> του πάνω στην
παπαρούνα

Christ was taking the cross and his <u>blood</u> spilt on the poppy

09 Afrodite: **και μετά ήρθε το άσπρο πουλί να του βγάλει το στεφάνι και έσταξε
πάνω του το αίμα**

And then the white bird came to take off the wreath (from his head) and the blood
spilt on it

10 Teacher: **πολύ ωραία παιδιά.** Μπράβο σας

Very good children. Well done

Both of these extracts indicate how a lesson can be developed creatively to build on existing knowledge, encourage children to speak in class, learn to summarize important points, create compounds with words they know and support their use of the standard variety during class time. In this excerpt the teacher begins this part in a similar manner as in Excerpt 1. During our interaction at the end of this lesson, she said that consistency is very important when teaching young children as they learn to associate roles, speaking styles and topics discussed with a particular variety. For instance, the fact that the teacher begins each part by holding up a picture of either a robin or a poppy followed by questions and prompts in SMG (as she began in Excerpts 1 and 2) indicates that she is suggesting to children to use the same variety when discussing specific issues concerned with the lesson. This order plausibly explains why children respond to the teacher's direct questions during the lesson in SMG, as in utterances 02, 03, 04 above, and the praise they all receive from the teacher immediately afterwards (utterance 05). It certainly also helps children in understanding 'teacher talk' and her teaching practices as actions that serve specific interactional and, in this case, learning goals. This sort of encouragement of using SMG suggests to children what the 'preferred' variety for school is.

Yet, this does not mean that all children respond in similar ways. For instance, Marilia in utterance 06 responds to the teacher's question by codeswitching between GCD and SMG. She used the GCD word (γαίμα 'blood' instead of the SMG 'αίμα') and concluded her contribution by using the conjunction [και] 'and' and the SMG [κόκκινο] 'red' instead of GCD equivalent [κότζινο]. This observation is similar to a pattern that was also observed in the previous example, in that the student shares a personal opinion and there does not seem to be a gap between utterances; both features were observed above where the learners feel confident to respond in GCD in a rather formal interaction between teacher and students.

Georgia in utterance 08 codemixes between SMG and GCD, but then Afrodite in utterance 09 switches to SMG completely. This extract indicates a rather harmonious existence between SMG and GCD which is more evident in preschool education, as opposed to classes with older learners (see Ioannidou 2009; Ioannidou and Sophocleous 2010; Sophocleous 2011), where teachers expect students to make use of the standard variety SMG more systematically than in kindergarten/preschool education for the reasons discussed above. Even though the teacher indirectly encourages the use of SMG during class time through her subtle insistence of using the standard in class (as seen in Excerpts 1 and 2 above), she nevertheless accepts children's contributions after their use of dialectal elements, hence, allowing GCD the space to serve as a medium of interaction in this formal learning environment. One might also suggest that the two responses in Excerpt 2 (06 and 08) where code switching is used are quite common in their type. These responses were the outcome of teacher's questions of a rather broader focus and of a more interpretative nature, as opposed to her more specific questions about asking what children see in a photograph. Specifically, in utterances 05 and 07, the teacher's general questions 'what do these two have in common?' (05) and 'who can remember this story to tell us about it?' (07) invite learners to rationalize and narrate, and this is where spontaneity is evident to a certain extent, hence accounting for the use of GCD elements. Both Excerpts 1 and 2 indicate how the teacher empowers preschoolers to participate in class interactions using GCD. She noted after this lesson that children need to feel safe and that the school environment is a continuation of the home, hence, the use of GCD is important in children's empowerment and self-confidence.

Excerpt 3: Souvlaki Takeaway

The following excerpt draws on a fun activity involving role-play that unfolded after children had a lesson focusing on food. It is typical for this age that their class is structured in such a way that they have different corners in the classroom where children can play different roles. For instance, they had a cooking corner where this example took place; they had another corner with a doctor's office and equipment, and another corner with tools for cars and mechanics. This is a useful example mimicking what is happening in GC society outside the formal environment of school. As already noted, the language variety used out of school is GCD so it is expected and natural that the imaginary conversation unfolding between a customer (the teacher) who went to buy souvlaki from the take-away shop will also take place in GCD. Here the roles change from being teacher to a customer and pupil to a cook and all employed the language that seems fit for the specific occasion, GCD. Interestingly, the teacher switched to SMG in the last part of utterance 03 to sound more polite as politeness is often associated with SMG (see Papapavlou 1998, 2001, Tsiplakou 2009). When she was asked why she switched to SMG, she suggested that she wanted to make her request sound more formal. In the following excerpt, the teacher is observed to allow space for GCD to serve a purpose during learning, in this way empowering children and acknowledging its use in this type of interactions.

01 Teacher: θέλω να παραγγείλω σουβλάκια!

   I want to order souvlakia!

02 Marilena: ναι, (0.2) τι να σας κάμω;

   Yes, (0.2) what can I make for you?

03 Teacher: θέλω μιαν μιξ σας παρακαλώ, με σσιεφταλιές τζαι σουβλάκια. **Σε πόση ώρα θα είναι ετοιμα;**

   I want a mixed (pitta) please, with shieftalies (local meat dish) and souvlaki. **In how long will they be ready?**

04 Alexis: σε 15 λεπτά

   In 15 minutes

05 Teacher: πόσα έννα στοιχίσουν;

   how much will they cost?

06 Alexis: 10 ευρώ

   10 euro

4. Discussion

The above excerpts have been selected for analysis as they provide fertile grounds for discussing the issue of empowering children in the formal learning environment where SMG predominates.

4.1 SMG and GCD in preschool education

During the entire five months of data collection, it was clear that both SMG and GCD are used in and out of the classroom. As Teacher M said, 'Language does not occur in a vacuum and it's impossible to leave GCD out of school.' GCD is the home variety, the first language acquired by children, hence its entire absence from school would be simply unrealistic. A myriad of instances has been observed when GCD was employed by children and they were all instances when they expressed themselves in spontaneous and unplanned speech, either in front of the entire class as a result of enthusiasm to share personal experience or when contributing to class discussion. The data collected suggest that personal and social identities are expressed with the use of GCD: children interact between themselves, spontaneously say something and engage in one-to-one interactions with the teacher in GCD. All these instances have been observed in the excerpts above suggesting that the use of GCD in the classroom empowers learner autonomy and confidence to share in front of the class their own opinion.

On the contrary, when they were careful of what to say and spoke in a more careful manner in class, they opted for SMG. The use of SMG was evident in interactions when children were responding to the teacher's specific questions relevant to the topic discussed at the time, such as 'what does this look like, describe it to me', 'what do you see here?' (see Excerpts 1 and 2). Yet, when they are asked to interpret situations, draw conclusions, provide their own opinion or summarize stories the teacher narrated to them, then GCD takes over, where syntax, lexis and pronunciation is in GCD. One might suggest that this is due to the fact that a request for general information gives them the liberty to express themselves in longer utterances, in more spontaneous and less planned speech, and this is indeed a fertile ground for the use of GCD.

GCD is also the variety that has been observed to be of use in situations where learners provide additional information outside the 'public' sphere of interaction in class. Even though these discussions also take place in class, they seem to be less 'public' and more 'private' when compared to others (see Gal 2002, 2005; Gal and Woolard 2001, on language and public/private spheres, and Sophocleous 2013 on the public/private distinction in language use at kindergarten). Examples of these instances include situations as in Excerpt 1, when the children were addressing only the teacher in class as a one-to-one interaction (see Excerpt 1, utterances 07, 15, 16) or addressing each other (utterance 03).

Additionally, during class observations, learners were observed to put on 'act' identities or 'performing' identities to suit the occasion at play (see Excerpt 3). This was often evident in follow-up activities where children were encouraged to take part in role-play, sing or recreate the story narrated to them. These are all activities that fall under 'structured play' that we have also observed in Excerpt 3 above (more on bidialectal children performing identities in Ioannidou (2017) and Sophocleous and Ioannidou (2020)). The data observed indicate that the order and patterns arising from class interactions suggest that even though the language learnt in class is SMG, children are nevertheless empowered to contribute to the lesson through their use of GCD as in structured activities that help them socialize more, develop self-confidence and feel worthy and important in terms of sharing opinions and being heard by their teacher and peers.

4.2 Empowering children through the use of GCD in formal education

As already noted, language policy in Cyprus regarding the use of the two language varieties is rather vague. The MoEC suggests that GCD can be used in certain cases in education but not to the disadvantage of mastering SMG. This vagueness is what causes the language policy to be described by many as a covert policy; yet, it is also the cause that allows the possibility for GCD to be used by both students and teachers in class and give it space to be used in formal education. Consequently, children are also empowered to feel confident in using their home variety to learn, socialize and be active participants in the learning environment.

Many teachers were observed to be in favour of the use of GCD in education as in the examples below from different sectors of formal education (see Sophocleous 2011):

A. 'I see that they can understand much more when I use the dialect in class. You become clearer because you speak their language' (female teacher from Pancyprian Gymnasium)
B. 'I have never tried to correct them in class, because I use the dialect myself as the medium of instruction' (Maths secondary school teacher from Pancyprian Gymnasium).
C. 'Instead of using pure SMG terms, which are written in our books, I speak the language of the market, like the carpenters speak in their factories, in their workshops. These are the terms that students need to learn and remember. They will not use the Greek equivalent terms unless they go to work in Greece' (Technology teacher, First Technical School).

4.3 Kindergarten teachers' expectations of children's language use

Kindergarten teachers, whose classes were observed in the past (see Sophocleous 2009) as part of a greater study examining teachers' language attitudes in the school environment, state that children bring with them to school GCD and not SMG, so it is unsurprising that GCD also has its place in Cypriot education. Kindergarten teachers are observed to use SMG when they seek students' attention, when they teach and when they encourage discussions relevant to class material (such as answering specific questions, retelling a story, repeating new words). They argue that these unwritten rules and obligations need to be met so that greater attention will be placed on what and how something is being said. However, there are other instances in class where GCD will be favoured instead, and these are instances when children's home background and culture will be the focus of their interactions. Since participation, self-confidence and encouragement are vital at this age, Mrs B, who participated in a kindergarten study, argues that children's talk forms the backbone of effective learning, which also includes language learning. Their language is always developed in relation to their environment and that implies that GCD will always serve a purpose in education. 'We encourage children to contribute in class by using the language they bring with them, by using GCD' (Mrs B from Makedonitissa Kindergarten, in Sophocleous 2009).

5. Conclusions

This chapter examined the use of the two varieties in preschool education in Cyprus and how specifically children are empowered and supported to use GCD in the learning environment where SMG serves as the main language of learning. The data suggest that the home variety, GCD, indeed serves a very important role: that of socialization between children and their teacher, forming a personal identity through expressing opinion and sharing ideas, and developing self-confidence. All of these are achieved via the use of the language they grow up with, namely GCD. Looking at GCD from this sociolinguistic perspective, we can appreciate the importance of permitting its use in education and hence, empowering the children who use it, particularly in Early-Years education where they begin to make sense of the world around them and their society. Crucially, the empowerment that takes place is the encouragement to preschoolers to use GCD precisely to transition them to using SMG. This is not a question of reductive multilingualism, where the children are expected to cease using GCD; the use of their 'home' variety is not encouraged with the expectation that they shift completely to SMG. This is not a modern-day equivalent to eighteenth- and nineteenth-century nation-building, predicated on a single language for a unified modern state. In other words, the use of GCD is not permitted so as to eventually erase it from the public space in Cyprus; the initial empowerment of preschool Cypriots is not intended to encourage their communication skills with a view to decreasing multilingualism on the island.

This study will be of interest to school educators, administrators and policymakers of other bidialectal, bilingual or multilingual education settings that seek to investigate and understand the complex relationship between different languages/varieties, the impact these have on learners' socialization activities and how the school can contribute to children's academic and personal development by encouraging linguistic diversity.

The case of Cyprus is rather unique, since all GCs speak GCD, being their first language acquired at home, and SMG, which shares similar features to GCD, is the acquired language of school. However, in multilingual communities where speakers of one language do not speak the majority language and school is a space of learning, acculturation, socialization and dealing with majority- and minority-related concerns, the learning environment and relevant issues become even more complex.

Since the early study of bilingual education, monolingual learning among bilingual speakers often resulted in learners having ambivalent attitudes towards the value of their own mother tongue and insecurity about their culture (Cummins 1981). This is also pertinent today where non-standard varieties are often labelled as 'linguistically deprived' (as in the case of Ebonics, see Delpit and Dowdy 2002, or Aboriginal languages in Canada, see Burnaby 2002). Such sociolinguistic stereotyping has a major influence on our impression upon these varieties and its speakers despite the very fact that all varieties (languages and dialects) are vastly complex structural systems with systematicity in grammar and syntax.

For this reason, modern-day literacy and education are striving for inclusion of all kinds, so students feel confident and welcomed to explore, engage and share as part of a whole in a classroom environment interacting with peers and teacher – and this is how empowerment of learners is achieved in a multilingual learning environment. As Freire (2000:72) puts it, 'education must begin with the solution of the teacher-student contradiction, by reconciling the poles of the contradiction so that both are simultaneously teachers and students.'

Note

1. Reference will be made to the two as two language varieties, not a standard language and a dialect. This perspective does not distinguish one as being superior than the other, but rather two of the same kind. As Max Weinreich used to say all languages are dialects in the same way all dialects are languages and began his famous speeches with 'A language is a dialect with an Army and a Navy'.

References

Auer, P. (2007), 'Introduction', in P. Auer (ed.), *Style and Social Identities: Alternative Approaches to Linguistic Heterogeneity*, 1–24, Berlin: Walter de Gruyter.

Bohrer, C. N. (2005), 'Libraries as Early Literacy Centers', *Public Libraries*, 44 (3): 127–32.

Burnaby, B. (2002), 'Reflections on Language Policies in Canada: Three Examples', in J. W. Tollefson (ed.), *Language Policies in Education*, 65–89, London: Lawrence Erlbaum Associates.

Casey, A., and Sheran, C. (2004), 'Early Literacy Skills Development'. Available online: http://www.ws.k12.ny.us/Downloads/EarlyLit.pdf (accessed 25 May 2018).

Country Report Cyprus (2004), *Language Education Policy Profile*. Republic of Cyprus. Ministry of Education and Culture, Cyprus. Language Education Policy Profile. Available online: http://www.coe.int/t/dg4/linguistic/Source/Country_Report_Cyprus_EN.pdf (accessed 20 February 2007).

Cummins, J. (1981), *Bilingualism and Minority-Language Children*, Ontario: Ontario Institute for Studies in Education.

Daimant-Cohen, D. (2007), 'First Day of Class: The Public Library's Role in 'School Readiness'", *Children and Libraries*, 5 (1): 40–8.

Delpit, L., and Dowdy, J. (2002) (eds), *The Skin that We Speak*, London: New Press.

Drigas, A. S., Kokkalia, G. K., Economou, E., and Roussos, P. (2017), 'Intervention and Diagnostic Tools in Preschool Education', *International Journal of Emerging Technologies in Learning*, 12 (11): 185–97.

Freire, P. (2000), *Pedagogy of the Oppressed*, London: Bloomsbury.

Gal, S. (2002), 'A Semiotics of the Public/Private Distinction', Differences: A Journal of Feminist Cultural Studies, 13 (1): 77–95.

Gal, S. (2005), 'Language Ideologies Compared: Metaphors of Public/Private', *Journal of Linguistic Anthropology*, 15 (1): 23–37.

Gal, S., and Woolard, K. (eds) (2001), *Languages and Publics: The Making of Authority*. Manchester: St Jerome's Press.

Hornberger, N. (2002), 'Multilingual Language Policies and the Continua of Biliteracy', *Language Policy*, 1 (1): 27–51.

Inglehart, R. (1990), *Culture Shift in Advanced Industrial Society*, Princeton, NJ: Princeton University Press.

Ioannidou, E. (2009), 'Using the Improper Language in the Classroom: The Conflict between Language Use and Legitimate Varieties in Education. Evidence from a Greek Cypriot Classroom', *Language and Education*, 23 (3): 263–78.

Ioannidou, E. (2017), 'Performing Registers and Registering Performance: Young Children's Linguistic Practices during Play in the Greek Cypriot Context', *Language and Communication*, 56: 55–68.

Ioannidou, E., and Sophocleous, A. (2010), '"Now, Is This How We Are Going to Say It?": Comparing Teachers' Language Practices in Primary and Secondary State Education in Cyprus', *Linguistics and Education*, 21 (4): 298–313.

Kymlicka, P., and Patten, A. (2003), 'Language Rights and Political Theory', *Annual Review of Applied Linguistics*, 23: 3–21.

MoEC (Ministry of Education and Culture) (1994), *National Curriculum for Primary Education*, Nicosia: Ministry of Education and Culture.

MoEC (Ministry of Education and Culture) (2002), The Greek Cypriot Dialect and Standard Modern Greek, circular sent to all schools on the island on 28 August 2002.

MoEC (Ministry of Education and Culture) (2016), Αναλυτικό Πρόγραμμα Προσχολικής Εκπαίδευσης, [Detailed Programme of Preschool Education]. Available online: http://archeia.moec.gov.cy/sd/270/dee_nip_proscholiki_ekpaidefsi.pdf (accessed 26 May 2018).

Pashiardis, P. (2007), 'Cyprus', in W. Hörner, H. Döbert, B. Von Kopp and W. Mitter (eds), *The Education Systems of Europe*, 202–22, Dordrecht, the Netherlands: Springer.

Papapavlou, A. (1998), 'Attitudes toward the Greek Cypriot Dialect: Sociocultural Implications', *International Journal of the Sociology of Language* 134: 15–28.

Papapavlou, A. (2001), 'Mind Your Speech: Language Attitudes in Cyprus', *Journal of Multilingual and Multicultural Development* 22: 491–501.

Papapavlou, A., and Pavlou, P. (2005), 'Literacy and Language-in-Education Policy in Bidialectal Settings', *Current Issues in Language Planning*, 6 (2): 164–81.

Papapavlou, A., and Sophocleous, A. (2009), 'Relational Social Deixis and the Linguistic Construction of Identity', *International Journal of Multilingualism*, 6 (1): 1–16.

Παυλίδης, Α. (1992), Ιστορία της Νήσου Κύπρου (τόμος τρίτος), Λευκωσία: Φιλόκυπρος [Pavlides, A. (1992), The History of the Island of Cyprus, 3rd volume), Lefkosia: Filokypros].

Ruiz, R. (1991), 'The Empowerment of Language-Minority Students', in N. H. Hornberger (2017) (ed.), *Honoring Richard Ruiz and His Work on Language Planning and Bilingual Education*, 259–69, Bristol: Multilingual Matters.

Sophocleous, A. (2009), 'Language Attitudes towards the Greek Cypriot Dialect: Social Factors Contributing to Their Development and Maintenance', Unpublished PhD thesis, Kingston upon Thames: Kingston University.

Sophocleous, A. (2011), 'Switching Code and Changing Social Identities in Face to Face Interaction', *Sociolinguistic Studies*, 5 (2): 201–33.

Sophocleous, A. (2013), 'Maya the Bee, Scooby Doo and Other Stories: How the Public and Private Distinction Is Depicted in Children's Bidialectal Interactions in Kindergarten', *Multilingua* 32 (5): 625–55.

Sophocleous, A., and Ioannidou, E. (2020), 'Young Children Performing Linguistic Varieties: Comparing Classroom and Play-time Language Use in the Bidialectal Context of Cyprus', *Language & Education*, 34 (6): 1–18. DOI: 10.1080/09500782.2020.1736093.

Tsiplakou S. (2006), 'The Emperor's Old Clothes: Linguistic Diversity and the Redefinition of Literacy', *International Journal of Humanities*, 2: 2345–52.

Tsiplakou, S. (2007), 'Linguistic Variation in the Cypriot Language Classroom and Its Implications for Education', in A. Papapavlou and P. Pavlou (eds), *Sociolinguistic and Pedagogical Dimensions of Dialects in Education*, 236–64, Newcastle-upon-Tyne: Cambridge Scholars.

Tsiplakou, S. (2009), 'Code-Switching and Code-Mixing between Related Varieties: Establishing the Blueprint', *International Journal of Humanities*, 6: 49–66.

Tsiplakou, S., Papapavlou, A. N., Pavlou P., and Katsoyannou, M. (2006), 'Levelling, Koineization and Their Implications for Bidialectism', in Frans Hinskens (ed.), *Language Variation – European Perspectives: Selected Papers from the Third International Conference on Language Variation in Europe*, 265–76, Amsterdam: John Benjamins.

Tsiplakou, S., Armosti, S., and Evripidou, D. (2016), 'Coherence "in the Mix"? Coherence in the Face of Language Shift in Cypriot Greek', *Lingua*, 172–3: 10–25.

Van Kleeck, A., Stahl, S. A., and Bauer, E. B.(eds) (2003), *On Reading Books to Children: Parents and Teachers*, London: Lawrence Erlbaum Associates.

Walzer, M. (1983), *Spheres of Justice: A Defense of Pluralism and Equality*, New York: Basic Books.

Yiakoumetti, A. (2006), 'A Bidialectal Programme for the Learning of Standard Modern Greek in Cyprus', *Applied Linguistics*, 27 (2). 295–317.

Yiakoumetti, A. (2007), 'Choice of Classroom Language in Bidialectal Communities: To Include or to Exclude the Dialect?', *Cambridge Journal of Education*, 37 (1). 51–66.

Zigler, E., Gilliam, W. S., and Jones, S. M. (2006), *A Vision for Universal Preschool Education*, Cambridge: Cambridge University Press.

Conclusion: Multilingualism in public spaces: Empowering and transforming communities

Robert Blackwood and Deirdre A. Dunlevy

Among its various contributions, this volume brings together research from different perspectives, including sociolinguistics, education and sociology, under the frame of looking at the public space both as a site for multilingualism and as a tool for empowerment. By foregrounding the community as the agency of empowerment, the chapters in this volume speak to the ways in which, even in contexts of conflict or linguistic tension, the embracing and promotion of multiple languages within our public spaces can transform not only the visual composition of public spaces, but also communities and their attitudes towards languages, their ideas of identity and their understanding of the world around them.

Language plays a central role in meaning construction, a fundamental cog in the powerhouse of our lived experiences. Language has the potential to transform and empower a community and its impact is dependent on innumerable social variables. Language and empowerment can be viewed from different perspectives, from personal empowerment through language use, which can shape and define a personal space and identity, to the empowerment of a community through language inclusion. In other words, language is a form of power that can be used to exclude groups, or to develop social cohesion in divided societies. This volume exemplifies how language can transform a community, through its empowerment or indeed, disempowerment. The chapters demonstrate how communities and speakers struggle to remove barriers to the recognition of multilingualism, such as the invisibilization or demoting of languages in public signage, in language policies, in the stigmatization of identities associated with languages. In the process, empowerment is enacted through efforts to transform these sources of tension or conflict into opportunities for the community. The volume demonstrates that it is within the conflict and struggle that the processes of empowerment can emerge, as speakers and communities strive to remove these obstacles for their community. At a time when many facets of European society are engaging with negative rhetoric about multilingualism, despite being an increasingly globalized community, the case studies presented in this volume purport the benefits of multilingualism at individual and societal levels. Empowerment is a complex and ever-changing process, by which the actors and actions are constantly changing through their actions, their evolving statuses and their societal roles. That is to say, empowerment is not actioned by any one individual or group of individuals, rather, it is a necessary collaboration involving awareness and involvement from many parties. Through acts of disempowerment, such as the negation of inclusion of a community's language in public spaces, a group can be incensed to take action, such as Ai'Ta! in Brittany, and to take control of the narrative around their own language and culture.

We noted in the introduction to this volume that we intend this volume to contribute to wider debates in the humanities and social sciences with the view to highlighting how sociolinguistics can inflect these discussions. We return now to the approaches identified by Carabine (1996: 17) and consider empowerment through the lens of sociolinguistics: how individuals self-identify as multilingual; how groups and communities practise multilingualism; and how others press their case for the extension of rights. These three methods of empowerment are interconnected and can be understood and interpreted by groups differently, but with the common objective of exercising their right to power through linguistic diversity.

Self-identification as multilingual as empowerment

Across the volume, examples abound of individuals who identify as speakers of more than one language, from second- and third-generation Gujarati shop owners in Leicester, through German-Italians in South Tyrol, to language activists in Brittany. In each of these cases, individuals and groups live out their identity as multilingual people, drawing on the languages of their repertoire as and when necessary or desirable. This is not to claim that self-identification as multilingual is unproblematic, and Sloboda highlights the cases of Slovak speakers who stress their confidence and abilities in Czech in Czechia in response to public narratives that privilege Czech over Slovak. We do not claim here that groups actively, vocally and proudly identify as multilingual; in a number of the cases explored in this volume, the fact of being multilingual has been unremarkable, and it is only with changing sociopolitical circumstances – and in light of the crisis in hospitality (Balch, 2016) in particular, as a successor to the enlargement of the European Union in 2004 – that self-identification as multilingual has become noteworthy, almost as a challenge to the rhetoric of monolingualism. That communities are being transformed is undeniable, not least as hypermobility accelerates the movement of groups across the continent; by way of example, we note how Opsahl's informants informally attest to increased presence of Polish in Oslo over the time between the start of the project and the completion of her chapter.

In some cases, self-identification as multilingual is recognized as a highly political act, and a process by which communities effectively perform an act of empowerment, in the cases of Northern Ireland and Brittany, for a different group to recognize. Identifying as multilingual challenges long-established narratives and disrupts specific perspectives that are decidedly political rather than linguistic. Not all self-identification as multilingual is undertaken with the same levels of collective self-awareness that Dunlevy notes in west Belfast in Northern Ireland, or that Blackwood highlights amongst Breton-language activists taking direct action in France. Without necessarily the metalanguage to self-identify as multilingual, pre-schoolers in Cyprus recognize cues from their teachers that they are, to use Sophocleous's term, bidialectal and happily live out this existence in play, song and conversation within their nursery school.

Practising multilingualism as empowerment

In each of the chapters here, multilingual groups live out their daily lives in more than one language, even if, in the case of Patrice Lumumba Square in Brussels, the breadth of languages spoken by the Congolese communities is erased from the discussions around the renaming of the square. In some cases, such as Poles in Norway as discussed by Opsahl, the dividing line between language practices are clearly maintained, and translanguaging, touched on by a number of contributors such as Gorter and Sophocleous, is not widely attested. In these examples, individuals use the linguistic resources at their disposal to live out multiple or compound identities which, at different points or in different circumstances, draw extensively on one of the discrete, named languages within their repertoire. Slovene speakers in Trieste province, as noted by Tufi, may privilege Italian in the arrangement of the public spaces they inhabit, but they also draw on Slovene, and position themselves as Slovene speakers, even if not as Slovene nationals. Tufi's findings are echoed in Sloboda's discussion of individuals, and in particular Slovak and Czech speakers, in Czechia where multilingualism is a lived reality, and one that challenges the resurgent narrative from across the continent that a modern nation state is predicated on a single national language. The visual arrangement of multilingualism, even with the most banal of examples such as the sign in Oslo identified by Opsahl which instructs workmen, in Polish and Norwegian, to close the gate after them, attests to the normalization of multilingualism as practised in the widest range of circumstances. Rather than leading to conflict, the mundanity of the examples of conspicuous multilingualism attested here – apart from those specific cases which are visibly contested in these chapters – suggest the potentiality for multilingualism as an everyday practice to testify to social cohesion.

Harrison's approach in this volume makes an important contribution to our understanding of rationales for individuals practising multilingualism, and her findings point to a range of motivations for written multilingual language practices. One of the first drivers for writing in more than one language identified by Harrison is community cohesion and the affective dimension of making public spaces multilingual. From a solicitor and a shopkeeper to the city council, multilingualism is practised, and by extension power is exercised, in order not to exclude but to include, to bring in all residents of the city, and to permit all individuals within the city to participate fully in life in Leicester.

Pressing for the extension of rights as empowerment

The act of calling for rights to use languages has a long and rich tradition within sociolinguistic scholarship, and it is inevitable that this dimension is reflected in this volume. Linguistic Landscape (LL) research in particular has explored the calls by ethnolinguistic groups to be represented visually in the public space, starting with Ben-Rafael, Shohamy, Amara and Trumper-Hecht's (2006) discussion of the symbolic construction of place in order to manage the presentation of self and as part of power relations between groups. Of these three approaches articulated by Carabine, this lobbying for the extension of rights is the one most clearly characterized by contesting the power held by others. As examined in this volume, this pressing for the extension of rights can be undertaken via direct action, as Blackwood notes in Brittany, France, where language activists argue that tampering with the visual arrangement of signs, or even their construction, is their only recourse, having pursued other methods. Blackwood explores how this proactive approach of the collective results not only in an immediate increase in the visibility of Breton in public spaces but also an awareness of the struggle for visibility and status of the language in the community. By the collective altering the signs themselves, they transform physical public spaces to emphasize the struggle for improved language rights in the region. The unofficial insertion of Breton in signs, and alteration of existing signage to include the local regional language also speaks to the attitudes of the local community and the central role the language plays in the construction of a local identity. As Dunlevy notes, there are less physically confrontational possibilities for speakers of Ulster-Scots or Irish in Northern Ireland, who need to petition their local council and obtain the support of two-thirds of their neighbours to have the street name rendered in the other language (in addition to English). However, despite a clear rubric for strict language management practices from the top-down, signs are altered by members of the community who feel the language choice reflected in signage does not index their identity, as with the case of Derry/Londonderry signage.

The advocating and campaigning for extensions of language rights emerges in the cases explored in detail by Ó Mainnín, who documents the concerted efforts to legislate for the inclusion of Irish in public spaces in place names in Northern Ireland. His analysis of the language management process within the devolved region of Northern Ireland emphasizes the central role that grassroots movements and language advocacy groups have had in pushing the agenda for increased language status for Irish at a legislative level.

Language and empowerment

In the introduction to this volume, we also considered Solomon's (1976: 6) definition of empowerment as 'a process whereby persons who belong to a stigmatized social category throughout their lives can be assisted to develop and increase their skills in the exercise of interpersonal influence and performance of valued social roles'. We return to this definition of the concept now in our reflection on the role of language in the process of empowerment. Empowerment emerges in many forms throughout the contributions in this volume, emphasizing the fact that it is a complex and multifaceted process, rather than a linear, once-off action. Empowerment can take many forms and be actioned by any actor, from a migrant worker to a child learning to read. Gorter considers how the process of empowerment can be theorized in its visibility in public spaces through the development of his cyclical model for understanding LL, 'Multilingual inequalities in public spaces' (MIPS). In his model, Gorter emphasizes the active role of the engaged community on language policy development. Sloboda takes the view that language policy development and empowerment are inextricably linked, as we see in Czechia that through their actions, social actors can restrict the visibility of another group's language, and understanding the tensions and contradictions of the relationship between languages in a multilingual space is central to transforming a situation from one of disempowerment to an empowered language community.

The process of empowerment for a community is connected to a sense of identity, as testified by Tufi in her exploration of the LL in border communities of north-eastern Italy, where the utilization of the LL as a form of identity expression has a transformative impact on multilingualism in the communities, highlighting the potential for community empowerment in multilingual settings. It is through direct action that identity norms and stereotypes can be challenged, as we learn of the activities of the Ai'Ta! collective in Brittany, France, who use the LL as a means of expressing their identity in order to readdress the imbalance of language status and to encourage force an improved status for the regional language. It is through active empowerment from the collective that the status of Breton is highlighted in public spaces, drawing the issue out of private fora and into the awareness of the broader community.

In considering this material, we can revisit Solomon's definition with a particular focus on the role of language and purport that, particularly in multilingual communities, language has a naturally central and active role in the process of empowerment. For a multilingual individual, developing and increasing the social roles of their language(s) in public spaces empowers that person to destigmatize their own language, while at the same time increasing the wider community's exposure to the language, normalizing its presence in public spaces and assisting in the development of that language having a valued social role in the community.

Empowering and transforming communities

We are writing this volume at a time when issues of empowerment have come to the fore in general social discourse through events like the murder of George Floyd and social movements such as the Black Lives Matter movement. As society as a whole educates itself on inequality of different forms, the increased awareness about the influence of power and existing social structures on how we perceive the world around us contributes to a collective empowering of the individual through knowledge. The significance of Van Mensel's discussion of the name of Patrice Lumumba Square / Square Patrice Lumumba is heightened as, during the final stages of preparing this volume, the statue of Leopold II in Antwerp was vandalized and subsequently removed, and King Philippe expressed his 'deepest regret' for Belgium's colonial rule in Congo. Questions of exercising power and changing societies are particularly prominent in public discourse.

The volume's centralizing of the issue of empowerment of communities through the prism of public spaces has potential impact for our understanding and reviewing assumptions regarding citizenship. The public space is a social arena that is theoretically open equally to all to utilize and contribute to its composition. However, as attested throughout this volume and elsewhere (Piller 2016; Skutnabb-Kangas and Phillipson 2017), the globalized modern world is inherently unequal, and how we consume and manipulate our public spaces often disempowers an 'other'. The paradox of empowerment, where one group's empowerment may result in another group feeling disempowered, is evident in the two chapters on Northern Ireland presented. Here, we learn how the processes of empowerment, through the seeking of legislative protection and support for the Irish language in place names (Ó Mainnín), although intended to improve a language situation for a minoritized community, can at the same time, lead to feelings of disempowerment or territorialization through the inclusion of the minority language in public spaces. At the same time, these actions prompt a perceived delegitimization of the out-group through their exclusion from the LL, as is evident in Dunlevy's chapter where she explores instances of inclusion of Irish or Ulster-Scots in the LL across Northern Ireland, and the difficulty of creating a shared space through language in a divided community.

The focus of the volume on public spaces permits us to consider how the transformation of the public space revolves around attempts to redefine the functions and values of what it is that composes the public space (Barnett 2014), including language. The very notion of a public space suggests there is a level of openness and accessibility to all and that there is a level of communality in the act of something being public rather than private. However, public spaces are not equally open, accessible and shared by all; tensions around controlling the space, living in the space and sharing the space emerge. When we consider languages in public spaces, we can identify the many roles that language can take spatially, socially and as an actor through combinations of practices, meanings and values, all of which are subject to tensions. Publicness is enacted through shared rituals, voting, being seen and heard, and active participation. Barnett (2014: 893) acknowledges that 'publics can be weak or strong, they can influence or exercise power, they can act as sieges against concentrations of power or a sluices enabling its more democratic regulation' and it is the multiplicity in balance of powers within public spaces that is explored throughout chapters in this volume. Sloboda tackles the legitimization of a language in public spaces in his chapter, positing that language choice management contributes to the reproduction of social divisions and to power inequality between groups. By focusing on more marginalized communities, such as Leicester's South Asian community (Harrison), the Irish- and Ulster-Scots-speaking communities of Northern Ireland (Dunlevy) or those for whom agency of power is not attainable, such as young children in Cyprus (Sophocleous) or the Polish migrant workers in Norway (Opsahl), the chapters here draw attention to the processes of disempowerment and delegitimization that occurs through the foci of language.

As such, by understanding these processes, we can begin to renegotiate and redress the imbalance in our public spaces, leading to the empowerment of communities. The renaming of Patrice Lumumba Square / Square Patrice Lumumba in Brussels is a case in point, where years of colonizing oppression are being reassessed, and the memorialization and commemoration of the first prime minister of the independent Republic of the Congo, Patrice Lumumba, is celebrated in Brussels, where previously only those who colonized, such as Leopold II, were commemorated (Van Mensel).

Social cohesion emerges as a common strand throughout the chapters presented here. The building of linguistic awareness in communities at a micro or macro level can be influential in increasing mutual understanding and reducing barriers through an appreciation and understanding of the importance of multilingualism and allowing for the embracing of diversity within the linguistic space. Our understanding of multilingualism is broad, and recognizes the breadth of both practices and interpretations of communities where more than one language is seen. Our exploration into the role of language in diverse settings (education, memorialization, policy and the LL) demonstrates the wide-reaching impact that awareness and tolerance of diversity in language can have on sectors where it is not traditionally valued.

References

Balch, A. (2016), *Immigration and the State: Fear, Greed and Hospitality*, Basingstoke: Palgrave Macmillan.

Barnett, C. (2014), 'How to Think about Public Space', in P. Cloke, P. Crang and M. Goodwin (eds), *Introducing Human Geographies*, 3rd edn, 883–98, London: Routledge.

Ben-Rafael, E., Shohamy, E., Amara, M. H., and Trumper-Hecht, N. (2006), 'Linguistic Landscape as Symbolic Construction of the Public Space: The Case of Israel', *International Journal of Multilingualism*, 3 (1): 7–30.

Carabine, J. (1996), 'Empowering Sexualities', in B. Humphries (ed.), *Critical Perspectives on Empowerment*, 17–34, Birmingham: Venture Press.

Piller, I. (2016), *Linguistic Diversity and Social Justice: An Introduction of Applied Sociolinguistics*, Oxford: Oxford University Press.

Solomon, B. (1976), *Black Empowerment: Social Work in Oppressed Communities*, New York: Columbia University Press.

Skutnabb-Kangas, T., and Phillipson, R. (2017), 'Linguistic Human Rights, Past and Present', in T.Skutnabb-Kangas and R.Phillipson (eds), *Language Rights: Critical Concepts in Language Studies*, vol. 1, 71–110, London: Routledge.

Index

Abousnnouga, G., 161
Abrassart, G., 162
activism, 177–193. *See also* France, language activism from; Linguistic Landscape activism
Act of Explanation, 61
Adams, R., 5
Advertisement Regulation Act, 41
Ager, D., 203
Ai'Ta! group in France, 177–193
Alderman, D. H., 161
Amara, M. H., 244
Amos, H. W., 23

Bagna, C., 114
Bailey, J., 32
Barni, M., 114
Belgium's public space, 162–166
　Leopold II in Brussels, 164
　memorials and street names in, 163
　(post-)colonial memory in, 162–166
Ben-Rafael, E., 160, 244
Ben Yakoub, J., 162
Berezkina, M., 113, 130
Bermel, N., 42
Berruto, G., 94
billboard campaign site signs, 123–125
Blackwood, R., 10, 97, 138
Blommaert, J., 18, 94, 206
Bock, Z., 188
Borba, R., 170
Bourdieu, P., 2, 120
Bragard, V., 164
Breton as a language of France, 179–180
Brittany, LL of, 180–182
　activism, 182–184
　Ai'Ta! group in, 183
　diachronic approach, 181
Bruyel-Olmedo, A., 16
Bygdas, M. E., 113
Byrnes, Giselle, 76

Carabine, J., 4, 244
Ciccolone, S., 102
communicative management, 32
communities, empowering, 241–247. *See also* empowering communities
complementary multilingual signs, 213–214
construction site signs, 121–123
Consumer Protection Act, 41
Cook, V., 16
Cooper, R. L., 210
Coulmas, F., 7
council signage policies, 140–142
Cyprus, preschool education in, 223–247
　data analysis, 228
　data collection techniques, 228
　Greek Cypriot dialect (GCD) in, 223–247
　　acrolectal feature, 225
　　basilectal feature, 225
　　empowering children through, 236
　　mesolectal feature, 225
　Greek Cypriot Dialect (GCD) in, 224
　importance and goals of, 226–227
　kindergarten teachers' expectations, 236–237
　Standard Modern Greek (SMG) in, 224
　structured play and its importance, 227
　transcription conventions, 229–235
Czech Republic (Czechia), 31–58
　communicative management, 32
　Czech-Slovak ethnonational lines, 35
　ethnic interests in a 'civic nation', 31–58
　'foreign'-language dominance issue, 40–47. *See also individual entry*
　language management, 32
　'macro' social order, 33
　'micro' social order, 33
　Prague Drivers' Register, 47–48
　public authorities' non-use of English, negative evaluation, 47–49

public/private lines, 35–40. *See also* individual entry
publicness, 33
sociocultural management, 32
socioeconomic management, 32
Czmur, S., 129

Dal Negro, S., 138
Davis, Thomas, 62
de Vieuzac, Barère, 179
De Witte, L., 162
Demoulin, L., 162
dialect speakers in formal education, empowering, 223–247. *See also under* Cyprus
direct action in France, 177–193. *See also* Brittany; France, language activism from
Down Survey, 61
Du Bois, J., 177, 178
Duchene, A., 130
Dunlevy, D. A., 10, 244
duplicating multilingual signs, 210–213
  Belgrave Neighbourhood Centre sign, 212
  Florist shop sign, 212
  informational function of, 215
  Leicestershire Police sign, 211

Edwards, J., 5
Eichinger, L., 93
empowering communities, 241–247
  extension of rights for, 244
  language and, 244–245
  multilingualism in, practising, 243
  self-identification as, 242–243
  transforming communities and, 245–246
empowerment in public space, 1–3
  Carabine on, 4
  Edwards on, 5
  exclusion, 6
  Fishman on, 5
  Gerodimos on, 3
  history, 3–4
  Humphries on, 3
  inclusion, 6
  Lim on, 5
  McLaughlin on, 3

plurality of, 3–4
power in, 2
(socio)linguistics and, 4–8
Stroud on, 5–6
Esch, E., 5
Espinosa-Ramírez, A. B., 161
ethnic interests in a 'civic nation', 31–58
Ethnographic Linguistic Landscape Approach (ELLA), 18
European Language Equality Network, 70
exclusion, 6

Fabrício, B. F., 170
Fishman, J. A., 5
Floyd, George, 245
Flusser, V., 2
'foreign'-language dominance, 40–45
  conditions for, 45–47
  English preference, 41
  German minority population, 41
  street-name signs, 41–42
  visual domination, 46
Foucault, M., 2
fragmentary multilingual signs, 206–209
France, language activism from, 177–193. *See also* Brittany
  Ai'Ta! group in, 177–193
  Breton in, 179–180
  contexts, 178–184
  as dialogue between powerful and voiceless, 188–189
  direct action, 177–193
  empowerment through, 184–186
  legitimize by the very act of emplacement, 186–187
  monolingual road signage, dismantling, 185–186
  in the name of justice, 187–188
Fraser, N., 6
Freire, P., 4, 238
Friberg, J. H., 112, 122, 129, 131
Friel, Brian, 62
Friuli-Venezia Giulia (VG), 89–110
  after Second World War, 93
  ethno-linguistic awareness, 99
  German featuring signs, 103–107
  language distribution in, 91–92
Fusco, F., 103

Gaelic/Irish script, 148
Gal, S., 6, 32, 49
Garvin, R., 23
Germanophone, 95
Gerodimos, R., 3
Gmaj, K., 115
Goddeeris, I., 162–163, 171
Goffman, E., 182
Golden Mile, Leicester, 195–222
  analysis, 204–214
  authors choosing messages in Gujarati, 215–216
  Bank of India sign, 205
  banners, 200
  business signs, 201–203
  complementary signs, 213–214
  Cossington Recreation Ground sign, 207
  duplicating signs, 210–213
    Belgrave Neighbourhood Centre sign, 212
    Florist shop sign, 212
    Leicestershire Police sign, 211
  fragmentary signs, 206–209
  Gujarati, visual presence of, 204–206
  influence of authors in, 195–222
  language order, 214
  language position, 214
  languages of, 200–203
  motivations of authors, 214
  multilingualism displayed, type, 206
  research methods, 203–204
Golden, A., 112, 114
Good Friday Agreement of 1998, 64–67, 72
Gorter, D., 8–9, 15, 116, 139, 153, 243
Greek Cypriot Dialect (GCD), 224–236
  in preschool education in Cyprus, 223–247. *See also under* Cyprus
Gujónsdóttir, G., 116
Guilat, Y., 161

Heller, M., 130
Hochschild, A., 162
Holder, Daniel, 69
Hornsby, M., 180
Hult, F. M., 16
Humphries, B., 3
Hyde, Douglas, 62
Hymes, D., 32

Iglicka, K., 115
inclusion, 6
indigenous languages in Ireland, 60–61
inequality, multilingual, 13–25. *See also* linguistic landscapes (LL); public spaces, multilingual inequality in
Inglehart, R., 223
Ioannidou, E., 236
Ireland, 60–61. *See also* Northern Ireland
  indigenous languages in, 60–61
  minoritized languages in, 60–61
Irish Language Act (ILA), 65, 137
Irish Language Bill, 69–71
Italian borderscapes, 89–110. *See also* Friuli-Venezia Giulia (VG); Trentino-Alto Adige/South Tyrol (ST)

Järlehed, J., 139, 149
Jaspers, J., 15
Jaworski, A., 161, 197
Jernudd, B. H., 32
Johnson, Cassels, 19

Kallen, J., 142, 148
Kaufmann, V., 95–96
Kennedy, Danny, 68
Kitis, E. D., 182, 183, 185
Klemensová, T., 46
Knittl, L., 42
Kraft, K., 113, 129
Kupec, P., 51

language, 19–20, 32, 244–245
  empowerment and, 244–245
  language-skill-based professional site, 120–121
  management, 32
  order in multilingual signs, 214
  policy processes, 19–20
  position in multilingual signs, 214
  recognition complexity in Northern Ireland, 137–157
Lázně, Mariánské, 40
Lefebvre, H., 161
legislation and politics in Northern Ireland, 63–66. *See also under* Northern Ireland

Leicester's South Asian community, 196–199. *See also* Golden Mile, Leicester
  development of, 196–199
  multilingual welcome sign at, 198–199
    Belgrave Library, 198
    St Margaret's bus station, 199
Leinonen, J., 116, 117, 128
Li, Wei, 15
Lim, L., 5
linguistic landscape (LL), 13–25, 32–33, 89–110, 144–151, 160–162. *See also* Multilingual Inequalities in Public Spaces
  English, advantages, 16
  ethnographic linguistic landscape approach (ELLA), 18
  memory and monuments names, 160–162
  minority languages, as subordinate, 17
  multilingual turn, 15
  onomastic signs in, 149–151
  place names, 160–162
  place-name signage and, 138–140
  recent approaches in, 18
  studies, trends in, 14–18
  towards a comprehensive model, 18–24
  towards inclusive model of, 13–25
  variationist linguistic landscape study (VaLLS), 18
Linguistic Landscape activism, 182–184
  of Brittany, 180–182
  as community empowerment means, 177–193
  as dialogue between the powerful and voiceless, 188–189
  direct action, 188
  empowerment through, 184–186
  to legitimize by the very act of emplacement, 186–187
  monolingual road signage, dismantling, 185–186
  in the name of justice, 187–188
  rationales for, 184–189
linguistic mobility, 89–110. *See also* transformative power of linguistic mobility
Local Government Act, 66
Local Government Order 1995, 140

Lou, J. J., 161
Lumumba, Patrice, 159–176

Machin, D., 161
'macro' social order, 33
Makoumbou, Rhode, 169
Malinowski, D., 195
Marten, H. F., 139
McLaughlin, K., 2–4
'micro' social order, 33
Milani, T., 182, 183, 185
minoritized languages in Ireland, 60–61
minority languages, issues with, 17
  ideologies, 17
  regional languages, 17
  visibility, 17
mobility, 89–110. *See also* linguistic mobility; transformative power of linguistic mobility
model multicultural city, multilingualism in, 195–222. *See also* Golden Mile, Leicester
  research methods and survey, 200–204
Moriarty, M., 149, 162
Morris, Ewan, 76
motility, theorization, 89, 95–96
  aptitude for movement, 96
  field of possibilities, 96
  movement, 96
  moving and being mobile, 96
  moving without being mobile, 96
  not moving and being mobile, 96
motivations of authors, 214–217
  messages in Gujarati, 215–216
  non-inclusion of written Gujarati, 217–220
  partial inclusion of written Gujarati, 216–217
Multilingual Inequalities in Public Spaces (MIPS), 13–25
  component parts, 19–25
  language policy processes, 19–20
  perception, seeing and reading, 23–24
  reflections, reactions and language practices, 24
  sign-making processes, 21–22
  unequal languages on signage, 22–23
multilingual turn, 15

Nábělková, M., 39
Nekvapil, J., 32, 49
Neustupný, J. V., 32, 49–50
1947 Independence of India Act, 196
1968 Prague Spring, 35
Northern Ireland, 137–157
  language recognition complexity in, 137–157
  Northern Ireland Act 1998, 64–68, 73
  Northern Ireland Human Rights Commission, 70
  Northern Ireland Statistics and Research Agency (NISRA), 143
  place names in, 137–157. *See also individual entry*
Northern Ireland, place names provisions in, 59–87
  community sensitivities, 72–75
  enactments, 66–72
  language, identity and place names, 61–63
  language legislation and politics in, 63–66
    Good Friday Agreement of 1998, 64–67
    Irish Language Act, 65
    Northern Ireland Act 1998, 64–69
    Respecting Language and Diversity Bill, 66
  Local Government Act, 66
  Irish Language Bill, 69
  political and legislative context, 59–87
  politics of naming, 72–75
  proposals, 66–72
  public responses, 66–72
  signage, 72–75
  visibility of naming, 72–75
Norway, poles in, 112–113
Norwegian Broadcasting Corporation (NRK), 114
notion of invisibility, 115–117

Ó Mainnín, Mícheál B., 8
O'Donovan, John, 63
Obojska, M. A., 112, 121, 125, 128–129
Onofri, L., 23
onomastic signs, 149–151
Opsahl, T., 9, 114, 243
Otheguy, R., 15

Patrice Lumumba Square in Brussels, 166–170
  Congolese community, 166–170
  Futur Place Lumumba, 167–168
  Square du bastion/Bolwerksquare, 167–168
Pavlenko, A., 160
perception, seeing and reading, 23–24
Petty, William (Sir William Petty), 61
place names in Northern Ireland, 137–157
  bilingual signage in Irish and English, 141–142
  council signage policies, 140–142
    Antrim and Newtownabbey Borough Council, 140
    Belfast City Council, 141
    Derry and Strabane district council, 141
    Mid Ulster District Council, 148
  Derry/Londonderry road sign, 150
  Gaelic/Irish script, 148
  Irish in, 147–149
  methodology, 142–143
  numbering policies, 141
  place-name signage, 138–140
  policies and practices, 151–153
  Shankill area, 150–151
  signage, 141, 144–147
  socio-political issue in, 140
  street naming, 141
  in Ulster-Scots, 141, 144–147. *See also individual entry*
Planche, S., 164
policy processes, 19–20
  council signage policies, 140–142
  numbering policies, 141
Polish in Norwegian public spaces, 111–136
  analysis, 120–126
  areas for observation, 118–119
  audible expressions, 118–119
  background, 113
  billboard campaign site, 123–125
  Bryggen image, 124
  categories, 120–126
  construction site, 121–123
  field observations, 118
  immigration history in Norway, 112
  interpretative subject role, 117

language-skill-based professional site, 120–121
market forces prevail, 130–131
methodology and data, 117–120
missing fifth and sixth site, 126
motivation, 113
mutually reinforcing ideologies, 128–129
notion of invisibility, 115–117
poles in Norway, 112–113
renovation and construction sites, 130
research questions, 113
urban space, 114–115
virtual LLs, 125
visual expressions, 118–119
Postcolonial re-memorization in public space, 159–176. *See also* Patrice Lumumba Square in Brussels
in Belgium, 162–166. *See also* Belgium's public space
memory and monuments names, 160–162
place names, 160–162
power in public space, 1–3
Bourdieu on, 2
communication and, 3
exploration, 2
Flusser on, 2
Foucault in, 2
language and, 2
McLaughlin on, 2
Weber on, 2
preschool education in Cyprus, 224–226
private space, 6–7
public spaces, multilingual inequality in, 6–7, 13–25. *See also* linguistic landscapes (LL)
impact of, 24–25
multilingualism in, 31–58
prerequisites for, 31
research agenda, 24–25
public/private lines, differentiations along, 35–40
signs, 36–38, 43, 49–52
spoken and written modes, 42, 49–52
urban spaces, 36, 49–52
visitors versus residents, 36, 49–52
publicness, 33
Puzey, G., 138–139

Rafael, Ben, 16
Reh, M., 203, 206, 213
recognition complexity in Northern Ireland, 137–157
re-memorization in public space, 159–176. *See also* Patrice Lumumba Square in Brussels; Postcolonial re-memorization
Respecting Language and Diversity Bill, 66
Rice, A., 172
Robert, Mireille Tsheusi, 169
Ruiz, R., 4, 6

Satinská, L., 40
Schegloff, E. A., 33
Scollon, R., 177, 178, 190
Scollon, S. W., 177, 178, 190
Seargeant, P., 148
Sebba, M., 195–196
self-identification, 242–243
Shohamy, E., 116, 161, 244
signage and language relation, 23
sign-making processes, 21–22
Skutnabb-Kangas, Tove, 76 n.1
Slake, A. L., 113
Sloboda, M., 9
Slovenophone, 95
Smith, A. D., 179
(socio)linguistic research, 4–8
Solomon, B., 3, 244–245
Sooryamoorthy, R., 217
Sophocleous, A., 236, 243
space for multilingualism, demarcating, 31–58
Czech context, 34–35. *See also* Czech Republic (Czechia)
methodology, 34
theoretical perspective, 32–33
Spalding, T., 160
spatial mobility, 95
Spolsky, B., 124–125, 210
Stanard, M. G., 162
Standard Modern Greek (SMG), 224–236
Statistics Norway (SSB), 112
Stjernholm, K., 114, 130
Street name signage in Northern Ireland, 141, 144–147
in Irish, 147–149

Stroud, C., 5–6, 188
Swift, Jonathan, 61

Thurlow, C., 161
Toivanen, M., 116, 117, 128
Toubon law of 1994, 180
transcription conventions, 229–235
    The Robin and the Poppy (Excerpt 1), 229–231
    The Red Poppy (Excerpt 2), 231–233
    Souvlaki Takeaway (Excerpt 3), 233–234
transformative power of linguistic mobility, 89–110
    data, 97–104
    Italian borderscapes, evidence from, 89–110
    theoretical background, 94–97
transforming communities, 1–10
translanguaging, 15
Trentino-Alto Adige/South Tyrol (ST), 89–110
    after Second World War, 93
    commercial signs, 98–101
    institutional spaces, language in, 99
    Italian-Slovenian, 99–102
    language distribution in, 90–91
    public signs, 98–101

Trumper-Hecht, N., 244
Tufi, S., 8–9, 97–98

Ulster-Scots name signage, 141, 144–147
    brown signs, 145
    place name signage, 141, 144–147
    street name signage, 141, 144–147
    in traditional areas, 144
    use of 'formerly' word, 144–146
unequal languages on signage, 22–23

Van Mensel, L., 10, 15, 245
Vandenbroucke, M., 160
Variationist Linguistic Landscape Study (VaLLS), 18
Vary, Karlovy, 40
Vigers, D., 180–181
Vingron, N., 23
virtual Linguistic Landscape, 125

Waksman, S., 161
Walzer, Michael, 223
Wand, A., 93
Wardahl, R., 114–116, 126
Weber, M., 2
Wierzejski, A., 115
Wodak, R., 4